Amos Oz's Two Pens

The Hebrew novelist and political essayist, Amoz Oz (1939–2018), arguably Israel's leading intellectual, was fond of describing himself as using two different pens — the first used to write works of prose and fiction, and the other to criticize the government and advocate for a political change. This volume revisits the two pens parable. It brings together scholars from various disciplines who assess Amos Oz's dual role in Israeli culture and society as an immensely popular novelist and a leading public intellectual. Next to offering an intellectual portrait, the chapters in this book highlight some of Oz's seminal works, examine their reception, evaluate key political and literary debates he was involved in, as well as trace some of the connections between the two realms of his activity. This book is a fascinating read for students, researchers, and academics of Israeli politics, history, literature, and culture.

The chapters in this book were originally published as a special issue of the *Journal of Israeli History* and are accompanied by a new afterword by the Israeli novelist Lilah Nethanel.

Arie M. Dubnov is Associate Professor of History and the Max Ticktin Chair of Israel Studies at the George Washington University, USA. His publications include the intellectual biography *Isaiah Berlin: The Journey of a Jewish Liberal* (2012), and two edited volumes, *Zionism – A View from the Outside* (2010 [in Hebrew]) and *Partitions: A Transnational History of Twentieth-century Territorial Separatism* (2019, co-edited with Laura Robson).

Amos Oz (1939–2018)

Photo by Dani Machlis; Courtesy of Heksherim Institute, The Ben-Gurion University of the Negev, Beer Sheva.

Amos Oz's Two Pens
Between Literature and Politics

Edited by
Arie M. Dubnov

LONDON AND NEW YORK

First published 2023
by Routledge
4 Park Square, Milton Park, Abingdon, Oxon OX14 4RN

and by Routledge
605 Third Avenue, New York, NY 10158

Routledge is an imprint of the Taylor & Francis Group, an informa business

Introduction, Chapters 1–9 © 2023 Taylor & Francis
Afterword © 2023 Lilah Nethanel

All rights reserved. No part of this book may be reprinted or reproduced or utilised in any form or by any electronic, mechanical, or other means, now known or hereafter invented, including photocopying and recording, or in any information storage or retrieval system, without permission in writing from the publishers.

Trademark notice: Product or corporate names may be trademarks or registered trademarks and are used only for identification and explanation without intent to infringe.

British Library Cataloguing in Publication Data
A catalogue record for this book is available from the British Library

ISBN13: 978-1-032-39811-2 (hbk)
ISBN13: 978-1-032-39814-3 (pbk)
ISBN13: 978-1-003-35150-4 (ebk)

DOI: 10.4324/9781003351504

Typeset in Minion Pro
by Newgen Publishing UK

Publisher's Note
The publisher accepts responsibility for any inconsistencies that may have arisen during the conversion of this book from journal articles to book chapters, namely the inclusion of journal terminology.

Disclaimer
Every effort has been made to contact copyright holders for their permission to reprint material in this book. The publishers would be grateful to hear from any copyright holder who is not here acknowledged and will undertake to rectify any errors or omissions in future editions of this book.

Contents

	Citation Information	vii
	Notes on Contributors	ix
	Introduction: Amos Oz's two pens	1
	Arie M. Dubnov	
1	Amos Oz and the politics of identity: A reassessment	27
	Eran Kaplan	
2	The greatness of smallness: Amos Oz, Sherwood Anderson, and the American presence in Hebrew Literature	43
	Karen Grumberg	
3	The American Oz: Notes on translation and reception	70
	Omri Asscher	
4	Amos Oz: A humanist in the darkness	95
	David Ohana	
5	"Now we shall reveal a little secret" first person plural and lyrical fluidity in the works of Amos Oz	115
	Vered Karti Shemtov	
6	"Like a cow that gave birth to a seagull": Amos Oz, Yoel Hoffmann and the birth of *The Same Sea*	134
	Neta Stahl	
7	Memory and space in the autobiographical writings of Amos Oz and Ronit Matalon	153
	Adia Mendelson-Maoz	
8	Amos Oz: The lighthouse	179
	Yigal Schwartz	

9	Love, compassion, and longing *Nurith Gertz*	186
	Afterword *Reading Amos Oz Today* *Lilah Nethanel*	194
	Index	202

Citation Information

The chapters in this book were originally published in the *Journal of Israeli History*, volume 38, issue 2 (2020). When citing this material, please use the original page numbering for each article, as follows:

Introduction
Amos Oz's two pens
Arie M. Dubnov
Journal of Israeli History, volume 38, issue 2 (2020), pp. 233–258

Chapter 1
Amos Oz and the politics of identity: A reassessment
Eran Kaplan
Journal of Israeli History, volume 38, issue 2 (2020), pp. 259–274

Chapter 2
The greatness of smallness: Amos Oz, Sherwood Anderson, and the American presence in Hebrew literature
Karen Grumberg
Journal of Israeli History, volume 38, issue 2 (2020), pp. 275–301

Chapter 3
The American Oz: Notes on translation and reception
Omri Asscher
Journal of Israeli History, volume 38, issue 2 (2020), pp. 303–327

Chapter 4
Amos Oz: A humanist in the darkness
David Ohana
Journal of Israeli History, volume 38, issue 2 (2020), pp. 329–348

Chapter 5
"Now we shall reveal a little secret" first person plural and lyrical fluidity in the works of Amos Oz
Vered Karti Shemtov
Journal of Israeli History, volume 38, issue 2 (2020), pp. 349–367

Chapter 6

"Like a cow that gave birth to a seagull": Amos Oz, Yoel Hoffmann and the birth of The Same Sea
Neta Stahl
Journal of Israeli History, volume 38, issue 2 (2020), pp. 369–387

Chapter 7

Memory and space in the autobiographical writings of Amos Oz and Ronit Matalon
Adia Mendelson-Maoz
Journal of Israeli History, volume 38, issue 2 (2020), pp. 389–414

Chapter 8

Amos Oz: The lighthouse
Yigal Schwartz
Journal of Israeli History, volume 38, issue 2 (2020), pp. 415–421

Chapter 9

Love, compassion, and longing
Nurith Gertz
Journal of Israeli History, volume 38, issue 2 (2020), pp. 423–430

For any permission-related enquiries please visit:
www.tandfonline.com/page/help/permissions

Notes on Contributors

Omri Asscher is Senior Lecturer at the Department of Translation and Interpreting Studies in Bar-Ilan University, Israel. His work deals with competing Jewish identities in Israel and the United States, primarily through the prism of literary and theological translation. He is the author of *Reading Israel, Reading America: The Politics of Translation between Jews* (2019).

Arie M. Dubnov is Associate Professor of History and the Max Ticktin Chair of Israel Studies at the George Washington University, USA. His publications include the intellectual biography *Isaiah Berlin: The Journey of a Jewish Liberal* (2012), and two edited volumes, *Zionism – A View from the Outside* (2010 [in Hebrew]) and *Partitions: A Transnational History of Twentieth-century Territorial Separatism* (2019, co-edited with Laura Robson).

Nurith Gertz is Emerita Professor of Literature and Film at the Open University of Israel. Her academic research deals with a wide range of topics such as Hebrew literature, Israeli and Palestinian cinema, Israeli society and culture, trauma and private and collective memory. Gertz was one of the first to study Amos Oz's works, and her book *Amos Oz: A Monography* (1980) paved the way for many of the subsequent studies. Gertz and Oz first met in 1973, shortly before the outbreak of the Yom Kippur War, and maintained friendly relations until his death in 2018.

Karen Grumberg is Arnold S. Chaplik Professor of Israel and Diaspora Studies and the Director of the Center for Middle Eastern Studies at the University of Texas at Austin, USA. She works primarily on modern Hebrew literature in comparative contexts and on global and international Gothic. She is the author of *Hebrew Gothic: History and Poetics of Persecution* (2019).

Eran Kaplan is the Rhoda and Richard Goldman Chair in Israel Studies at SF State, USA. Professor Kaplan teaches courses on Modern Israel, the Arab Israeli Conflict, Israeli Cinema, Modern Hebrew Culture, and the History of Jerusalem at SF State. He is the author, most recently, of *Projecting the Nation: History and Ideology on the Israeli Screen*.

Adia Mendelson-Maoz is Professor in Israeli literature and culture at the Department of Literature, Language and Arts, Open University of Israel. She investigates the multifaceted relationships between literature, ethics, politics, and culture, mainly in the context of Hebrew Literature and Israeli culture. Her book, *Territories and Borders in the Shadow of the Intifada: Ethical Reading of Hebrew Literature 1987–2007* (2020) is a Hebrew adaptation of *Borders, Territories, and Ethics*.

Lilah Nethanel is an Israeli writer and literary scholar. With Youval Shimoni, she is the joint editor of David Vogel's *Viennese Romance* (2013).

David Ohana is Professor at The Ben-Gurion Institute for the Study of Israel and Zionism at Ben-Gurion University of the Negev, Israel, and a Life Member at Clare Hall College at the University of Cambridge, UK. His many books include: *The Origins of Israeli Mythology* and most recently *The Fascist Temptation* (Routledge 2021).

Yigal Schwartz is Professor of Literature at Ben-Gurion University of the Negev, Israel where he serves as the director of "Heksherim": The Research Institute for Jewish and Israeli Literature and Culture. Additionally, he serves as the editor-in-chief of the Kinneret Zmora-Bitan Dvir publishing house. He edited several of Oz's books and wrote extensively about Oz's literary work. His most recent book is *Why the Puss has Boots* (2021).

Vered Karti Shemtov is the Chernov Lokey Senior Lecturer at the Department of Comparative Literature, Stanford University, USA, and the Editor-in-Chief of *Dibur Literary Journal*. Shemtov is the author of *Changing Rhythms: Towards a Theory of Prosody in Cultural Context*. Some of her more recent publications in English are *Utopia, Dystopia, Limbotopia* with Elana Gomel, and *Poetry and Dwelling: From Martin Heidegger to the Songbook of the Tent Revolution in Israel*.

Neta Stahl is Associate Professor at the Department of Modern Languages and Literatures and the Director of the Stulman Program in Jewish Studies at Johns Hopkins University, USA. Her primary research interests lie at the intersection of literature, religion, and culture. She works on a broad range of modern Hebrew writers, from S.Y Agnon and Uri Zvi Grinberg to the contemporary author Yoel Hoffmann. Her most recent book, *The Divine in Modern Hebrew Literature* was published in March 2020 with Routledge.

Introduction: Amos Oz's two pens

Arie M. Dubnov

ABSTRACT

Often regarded as the country's leading intellectual, the Israeli novelist and political essayist Amos Oz (1939–2018) was fond of describing himself as using two different pens, the first used to write work of prose and fiction, and the other – to criticize the government and advocate for a political change. The idea behind this special issue is to revisit the two pens parable by bringing together scholars from various disciplines to assess Amos Oz's dual role in Israeli culture and society as an immensely popular novelist and a leading public intellectual. Next to offering an intellectual portrait, this introduction highlights some of Oz's seminal works, examines their reception, revisits key political and literary debates he was involved in, and traces some of the connections between the two realms of his activity.

In 2008, the Parisian *Salon du livre*, one of the most celebrated literary festivals in France, hosted a special panel with the three tenors of Israeli literature – A. B. Yehoshua (b. 1936), David Grossman (b. 1954), and the late Amos Oz (1939–2018). Outside their outstanding literary accomplishments, all three inveterate fabulists are known for their civic engagement and political commitments. They channeled their ideas to the broader public, never shying away from addressing issues of the day, even if they involved a robust commentary on Israeli governments and policies. With these trademarks in common, the panelists were asked to discuss what comes first, the literary author or the engaged intellectual, and how they balance their literary and political appetites. In his reply, Amos Oz described his writing instruments:[ ]

> I have two pens on my writing desk, one black, the other – blue. I use one pen when I want to tell the government to go to hell. I would use it when I write an article to the newspapers: "Dear government, go to hell." Surprisingly, and I do not know precisely why, they would refuse to go to hell. When I want to write a story, however, I use the other pen. I never mix between the two pens.[1]

It was not the first time Oz spoke of his two pens. A frequently employed trope, it became one of the author's emblems. When Oz passed away ten years later, in December 2018, the trope found its way into numerous obituaries and articles commemorating him. Oz's insistence on the separation and semi-autonomy of each field was often scrutinized by commentators, even by close colleagues and friends. Indeed, during the same 2008 event, A. B. Yehoshua, who was accustomed to hearing Oz using the two pens parable, could not resist addressing the Parisian audience in French, triggering a burst of great laughter when declaring: "I have known Amos for many years, and I can assure you: he is not using two pens." Perhaps the two pens story was a helpful ploy to conceal what was, in fact, an interdependency of the esthetic and the political? Oz perceived history and politics as a series of melodramatic confrontations. Recurrently, he would construe it as an enthusing interpersonal conflict between humans with grand ambitions and egos but equally great human flaws. His political essays, speeches, and newspaper articles – sometimes more than his fiction – provided him with the arenas he needed to make the grand ideological narratives an object of suspicion. At the same time, political conflicts were frequently relocated into Oz's fiction. Literary prose, and not only the op-ed and the essay, were mediums he used to cut through particular political dilemmas.

The idea behind this special issue is to revisit the two pens parable by bringing together scholars from various disciplines to assess Amos Oz's dual role in Israeli culture and society as an immensely popular novelist and a leading public intellectual. Oz, who passed away in December 2018, was recognized from an early stage of his career as one of Israel's top writers and intellectuals. His books have been translated into some 45 languages (more than any other Israeli author), he won dozens of awards for his work, including the Israel Prize for Literature in 1998, Prix Femina, the Frankfurt Peace Prize, the Goethe Prize, the Primo Levi Prize, and the National Jewish Book Award, and was nominated for the Nobel Prize. Far more than a famous author, he was revered by many who considered him the embodiment of a humanistic or liberal Zionism, a simultaneously patriotic and critical if not prophetic thinker, one of those "unacknowledged legislators of mankind," as Shelly famously put it.[2]

Oz's frequent interventions in politics, public commentaries, and media appearances, and not only his prose, contributed greatly to his canonization. Influential liberal journalists outside Israel embraced Oz with particularly strong admiration. He was compared to Václav Havel, the Czech novelist-dissident-statesman who stood behind the Velvet Revolution, and described as "a bleeding-heart liberal constantly scolding the nation for its ongoing occupation of Palestinian lands," and a fearless humanist who, even when denounced as a traitor, regarded the insult "as nothing less than 'a badge of honor,' putting him in the same company as Jeremiah, [and] Abraham Lincoln."[3] Even his physique did not escape the scrutiny of non-Israeli observers, who commented on Oz's "rugged, emblematic looks," "his face battle-scarred by service in Israel's 1967 and 1973 wars." The "novelist-kibbutznik," they concluded, "could have been a model of the 'new Jew' the first Zionists longed to forge in the Mediterranean sun," "part of the mid-century Zionist iconography."[4] For many Israelis, Oz's long industrious career, his frequent media appearances, and the fact he accompanied Israeli culture for so long seem to have had that curious effect: even when becoming old, he seemed eternal. As far as his popular appeal goes, it would be safe to speculate that Oz turned into an icon not because anyone took the alleged separation between the pen of the novelist and the pen of the public moralist seriously, but precisely because the compendium of esthetics and politics became his insignia: His novels were read as forming a literary map of Israel and as a running commentary on where the Zionist project was at odds with its own declared values, and his speeches and essays scorning Israeli governments and policies accompanied them and were taken more seriously thanks to the symbolic capital he earned as a novelist who was interested in the universal predicaments of the human condition.

For other, more denigrating critics, there was nothing intrinsically universal about Oz. He was described as the literary warden of Zionist settler-colonialism, taking a similar role to the one Albert Camus took on himself when defending the French *pied-noirs* in Algeria, offering, as Perry Anderson put it, "a mixture of machismo and schmaltz," while promoting through his art and tireless defense of the two-states solution politics of Jewish-Arab separation and partition that could not transcend the iron cage of nation-statism.[5] Expressions of animosity and contempt toward the towering figure also came from within Israel. Obsessed with masculine beauty, critic Yitzhak Laor argued, Oz continued and brought to a pinnacle the paramount effort of modern Hebrew literature to construct the Sabra as a distinct subject that is defined through negation, by that which he is not (not "exilic," not "Mizrahi," not religious, not feminine), producing ingenious novels with a plot that could be recapped with the tagline "the sex life of Israel's security forces veterans."[6] The collapse of the Oslo Accords into an orgy of violence placed Oz in particular, and liberal Zionism in general, under a critical eye. Oz's well-rehearsed speeches against the "fanatics on both sides" were dismissed by Tzvi Ben-Dor Benite and others for offering a false symmetry masquerading asymmetry of power and control. Oz's insistence that curbing the extremist on both sides would transform an irreconcil-able, venomous holy war between Jews and Palestinians into a "real-estate dispute" that could be solved pragmatically was equally dismissed as a convenient rhetorical device that was predicated on the false assumption that fanatism is the trait of the Palestinian, the Mizrahi, the traditional or observant Jew ("in vain, you turned every tefillin wearer into a sorcerer"), which conveniently helped Oz to clear the old kibbutz leadership and the secular Ashkenazi hegemony from any blemish of intolerant extremism.[7] As Eran Kaplan's article in the present volume reminds us, such criticisms neither faded away nor were they ever divorced from the ideological, social, and political schisms of Israeli society.[8] Tinted by contemporary identity politics and the sharpening of political divides, "anti-obituaries" produced after Oz's passing took pleasure in describing him mockingly as the "[secular] Chief Rabbi" and even "Admor (Hassidic leader)" of an old guard and as the unelected "President of the White Tribe,"[9] i.e., an anachronistic symbol of a bygone era of Ashkenazi labor-Zionism. Poignantly, the accusation that Oz's iconic status was a remnant of what the late Israeli sociologist Bruch Kimmerling described as "the age of the *Ahusalim*" (an acronym denoting the Ashkenazi, secular, socialist, and nationalist vanguard that founded the country) provided the crux of many of those postmortem critiques.[10] Oz was understood as spokesman of the country's old self-assigned cultural aristocracy, producing high-table and dreamy self-gratification talk about liberal plural-ism that failed to capture or to challenge the everyday experience of discrimination and the unbridgeable gaps separating different sectors of the far from homogenous Israeli society.

In conceiving this special issue, my aspiration was to avoid the double traps of either producing an *In Memoriam* hagiographic tribute or falling prey to an iconoclastic desire to remove a deceased suzerain from his plinth. Neither nostalgic nor angry, my intention was to reexamine Oz's oeuvre as a fascinating blend of esthetic expressions and political formations and thus challenge the "two pens" myth. I hope this issue would serve as an invitation to reevaluate Oz by placing him in broader historical, cultural, and literary contexts while avoiding the dual pitfalls of a hagiographic extolment of the virtues on the one hand and the equally zealous dismissive iconoclasm, on the other hand.

It is, to be sure, a tricky balancing act. What makes it particularly challenging from this historians' point of view is the fact Oz's literary estate is still not open to researchers and that he destroyed a vast majority of his unpublished papers and drafts, as he self-proclaimed in his conversations with Shira Hadad, one of his former editors: "I do not archive [my unpublished papers], I destroy. I'm not an archivist. I tear into tiny pieces, throw them to the toilet, drain the water. Because I cannot start a fire in the house, and I'm scared throwing it in the trash, pages might fly away; someone might find [something], I do not want to [take the risk]."[11] Oz was acutely aware of his celebrity status in Israel and beyond it, a product of tireless manufacturing and marketing of a distinctive public persona, which he groomed and maintained through numerous carefully curated interviews and documentaries, and, of course, through his best-selling 2002 autobiographical novel, *Tale of Love and Darkness* (*Sipur al ahavah ve-hoshekh*) that was made into a Hollywood film. Oz was not the first fiction writer to dislike academics and fact-checkers sniffing around his work, but his aversion took the form of a principled stance. To leave no room for doubt, he included in his autobiography an entire chapter consisting of the admonition of the "bad reader" who seeks to unearth the facts buried underneath the fictional self-fashioning. Oz regarded the "good reader," suggests Vered K. Shemtov, as a reader who intuitively apprehends that the real gap is not the one separating between the text and the life of his author but the gap between the text and the reader.[12] Yet the metaphors and similes Oz employed in Hebrew to slam "bad readers" are revealing: they are gossip-monger readers of tabloids; they approach the author equipped with "plastic handcuffs" (an object reminding the Israeli reader of the first Intifada, and ubiquitous images of Palestinian youths detained by Israeli soldiers) trying to "arrest" him; they are "priggish-Puritans" whose main desire is to uncover the unredeemed sinner that the fiction author tries to conceal (hence believing that Dostoevsky must have murdered old ladies, Faulkner was involved in incest, Nabokov was a pedophile and so on); they are dangerous rapists:

> The bad reader comes and demands from me to peel away the layers of the book which I wrote . . . The bad reader is like a psychopathic lover who pounces on and tears the clothes off a woman who fell into his hands, and when she is totally naked he continues to rip off her skin and impatiently sets it aside and chomps at it between his gross yellow teeth – only then he comes to his satisfaction: 'that is it,' he says. 'Finally, I'm inside, I'm really inside. I've arrived.'[13]

This is an extraordinarily brutal, pornographic-turning-homicidal description. Intriguingly, the entire chapter from which this passage was taken (chapter 5 in the Hebrew edition) was omitted from Nicholas De Lange's elegant English translation, perhaps due to its gruesome language. Such a categorical authorial proclamation frames the original Hebrew edition and leaves little room for guessing. Oz envisioned a hierarchical and authoritative relationship with his audience: while demanding full attentiveness and unquestioning allegiance from his readers, the autobiographical narrator was not willing to gesture that he is committed to making a sincere effort of providing a truthful account of himself and condemned categorically any attempt of checking his narrative's veracity as a heinous "bad reading" crime. This is a peculiar "user manual," especially in a work that derives its power from the presumable fact that the author is not hiding behind an invented character but is the main protagonist of his tale. In that sense, Oz breaches, straightforwardly and rather stunningly, what the French theoretician Philippe Lejeunian famously dubbed as an "autobiographical pact" between the author and his readers.[14] As a result, we must take all he tells us about himself with a grain of salt. More than an ingenious narrative of the being-in-itself of the past, or an amalgamation of introspection and a claim for truth, *Tale of Love and Darkness* is an aestheticized self-portrait of a magisterial author at the autumn of his life, a marvelous blend of half-truths and inventions. His harsh dismissal of "bad readers" serves as an ultimatum, a threat. It joins Oz's numerous attempts to control the way he would and should be remembered. We have no choice but to reject this ultimatum and bring back *Geschichte* into the highly stylized and acutely self-aware *Lebensgeschichte*.

Unexpectedly, the historico-literary project has turned out to be even more challenging in light of the public controversy that erupted while the present volume was in advanced stages of production, following the publication of a revelatory memoir by Oz's youngest daughter, Galia Oz (b. 1964), accusing her late father of tyrannical to abusive behavior that included physical and verbal violence.[15] This controversy, which aired family feuds and secrets in public and generated an important conversation about abusive parenting, has not yet ended. The Israeli literary circles, including past editors and colleagues, joined the stormy debate that cast a heavy shadow over Oz's reputation and reexamined the gaps separating literature from life.

Not stirring away from the present storm, the quarrel makes some of our guiding questions clearer: why do Oz's name and work evoke such strong emotional responses? How did he achieve such an iconic status, as a literary paterfamilias revered as a saint by his followers, representing all that is bad by his detractors? When and how did Oz's name and ideas enter into the Israeli culture's bloodstream? What explains his transformation into a cultural icon, an institution, a trademark? What was the mechanism, and who were the agents who helped him receive such recognition and enjoy such a reception in Israel and beyond it? I wish the present issue to open a conversation based on this set of questions. The articles assembled under this roof seek to start answering some of these questions. Carving out space for cross-disciplinary dialogue between historians and literary scholars, willing to acknowledge the interdependencies and interaction between their fields of study on the one hand and connections between the two layers of Oz's work, on the other hand, can help us start answering these questions.

Born Amos Klausner on May 4, 1939, Oz's long career and life story offer a cross-sectional view of some of the chief political and ideological vectors that shaped Israeli history. His parents, Yehuda Arieh Klausner (Odesa 1910 – Jerusalem 1970) and Fania Mussman (Rovno [today's Rivne] 1913–Jerusalem 1952) were Eastern European Zionist immigrants who arrived in Palestine six years prior to his birth and settled in Jerusalem. He studied at Tahkemoni, a religious elementary school affiliated with the Mizrachi Zionist movement, where the poetess Zelda (Zelda Schneurson Mishkovsky; 1914–1984) was one of his teachers. From there continued to the Rehavia Gymnasia (ha-gymnasia ha-ivrit be-Rehavia), Jerusalem's first modern Jewish high school.

Though poor, the prevailing atmosphere of his childhood house was reputably middle class, well-educated if not bookish, and decisively political. Through his father

Yehuda Arieh, who studied history and literature in Vilnius and worked as a librarian, Oz was related to Joseph Klausner (1874–1958), the well-known former editor of the Hebrew literary magazine *Ha-Shiloah* (published between 1896 and 1926), who moved to Palestine in 1919, becoming a key figure at the newly established Hebrew University, known for his monumental and controversial biography of Jesus, his work as a literary scholar, and as the chief redactor of the *Encyclopedia Hebraica*.[16] Notably, Joseph Klausner was, like Amos Oz's father Yehuda Arieh, also an outspoken Revisionist Zionist, a fierce critic of labor Zionism as well as the bi-nationalist group Brit Shalom, who, in 1949, ran against Chaim Weizmann in the first elections for the Israeli President. During the mandatory period, the literary-political circle that orbited around "Uncle Joseph," as Amos Oz would later describe him, included the poet Shaul Tchernichovsky, who Klausner admired and considered to be the true Zionist poet laureate, and Hayim Nachman Bialik. They were joined by numerous students, authors, translators and Revisionist activists such Shmuel Werses (1915–2010, who later became a renowned scholar of Haskalah literature), Joseph Lichtenbaum (1895–1968, poet, literary critic, and Hebrew translator), Joseph Nedava (1915 – 1988, a leading figure in the Revisionist movement, later professor of political science) and Benzion Netanyahu (*né* Mileikowsky, 1910–2012, who was a Revisionist journalist at the time, appointed to serve as Jabotinsky's last private secretary the year Oz was born and remembered today primarily thanks to his studies of Don Isaac Abravanel and as the father of Binyamin Netanyahu, the current Israeli prime minister). It was a group of embittered contrarians that had assembled on the edge of the Yishuv, promoting radical politics and believing passionately, perhaps credulously, in the power of words. It is difficult to escape the impression that the young Amos absorbed similar beliefs by osmosis.

But more than "Uncle Joseph," it was the tragic story of his mother Fania that shaped Oz's early life. "Every true writer becomes a writer because of a profound trauma experienced in youth or childhood," Oz declared in later years, in one of his lectures on S. Y. Agnon.[17] More than an observation about the impulses that drove the great Galicianer storyteller to produce his books, this veiled autobiographical hint became clearer in later years when Oz told in his memoir how he was orphaned at the age of twelve following his mother's suicide. The disaster fragmented the family and scarred the adolescent boy. Two years following the tragic event, the estranged and angry Amos left the dimly lit study rooms of Jerusalem, cut himself from his Revisionist family, and restarted his life as a kibbutz member. Nurith Gretz, Oz's authorized biographer-friend, found in this constitutive early loss a key to his soul and literary creativity. According to her, Oz's unceasing yearning to be loved and adored grew out of this formative injury, and the deep sense of abandonment and maternal betrayal also explains the fact his sense of self-worth remained lacking despite the recognition and the numerous honors bestowed on him over the years.[18]

Leaving a Revisionist Zionist home at a young age and replacing it with a kibbutz had another dimension. Not yet an artist, this self-reinvention was, perhaps, Oz's first artistic design. He chose to "walk in the fields" of Huldah, one of the kibbutzim established by the socialist Gordonia movement, which considered manual labor to be the path to redemption. A blazing transfiguration of self, this was, perhaps, the furthest ideological distance he could travel away from his family while remaining within the Zionist realm.

Reportedly, it was around that stage that he also adopted his new surname Oz, a word carrying a resilient biblical ring, meaning courage, heroism, and strength.

Oz's fiction revisited these attempts of self-reinvention, fueled by a mixture of heart-break and hope. The kibbutz, a locus classicus he kept revisiting, was considered by him as the prime site of this radical reincarnation. As Karen Grumberg showed, Oz's literature offers a fascinating test-case to examine how Zionist ideology has influenced representations of geography and space in Israeli culture.[19] Grumberg further develops this thesis in the present issue, showing through a comparative reading of Oz's stories and Sherwood Anderson's *Winesburg, Ohio*, how Oz was influenced by the American author, and translated and adapted representations of small-town America to reflect and describe Israeli landscape.[20]

At the very same time, the kibbutz was also a site of violent repression. This rejuvenation/suppression duality was expressed in *A Perfect Peace* (*Menuha nekhona*, orig. 1982), for example, through the figure of the 27-years old Yonatan Lifshitz, a second-generation young kibbutznik struggling to find his individuality vis-à-vis his dismissive and monstrous pioneer father, who was full of righteousness, highfalutin ideals, and mockery of the young, whom he constantly belittled and dismissed as a spoiled generation that failed his expectations.[21] Oz returned to the theme four decades later, in the eight interconnected short stories of *Between Friends* (*Bein Haverim*, orig. 2012), describing the pettiness, everyday banal cruelty, the ambiguous love-hate relationships between parents and children, the constant gossip and ridicule that characterized life in the fictitious kibbutz Yekhat, a collectivist panopticon where everything is visible and known to the crowd, and where there is no escape from deep loneliness, sense of loss and despair.[22] Literary critic Abraham Balaban (himself a former member of kibbutz Huldah) suggested reading this duality through a Jungian lens, as indicating an undeniable religious element to Oz's prose, into which Kabbalistic motifs and symbols were woven. According to that reading, Oz's unceasing effort to delve ever deeper into the dark side of consciousness, and the use of Kabbalistic terms in later novels such as *To Know a Woman* (*La-da'at ishah*, orig. 1989) and *Fima* (*Ha-matsav ha-shelishi*, orig. 1991), were part of a voyage toward holiness that could be achieved only through unity between opposing, contradictory psychic forces.[23]

It remains unclear if Oz would have subscribed to this dialectical and somewhat mystic reading of his fiction. As a public intellectual, however, he returned and explicitly referred to the kibbutz as a bold social experiment and highlighted the fact it embodied an essential paradox: a new, utopian secular order, expressed and promoted through a great deal of messianic and redemptive fervor. Indeed, to a greater extent, for Oz the intellectual, the kibbutz and its internal contradictions served as an overarching metonym of Israeliness: "The kibbutz is perhaps the most remarkable attempt to construct a model of an extended family without coercion in the entire twentieth century," Oz declared in a 1994 interview. "The mistake [of its founders] was to make too many assumptions about the state of human nature and the chances of altering it." Even when taking over the management of the kibbutz affairs, the sons "continued giving more weight to their fathers than to their children: it was more important to them to fulfill the fathers' dreams than those of their children. They lived with their faces to their parents' imaginations and with their backs to their children. In this, they were no different from a religious community."[24]

The kibbutz, in other words, was seen by him as the key arena in which the burning desire to forge a new self was coupled with idealistic hopes of building a new social order. He admitted in retrospect that there was an undeniable element of violent fanaticism in both projects. Before harming others, it was a form of self-injury, having a stifling effect on the sons' generation, impotent and crushed under the heavy burden of the fathers and Israel's founding myths. Turning the kibbutz into a symbol of the Israeli condition, however, was also indicative of certain characteristic blinders of the Israeli labor movement. Understood from this prism, Oz's Israeliness was at its core socialist, secular, Zionist, male, and Ashkenazi. As it was often noted, only in later stages did his prose open up to accept other shapes and colors. By the time Oz began embracing the diversity of Israeli life, the old way of life represented by the kibbutz was defeated and practically obsolete. He nevertheless remained one of its most conspicuous apologists:

> I identify quite a bit with those who are now put in the defendant's chair and are blamed for all our disasters: precisely with '*Eretz Yisrael ha-ovedet*' [literally: 'working Israel,' codename for Labor Zionism] that for thirty years of my life I wrote quite a bit about, [including about] its internal contradictions and hypocrisy and ugliness and arrogance. Now that it has been defeated, I am not sure that its successors from Shas or the settlement movement or the post-Zionist caravan are better than it is. I think not.[25]

Oz's political appetites were also evident from an early stage, and in his early political interventions, one can detect undeniable generational tensions as well. Though he began writing stories in his twenties, a handwritten letter he sent in April 1954 to David Ben-Gurion is, perhaps, a record of his first audacious and opinionated intervention in political affairs. Triggered by a comment made by the former Prime Minister who retired from politics to Sde Boker and reportedly wrote that he could not find true passionate Zionism in the ranks of those younger than him, the 15-year-old Oz rushed to his desk and authored a letter condemning the premier for his dismissive comment, arguing that the youth is not to be blamed but praised for fighting "corruption, degradation, and careerism," and lacks leadership and "moral guidance."[26] Put in context, the letter reads like a mix of fearlessness and flattery, praising Ben-Gurion and pointing the finger at his successors. The fact the letter was not destroyed suggests that its rhetorical power impressed Ben-Gurion, who composed in less than a week a carefully crafted reply to the gallant young author.[27] Interestingly, the young Oz signed the letter using his new last name but listed his old Jerusalem home address and highlighted the fact he was a proud member of the Jerusalem Scouts.

Six years later, at the height of the Lavon Affair with Ben-Gurion back in the office, Oz sent another letter. This time it was an essay-long open letter, sent to the daily *Davar*, disapproving with Ben-Gurion's analysis of the state of the kibbutz movement.[28] Once again, the old man was prompted to respond in writing to the opinionated young man.[29] As Oz reports in *Tale of Love and Darkness*, criticizing openly the Prime Minister and Minister of Defense was an audacious if not rash move, and he feared that he might be disobeying some unknown military order (Oz was still a soldier at the time, about to end a relatively uneventful compulsory service in the Nahal brigade). As the memoir makes it clear, Oz considered this to be his début appearance as a spirited democratic critic, speaking truth to power and fighting against the arbitrary use of political power. He recalled vividly how he, nerve-wracked and inexperienced, met in person with "The

Father of the Nation," and how awed and surprised he was by Ben-Gurion's "strange, hypnotic form" and by the unanticipated cascade of questions that gushed from him about Spinoza, the philosopher whom Ben-Gurion famously admired the most. The long philosophical lecture, in which Ben-Gurion "had explained once and for all, in one crushing blow, everything that had been left unexplained in the thought of Spinoza," transmuted into an equally passionate sermon about other matters: "the loss of Zionistic fervor in our youth, or modern Hebrew poetry, which was dabbling in all kinds of weird experiments instead of opening its eyes and celebrating the miracle that was happening here daily in front of our eyes: the rebirth of the nation, the rebirth of the Hebrew language, the rebirth of the Negev Desert!"[30]

This is a marvelous account. It is, nonetheless, fabricated. The exchange of letters published in *Davar* and the protocol of the meetings that took place in Ben-Gurion's office in Tel Aviv on March 15 and 23, 1961, tell a rather different story. Conspicuously, Oz not only forgot to mention in his memoir the fact there were two meetings, but also failed to acknowledge the presence of nine and later eleven other kibbutzniks, representatives of the young guard of *Ihud Ha-Kvutzot Ve-Hakibbutzim* (Union of the kvutzot and the kibbutzim) the prime minister has asked to meet.[31] The ostensibly long monologue on Spinoza has no record in the protocols of the meetings, nor is the name of the philosopher mentioned once in the newspaper exchanges. The one-man-show and sermon were, in fact, a dialogue, during which Ben-Gurion, acknowledging his weakness in light of the Lavon affair, listened carefully and respectfully to the youth, trying to apprehend their outlook. Evident as well is the discrepancy between the casting of Ben-Gurion as a harsh, uncompromising ideologue and the young Oz as a broad-minded liberal-in-the-making in the novel and the contents of the historical documents. What prompted Oz to write his letter to *Davar* was an essay by Ben-Gurion, written for the jubilee of the establishment of Degania, the first kibbutz, reflecting on a half-century of Zionist labor and communal living, in which he suggested that full equality is an unreachable aim that could easily collapse into totalitarianism. The more modest aim of establishing cooperatives is the pragmatic and noble track worth pursuing, Ben-Gurion suggested. Oz, attempting to be holier than the Pope, insisted that any departure from the idea that the kibbutz aspires to full equality is a jarring ideological heresy and that although "equality cannot be fully realized, and that the fulfillment of the [ideal] of absolute equality would create an inhuman society," faith in absolute ideals and struggle for them provide the essence of the kibbutz. For in the kibbutz one finds, in the most refined form, that epic

> war of man against his own nature, against his passions, against his instincts, against the animal in him, against the 'natural' of his soul. The resurrection of Israel is a magnificent example of these two fronts of the human war against nature: [a war] against the "natural" laws of history and against the nature of the Jewish soul itself. [. . . .] It is the *kvutzha's* [collective commune] attempt to fulfill the unnatural and the impossible, to establish a utopia on earth, that gives the life of the *kvutzha* a meaning of a Gospel."[32]

Not less fervent were his comments during the group meetings. In response to Ben-Gurion's assertion that not all new immigrants are motivated by the same pioneer zeal and that some accommodations are required, Oz warned that willingness to offer special treatments, more than any political debacle, would cause him to leave the party. The exchange on the subject became heated. "You talk about aliyah [immigration to Israel] as one of the tenets of [faith], but that's not the point. The problem is what would be the profile of this aliyah," Oz proclaimed. Ben-Gurion answered: "No. First of all, let these Jews come to Israel, rather than them living either in America or in Russia." To this, Oz replied in the negative, pointing to the development towns to which Mizrahi immigrants were sent: "I am Epicurean [a heretic] when it comes to this matter. If we are to become a Levantine state, they better not come in the first place!"[33]

It is not difficult to understand why Oz, the sentimental memoirist of 2002, airbrushed the prejudiced and highly disturbing comments made by the younger Oz of 1961, an overzealous and arrogant kibbutznik. The episodic, selective memory, the fictitious account of a tête-à-tête conversation with the grand man based on concealment of the presence of others, the retrospective presentation of self as early blooming moderate humanist fighting the atavistic hyper-nationalist trends of young Israel: all these are testimonies to Oz's talent for melodrama and gifts as a storyteller. They are also testament to his tireless attempts to inject himself into the "good side" of history and to construct and later maintain his image as a lonely liberal and a pluralist, committed to fighting all types of religious and ideological zealotry.

A short time after his exchange and meetings with Ben-Gurion Oz returned to Jerusalem, to attend the Hebrew University, where he studied Hebrew literature and philosophy. Among his professors were the then-prominent literary scholar and critic Dov Sadan (1902–1989), the poet and translator Simon Halkin (1898–1987; who succeeded Joseph Klausner as Professor of Modern Hebrew Literature in 1949), and the philosopher Nathan Rotenstreich (1914–1993). After graduation he returned to Huldah, where he married his wife Nily (*née* Zuckerman) and where he would remain a kibbutz member for nearly three decades (1957–1986), earning his living as a teacher at the local high school. His first short stories were published in 1962 in *Keshet* (1958–1976), Aharon Amir's literary magazine that provided a stage for a new generation of authors such as Oz, A. B. Yehoshua, Yitzhak Ben-Ner, Yehoshua Kenaz, and others. One of his earliest stories told of a paratrooper killed in a parachute accident during the Independence Day demonstration, while another dealt with a 1950s reprisal operation. Both were set against a familiar, quintessential Israeli landscape and centered on kibbutz life. They could be read as modern commentaries on sacrifice with references to the biblical story of the binding of Isaac or as bold rebuffing of Israeli jingoism, or as a mixture of both.[34] In May 1962, the same year he acquired a status of a writer, he joined *Min Ha-Yesod* (literally: from the foundations), the ideological circle established during the Lavon affair by Rotenstreich, Eliezer Schweid, Shlomo Grodzensky, and others. An internal opposition working from within the labor Zionist movement, the group became famous for criticizing Ben-Gurion's quasi-authoritarian leadership style, defending Pinchas Lavon, and calling for a renewal of the social-democratic values and ethos that underpinned the labor movement in the early days. By the time Oz's first collection of stories, *Where the Jackals Howl*, was published in 1965, he was already known to be an author holding two pens.

His first short story collection, *Where the Jackals Howl* (1965) and the novel *Elsewhere, perhaps* (1966), both describing kibbutz life, won instantaneous critical acclaim. *My Michael* (1968), his second novel, became a bestseller and secured Oz's status as representing the "new wave" of modern Hebrew literature, alongside Yehoshua, Amalia

Kahana-Carmon, Shulamit Hareven, and Aharon Appelfeld. In all three cases, Oz was praised for the depth of psychological insight, his linguistic virtuosity, as well as his razor-sharp parody of the arrogance and condescension of the fathers' generation. The lack of pathos, and Oz's nuanced, captivating and thick descriptions of the emptiness of kibbutz life simultaneously impressed and annoyed Baruch Kurzweil (1907–1972), the influential and notoriously polemic literary critic. He described Oz's early short stories as a "gateway to an epic Waste Land," an acidic compliment comparing the young author to T. S. Eliot, the grandmaster of literary modernism, while condemning the valueless wilderness of him and the young generation of Israeli authors he was part of.[35] Many eyebrows were raised also by readers of Oz's short story "Nomad and Viper," in which a young woman from a kibbutz who plans, like Potiphar's wife, to accuse a Bedouin nomad of rape after he rejects her advances. Seduction by the potentially violent "Other" and intense erotic desires was further developed in *My Michael*, which was adapted to the cinema (1976), translated into 30 languages, and considered a classic. Written in a feminine first person, it contained vivid descriptions of the erotic hallucinations of the main protagonist, Hannah Gonen, who was fleeing in her dreams away from her unexciting and sexually unsatisfying marriage, into a world of fantasy, where Jules Verne's novels and the Arab twins Khalil and Aziz provided compensation and escape. Its famous opening line – "I am writing this because people I loved have died" – was oft-quoted and acquired additional meaning when Oz's mother's personal story came to light in later years. Kurzweil, once again, was dissatisfied: he accused Oz of indulging in narcissistic self-flagellation and showing off his virtuoso style, while failing to capture the spirit of the age or the inner life of his protagonist.[36] Oz, it is worth noting, was not the sole object of Kurzweil's venomous critique, as much as he was regarded, alongside S. Yizhar, as articulating in extreme the "anti-canonical" qualities he abhorred in the new secular Israeli literature. This new wave, he famously believed, was obsessed with the "literarization" of everyday life, devoid of any vision of the sublime, and detached from the authenticity of Jewish historical experience over the ages and from the esthetic heights European novel alike. The young authors disparaged so ruthlessly by Kurzweil agonized and often protested (Kurzweil was heavily influenced by Karl Kraus's merciless satirical style) but those debates also demarcate boundaries between the "new" and "old" literature, that in Kurzweil's case mapped on the divisions between "secular" versus "religious," "socialist" and "bourgeois," "rupture" and "tradition."[37]

The erotic fantasies that stood at the heart of many of these early stories, tangled up with politics – often, it was a Jewish-Israeli gaze at the Bedouin or the Palestinian "enemies" (the British nemesis joined the list with Oz's 1976 novella, *The Hill of the Evil Counsel*) – seem to have divided Oz's readers between those who admired his boldness and those shocked and repulsed by it. But they also gave Oz's early prose one of its distinctive trademarks: Unlike A. B Yehoshua, who described Zionism as a project of normalization making Jews like any other nation, the plots Oz's early stories took place in proximity to a real or imagined political frontier (his childhood neighborhood Kerem Avraham in Jerusalem, the fictional frontier kibbutz of Metsudat Ram in *Elsewhere, perhaps*), dwelled on the liminal spaces between sanity and abnormality, and their protagonists were longing for something else, eager to be liberated, anticipating things that are not yet to come true. In almost all of these early stories stood a sharp contrast between the grim everyday realities on the one hand, and the phantasm, the allure of remote places, and the unsatisfied yearning to experience a re-enchantment on the other hand. Whether he was describing the repetitive, wearisome rhythm of kibbutz life or the dull petite bourgeois existence of Jerusalemite families – the two "geographical axes" of Oz's life's story revolved around, as Nurith Gertz put it in one of the first academic studies of Oz's prose[38] – his insistence on describing a gray reality, hollowed of meaning, was far removed from the haughty utopian imageries of the new society offered by Zionist orators.

These early experiences notwithstanding, Oz's true sanctification as a fledgling intellectual took place in the wake of the 1967 Six-Day War. Quick to respond, Oz published a series of forceful op-eds and articles criticizing the euphoric if not Messianic exultation atmosphere in Israel in the immediate aftermath of the war, setting himself against the Israeli government and the newly formed Movement for Greater Israel alike. In "The Defense Minister and the Living Space" (August 1967), Oz criticized Moshe Dayan for rejecting the suggestion that Israel should withdraw from the occupied territories in exchange for peace agreements, not fearing to deploy the loaded German concept of *Lebensraum*, denoting the territories needed by a nation for its "natural development" so infamously associated with Nazi policies.[39] Eastern Jerusalem, that Israeli nationalists were quick to call "liberated" and assembled into the municipal boundaries of the capital of Israel, was portrayed by him as "an alien city" that had nothing to do with the "adored, terrifying Jerusalem" he grew up in as a child (September 1967).[40]

Siah lohamim (literally: combatants' talk, translated as *The Seventh Day*) remains the most recognized among these post-1967 works.[41] The anthology, a product of Oz's partnership with Avraham ("Pachi") Shapira (1935-), comprised interviews with combat soldiers who returned from the frontlines to share their experiences, unfiltered. From the outset, Shapira and Oz declared, they did not intend to produce yet another victory album of the kind that reached almost every home in Israel in those days, but a kind of "spiritual testimony": not to reconstruct the military maneuvers of the victorious commanders, but to capture how ordinary warriors experienced the war and its immediate aftermath and explain why so many of them were mourning, or at least confused, instead of joining the cheering and celebrating crowds. The testimonies shed light on the dark side of the war, as the interviewees talked openly about the death of close friends, expressed fear, anxiety and hinted at war brutalities. The odd mixture of eyewitness accounts, lamentation, grief, soul-searching, and intimate reflection stood in contrast with the prevailingly arrogant, triumphant mood that swept Israel in summer 1967. Notably, the original 1967 compilation consisted only of interviews with kibbutzniks and emerged, as Alon Gan showed, as an initiative of the kibbutz movement affiliated with Mapai, the ruling labor Zionist party.[42] Avraham Shapira, Oz's partner and the editor of the volume, played a pivotal role here: a former student of Kurzweill's who joined kibbutz Yizre'el, he served as the founding editor of *Shdemot* (*Fields*, established 1960), a kibbutz movement periodical that gradually transformed during the 1960s into a quasi-literary quarterly, publishing excerpts from the writings of Jewish philosophers and intellectuals such as Martin Buber, Shmuel Hugo Bergmann, Eliezer Schweid, Akiva Ernest Simon, Nathan Rotenstreich and others alongside brochures whose main purpose was to help train youth movement counselors in the kibbutzim. In doing so, *Shdemot* was offering the young, second-generation kibbutzniks not only a taste of the acumen of the wise men of the Hebrew University (many of whom were associated with groups like *Brit Shalom* and *Ihud* during the mandatory period) but also, and perhaps far more significantly, a taste of an unassertive, humble Jewish "spirituality," which helped nourish a new sensibility that stood in sharp contrast with the crude anti-religiosity of the official kibbutz ideology and the "fathers' generation."[43] It thus helped to generate a certain mood, a new sensitivity among some kibbutzniks, which provided, at least partially, the backdrop against which the inimitable style of *Siah lohamim* emerged.

The book inaugurated, arguably, a quintessentially Israeli subgenre of "soldier testimonies" that left an indelible mark on the shape of political debates about war and peace in Israel to this day. At the time of its publication, *Siah lohamim* served as a reminder of the unique status of the kibbutzniks – about 25% of the soldiers who died in the war were kibbutz member despite the fact they constituted less than 4% of Israel's general population at the time – and reaffirmed a certain *noblesse oblige* ethos among the members of this select class, Oz included. Despite its unheroic, lyrical tone and the palpable dovish political stance Oz promoted, the book was well-received at the time, praised by many as a generation-shaping document and even translated into English and several other foreign languages by the Israeli Ministry of Foreign Affairs who found the book to be a helpful propaganda tool, displaying the consciousness and humanistic voice of the Israeli soldiers in order to counter the increasing denunciations of Israel's brutality and illegal occupation.

Outside Israel, Oz acquired his unique status as the prominent Hebrew author who is also the moral voice of Israel in this post-1967 context as well. As Omri Asscher's article in the present volume shows, Oz was exceptionally quick in gaining critical acclaim overseas and in particular in the English-reading world, as all his major works have been published in translation, beginning with *My Michael* which appeared in 1970.[44] His nuanced political stance – a critic of Israeli policies at home, yet, at the same time, a cultural ambassador of the Israeli republic abroad – was interwoven with his literary accomplishment, helping him to secure a visiting position at St Cross College, one of Oxford University's new colleges, in 1969–70. Subsequent visiting positions and prestigious fellowships were offered by UC Berkeley (1980), Colorado College (1984–5), Boston University (1987), Princeton University (1997), University of Indiana (2001), Tübingen (2002) and Stanford (2007). Isaiah Berlin, who became a friend, admired Oz for his temperate liberalism and erudition, and customarily subscribed to Oz's interpretations of the Israel-Palestine conflict. "[T]here are two ways of ending tragedies," Berlin once paraphrased Oz: "the Shakespearian, and the Chekhovian – in the first, everybody in the end is dead; in Chekhov they are all miserable, but alive. The second is preferable, and the first is never unavoidable – that is the degree of his and my optimism – but still it is something."[45]

Whether agreeing with him or not, many Israelis too came to regard Oz as the spokesman of the moderate, dovish "Peace Camp," treating *Siah lohamim* as urtext of the post-1967 Zionist Left. The book joined Oz's collections of his political articles such as *Under This Blazing Light* (*Be-or ha-tkhelet ha-aza*, orig. 1979) and *The Slopes of Lebanon* (*Mi-mordot ha-Levanon*; orig 1988), and his travelogue *In the Land of Israel* (*Poh va-sham be-Erets-Yisra'el*; orig. 1983) offering a sober analysis of the growing social tensions within Israeli society, the pitfalls of hyper-nationalism, alongside Oz's analyses on the Israeli-Palestinian conflict and his uncompromising critique of the messianic fervor of Gush Emunim and the settler movement.[46] Put together, provided a language for those who wished to remain "loyal critics," working from within the acceptable confines of Zionist ideology, and contributed greatly to Oz's reputation as "a humanist in the darkness," as David Ohana, one of the participants in the volume, phrases it.[47] The reportage-like style of many of these writings is also telling: no longer a spokesman for a self-congratulatory and hegemonic socialist Zionism, the narrator in these books conveyed deep feelings of discord. Oz recast himself as an author who became a stranger in his own land and compelled to go into a journey, just like John Steinbeck and his poodle Charley did in America, to witness firsthand and learn anew his own terrain. At times, the journey becomes a one-man crusade, as on the way to meet with the settlers of Ofra: "I remind myself that if my hosts [in Ofra settlers] succeed in their cause, they may drag me and my children with them, to kill and die in a perpetual unnecessary war, or perhaps to turn Israel into a monster like Belfast or South Africa. For this argument is not an intellectual exercise: it is a matter of life and death, pure and simple."[48] The journey as a series of impassioned disputes on life and death, a prophetic polemicist on wheels.

Underlying these post-1967 political writings were at least two principal trademark arguments. First is the conception of 1967 as a mythical frontier between two eras. The settlement movement in particular, and the rise of the Israeli Right-wing Likud party more generally, were regarded in them as distorted and fraudulent irredentist projects that violated the form, contents and norms of pre-1967 Israel. It would be difficult to underestimate the power of this commanding didactic historical narrative. In parallel, these writings facilitated Oz's famous conception of Israel/Palestine as the land of colliding dreams, in which two groups, with equal and legitimate aspirations to nation-hood and recognition, struggled with each other over a tiny but culturally and religiously significant piece of territory. Oz was among the first to acknowledge that culture, religious sentiment and collective memory could not be ignored, but he also came to realize that they often added fuel to the fire. Ultimately the conflict is neither religious nor ethnic, but territorial, "a dispute over property: whose house? Who is going to get how much of it? Such conflicts can be resolved through compromise."[49] Both notions were predicated on the idea of a two-state solution. Such a partition, Oz came to the conclusion, was the only solution to this "tragic clash between right and right."[50]

Unsurprisingly, not everyone found these accounts cogent. Hillel Weiss, a religious settler from Elkana and a professor of Hebrew literature at Bar-Ilan University, expressed the resentment of many of his constituency when accusing Oz of boosting hatred for the Israeli Right, whose supporters were portrayed as tribal and primitive, and for producing essays rife with expressions of "Judeophobia, hatred of Jews and fear of Judaism, Shylockism and Shasnikism." In Oz's writings he saw how the call" "Beat the Jew!" has recently metamorphosed into "Beat the Settler!" For Weiss there was no gap separating Oz's fiction from his political writings, for both were symptoms of cynical despair, instability and "growing nihilism." He described the typical protagonist of Oz's story mockingly: "a grotesque political impotent scarred by some primeval trauma, usually a complex involving the character of a mother-pervert who has abandoned her family," who suppress his suffering and expresses "a total reduction of all earnest values."[51] On the other end, Palestinian activists and scholars applying the settler-colonial paradigm discarded the very framing of the conflict as a symmetrical struggle between two national movements, nor did they find Oz's glowing description of Israeli politics before 1967 to be particularly convincing. This line of critique became noticeable during the early 1990s, at a time when the unsettled disputes surrounding the Oslo Accords created a visible gap between the PLO leadership's supporters and leading Palestinian intellectuals who were opposed to the agreements. Edward W. Said was particularly upset by Oz's description of the agreement between Rabin's government and the Palestinian Authority as "the second biggest victory in the history of Zionism," dubbing it a "Palestinian Versailles" instead.[52] Postcolonial studies scholars followed suit: Oz's was indicted of erasing Palestinian Arabs almost entirely from his literary work, except in the form of an occasional two-dimensional abstract symbol of the "Other," and constructing in his political essays a meta-narrative that failed to face up adequately with the mass ethnic cleansing of 1948, Zionism's original sin.[53] In the volatile circumstances of the conflict, the translations of Oz's works to Arabic could not but have a political insinuation, raising the thorny question whether the act of translation is a move toward peacebuilding or a surrender to an arrogant enemy literature.[54] Often, summit meetings of Oz with influential Arab and Palestinian intellectuals did not take place in Israel-Palestine but had to be mediated by European institutions, such as in the case of the Siegfried Unseld Prize that was awarded jointly to Oz and Sari Nusseibeh in Berlin in 2010.[55]

The ways in which Oz addressed intra-Jewish ethnic relations between Mizrahim and Ashkenazim prompted an equally calamitous response. While Oz's description of his visit to Beit Shemesh in *In the Land of Israel*, where he witnessed the deep-seated sense of insult and rage of the Mizrahi residents, was greeted by many other Ashkenazi commentators as a wakeup call and an invitation to start recognizing past grievances, a next generation of Mizrahi novelists and poets such as Dror Mishani, Almog Behar and Mati Shemoelof, wondered if Oz, instead of relinquishing the traditional Orientalist and paternalistic role assigned to the Ashkenazi intellectuals, and fighting discrimination in earnest, reaffirmed traditional power relations by speaking on behalf of the Mizrahim, who were seen worthy of empathy but yet incapable of self-representation.[56] Far more contentious was the reception of Oz's epistolary novel *Black Box* (*Kufsah shehorah*, 1987). The novel was set in 1976, on the eve of the Likud party's ascent to power, and described the end of a tenuous marriage between Dr. Alex Gideon, an Ashkenazi veteran military officer turned a dovish academic, and his wife Ilana (*née* Halina), smitten by the charms and unpretentious warmth of Michel Sommo, the observant and Right-wing Jewish immigrant from Algeria. It was difficult to avoid the impression that in addition to a series of Manichean binarisms – the tall, righteous, cold and haughty secular and educated Ashkenazi mirroring the short, somewhat boorish but devout and affectionate Mizrahi committed to the Greater Land of Israel ideology – Oz made the entry of the Mizrahi into the life of a dysfunctional Ashkenazi family a symbol of the collapse of the Israeli society he dreamt of. Mizrahi activist Ofra Yeshua-Lyth was furious: "Oz captures well the fears of the Ashkenazi Israeli elite form the possibility that people from the Mizrahi community [*yotzei edot ha-mizrah*] would express their true power within the confines of the existing democratic process." The fictional character of Michel Sommo, who initially seems pleasant and humble but reveals a huge appetite and talent for a takeover of the Israeli aristocracy's wealth as the plot thickens, was regarded by her as the brainchild of distorted, slanderous stereotypical thinking. She saw clear parallels between the mini-controversy sparked by Oz's novel and the scandal that broke out in Germany around Rainer Werner Fassbinder's play *Garbage, The City and Death* (*Der*

Müll, die Stadt und der Tod, 1976) and concluded: "What will Amos Oz say if some German writer would have written about a dwarf Jew, hairy as a monkey, extorting money from a member of a 'noble' Aryan family as 'reparations for the suffering of the Jews in the Holocaust'?"[57] Literary scholar Ariel Hirschfeld was also taken aback:

> Oz turns the story of Alexander [Gideon] into an aristocratic decadence from the last days of the Romanov dynasty. It is hard not to hear the voices of Russian princes in the words of his only son, the heir Volodya Godonsky, and Oz gives his family enormous landed estates spread over the entirety of '*Eretz Yisrael Ha-ovedet*' as a kind of latifundium. Luckily, he has no feudal peasants for sale. The exiled prince, in his icy palace, engages in "fantasies" in a spiritual scientific manner, and remotely sponsors, using the property of his "ancestors" (his father only) the growth of right-wing Sephardism, cunning as a fox, small as a rat, sexually-stimulating as a goat, exilic as a Jew. Subdued, racist and forceful hatred is dripping throughout the pages of this book towards the Sephardi alongside an admiration of his power and great trepidation. Oz is unwilling to detach himself from the ancient dimensions of the uniform portrait of Israel the Mother, and thus he is forced to impart to the Ashkenazi aristocratic, quasi-poetic dimensions, in order to balance the mythological demons emerging from the Sephardic side.[58]

The poet David Avidan, who ran a popular weekly newspaper column at the time, concluded dismissively: "Amos Oz's inflationary status, the pose of the political guru (which he inherited from [the poet] Chaim Guri) and the relative abundance of translations of his books into other languages make him a nuisance in Hebrew prose and a barrier to its further development."[59] Notwithstanding the fact it was slammed by critics, the book was embraced by the general public and turned out to be a huge commercial success. Indeed, for the next decade and a half, this pattern – popular demand accompanied by an increasing hostility from the Israeli intelligentsia – repeated itself. Until 1999, Oz argued in later years, "there was almost a consensus, not only among literary critics, but also in the literature department, to dismiss or cancel my writing. Take for example [the novels] *To Know a Woman* [*la-da'at ishah*; 1989] or *Don't Call It Night* [*al tagidi lailah*; 1994]: these were books that were panned by almost everyone. Oh, yes: hatred. That's the accurate word for it."[60]

The Mizrahi characters that populated Oz's later works, however, were more conciliatory, and less cartoonish. The stark Ashkenazi (West) vs. Mizrahi (East) binarism was replaced by new poetics and esthetics of Mediterraneanism (*yam tikhoniyut*) and an attempt to forge a more inclusive Israeli identity, an Israeliness still founded on the tenets of Jewish ethnonationalism, but one that sees "Zionism as surname."[61] Artistically, Oz's Mediterraneanism reached its peak in *The Same Sea* (*Oto ha-yam*, 1999), a short, lyrical novel that was written in an unusual, almost rhyming poem.[62] Next to a colorful gallery of characters, the author himself also makes cameo appearances in the novel, receiving phone calls from his characters, who complain about the way he presents them in his work. Many suggested that *The Same Sea* prepared the ground for Oz's epic autobiography, *A Tale of Love and Darkness*: an intimate chamber music for quartet that precedes the master's grand symphony. The short-lived optimism of the 1990s, the hope that the politics of mutual negation would be replaced by interaction provides, perhaps, the political context for Oz's unconventional novel. The experimental style, the free jumps between the first-person singular and the first-person plural ("I-Us" in Vered Shemtov's terms), and the genteel nods toward postmodern fluidity and polyphony disclose Oz trying to reinvent himself and, as Neta Stahl suggests in the present issue, to adapt to new literary fashions and norms.[63] At the very same time, as Adia Mendelson-Maoz shows, the first-person, confessional narrative that aims "giving witness to oppression" reverberates in later Israeli autobiographical texts such as Ronit Matalon's *The Sound of Our Steps* (*Kol tsa'adenu*; 2008). Although Matalon's emotionally powerful novel describes a very different historical and cultural experience (that of a daughter of a fractured Egyptian-Jewish immigrant family speaking Arabic and French) the same key themes provide the kernel of the novel: trauma of immigration, emphasis on childhood experiences, an ambivalent figure of the mother, and a deep sense of loss.[64]

The acrimonious intra-Jewish quarrels surrounding Oz's publications from the 1980s and 1990s disclose resentment and envy, which attests to the unique national celebrity status the author has acquired. At the same time, it also revealed that the labor Zionist intelligentsia has lost its unique access to the corridors of power it enjoyed in earlier years. Emblematically, a week after judging Oz's *Black Box* so harshly, David Avidan bewailed the fact prime minister Yitzhak Shamir invited none of the poets and novelists associated with the labor movement, Oz included, to a special party he hosted at his residence.[65] Authors and poets never had genuine political power in Israel, Oz argued in later years, just the delusion of influence: "Until 1977, [Israeli] literature had the illusion of a child who claps his hands once every minute and a half and is certain that all the city's traffic lights are changing due to his clapping. From 1977 this illusion was also shattered. [. . .] Just as Sartre did not pull France out of Algiers and it was not Norman Mailer was not the one who took America out of Vietnam, neither S. Yizhar nor A. B. Yehoshua can take Israel out of the territories."[66]

The writing of *A Tale of Love and Darkness*, the magnificent opus that eclipses much of Oz's work today, should be understood also in this context: a reaction to a longstanding anxiety about the decreasing voice of the liberal Zionist, an endeavor to restore the author's privileged point of view and self-assigned role as the nation's narrator by making the autobiography one with the national epic: a life of a boy born into a historical turmoil, whose personal disasters and triumphs become inextricably linked to that of his nation. Yigal Schwartz, Oz's former editor, who became his main researchers, recognized almost instantly that the personal autobiographical novel has turned into a cult book. Oz was flooded with an unstoppable stream of letters, in which readers revealed personal, and often dramatic and tragic stories from their own lives. Oz, Schwartz argued, "cast himself in the role of the chosen son and wizard of the tribe," prompting his readers to produce no less intimate confessions.[67] We have included in the present volume a translation of Schwartz's obituary, originally published in Hebrew, providing the former editor's bird-seye view of the long and prolific career.[68]

While the publication of *A Tale of Love and Darkness* became a major cultural event and a proof that Oz's virtuoso qualities as a storyteller did not diminish, the charm of his political, didactic messages faded over the years. In recent years, a growing number of Israeli progressive intellectuals began scrutinizing the underlying political assumptions of Oz's master narratives. In particular, many who revisited *Siah lohamim* dismissed it as a book generating a quintessentially Israeli subgenre of "shooting and weeping," claiming that it might have provided a catharsis for the warriors but failed to offer a categorical moral warning that would prevent future generations of soldiers from running into battle and dutifully obeying orders and did not help to bring to an end Israel's occupation of the

West Bank and Gaza. "Doubt is allowed; Challenge is forbidden," the Israeli historian Aviad Kleinberg recapped the message of the book.[69] The fact that military service, preferably in a combat unit, is taken as the precondition for voicing any criticism was not less dubious. Moreover, the suspicion that when assembling the testimonies Shapira and Oz acted as a self-appointed vigilance committee – historians Tom Segev and Alon Gan argued that some of the participants' testimonies were censored, in some cases at their request, that some expressions were tainted before printing, and in extreme cases, testimonies were distorted to match the desirable image of the benevolent warrior-humanist the editors had in mind – added to the dark clouds hovering above the book.[70] *Censored Voices*, Mor Loushy's 2015 documentary, confirmed some of those suspicions.[71] Shortly thereafter, a revised and expanded edition of the anthology was published. This time it included interviews conducted with some religious Zionist soldiers who studied at the Merkaz Harav yeshiva, that were edited out from the original publication because they were perceived by the editors as including unacceptably harsh and shocking expressions.[72] It became an ambivalent legacy indeed: The 1967 anthology seems to have shown a certain openness of talk, freed from official propaganda, and, at the same time, exposed the clear limits to swimming against the current and the power of social censorship. Revising it circa 2015–18 served as an epitaph to the declining prominence of the kibbutz movement in the Israeli military forces and society alike, and a reminder of the dynamics of exclusion and silencing of earlier years.

The reentry of *Siah lohamim* to Israeli public discourse in 2015 was not coincidental, but linked to the tempestuous debates surrounding "Breaking the Silence" (*Shovrim Shtika*). The NGO, established in 2004 by IDF veterans who served in the West Bank, records and disseminates soldiers' testimonies in an attempt to increase public awareness of the harsh conditions in the occupied territories. Oz lent his support to the NGO, alongside Peace Now (established in 1978, also originating in the political activism of veteran and reservist soldiers and officers), B'Tselem (an NGO documenting human rights violations in the occupied territories), and the New Israel Fund. In November 2016 Oz placed himself at the eye of yet another public storm, when speaking in favor of "Breaking the Silence" at a public event at Ben-Gurion University. "Sometimes, throughout history, individuals who were branded as 'traitors' among the majority of their people were revealed to be teachers over the years," Oz declared in his speech.[73]

Oz's reference to treason was, unmistakably, an echo of and response to the harsh rhetoric employed by Israeli officials, including prime minister Netanyahu, who denounced the group and tried to outlaw its activity. Such scolding stood in bleak contrast to the warm hug Oz and his peers received in the late 1960s and 1970s, and exposed the limits, and perhaps also the archaic irrelevance, of the old mode of patriotic conscientious objection coming "from within," from the men and women in uniform. But treason made its way into much of Oz's late prose, which once again allied his politics. Treason appeared in his memoir in which he recalled how, as an eight-year-old boy, he was called a traitor after befriending a British soldier who served in mandatory Jerusalem. The same theme was explored a few years earlier in *Panther in the Basement* (1995), a scintillating young adult novel telling the story of a friendship between a twelve-year-old Jewish Jerusalemite kid and the clumsy, and ostensibly unheroic and vulnerable Sgt. Dunlop who captures him when he strolls the streets after curfew.[74] The theme is further developed in *Judas*, his 2014 novel, whose main protagonist is an incorrigibly idealistic yet perplexed graduate student trying to write a seminar paper on the Jewish views of Jesus, who finds himself fascinated to the point of obsession with the story of Judas Iscariot.[75] Set in Jerusalem of the 1950s, the novel provided Oz the opportunity to revisit the work of his great uncle Klausner who stirred a controversy when insisting to describe Jesus as a Jew (a kind of mystic visionary, perhaps, but yet very much a product of Judaism of his time), to reflect on the meaning of perfidiousness in its various theological and political transmutations (from "perfidis Judaeis," the potent insulting phrase marking Jewish faithlessness and betrayal in the Christian world, to "perfidious Albion," the pejorative slogan used by the Revisionist Zionists, accusing Britain of duplicity, and treachery), but above all: to examine, albeit allegorically, the meanings of notions of disloyalty, faithlessness, and treachery in Israel of his time. The extended bookish dialogs between the fictional protagonists and the political writings of the late Oz used the same vocabulary, revisited the same moral issues, and toured the same political terrains. A nearly cannibalistic plagiarism, the words put by Oz in the mouth of *Judas's* main protagonist, telling his interlocutor that even Jeremiah the prophet, Abraham Lincoln, Theodor Herzl, Charles de Gaulle and were called traitors, reoccurred in Oz's 2016 political speech, quoted almost word by word.[76] Most likely, they were also written using the same pen.

A prolific writer who remained omnipresent over more than five decades, the reading of Oz's works makes a cross section of Israeli history. As it often happens with boldly stated ideas, many of the views expressed by Oz that might have been au courant at the time seem hopelessly out-of-date today. Oz allowed the inconsistencies in his own life to become identical to the dramatic twists and turns of Israeli history. The aim of the present article, and the special issue more generally, is not to provide a definitive overview of neither Oz's life and work, nor the long years of Israeli history he took part in. Instead, we would like to initiate a cross disciplinarity dialogue that would enrich our understanding of both. Like in the case of *Eminent Victorians*, Lytton Strachey's notoriously controversial group portrait of the towering figures of the age that preceded him, there is an element of disenchantment and a deliberate effort to go beyond pretentious rhetoric in sketching the portrait of this eminent Israeli novelist. Victorian studies developed enormously since the time of Strachey's iconoclastic book, becoming, especially during the 1990s and the early 2000s, a site of lively dialogs between historians and literary scholars. Fresh insights and a bold reassessment of the very category "Victorianism" could be provided only once the formal disciplinary boundaries ceased to be policed in a dogmatic way.[77] New kinds of academic conversation are, hopefully, becoming possible in the field of Israel Studies as well.

Notes

1. Yehezkel Rahamim, "Shloshet ha-tenorim [The Three Tenors]," *Ynet*, March 15, 2008. https://www.ynet.co.il/articles/0,7340,L-3519263,00.html. Accessed May 17, 2021 (Unless mentioned otherwise, all translations from Hebrew in this article are mine, AD).
2. Shelley, "A Defence of Poetry," 57.
3. Jonathan Freedland, "Amos Oz: The Novelist Prophet Who Never Lost Hope for Israel," *The Guardian*, December 28, 2018. https://www.theguardian.com/books/2018/dec/28/amos-oz-israel-novelist-prophet-never-lost-hope. Accessed May 20, 2021.

4. David Remnick, "The Spirit Level: Amos Oz Writes the Story of Israel," *The New Yorker*, November 8 2004. https://www.newyorker.com/magazine/2004/11/08/the-spirit-level. Accessed May 20, 2021; Jonathan Freedland, "The Radical Empathy of Amos Oz," *The New York Review of Books*, January 142,019. https://www.nybooks.com/daily/2019/01/14/the-radical-empathy-of-amos-oz/.
5. Perry Anderson, "Scurrying Towards Bethlehem," *New Left Review*, July/Aug 2001, 23, n. 23. https://newleftreview.org/issues/ii10/articles/perry-anderson-scurrying-toward-bethlehem. Accessed May 20, 2021; Piterberg, "Literature of Settler Societies," 1–52; Cleary. *Literature, Partition and the Nation-State Culture and Conflict in Ireland, Israel and Palestine*, chap. 4.
6. Laor, "Haiye ha-min shel kohot ha-bitahon," 75–104.
7. Zvi Ben-Dor Benite, "Lekh la-azazel, Amos Oz [Go to Hell, Amos Oz]," *Ha-oketz*, December 16, 2008. Accessed May 20, 2021. https://www.haokets.org/2008/12/16/%D7%9C%D7%9A-%D7%9C%D7%A2%D7%96%D7%90%D7%96%D7%9C-%D7%A2%D7%9E%D7%95%D7%A1-%D7%A2%D7%95%D7%96/.
8. Eran Kaplan, "Amos Oz and the Politics of Identity: A Reassessment," *Journal of Israeli History* 38, no. 2 (2021): 259–274. See also idem, "Amos Oz's a Tale of Love and Darkness and the Sabra Myth," 119–43.
9. Dror Eder, "Ha-hitnas'ut shel Amos Oz [Amos Oz's condescension]," *Israel ha-yom*, February 15, 2015, Accessed May 20, 2021, https://www.israelhayom.co.il/article/258957; Benny Ziffer, "Amos Oz 1939–2018: Met nasi ha-shevet ha-lavan [Amos Oz, 2018–1939: The President of the White Tribe has died]," *Haaretz*, December 28, 2018, Accessed May 20, 2021 https://www.haaretz.co.il/gallery/literature/.premium-1.6788133.
10. Kimmerling, *Kets shilton ha-ahusalim*.
11. Oz and Hadad, *Mi-mah Asui ha-tapuah?*, 39.
12. Vered Shemtov, "'Now We Shall Reveal a Little Secret': First Person Plural and Lyrical Fluidity in the Works of Amos Oz." *Journal of Israeli History* 38, no. 2 (2021): 349–367.
13. Oz, *Sipur al ahavah ve-hoshekh*, 37.
14. Lejeune, "Le Pacte Autobiographique," 13–46. Taking my cue from Michael Stanislawski, I also regard Oz's autobiography, like so many other Jewish autobiographies, as memory agents: an explicit attempt of their authors to write the histories of their time. See Stanislawski, *Autobiographical Jews*. Noteworthy in this context is Marcus Moseley's magisterial study of the emergence of Jewish autobiographical writing, which also follows Lejeune's working definitions of autobiography: Moseley, *Being for Myself Alone*.
15. Oz, *Davar she-mithapes Le-Ahava*.
16. Klausner. *Jesus of Nazareth*. The two-volume book was first published in 1922 and went through six editions by 1954.
17. Oz, *The Silence of Heaven*, 3. In the Hebrew original Oz did not use the word trauma but *pzi'a*, an injury. He recited the formula – authors are created due to some severe injury–in various interviews.
18. Gertz, *Mah she-avad ba-zeman*. See also Gertz's contribution to the present volume "Love, Compassion, and Longing." *Journal of Israeli History* 38, no. 2 (2021): 1–8. Noteworthy, Gertz's biography was revised shortly after its publication, in response to the publication of Galia Oz's memoir. As mentioned above, the production of the present volume was underway at the time Galia Oz's book was published, opening a controversy that has not yet ended.
19. Grumberg, *Place and Ideology in Contemporary Hebrew Literature*.
20. Karen Grumberg, "The Greatness of Smallness: Amos Oz, Sherwood Anderson, and the American Presence in Hebrew Literature," *Journal of Israeli History* 38, no. (2021): 275–301.
21. Oz, *A Perfect Peace*.
22. Oz, *Between Friends*.
23. Balaban, *Between God and Beast*.
24. Oz, *Kol ha-tikvot*, 21. The excerpt is taken from a 1994 interview.
25. Oz, *Be'etsem yesh kan shete milhamot*, 139.

26. Ben-Gurion Archive/Correspondences/Amos Oz to David Ben-Gurion [handwritten], April 23, 1954.
27. Ben-Gurion Archive/Correspondences/David Ben-Gurion to Amos Oz [typewritten], April 28, 1954.
28. Oz, "Shituf eino tahlif le-shivyon [A Cooperative Is Not a Substitute for Equality]," *Davar*, February 20, 1961, 3.
29. David Ben-Gurion. "Hagigim nosafim [Additional Meditations]." *Davar*, February 24, 1961, 2. The exchange was reprinted decades later in the Bulletin of the Department of Education of the Kibbutz Artzi movement: Ben-Porat, "Ma'arch limudi al shivyon ve-shituf ba-kibbutz," 94–106.
30. Oz, *A Tale of Love and Darkness*, 454.
31. Ben Gurion Archive/Protocols/Protocol of Meeting between the Prime Minister and Minister of Defense with Members of *Ihud Ha-Kvutzot Ve-Ha-Kibbutzim*, at the Ministry of Defense, Ha-Kirya [Tel-Aviv], March 15, 1961, 75pp, and March 23, 1961, 45pp.
32. Oz, "Shituf eino tahlif le-shivyon," 3.
33. Protocol of the March 15, 1961 Meeting, on p. 45.
34. The standard study of this biblical-turned-literary *topos* remains Feldman, *Glory and Agony*. Feldman suggested reading Oz's and A. B. Yehoshua's works against a backdrop of intensified Oedipal tensions between the fathers' and sons' generations, which further stressed the violent and masculinist elements in Israeli culture, brought the notion of filicide to center stage, and informed the way in which the young Oz parodied the lofty rhetoric of the founding fathers and sought to explore the liminal spaces separating sanity from abnormality. See also Feldman, "Our Primary Myth of Violence," 546–7.
35. Kurzweil, "Ha-sipur ha-Yisraeli ba-shanim ha-aharonot, I [the Israeli Story During the Last Years, Part 1]," *Ha'aretz*, March 4 1966. Reprinted in idem, *Hipus ha-sifrut ha-Yisraelit*.
36. Kurzweil, *Hipus ha-sifrut ha-yisraelit*, 298–306. The chapter on Oz was based on a review originally published in May 1968.
37. Diamond, *Barukh Kurzweil and Modern Hebrew Literature*; Laor. *Ha-ma'avak al ha-zikaron*, 282–295.
38. Gertz, *Amos Oz*, 25.
39. Oz, Amos. "Sar ha-bitahon ve-merhav ha-mihya [The Defense Minister and the Living Space]," *Davar*, August 221,967. An edited version of the article was included in Oz's essay anthology *Be-or Ha-Tekhelet Ha-`Azah: Maamarim U-Reshimot*. Tel Aviv: Sifriyat Poalim, 1979. An English translation appeared under the title "Moshe Dayan and 'Lebensraum'." Translated by Hersh Rabnovich. *Jewish Currents*, 22, no. 2 (February 1968): 18–21. Interestingly enough, the essay did not find its way into the English translation of *Under This Blazing Light: Essays*.
40. Oz, "An Alien City." In *Under This Blazing Light*, 173–81. The article was first published as part of *Siah lochamim*.
41. Shapira, *The Seventh Day*. Full original title: *Siah lohamim: pirke ha-kshavah ve-hitbonenut*.
42. Gan, "The Tanks of Tammuz and the Seventh Day."
43. Some scholars, such as Shalom Ratzabi, went as far as suggest that the romantic German Zionism of the Jerusalemite professors was the true origin of the dovish Zionism that Oz represented so well. See Ratzabi, "Romantic Nationalism as the Source of Political Moderation." Nevertheless, outside recollections of former *Shdemot* members, very little scholarly work has been done on the subject. See Ufaz, "Zikat ha-kibbutz li-mkorot ha-yahadut be-mahshevet 'Hug Shdemot'"; Katz and Kedar, "Judaism from the Perspective of Secular Israeli Intellectuals."
44. Omri Asscher, "The American Oz: Notes on Translation and Reception," *Journal of Israeli History* 38, no. 2 (2021): 303–327.
45. Isaiah Berlin to Steven Lukes, February 28, 1994, In: Supplementary Letters 1975–1997, The Isaiah Berlin Virtual Library. The webpage contains letters that have been discovered after the publication of Berlin's letters. I would like to thank Henry Hardy for turning my

attention to this unpublished letter and the Isaiah Berlin Literary Trust for the permission to quote from it. http://berlin.wolf.ox.ac.uk/published_works/a/l4supp.pdf.

46. Oz, *Under This Blazing Light*; Oz, *The Slopes of Lebanon*; Oz, *In the Land of Israel*.
47. David Ohana "Amos Oz: A Humanist in the Darkness," *Journal of Israeli History* 38, no. 2 (2021): 329–348.
48. Oz, *In the Land of Israel*, 127.
49. Oz, *Under This Blazing Light*, 7.
50. Oz, *How to Cure a Fanatic*.
51. Weiss, *Alilah*, 77, 83, 87.
52. Said, "The Morning After," 3. The essay was reprinted in Said's collection, *Peace and Its Discontents: Essays on Palestine in the Middle East Peace Process*. New York: Vintage Books, 1995.
53. Cleary, *Literature, Partition and the Nation-State Culture and Conflict*, chap. 4; Bernard, *Rhetorics of Belonging*, chap. 4.
54. While some translations of Oz's works into Arabic appeared in Israel, only three of Oz's adult novels were published in Arab capitals: *My Michael* (published in Cairo by al Dar al Arabia, 1994 and Baghdad: Manšūrāt al-ğamal, 2013), *Unto Death* (Amman: Dar al-Tanuir al-ʿElmi, 1995), and *A Tale of Love and Darkness* (Beirut: Menshewrat Alejmel, 2010; Baghdad: Manšūrāt al-ğamal, 2010). The Arabic translation of Oz's memoir was funded by the family of George Khoury, a Palestinian citizen of Israel and a student at the Hebrew University, who was killed in 2004 by a Palestinian militant, who mistook him for a Jew. The Jordanian novelist and literary critic Ghalib Halasa included in his study of Oz's literature a translation of the 1971 novella "Crusade" (included in *Unto Death*). See Halasa, *Naqd Al-Adab Al-Sihyuni*. Countering strong anti-normalization demands, the Lebanese poet and literary critic ʿAbdo Wazin, cultural editor of the newspaper *Al Hayat*, praised the book and Oz's other works, while acknowledging the problem of separating literature and political identity. See Wazen, "Al'iisrayiyli Eamus Eawz Ma Barah Yuhrij Alsahafat Althaqafiat Alerby ... Barawayatih Almuhima [Arabic: The Israeli Amos Oz Continues to Embarrass the Arab Cultural Press ... With His Important Novels]." *Independent Arabia*, June 11, 2019. I would like to thank Yoram Meital and Anton Shammas for providing me with these references.
55. For their acceptance speeches see Oz, Amos, and Sari Nusseibeh. "Two Views on Mideast Peace." *New York Review of Books*, October 13, 2010, Accessed May 23, 2021, https://www.nybooks.com/daily/2010/10/13/two-views-mideast-peace/.
56. Mishani, *Be-khol Ha-inyan ha-mizrahi yesh eyzeh absurd*, chap. 3; Almog Behar, "Mi-po u-misham, mi-sham u-mipo, Eretz Yisrael ve-ha-elbon [From Here to There, from There Tohere, the Land of Israel and the Insult]," *Ha-okets*, July 29, 2009; Mati Shemoelof, "Lamah la-sofer Amos Oz lo megi'a pras Nobel le-sifrut? [Why Does Oz Not Deserve the Nobel Prize for Literature?]," *Nrg*, October 4, 2009, Accessed May 23, 2021, https://www.makorrishon.co.il/nrg/online/47/ART1/949/744.html.
57. Ofra Yeshua-Lyth, "Mishel sheli: Ha-kufsa, ha-ashpa, ve-ha-yehudi [My Michelle: The Box, the Trash, and the Jew]," *Ma'ariv*, July 17, 1987, 2, 4 on 4. On the parallel controversy in Germany see: Schappach, "Why Rainer Werner Fassbinder's Play *Garbage, the City, and Death* Could Not Be Performed in Germany." As far as we know, Oz did not respond to this critique. The only published response came from the poetess Nily Carmon-Plumin (spouse of the poet Natan Yonatan), who was infuriated by Yeshua-Lyth's analogy: Carmon-Plumin, Nily. "Amos Oz natan la-metziut le-daber [Amos Oz Allowed Reality to Speak]." *Ma'ariv*, July 31, 1987, 70.
58. Hirschfeld, "Nigmeret zehut u-mathila aheret," 452. The essay was originally published in 1990.
59. David Avidan, "Ha-kufsah lo s'hora [Hebrew: The Box Is Not a Commodity]," *Hadashot*, January 23, 1987, 10.
60. Oz and Hadad, *Mi-mah asui ha-tapuah?*, 110.
61. Oz quoted in Ohana, *Ha-yisraelim ha-aharonim*, 12.

62. Oz, *The Same Sea*.
63. Neta Stahl, "'Like a Cow That Gave Birth to a Seagull': Amos Oz, Yoel Hoffmann and the Birth of the Same Sea," *Journal of Israeli History* 38, no. 2 (2021): 369–387.
64. Adia Mendelson-Maoz, "Memory and Space in the Autobiographical Writings of Amos Oz and Ronit Matalon," *Journal of Israeli History* 38, no. 2 (2021): 389–414. Mendelson-Maoz borrows the phrase "giving witness to oppression" from the writings of Gayatri Chakravorty Spivak.
65. David Avidan, "Shamir et Shamir ve-shot. [Shamir & Shamir & Co.]," *Hadashot*, January 30, 1987, 10.
66. Oz, *Kol ha-tikvot*, 17–8. Oz retired to the same analogy years later in his conversations with Shirah Hadad: Oz and Hadad. *Mi-mah asui ha-tapuah?*, 153–4.
67. Schwartz, *Zemer nuge shel Amos Oz*. A similar metaphor was employed recently by the Israeli novelist Ruby Namdar: Namdar, "The Wizard of Words and the Baggy Monster: Rereading Amos Oz's a Tale of Love and Darkness."
68. Yigal Schwartz, "Amos Oz: The Lighthouse," *Journal of Israeli History* 38, no. 2 (2021): 415–421.
69. Aviad Kleinberg, "Siah lohamim u-vokhim [Soldiers Talk and Weep]," *Yediot Aharonot*, June 3 2015, as reprinted in his blog https://aviadkleinberg.com/.
70. The omitted religious Zionist testimonies were published separately in summer 1968 in vol. 29 of *Shdemot*. Avraham Shapira sent a copy of that issue to his mentor, Gershom Scholem, who was dismayed by what he considered to be a poor command of Hebrew and stuttering that revealed the "complete degeneration of the language in the mouths of these Torah learners," but refrained from commenting directly about the contents of their ideas. Shapira would later reproduce this letter: Scholem, "Mikhtav be-ikvot Siah lohamim," 533. See also Segev, *1967*, 442–48; Gan, "The Tanks of Tammuz and the Seventh Day."
71. Loushy,"Censored Voices." The documentary was released in Israel under the title "Siah lohamim: Ha-slilim ha-gnouzim [Soldiers' Talk: The Redacted Tapes]."
72. Shahar, Shapira, Alberton, and Gries, eds. *Siah lohamim*. For discussion see Sagi, "Siah lohamin."
73. An English translation of the speech was published online: Oz, Amos. "Breaking the Silence – a Jewish Tradition." New Israel Fund Australia, 2016, Accessed May 23, 2021, https://www.nif.org.au/amos_oz_breaking_the_silence_a_jewish_tradition.
74. Oz, *Panther in the Basement*.
75. Oz, *Judas*.
76. Ibid., 248–9.
77. Howsam, "Victorian Studies and the History of the Book: Opportunities for Scholarly Collaboration"; Boyd, Kelly, and Rohan McWilliam, eds., *The Victorian Studies Reader*. London: Routledge, 2007.

Acknowledgments

I would like to thank Adi Portugez of the Ben-Gurion and Research Center, Ilan Bar-David of Heksherim, the Research Institute for Jewish and Israeli Literature and Culture at the Ben-Gurion University, which also houses the Oz Papers, for their assistance. Omri Asscher, Mikhal Dekel, Hanan Harif, Giddon Ticotsky, Yoav Ronel, Neta Stahl and Orian Zakai provided valuable feedback on an earlier draft of this essay.

My heartfelt thanks are to Anita Shapira and Derek J. Penslar, the general editors of the journal, who have been inspirational, supportive and patient during the long gestation period of this project. As they hand over the baton to new editors, additional special thanks are due for long years of assiduous work and stewardship.

Disclosure statement

No potential conflict of interest was reported by the author(s).

Bibliography

Balaban, Abraham. *Between God and Beast: An Examination of Amos Oz's Prose.* University Park: Pennsylvania State University Press, 1993.

Ben-Porat, Iron. "Ma'arch limudi al shivyon ve-shituf ba-kibbutz [Lesson Plan on Equality and Cooperation in the kibbutz]." *Ha-hinukh ha-meshutaf* 57 (1986): 94–106.

Bernard, Anna. *Rhetorics of Belonging: Nation, Narration, and Israel/Palestine.* Liverpool, UK: Liverpool University Press, 2013.

Cleary, Joe. *Literature, Partition and the Nation-State Culture and Conflict in Ireland, Israel and Palestine.* New York: Cambridge University Press, 2002.

Diamond, James S. *Barukh Kurzweil and Modern Hebrew Literature.* Chico, California: Scholars Press/Brown Judaic Studies, 1982.

Feldman, Yael. "'Our Primary Myth of Violence': Shulamith Hareven and the Psycho-Political Discourse in Israel." In *Rega shel huledet : Mehkarim be-sifrut Ivrit u-ve-sifrut Yiddish li-khevod Dan Miron* [Moment of Birth: Studies in Hebrew and Yiddish Literatures in Honor of Dan Miron], edited by H. Hever, 539–563. Jerusalem: Mosad Byalik, 2007.

Feldman, Yael S. *Glory and Agony: Isaac's Sacrifice and National Narrative.* Stanford, Calif.: Stanford University Press, 2010.

Gan, Alon. "The Tanks of Tammuz and the Seventh Day: The Emergence of Opposite Poles of Israeli Identity after the Six Day War." *Journal of Israeli History* 28, no. 2 (2009): 155–173.

Gertz, Nurith. *Amos Oz: Monografyah* [Amos Oz: Monograph]. Tel-Aviv: Sifriyat Po'alim, 1980.

Gertz, Nurith. *Mah she-avad ba-zeman: Biographia shel yedidut* [What Was Lost to Time: A Biography of A Friendship]. Tel-Aviv: Kinneret Zmora Bita, 2020.

Grumberg, Karen. *Place and Ideology in Contemporary Hebrew Literature.* Syracuse, N.Y.: Syracuse University Press, 2011.

Halasa, Ghalib. *Naqd Al-Adab Al-Sihyuni : Dirasah Idiyulujiyah Wa-Naqdiyah Li-a`Mal Al-Katib Al-Sihyuni `Amus `Uz* [Criticism of Zionist Literature: An Ideological and Critical Study of the Works of the Zionist Writer Amos Oz]. Beirut: `Amman: al-Muassasah al-`Arabiyah lil-Dirasat wa-al-Nashr; Dar al-Tanwir, 1995.

Hirschfeld, Ariel. "Nigmeret zehut u-mathila aheret [An Identity Ends and a New One Begins]." In *Yofyam shel ha-menutsahim : Bikoret u-mehkar Al yetsirato shel Yehoshu`a Kenaz* [The Beauty of the Defeated: Critical Essays on Yehoshua Kenaz], edited by C. Strass and K. Dotan, 441–459. Tel Aviv: Am Oved, 2016.

Howsam, Leslie. "Victorian Studies and the History of the Book: Opportunities for Scholarly Collaboration." *Victorian Review* 22, no. 1 (1996): 65–70.

Kaplan, Eran. "Amos Oz's a Tale of Love and Darkness and the Sabra Myth." *Jewish Social Studies* 14, no. 1 (2007): 119–143.

Katz, Gideon, and Nir Kedar. "Judaism from the Perspective of Secular Israeli Intellectuals." *Democratic Culture* 14 (2012): 93–152.

Kimmerling, Baruch. *Kets shilton Ha-ahusalim* [End of Ashkenazi Hegemony]. Jerusalem: Keter, 2001.

Klausner, Joseph. *Jesus of Nazareth: His Life, Times, and Teaching.* Translated by Herbert Danby. Boston: Beacon Press, 1964.

Kurzweil, Baruch. *Hipus ha-sifrut ha-Yisraelit: Masot u-ma'amarim* [In Search of Israeli Literature: Essays and Articles]. Edited by Zvi Luz and Yedidya Itzhaki. Ramat-Gan: Bar-Ilan University, 1982.

Laor, Dan. *Ha-ma'avak al ha-zikaron* [Hebrew: The Struggle for Memory]. Am Oved: Tel Aviv, 2009.

Laor, Yitzhak. "Haiye ha-min shel kohot ha-bitahon [The Sex Life of the Security Forces]." In *Anu kotvim otakh moledet: Masot al sifrut Yisraelit [Narratives with No Natives: Essays on Israeli Literature]*, 75–104. Tel Aviv: Ha-Kibbutz Ha-Meuhad, 1995.

Lejeune, Philippe. "Le Pacte Autobiographique." In *Le Pacte Autobiographique*, edited by P. Lejeune, 13–46. Paris: Seuil, 1975.

Loushy, Mor, (director). "Censored Voices." 84 mins: Music Box Films (distributor), 2015

Mishani, Dror. *Be-khol ha-inyan ha-mizrahi yesh eyzeh absurd: Hofa'at ha-mizrahiyut ba-sifrut ha-ivrit be-shenot ha-shemonim* [Ethnic Unconscious: Emergence of 'Mizrahiut' in the Hebrew Literature of the Eighties]. Tel Aviv: Am Oved, 2006.

Moseley, Marcus. *Being for Myself Alone: Origins of Jewish Autobiography.* Stanford, Calif: Stanford University Press, 2006.

Namdar, Ruby. "The Wizard of Words and the Baggy Monster: Rereading Amos Oz's a Tale of Love and Darkness." *Jewish Review of Books* 11, no. 3 (Fall 2020): 30–32.

Ohana, David. *Ha-yisraelim ha-aharonim* [The Last Israelis]. Tel-Aviv: Ha-Kibbutz Ha-Meuhad, 2001.

Oz. *The Slopes of Lebanon.* Translated by Maurie Goldberg-Bartura. Boston: Houghton Mifflin Harcourt, 2012.

Oz, Amos. *Be-or Ha-Tekhelet Ha-'Azah: Ma'amarim u-reshimot.* Tel Aviv: Sifriyat Poalim, 1979.

Oz, Amos. *A Perfect Peace.* Translated by Hillel Halkin. San Diego: Harcourt Brace Jovanovich, 1985.

Oz, Amos. *In the Land of Israel.* Translated by Maurie Goldberg-Bartura. San Diego: Harcourt Brace Jovanovich, 1993.

Oz, Amos. *Under This Blazing Light: Essays.* Translated by N. R. M. De Lange. Cambridge, New York, N.Y: Press Syndicate of the University of Cambridge, 1995.

Oz, Amos. *Panther in the Basement.* Translated by Nicholas De Lange. London: Vintage, 1997.

Oz, Amos. *Kol ha-tikvot: Mahshavot al zehut Yisraelit [All Our Hopes: Essays on the Israeli Condition].* Keter: Jerusalem, 1998.

Oz, Amos. *The Silence of Heaven: Agnon's Fear of God.* Translated by Barbara Harshav. Princeton, NJ: Princeton University Press, 2000.

Oz, Amos. *The Same Sea.* Translated by Nicholas De Lange. New York: Harcourt, 2001.

Oz, Amos. *Be'etsem yesh kan shete milhamot* [But These are Two Different Wars]. Jerusalem: Keter, 2002.

Oz, Amos. *Sipur al ahavah ve-hoshekh* [A Tale of Love and Darkness]. Jerusalem: Keter, 2002.

Oz, Amos. *A Tale of Love and Darkness.* Translated by Nicholas De Lange. Orlando: Harcourt, 2004.

Oz, Amos. *How to Cure a Fanatic.* Translated by Nadine Gordimer. Princeton: Princeton University Press, 2010.

Oz, Amos. *Between Friends.* Translated by Sondra Silverston. Boston: Houghton Mifflin Harcourt, 2013.

Oz, Amos. *Judas.* Translated by Nicholas De Lange. London: Houghton Mifflin Harcourt, 2017.

Oz, Amos, and Shirah Hadad. *Mi-mah asui ha-tapuah?: Shesh sihot al ketivah ve-al ahavah, al rigshe ashmah ve-ta'anugot aherim [What's in an Apple?: Six Conversations about Writing and about Love, about Guilt and Other Pleasures].* Ben Shemen: Keter, 2018.

Oz, Galia. *Davar she-mithapes le-ahaava* [Something Disguised as Love]. Modi'in: Kinneret Zmora Bitan, 2020.

Piterberg, Gabriel. "Literature of Settler Societies: Albert Camus, S. Yizhar and Amos Oz." *Settler Colonial Studies* 1, no. 2 (2011): 1–52.

Ratzabi, Shalom. "Romantic Nationalism as the Source of Political Moderation." *Democratic Culture* 2 (1999): 137–167.

Sagi, Avi. "Siah lohamin: Ben siah reflektivi le-siah pastorali [Siah Lohamim: Between Reflective Discourse and Pastoral Discourses]." *Reshit: Studies in Judaism* 3 (2019): 73–91.

Said, Edward W. "The Morning After." *London Review of Books* 15, no. 20 (1993): 3–5.

Said, Edward W. *Peace and Its Discontents: Essays on Palestine in the Middle East Peace Process.* New York: Vintage Books, 1995.

Schappach, Beate. "Why Rainer Werner Fassbinder's Play *Garbage, the City, and Death* Could Not Be Performed in Germany." In *Theatre Scandals: Social Dynamics of Turbulent Theatrical Events*, edited by V. A. Cremona, P. Eversmann, B. Rowen, A. Saro, and H. Schoenmakers, 163–174. Leiden: Brill, 2020.

Scholem, Gershom. "Mikhtav be-ikvot Siah lohamim, 11. 7.68[Letter following Siah lohamim, July 11, 1968]." In *Devarim be-go : Pirke morashah u-tehiyah* [Explications and Implications], edited by A. Shapira, 533. Tel Aviv: Am Oved, 1990.

Schwartz, Yigal. *Zemer nuge shel Amos Oz: Pulhan Ha-sofer ve-dat ha-medina* [Melancholy Song by Amos Oz: Cult of the Author and the State Religion]. Tel Aviv: Kinneret Zmora-Bitan Dvir, 2011.

Segev, Tom. *1967: Israel, the War, and the Year that Transformed the Middle East.* Translated by Jessica Cohen. New York: Metropolitan Books, 2007.

Shahar, Yuval, Avraham Shapira, Yair Alberton, and Zeev Gries, eds. *Siah lohamim: Pirke ha-kshavah ve-Hitbonenut: Mahadurah mehudeshet u-murhevet bi-melot shiv'im shanah li-Medinat Yisrael* [Soldiers' Talk: A Record of Conversation and Reflection: A Revised Edition on the Occasion of the Seventieth Anniversary of the State of Israel]. Jerusalem: Carmel, 2018.

Shapira, Avraham, ed. *The Seventh Day: Soldiers' Talk about the Six-Day War.* New York: Scribner, 1971.

Shelley, Percy Bysshe. "A Defence of Poetry." In *Essays, Letters from Abroad, Translations and Fragments*, edited by M. W. Shelley, 1–57. London: Edward Moxon, 1852.

Stanislawski, Michael. *Autobiographical Jews: Essays in Jewish Self-Fashioning.* Seattle: University of Washington Press, 2004.

Ufaz, Gad. "Zikat ha-kibbutz Li-mekorot ha-yahadut be-mahshevet 'Hug Shdemot' [The Ties of the Kibbutz to Jewish Sources as Expressed in the Thought of the 'Shdemot Circle']." Unpublished PhD thesis, Tel Aviv University, 1986.

Weiss, Hillel. *Alilah: Sifrut ha-kilayon ha-Yisraelit* [Plot: Demise in Contemporary Hebrew Literature]. Bet-El: Sifriyat Bet-El, 1992.

Amos Oz and the politics of identity: A reassessment

Eran Kaplan

ABSTRACT

If early in his career Amos Oz was regarded as the epitome of the new Israeli or Hebrew, later critics tended to reduce Oz's image to that of a member of a specific group – Ashkenazi Laborites – that was once the hegemonic group in Israel but has seen its status decrease in recent years. This article seeks to show that in his career, Oz exhibited views on Jewish history and the future of the Jewish state that went beyond the narrow confines of Labor Zionism, and that he offered some keen political insights that transcended the limits of identity politics.

On the day that Amos Oz passed away, Benny Ziffer, the literary editor of *Haaretz*, published an article titled "Amos Oz 1939–2018: The President of the White Tribe has Died."[1] While the article, which was featured prominently on the newspaper's website, was somewhat less acerbic than the title may have intimated, it created a maelstrom of sorts, with angry readers accusing the newspaper, and Ziffer, of poor taste.[2] Ziffer underscored the singular position of Oz as a public intellectual in Israel (he was the only non-politician who gave a eulogy at Shimon Peres's funeral), and he asserted that his death has shocked the public in the same manner that the deaths of Bialik, Herzl, or Jabotinsky had in the more distant past. But Ziffer also questioned whether the quality of Oz's writings actually matched his outsized position in Israeli public life; and perhaps more upsettingly, especially to the readers of *Haaretz*, he undermined Oz's universal appeal as a writer and intellectual, describing him as the representative, or president, as the title suggested, of a specific group in Israel: white (Ashkenazi), secular Jews, devoted to the values and political vision of the nation's founding fathers.

Since the 1990s, with the emergence of critical Israeli sociologists and historians, but perhaps more importantly with the end of the old melting-pot ethos and the rise to dominance of the neoliberal order and its multi-cultural ideology, the view of Israeli society as consisting of distinct social or ethnic groups that adhere to different, often conflicting, political ideals, has seemed to take over the public discourse in Israel. From this perspective, the group that the sociologist Baruch Kimmerling described using the acronym "*ahuslim*," which stands for Zionist, socialist, secular Ashkenazim, the traditional Israeli elite, has once been the dominant or hegemonic tribe, whereas other groups – religious Jews, Mizrahim, new immigrants from the former Soviet Union and

Arabs – have been marginalized or silenced; they were the subalterns in the theoretical jargon of the 1990s.[3] But, as Kimmerling and others have observed, since the 1970s, the *ahuslim*, whose political base has been the Labor party and other liberal parties, have been losing their grip on the country's political reins, ceding power to the Likud and other right-wing parties in an Israel that is seemingly more open to different voices, sounds, and tastes.

Ziffer may have been ideally situated in the Israeli public sphere to comment on these changes. An erstwhile card-carrying member of the "white tribe" (he has been after all the literary editor of *Haaretz* since 1988, the all but official voice of that tribe), Ziffer has developed in recent years a close personal relationship with Benjamin Netanyahu and his wife Sarah, which has been followed by a public embrace of right-wing, Greater Land of Israel ideology and an ongoing campaign – first in print and then online – against the "holy cows" of what he dismissively has referred to as the detached Tel Aviv elite. Now, a self-appointed mouthpiece for the groups that were once marginalized by the now withering Laborite elite, Ziffer singled out in his article Oz's 1982 book *In the Land of Israel*, a travelogue of sorts, in which under the guise of a reporter, Oz traveled throughout Israel, to what was once called "the second Israel" – an ultra-orthodox neighborhood, development towns, settlements in the West Bank – to explore a changing Israel. As Ziffer put it, "What is upsetting about the book is precisely what Amos Oz has actually been, a member of the white tribe who goes out to discover the Israeli jungle."

In recent years, Oz himself made it easier for people like Ziffer to reduce his legacy to that of a member of a specific group in the Israeli public sphere – identity politics as the ultimate way of mapping ideology in our neoliberal age. In his last TV interview, from October 2018, a frail-looking Amos Oz was asked about his ability to affect change in Israel. In his response, Oz admitted that, "It is clear to me that today the message should not be coming from an old, privileged, male Ashkenazi from a long-gone age. The message today has to come from much younger women and people who come from a background that is very different from mine."[4]

While it may seem that in his later years, Amos Oz has embraced the jargon of identity politics lock, stock, and barrel – he saw himself as belonging to a specific group or tribe in the broader Israeli cultural matrix – earlier in his career and public life, he personified a more universal Israeli position.[5] He was the embodiment of one of the dominant ideological tenets of the time – the negation of exile and the creation of a new all-encompassing Hebrew identity. He presented an updated version of Elik who was born from the sea, though in Oz's case, reborn was more accurate.

I have suggested elsewhere that the younger Oz was regarded – not only in Israel but perhaps just as much, if not more so, outside of it – as the ideal Sabra. In his prose, but also in interviews and in autobiographical pieces, he came across as a new breed of Zionist/Israeli pioneer.[6] In his 1976 novella *The Hill of Evil Counsel*, which combines autobiographical elements from Oz's childhood with a touch of magic realism, he offered the following biographical sketch of the young protagonist's (who is based on the young Oz) fictional father's first years in Palestine: "In 1932, he had emigrated to Palestine with the intention of establishing a cattle farm in the mountains ... For three months he stayed in a guesthouse in the small town of Yesod Ha-Ma'ala, and spent whole days wandering alone from morning to night in Eastern Galilee looking for water buffalo in the Huleh Swamps. His body grew lean and bronzed, his blue eyes, behind his round spectacles, looked like lakes in a snowy northern land."[7] This was the classic Zionist trope of the exilic Jew shedding his past – of passivity, frailty and detachment from nature and being reborn as a virile, healthy, pioneer – the New Hebrew who embraces the *vita activa* and throws off the yoke of centuries of idealization of the *vita contemplativa* and its detachment from nature (with an emphasis of just how European this ideological image had been with the emphasis on the father's blue eyes).

Amos Oz, né Klausner, was born in mandatory Palestine and his father was never a pioneer in the Galilee – but a bookish academic and librarian. And it was Oz himself who rebelled against the exilic traits that his father embodied (as well as trying to overcome the trauma of his mother's suicide) by moving away from Jerusalem to a kibbutz at the age of fourteen and embracing Labor Zionism as his political home after growing up in a predominantly Revisionist Zionist household. And this was the story that Oz related to his readers and the broader public: the frail, bookish child became a pioneer, a worker of the land, and later a wordsmith committed to the ideals of the kibbutz and its utopian commitments. And in many ways, this was the journey that all Israelis were called upon to make in those years: to shed their past and embrace a new Israeli identity. If Oz were to pass away prematurely in the 1960s or 1970s, he may have been regarded as the "president of the (universal) Israeli tribe." By 2019, after years of Likud political power and the emergence of identity politics, Oz had been reduced, at least by some, to the leadership of a specific group or tribe.

As noted earlier, Oz seemed to embrace this position recently by employing the contemporary vocabulary of identity politics. And perhaps just as importantly, by moving away from the old Zionist maxim of the negation of exile and embracing his family's Eastern European heritage in his 2002 memoir *A Tale of Love and Darkness* and by presenting himself as a product of that legacy, Oz has seemed to be restricting himself to the position of a spokesperson of a specific group, Ashkenazim, rather than some universal Israeli subject. So, with all these changes in his public persona and reception, was Oz indeed the quintessential representative of the *ahusl* tribe? Was he the ultimate symbol of the Ashkenazi Laborite camp? This is what this article seeks to explore and bring into question. By focusing on two issues that Ziffer underscored in his article: the Laborite bona fides of Oz, his commitment to an ideological creed that has lost its relevance in recent years, and by analyzing his allegedly dismissive attitude toward non-*ahuslim*, especially Mizrahim and to a lesser extent settlers in the 1980s (focusing on two texts that drew much of Ziffer's and others' ire: *In the Land of Israel* and *Black Box*) this article will posit that Oz held a much more nuanced ideological and political position that defies the simple (if not simplistic) caricature of him as a member of a privileged class and a champion of its political ideology that seeks to exclude and resist any real social or political change.

While Oz was born and raised in what was a predominantly Revisionist Zionist home, when he emerged as a public figure he was associated with Labor Zionism and the kibbutz movement and later with the Israeli peace camp. In June 1977, a month after the Likud under the leadership of Menachem Begin dethroned Labor, Oz was terrified of what may become of Israel: "And bad days are upon us now, the petit-bourgeois ethos, which has been gaining power in our lives for several years now will become the official political ideology ... And it will be accompanied by the beating drums of some tribal ritualism, of land and blood and of impulses, and various wars of purity and other defilements, fanaticism with dark secrets ... The pettiness of the diaspora mentality disguised as a strong-willed stance with all the language of health and virility."[8] A champion of the Likud and Begin's brand of nationalism he was not.

Two years later, in 1979, Oz published *Under the Blazing Sun*, a collection of political, personal, and literary pieces. The literary critic Dan Laor described the book as Oz's rejection of the ideological and political message of Revisionist Zionism, instead championing a society based on the values of secularism and social democracy. As opposed to the Revisionist worldview of blood and fire, Oz called for the renewal of the original values of the Labor movement: a humanistic and democratic movement for social change, that will create a productive and just society that will bring about the salvation of all people including the healing of the Jews.[9] With that, in his review of *Under the Blazing Sun*, Laor has offered a surprising observation: ultimately, Oz's writings and worldview are a continuation of the ancient Jewish neurosis, of an existential fear that the Zionist guise cannot overshadow. For Laor there are two Amos Oz: one who writes political essays, where he is clearly committed to a certain, Laborite brand of Zionism, and another, the novelist who unravels the national project and uncovers the neurotic forces that continue to haunt the Jewish community in Israel: forces that betray a certain primeval, Revisionist ideological disposition. This is indeed an important observation, though it is not necessarily limited to Oz's fictional works; in some of his political essays and interviews throughout his career these ideological instincts and tendencies have also come to the surface.

Ilan Peleg, in his study of Menachem Begin's ideological worldview, which Peleg has called Neo-Revisionism, has described Begin's ideology as an effort to glorify the past, emphasizing national catastrophes as the bedrock of the Jewish experience.[10] But what mostly has set Neo-Revisionism apart from traditional, mainstream Zionism has been its attitude toward what Peleg describes as a normal Jewish existence in the Jewish State. According to Peleg, Zionists, from Herzl onward, championed the return of the Jews to their land as an attempt to achieve normalcy; "Neo-Revisionism, on the other hand, has firmly rejected the state of normalcy not only as fundamentally unachievable but even as inherently un-Jewish."[11] This is a political philosophy rooted in fear and distrust of the non-Jewish world that sees danger and catastrophe lurking everywhere.

Nurith Gertz, in a study of Menachem Begin's campaign speeches, has reached similar conclusions. According to Gertz, in the 1980s, two ideological narratives were battling for primacy in Israeli political culture: a narrative that places Israel among the nations and one that offers a fundamental divide between Israel and the rest of the world and presents Jewish and Israeli history as the unresolved journey of the chosen people through catastrophic events, as an unending tale of destruction and redemption. While the first narrative represents the secular forces of Zionism according to Gertz, the latter represents as mixture of traditional, religious Jewish ideas with right-wing political goals, which became the hallmark of Begin's worldview: a battle for survival of the few against the many, a total confrontation that will only be resolved through destruction and redemption.[12]

In a similar vein, historian David Myers, writing about the intellectual legacy of Benzion Netanyahu, the father of Israeli prime minister Benjamin Netanyahu, who was a prominent scholar of Jewish history and a leading (Neo-)Revisionist intellectual, made the following observation:

The elder Netanyahu held to what the greatest of 20th century Jewish historians, Salo Baron, called the "lachrymose" – or tearful – conception of Jewish history. This view can be readily summarized in a line uttered by Benzion Netanyahu to David Remnick for a 1998 profile of Bibi in The New Yorker: "Jewish history is in large measure a history of holocausts." We might call this the Amalekite view of Jewish history, referring to the hated biblical foes of the Israelites whose existence – and even memory – should be blotted out (Exodus 17:14)... [I]t inspired his own militant Zionism, which demanded a persistent willingness to wage war against one's enemies.[13]

Moreover, Daniel Gordis in his biography of Menachem Begin, while discussing the struggle between Begin and Ben-Gurion over the reparations agreement with Germany, offered the following assessment: "For Ben Gurion, the Jewish State was about looking forward, acknowledging the horrors of the European past but moving past it ... Begin was no less committed to the Jewish future, but for him, the past animated the future. Whatever strength Israel might eventually muster, it would do so because the Jewish past would forever remind Jews of why they needed a state."[14] These are two distinct ways of locating the role of Zionism and the Jewish state within the broader arch of Jewish history. And while Laborites, and Ben-Gurion certainly among them, were well-versed in Jewish history and its many traumatic events, they were committed, ideologically and rhetorically, to the notion of the negation of the past, of overcoming the past and creating a new Hebrew or Israeli identity that is devoid of neuroses rooted in past traumas. Whereas in the Revisionist imagination from the 1940s onwards, the past has continued to be the focal point: future action should be guided and motivated by an understanding the traumatic core of the Jewish experience. Benjamin Netanyahu put this worldview on full theatrical display in his 2015 address to the UN General Assembly:

> For in every generation, there were those who rose up to destroy our people. In antiquity, we faced destruction from the ancient empires of Babylon and Rome. In the Middle Ages, we faced inquisition and expulsion. And in modern times, we faced pogroms and the Holocaust. Yet the Jewish people persevered. And now another regime has arisen, swearing to destroy Israel. That regime would be wise to consider this: I stand here today representing Israel, a country 67 years young, but the nation-state of a people nearly 4,000 years old. Yet the empires of Babylon and Rome are not represented in this hall of nations. Neither is the Thousand Year Reich. Those seemingly invincible empires are long gone. But Israel lives. The people of Israel live.[15]

Amos Oz, on many an occasion, presented himself as the champion the ideological lynchpins of his adopted home, the kibbutz, celebrating the universal, optimistic mission of Zionism. For example, in 1973, he offered the following words: "Our experiment is not merely, as Buber suggested, the only twentieth century experiment in a socialist mending of the world that has not failed ... We have an awesome duty not only for the people of Israel and the redemption of this particular wilderness but also for the entire world that is devoid of a message and is yearning for salvation."[16] But he also expressed throughout his public career some of the core principles of what Peleg and Gordis have described as Begin's brand of Neo-Revisionism, the ideological milieu in which he grew up.

In 1972 Oz participated in a conversation with Dan Ben-Amotz, the writer and public figure, who a generation before Oz brought the notion of negating the diasporic past and creating a New Hebrew identity to perhaps its most radical manifestation,[17] about the future of the Jewish national project. In this exchange, Oz articulated to an English-reading audience his Zionist worldview. Oz claimed that he wanted to believe in a world without borders, where individuals can move freely without the need for passports, without any kind of barriers or divisions, without the instruments of power that the modern state possesses. But he was not quite ready to do so. He did not want to bear the cross of internationalism on his back. For him, the Jewish experience in the diaspora was an exercise in internationalism, and that the Jews paid dearly for it. He told Ben-Amotz, who presented a universalist version of Zionism in the exchange (not at all the different from the above quote of Oz from 1973), that: "I would also like to live a national life in an unlocked house, but I am not prepared to be the first to break through the door and throw away the key into the sea. Not the first in the world and not the first in my neighborhood."[18]

Four months after his conversation with Ben-Amotz, in an interview with the socialist daily newspaper *Al Ha-Mishmar*, Oz offered similar thoughts to the Hebrew-reading public: "I am a Zionist, but I am a sad Zionist. I am a Zionist in that fundamental sense that, though I hold that nationalism is an anachronistic and violent concept, I cannot allow myself, as a father, to become a sort of launching pad of internationalism. If I can quote Ivan Karamazov, on an entirely different matter, 'I cannot yet allow myself.' Let others try it. I will not be the first one to give up on the status of the nation state and the mechanisms of the state: an army and defense systems. Not the first in the world and certainly not the first in the Middle East. I'd be happy if I could be the second or third. In that sense I do not wish to be a pioneer, not after Auschwitz."[19] As both Peleg, Gertz and Gordis have pointed out, this is the basic Beginist formulation of the unending bond between destruction and salvation in Jewish history. This is not a dialectical approach to Jewish history, what Gordis has described as acknowledging the past, but looking forward beyond the horrors of the Jewish experience in Europe; this is a worldview fueled by fear of the non-Jewish world that regards Jewish history as a journey from one catastrophe to another.

In his 1971 novella *Crusade* that was published in the book *Unto Death*, Oz described the interaction between the crusaders and the Jews in 1096 on their way to the Holy Land from the point of view of the Christians. According to Gershon Shaked, in this text, Oz described the Jews in the eyes of the Christians as the source of evil that needs to be eradicated.[20] From the crusades, to Auschwitz, to the struggle with the Arab world Oz has presented Jewish history, not unlike Benzion Netanyahu and his son, as a struggle for survival, as an eternal battle between the Sons of Israel and the Amalekites, between the Jews and their many haters.

And Oz continued to express these views on Jewish history and the role of Zionism until his last years. In a lecture at Tel Aviv University in 2018, Oz said: "I am not against employing a big stick. I am not a pacifist. As opposed to my colleagues in Europe and North America, who sometimes embrace me for the wrong reasons, who call me their brother, 'make love not war' [he said that in English, E.K.], as opposed to them I always thought that aggression is the root of all evil and aggression can only be stopped by force . . . Two female members of my extended family, Jews from Germany, in their teens, spent time in Nazi concentration camps; and it was not peace activists with olive branches and doves, but Allied soldiers with helmets and submachine guns [who saved his]. Therefore, I am not a pacifist . . . If the State of Israel, the Jewish people, did not have eventually a big and strong stick not one of us would have been here. We would either be dead in the ground or driven away from by force."[21] Not only did Amos Oz distance himself from the naïve, according to him, peace camp,[22] but he drew a clear distinction between the irrational, primeval forces in history (that a Jew can't and should never ignore) and the forces that should be used to repress them – the military might of the Jewish state. This sounds more like a Menachem Begin political rally – and in his memoir *A Tale of Love and Darkness*, Oz revealed the indelible impression that a Begin political rally has had on him in his youth[23] – than a Laborite one.

If, in many ways, Oz internalized the Zionist maxim to expunge the past and create a new identity that looks forward toward a utopian new beginning (this happened following his physical move to the kibbutz, the cradle of Labor Zionism); it appears that he could not fully purge the Revisionist view of Jewish history that informed so much of his worldview, growing up among such people as his uncle, the Hebrew University historian Yosef Klausner, and other Revisionist intellectuals and political leaders.

Dan Laor was indeed right: there were two Amos Oz. But the internal rift was not necessarily between Oz's political writings and his fictional prose – but perhaps between two ideological poles that shaped his views about Jewish history and the future of the Jewish State. In a 1974 interview to a cinema magazine about his breakout novel *My Michael* (at that time a film version of the novel was being produced), Oz made the following observation: "There was a country here sure of itself, sometimes arrogant, sometimes very arrogant: a certain mixture of James Bond and Nimrod the hero hunter. At night it revealed itself for what it really was – a refugee camp filled with people who were haunted ... And full of people who suffered through terrible things, who are afraid that they may suffer horrible things."[24] With Oz, the confidence and the assertiveness, the utopian gaze toward the future, which was such an important part of the early Zionist pioneering ethos, was accompanied by a certain Revisionist-influenced traumatic core that could not escape the horrors of the past. This is not necessarily the ideological purity that one would associate with president of the Laborite tribe – even one who was a leader of the Peace Now movement and who was in involved in leftist politics throughout his adult life. In fact, it was a far more complex ideological position that embodied the various sides of the Zionist view of the Jewish past and its legacies, and in this regard was much more universal (or multi-tribal) within the overall Zionist and Israeli context.

In 1982, while working for the Labor daily newspaper *Davar*, Oz, as one of the leading public voices of the Zionist Left, set out to discover and uncover the new political and ideological forces that were unleashed in Israel in 1977 and brought the Likud to power. That collection of reports would become the volume *In the Land of Israel*. Benny Ziffer, as we noted above, described Oz's effort as a kind of Kipling encountering the natives in their wild habitat, seeking to redeem them from their ignorance. Ziffer was not the first writer to describe this volume in this type of manner. In 1983 Doron Rosenblum described it thusly, "They – the ugly Israeli. He – the beautiful Israeli."[25] Dan Laor, in a somewhat more measured manner, described the volume as Oz's attempt to map the polarizing political forces that have come to undermine a kind of "sane" constructive, liberal Zionism, as Oz understood it.[26]

Arguably, the most volatile encounter in the book takes place in Bet Shemesh, a working-class development town with, then, a predominantly Mizrahi population (development towns, *ayarot pitu'ah*, were built in Israel's early years to absorb the new immigrants who arrived mainly from Arab and Muslim countries). And throughout this encounter, which happens mostly in a local coffee shop, Oz recorded heated exchanges that again and again resort to ethnic stereotypes that came to dominate the Israeli political landscape in those years.

Here is how Oz described this meeting in Bet Shemesh:

> I sit down at a café that has four or five tables outside . . . Young men are drinking beer . . . One turns to me and asks if I have come to look into 'Project Build-Your-Home' . . . Someone else comments acidly, 'One thing's for sure: this here is an Alignment [the name of the Labor political list in the 1970s and 1980s, E.K.] type.'"[27] For the Mizrahi patrons of the café, Oz, whom they recognize vaguely from appearances on TV, with his distinct Ashkenazi features – blue eyes and light complexion – is immediately classified as a Laborite. And when he confronts them with the question of what a typical Likudnik looks like, "Now the table erupts, as five or six men talk at once, their faces distorted by anger . . . 'A Likud face? Sure – black, a delinquent, Khomeini. A punk. Violent. That's what Shimon Peres (he pronounces it 'Peretz') called us at his rally, before the elections.

What we hear in this exchange are echoes of the volatile election campaign of 1981, in which the Likud, under Begin's leadership, narrowly defeated Labor, under Shimon Peres's leadership, and in which intra-Jewish ethnic tensions played a crucial role. One of the most dramatic developments in Israeli politics, leading up to the Likud's victory in 1977, was the shift of Mizrahi voters away from Labor to the Likud.[28] By the early 1980s this shift has become so pronounced that the two leading political parties then, Likud and Labor, became associated with Mizrahim and Ashkenazim respectively. For many Israelis, the 1981 campaign is associated with the term *tchach'tchachim*, an ethnic slur that refers to punks, or hoodlums, with a distinct ethnic, Mizrahi association.[29] In a Labor (or Alignment) rally a few days before the election, the popular comedian Dudu Topaz called Likud supporters *tchach'tchachim*. The following night, in the Likud's final rally of the campaign, Begin pounced and invoked the comedian's use of the term to spur his supporters in a riveting, emotional speech that was a tour-de-force of populist political agitation. The heated atmosphere of that campaign continued to reverberate in the fall of 1982. And Oz was certainly attuned to these tensions, allowing his interlocutors to vent their frustrations. Though, by being an all but silent observer, he comes across as detached or even patronizing. As Michael Shesher rather perceptively observed, "Actually Oz does not conduct a genuine dialogue with these people, because ultimately he does not come out of his own shell."[30]

But was Oz's encounter with the angry Mizrahi residents of Bet Shemesh no more than a rehashing of ethnic stereotypes, describing Mizrahim as emotional, irate, resentful, while he, the Ashkenazi, the Laborite, keeps his distance and cool? Did it offer any social or political insights that may explain the raging anger that he encountered? In fact it had, though this aspect of Oz's reporting has received scant attention if at all.

After the loud exchange with the café's patrons, Oz hears from a forty-five-year-old Moroccan Jew, who begins to speak where the group that erupted at Oz leaves off, complaining about the fact that during his military service all the officers were from the kibbutz while, we, "the Moroccans," were the corporals. Then Oz's interlocutor goes on to complain about a long history of ill-treatment of the Mizrahim by successive Labor governments – who on the one hand provided housing and education, but at the same time restricted the new immigrants to dirty, menial jobs and took away the Mizrahi immigrants' self-respect. The man then boldly asks Oz why did the Labor governments decide to bring the Mizrahim to Israel in the first place? And he answers his own query in the following manner: "But wasn't it to do your dirty work? You didn't have Arabs then [before the 1967 occupation of the West Bank and Gaza, E.K.], so you needed our parents to do your cleaning and be your servants and your laborers ... You brought our parents to be your Arabs."[31] The hierarchical stereotypes are still at play here – but there is also a historical explanation here. When Israel was founded, it still held on to the Labor Zionist values of Hebrew Labor. This principle was one of the reasons that the Jews in pre-state Palestine, since the days of the Second Aliya, and through the early years of the state, tried, and largely succeeded, in creating a separate Jewish economy from that of the Palestinian Arabs. Early Labor Zionists glorified manual labor (farming, road construction, factory work – what the man talking to Oz described as "dirty labor") as the highest form of pioneering. Young Jews from Eastern Europe were the working class. When they established themselves and came to own properties, land, businesses, they needed, from the point of view expressed in this exchange, a new class of laborers, but this time one that mostly provided services to the new Israeli middle class, which was almost exclusively made of veteran Ashkenazim. And the new working class was comprised of the new Jewish immigrants (Arabs, who now comprised 20% of the population of the new state, were still largely kept out of the main economic fields, chiefly through a series of emergency, martial laws that kept them away from Jewish areas). After the 1967 War, when Israel came to control a large number of Palestinians in the territories, which it occupied though did not annex, it allowed Palestinian Arabs to come into Israel, with hardly any restrictions, as day laborers, and within a few years, Palestinian Arabs took over the construction, farming, and service industries.[32] And what happened to the Mizrahim as a result, as Oz's converser explains to him: "But now I'm a supervisor. And he's a contractor, self-employed. And that guy there has a transport business. Also self-employed." The new Israeli capitalist ethos, which was fueled by cheap Palestinian labor, has offered Mizrahim upper social mobility: it gave them that sense of self-respect that the old Laborite establishment had deprived them of.

And why is the new Mizrahi middle class now (1982) so opposed to Labor, which has long shed its commitments to any perceived from of socialism and became identified with the peace camp, with calling for a territorial compromise with the Palestinians? Oz's interlocuter provided his perspective: "If they give back the territories, the Arabs will stop coming to work, and then you'll put us back into the dead-end jobs, like before ... look at my daughter: she works in a bank now, and every evening an Arab comes to clean the building. All you want is to dump her from the bank into some textile factory, or have her wash the floors instead of the Arab. The way my mother used to clean for you. That's why we hate you here." This is not identity politics; this is not helping to preserve privilege by way of cultural marginalization – what in essence Ziffer and others have accused Oz of doing in this text in particular. This is political analysis par excellence. This is not a detached anthropologist observing the exotic natives. This is informed and insightful political reporting. It explains the root causes of the type of rage and hatred that Oz encountered in the café and which had swept the country in the lead up to the 1981 campaign, and which he set out to understand. And if we were to allude to the earlier part of this article, Oz may have come here closest to a Marxist scribe – understanding social and cultural phenomena through the prism of class struggle. Here we encounter a kibbutznik in full.

Another ideologically charged visit described in *In the Land of Israel* took Oz to the West Bank settlement of Teko'a, where he interviewed Menachem and Harriet, a married couple and parents of five children. Harriet was born in New York and her journey to Teko'a was fueled by a certain messianic awakening – what many people associate as the prime reason that people moved to the settlements. She immigrated to Israel after the 1967 War, inspired by the overwhelming Israeli victory. And she eventually settled in the West Bank because that is where Jews can still make personal sacrifices for the sake of redemption. For Harriet, she was living out some kind of biblical prophecy.[33] And her tale, as presented by Oz, is the traditional, if not stereotypical, depiction of the settler movement from a liberal perspective: religious fanatics in search of redemption. But Oz also recounted Menachem's journey's to Teko'a in his report.

Menachem is Mizrahi Jew from Jerusalem. He grew up in a lower-middle class home and even spent some time in kibbutzim. Seeking new opportunities, he went to London in 1960 and spent there eight years pursuing various business ventures. He too retuned to Israel after the War, but for him it was not a religious calling: he sensed that the victory signaled change in Israel, that it created new economic opportunities. He and Harriet first lived in the Tel Aviv area, but he did not find professional success. And in 1975 they moved to the West Bank, first to Kiryat Arba. As Oz explained to his readers, "This had nothing to do with ideology: he simply saw an opportunity to move up when he was offered the managership of a small factory there."[34] Social mobility as the engine driving ideological decisions. Menachem may not have been driven by messianic ideology, but he was driven by ideology nonetheless: the free market. Just like in the encounter in Bet Shemesh, Oz exposed here the relationship between class, social mobility, and support for right-wing political causes. From Menachem's perspective, territorial compromise would mean an end to the West Bank as the new Israeli economic and social frontier.

In fact, in his conversation with Menachem, Oz underscored another important factor in the appeal of the settlements for Israelis seeking social mobility. As Israel, especially after the 1967 War, moved away from the state-controlled economic model that dominated the state's early years, which also included extensive social programs, and embraced a more deregulated and privatized economic vision: the welfare state, one of the great social legacies of Labor Zionism, began to come undone. As Daniel Guwein has shown, while the welfare state was being privatized in pre-1967-lines Israel, in the settlements it was flourishing.[35] The settlements offered government subsidies, lower taxes, better mortgages, public investment in businesses, as incentive to draw people to them. They in effect became a kind of compensatory mechanism for poor Israelis who were seeking the kind of opportunities that were no longer available to them in Israel behind the Green Line – the settlements offered the type of government support that helps people achieve middle-class status. And here is how Oz explained Menachem's ability, after he moved to Teko'a from Kiryat Araba, to become the owner of a small factory: "Most of the investment in his building and machinery was made mostly by the government and the Jewish Agency, a little by the community and a little by himself." That's the welfare state in the service of social mobility. Again, Oz here offered a keen political observation that defies cultural conventions – the settler as the irrational fanatic – in favor of economic and social analysis: far from the caricature that *In the Land of Israel* has come to occupy in the Israeli imagination. Perhaps critics, who are themselves captives of identity or tribal politics, have failed to appreciate in full the intricacy and insightfulness of that text – and just how timely it was in understanding processes and developments that critical scholars would begin to address only decades after its publication.[36]

Five years after *In the Land of Israel*, Oz published a novel, *Black Box*, that again touched on the nexus of the Ashkenazi-Mizrahi divide and the settlement project. An epistolary novel, it tells the story of the dissolution of the marriage of an Ashkenazi couple, and the subsequent, tumultuous marriage of the wife to a religious, Mizrahi Jew. (In true Ozian fashion, there is also an abandoned son, who spent some of his formative years on a kibbutz.) Many critics were unkind in their reaction to the novel. The literary scholar Dan Miron held no punches, comparing the novel (in fact all of Oz's oeuvre) to an opera: ornate, flashy, overly dramatic, and bombastic. More specifically, Miron drew comparisons between *Black Box* and Wagner's *Twilight of the Gods*, the culminating part of *The Ring Cycle*, that shows the destruction of Valhalla, the great hall of the Norse gods. To Miron, the novel was an allegory depicting the decline of the old, Ashkenazi elite (the Norse gods of Israeli mythology) and the emergence of new social forces in their stead.[37] In the novel this decline is symbolized by the character of Alec Gideon, a dying academic – cold, detached, patronizing in his tone – who left Israel and lost his younger wife, Ilana, to Michel Somo, a North-African Jew, who lives up to certain ethnic stereotypes (short-tempered, prone to violence, overly ornate in his language betraying a certain sense of intellectual inadequacy).

Here is Somo writing to Boaz, Ilana's and Gideon's son, an obstinate, rebellious young man: "That is why I said to you above that you are not a man. Certainly not a Jew. Perhaps it would really suit you to be an Arab. Or a gentile. Because to be a Jew, Boaz, is to know how to stand to adversity and to practice self-mastery and to keep treading our ancient path. That is the whole Torah on one leg: self-mastery."[38] This is a new version of Zionist pioneering cloaked in biblical allusions and ethnic stereotypes. And this type of prose led some critics, like Rami Kimchi, to describe *Black Box* in the following manner: "The characters in the novel are being crushed under an allegorical steamroller of racism and stereotypes."[39]

Under the, at times, awkward veneer of overly stylized language and characters that often seem cartoonish, though, lies a keen observation about the relationship among power, land and politics. In her review of *Black Box*, Dalia Amotz summarized the dramatic core of the novel thusly, "Essentially this book deals with the selling and buying of land. Michel wants to buy the land and Gideon wants to sell it."[40] The old, Ashkenazi elite's power was not the result of monopoly over cultural capital – they came first and therefore had access to the best available land. They had homes in the central areas (the key to middle-class status) and they established farming communities on the most productive land that was later privatized. When the immigrants from Middle-Eastern countries came to Israel, they only had access to the periphery, where real estate was not nearly as lucrative as in the veteran Ashkenazi enclaves. And so, when Oz describes the decline of the old elite, it is both dying (Gideon has terminal cancer), and it is also moving away from the country – Gideon has an academic post in America, and he is in the process of selling his property in Israel. The new social forces are going in the opposite direction. Michel moved to Israel from Paris, and he is engaged in a secretive plot to buy cheap land in the West Bank, the space that as Oz already described in In *The Land of Israel* was the area that allowed Israelis from the periphery the opportunity, through heavy subsidies and other incentives, to move up the social ladder.

Here is how Michel explains in the novel his reason for moving to Israel and the way he was absorbed in the country: "When I was a young man I worked as a waiter and there were some customers, including Jews, who mistook me for an Arab ... That is why I came to live here, full of faith that in Israel we would all be brothers and the Messiah would come to rule over us. And how did his country receive an idealistic young man who came, for your information, from the Sorbonne? Builder. Night watchman. Cinema ticket seller. Regimental policeman. In a word, the tail of the fox."[41] The cultural markers here are unmistakable: rage and humiliation that translate into hatred of the old elite: the typical representation of North-African Jews in Israeli culture. The writer and critic Yitzhak Laor has argued that this has been a prominent trope in Oz's writings:

> He is not only interested in building the myth [of the ideal, Ashkenazi, secular Israeli subject, E.K.] that is consumed with a burning love for the 'salt of the earth' ... but he cannot distance himself, not even when judging himself, from the objects of his desire, and so he bundles together an all-consuming love for the physical self, the Sabra, and a searing hatred for what has been left 'outside of the ego,' beyond the physicality of the 'Israeli ... ' a hatred against the religious, against Shas, against 'Khomeinism,' hatred that fuels the poisonous growths of the Zionist Left and insures that it will remain in the political wilderness for many years.[42]

For Laor, Oz represented an *ahusli* rejection of the other, which would later translate, as the "others" – Mizrahim, religious, settlers – become the majority in Israel, into a powerless political minority. And Michel Somo is a composite of all these foreign forces – he is a Mizrahi, religious Jew who is buying land in the West Bank, what Benjamin Netanyahu has been referring to as his natural coalition partners.

But in *Black Box*, beyond the cultural symbolism, beyond the markers of identity politics, there is also politics of economic power: who has control over resources. And the physicality that concerned Oz went beyond the representations of the body (the blond blue-eyed Sabra haunted by dark, skull-capped "others"), by who controlled the land, who worked the land. And he understood how the colonization of the West Bank, the most dramatic political development in Israel since 1967, has been not only some religious quest, the result of a messianic awakening, but an opportunity, for those who have been marginalized before, to move up socially, to become masters of their own land and property. And as these forces were moving up, the old elite, which was losing its control over the political levers, started to move out to the country in an attempt to integrate into a new globalized order in which attachment to a specific locality is no longer paramount. The messianic fervor of Michel Somo is precisely the same pioneering spirit of the Second Aliya; it is the ideological rationalization of a movement to acquire and control land. Coming from Oz, Michel Somo may sound contrived – Oz was ideally suited to write about kibbutz members or Hebrew University professors. But his actions are real and capture in real time the true political drama that was unfolding in the 1980s: the settlement of the West Bank, which may be the root cause for the political decline of the Zionist Left, which Laor alluded to (not because Israel ceased to be a moral state as a result of the occupation; but because the occupation paved the way for new social forces to advance and ultimately replace the old dominant groups).

In our neoliberal order, politics have been relegated to the cultural realm, as some kind of performance art. The underlying ideological assumption has been that real political change is impossible: the market and its needs will dictate everything, all that is left to do is to battle as to which voices gain access to the public sphere. Or as Alain Badiou described it, the ideological injunction of our time, when consumption is regarded as a civic duty, is to create more and more identities, so we can consume more and more and have an ever-increasing number of options to support, to identify with to vote for.[43] In his later years, especially in his final TV interview, Oz seemed to have operated within this ideological matrix, seeing himself as the voice of one of the many groups vying for position in the chaotic marketplace of identities. But when he was describing in the 1980s the kind of changes that were happening to Israeli society, namely the decline of Labor and the rise of new political and social forces, he was describing political and social transformations that were then, as they are today (in our still postmodern moment), pushed to the side, or simply ignored, in the face of the more immediate and easily to consume politics of identity.

Ever the provocateur (and a master generator of clickbait in our digital media age), on the thirty-day anniversary of Oz's death, Benny Ziffer published on the pages of the *Haaretz* literary supplement a lengthy article by Dan Miron, which offered a harsh, even dismissive, assessment of Oz's contribution to Israeli belle-letters (earlier in this article we saw Miron's derisive takedown of Oz's novel *Black Box* – Ziffer knew precisely what he was going to get from Miron).[44] The article generated the kind of buzz and anger that one would assume Ziffer had hoped for – and predictively the tribe came to protect the legacy of its hero.[45] In this article, I did not set out to judge the quality of Oz's prose or his place in the modern Hebrew literary canon. Rather, I tried to assess the position of Oz as one of the more prominent public intellectuals in recent Israeli history. For someone like Ziffer, who did a public about face and adopted a new ideological and political home, renouncing the old home as a site of decadent privilege seems par for the course (and Ziffer is not alone here: other public figures in Israel like the media personality Avri Gil'ad, the writer Eyal Megged, and Gadi Taub, have undergone similar ideological transformations and have taken to attacking their erst-while fellow travelers). Unlike Ziffer and others though, Oz, who also as a young person underwent an ideological awakening of sorts, and who was a fierce critic of the camp which was the ideological milieu in which he grew up continued to express and adhere to some of the tenets of the Revisionist worldview that shaped his childhood, revealing again and again the complexity and multifacetedness of the Zionist relationship with the Jewish past and the political conditions in the Middle East. It seemed convenient for someone like Ziffer to associate Oz with an ideology and a camp that he himself has left behind, an ideology and social group that no longer seem vital in Israel – but Oz's worldview, at crucial times, also reflected a deep connection to the ideology that Ziffer and others have adopted as a way to capture the public sentiments in 21st Century Israel. Indeed, it is hard to reduce Oz and his writings, both fiction and nonfiction, to a simple formula. He was both a keen observer of social and political changes, and he had a complicated relationship with Jewish history that defied straightforward party or ideological affiliation. He was a champion of leftist causes and involved in leftist politics, but core Revisionist instincts continued to shape his thinking throughout. He was aware that Israel since the 1970s was no longer a melting-pot aimed to produce a single Israeli identity, but rather a complex tapestry of groups and traditions; and at the same time he was attuned to the social and economic undercurrents that created this new ideological order. A president of the white tribe? Perhaps the chronicler of the reasons for its decline would have been more apt.

Notes

1. Benny Ziffer, "Amos Oz 1939-2018: Met nasi ha-shevet ha-lavan [Amos Oz 1939-2018: The president of the white tribe has died]," *Haaretz*, December 28, 2018 https://www.haaretz.co.il/gallery/literature/.premium-1.6788133. Accessed: August 17, 2020.

2. See for example a piece by a fellow *Haaretz* columnist: Uri Misgav, "Ziffer tzodek be-davar ehad: 'Po va-sham be-Eretz Yisrael' Hu akhen sifro ha-hashuv be-yoter shel Amos Oz [Ziffer is right about one thing: 'In the Land of Israel' is Amos Oz's most important book]," *Haaretz*, December 29, 2018. https://www.haaretz.co.il/gallery/.premium-1.6788751. Accessed: August 17, 2020.

3. Kimmerling, *Ketz shilton ha-ahuslim*.

4. The interview was broadcast on Kan, the Israeli public broadcasting corporation, on October 26, 2018. It is available online https://www.youtube.com/watch?v=x5ds2w5LZN0; Accessed June 5, 2019.

5. Žižek's observation about the demise of universalism under identity politics is useful here: "Identity politics reaches its peak (or, rather, its lowest point) when it refers to the unique experience of a particular group identity as the ultimate fact which cannot be dissolved in any universality." See: Žižek, "Troubles with Identity," *The Philosophical Salon*, May 28, 2018. http://thephilosophicalsalon.com/troubles-with-identity/. Accessed: August 17, 2020.

6. Kaplan, "Amos Oz's A Tale of Love and Darkness and the Sabra Myth," 120.

7. Oz, *The Hill of Evil Counsel*, 8.

8. Ya'akov Shavit, "Oz al ha-tupim [Oz on the drums]," *Yedioth Ahronoth*, June 17, 1977, Gnazim Archive, Amos Oz Newspaper Clippings Collection.

9. Dan Laor, "Ha-tzel rodef ahrei be'alav [The shadow chases after its owner]," *Haaretz*, August 17, 1979, Gnazim Archive, Amos Oz Newspaper Clippings Collection.

10. Peleg, *Begin's Foreign Policy, 1977-1983*, 54.

11. Ibid., 56.

12. Gerz, *Shvuya be-haloma*, 67-8.

13. David Myers, "Benzion Netanyahu: In Life and Death," *Jewish Journal* May 15, 2012. https://jewishjournal.com/opinion/104121/accessed October 6, 2020.

14. Gordis, *Menachem Begin*, 110-111.

15. See: Benjamin Netanyahu, "PM Netanyahu addresses the UN General Assembly," https://mfa.gov.il/MFA/PressRoom/2015/Pages/PM-Netanyahu-addresses-the-UN-General-Assembly-1-Oct-2015.aspx accessed: August 17, 2020

16. Unknown author, "Sihah im Oz [A Conversation with Oz]," *Hedim*, February 1973, Gnazim Archive, Amos Oz Newspaper Clippings Collection.

17. Born in 1928 as Moshe Tehilimzeiger in what was then a part of Poland, he arrived by himself in Palestine a decade later and not only adopted a new Hebrew name but also for many years presented himself a Sabra, a native-born Israeli.

18. Unknown author, "Amos and Dan," *Lilit* (January 1972), Gnazim Archive, Amos Oz Newspaper Clippings Collection.

19. Unknown author, *Al Ha-Mishmar*, May 5, 1972, Gnazim Archive, Amos Oz Newspaper Clippings Collection.

20. Shaked, *Gal hadash ba-sifrut ha-ivrit*, 201.

21. Amos Oz, "Kol ha-heshbon od lo nigmar," [We have yet to reach the bottom line],", a lecture given at Tel Aviv University, June 3, 2018. The lecture is available online at https://www.youtube.com/watch?v=Pqrd4c8ZT1E; accessed May 19, 2019.

22. In similar vein, in 1983, Oz maintained that, "As long as the others have tanks and planes, I also have to play the game according to its damned rules." Unknown author, "Tziyonut im tankim u-metosim [Zionism with tanks and planes]," *Yedioth Ahronoth*, November 14, 1983, Gnazim Archive, Amos Oz Newspaper Clippings Collection.

23. Oz, *A Tale of Love and Darkness*, 425-426.

AMOS OZ'S TWO PENS (header omitted)

24. "Michael sheli, shnot ha-himishim be-Yerushalayim: Re'ayon im Amos Oz [My Michael, the 1950s in Jerusalem: an interview with Amos Oz]," *Kolno'ah* (1974), Gnazim Archive, Amos Oz Newspaper Clippings Collection.
25. Doron Rosenblum, "Dyokan ha-sofer ke-ish ha-hevrah le-haganat ha-teva [A portrait of the writer as a member of the committee for the preservation of nature]," *Koteret Rashit*, May 11, 1983, Gnazim Archive, Amos Oz Newspaper Clippings Collection.
26. Dan Laor, "Min ha-bdaya el-ha-mamashut [From fiction to reality]," *Haaretz*, June 10, 1986, Gnazim Archive, Amos Oz Newspaper Clippings Collection.
27. Oz, *In the Land of Israel*, 30-31.
28. See on that: Shapiro, *The Road to Power*; Cohen and Leon, "The Mahapach and Yitzhak Shamir's Quiet Revolution."
29. See: Kaplan "Begin, *Chach'chachim*, and the Birth of Israeli Identity Politics."
30. Michael Shesher, "Etmol ve-ha-yom be-Eretz Yisrael [Yesterday and today in the Land of Israel]," *Maariv*, April 6, 1984, 37.
31. Oz, *In the Land of Israel* 36.
32. For a succinct but insightful analysis of this socioeconomic changes in Israeli history, see: Mahozai, "She-Abu Mazen yeshalem lahem bitu'ah le'umi." For a detailed and comprehensive description of these transformation see: Shafir and Peled, *Being Israeli*.
33. Oz, *In the Land of Israel*, 58-9. For a comprehensive study of the ideology of American Jews who settled in the West Bank, see: Hirschhorn, *City on a Hilltop*.
34. Oz, *In the Land of Israel*, 55-6.
35. Daniel Gutwein, "Some Comments on the Class Foundations of the Occupation." MR Online June 16, 2006. http://mrzine.monthlyreview.org/2006/gutwein160606.html. Accessed May 16, 2019.
36. For a comprehensive discussion of these issues, see: Allegra, Handel, and Maggor, (eds.) *Normalizing Occupation*. See also Lustick, "The Occupation after 51 Years."
37. Dan Miron, "Erev ba-opera [A night at the opera]," *Davar* November 25, 1988, Gnazim Archive, Amos Oz Newspaper Clippings Collection.
38. Oz, *Black Box*, 47-8.
39. Rami Kimchy, "Kufsa sh'hora: ha-roman ve-ha-seret [Black Box: the novel and the movie]." *Maariv*, December 10, 1993, Gnazim Archive, Amos Oz Newspaper Clippings Collection. For a notably different, and rare, laudatory critical assessment of the novel, which argues that in fact Oz gave a voice in this novel to the otherwise suppressed groups in Israel, while creating complex characters, see: Getz and Beebee, "The Epistolary Politics of Amos Oz's *Black Box*."
40. Dalia Amotz, "Ptichat ha-kufsa ahrei ha-nefila [Opening the box after the fall]." *Proza* 81 (July, 1987), Gnazim Archive, Amos Oz Newspaper Clippings Collection.
41. Oz, *Black Box*, 215.
42. Yitzhak Laor, "Yonatan hashav al ha-milim hiruf nefesh [Yonatan thought about the words sacrificing oneself]." *Davar* May 15, 1992, Gnazim Archive, Amos Oz Newspaper Clippings Collection.
43. Badiou, *Saint Paul*, 9-11.
44. Dan Miron, "Keitzad yakhol Amos Oz lehorot derekh le-mishehu [How can Amos Oz show the way to anyone?]," *Haaretz*, January 22, 2019. https://www.haaretz.co.il/literature/prose/.premium-1.6866760. Accessed: August 17, 2020.
45. See for example: Orin Morris, "Ha-im yahol Dan Miron leharot et ha-derekh le-mishehu? [Can Dan Miron show the way to anyone?]," *Haaretz*, January 31, 2019. https://www.haaretz.co.il/opinions/.premium-1.6896452. Accessed: August 17, 2020.

Disclosure statement

No potential conflict of interest was reported by the author(s).

Bibliography

Allegra, M., A. Handel, and E. Maggor, eds. *Normalizing Occupation: The Politics of Everyday Life in the West Bank Settlements*. Bloomington: Indiana University Press, 2017.

Badiou, A. *Saint Paul: The Foundation of Universalism*. Stanford: Stanford University Press, 2003.

Cohen, U., and N. Leon. "The Mahapach and Yitzhak Shamir's Quiet Revolution: Mizrahim and the Herut Movement." *Israel Studies Review* 29, no. 1 (2014): 18–40. doi:10.3167/isr.2014.290103.

Gerz, N. *Shvuya be-haloma: mitusim ba-terbut ha-Yisraelit* [Captive of Her Dream: Myths in Israeli Culture]. Tel Aviv: Am Oved, 1995.

Getz, J. M., and T. O. Beebee. "The Epistolary Politics of Amos Oz's *Black Box*." *Prooftexts* 18, no. 1 (1998): 45–65.

Gordis, D. *Menachem Begin: The Battle for Israel's Soul*. New York: Schocken, 2014.

Gutwein, D. "Some Comments on the Class Foundations of the Occupation." *MR Online*, June 16, 2006. http://mrzine.monthlyreview.org/2006/gutwein160606.html

Hirschhorn, S. Y. *City on a Hilltop: American Jews and the Israeli Settler Movement*. Cambridge, MA: Harvard University Press, 2017.

Kaplan, E. "Amos Oz's A Tale of Love and Darkness and the Sabra Myth." *Jewish Social Studies* 14, no. 1 (2007): 119–143.

Kaplan, E. "Begin, *Chach'chachim*, and the Birth of Israeli Identity Politics." *Israel Studies* 23, no. 3 (2018): 68–75. doi:10.2979/israelstudies.23.3.10.

Kimmerling, B. *Ketz shilton ha-ahuslim* [The End of the Reign of the Ahsulim]. Jerusalem: Keter, 2001.

Lustick, I. S. "The Occupation after 51 Years." *Israel Studies Review* 33, no. 3 (2018): 140–151. doi:10.3167/isr.2018.330309.

Mahozai, Y. "She-Abu Mazen yeshalem lahem bitu'ah le'umi: ha-burganut ha-Yisraelit va-ha-shinui be-yahasa shel ha-medina klapei ha-medina ha-Falestinit [Let Abu Mazen Pay Them Social Security: The Israeli Bourgeoisie and Its Changing Attitudes Towards a Palestinian State]." *Mita'am* 4 (2005): 36–44.

Oz, A. *Black Box*. Translated by Nicholas de Lange. New York: Harcourt, 1988.

Oz, A. *The Hill of Evil Counsel: Three Stories*. Translated by Nicholas de Lange. New York: Harcourt, 1991.

Oz, A. *In the Land of Israel*. Translated by Maurie Goldberg-Bartura. Orlando: Mariner Books, 1993.

Oz, A. *A Tale of Love and Darkness*. Translated by Nicholas de Lange. Orlando: Mariner Books, 2004.

Peleg, I. *Begin's Foreign Policy, 1977-1983: Israel's Move to the Right*. Westport: Praeger, 1987.

Shafir, G., and Y. Peled. *Being Israeli: The Dynamics of Multiple Citizenship*. Cambridge: Cambridge University Press, 2002.

Shaked, G. *Gal hadash ba-sifrut ha-ivrit* [A New Wave in Hebrew Literature]. Tel Aviv: Sifriyat Po'alim, 1974.

Shapiro, Y. *The Road to Power: Herut Party in Israel*. Albany, NY: State University of New York, 1991.

Žižek, S. "Troubles with Identity." *The Philosophical Salon*, May 28, 2018. http://thephilosophical salon.com/troubles-with-identity/

The greatness of smallness: Amos Oz, Sherwood Anderson, and the American presence in Hebrew Literature

Karen Grumberg

ABSTRACT

This article offers a comparative reading of stories by Amos Oz and Sherwood Anderson to propose "smallness" – evoked by genre, setting, and literary devices – as a vital literary strategy structuring Oz's works. Manifestations of smallness, fundamental to the twentieth-century American literary imagination, are indispensable in Oz's stories. Paradoxically, both Oz's literary modernism and his status as a "world author" can only be understood in the context of the small, the provincial, and the local that Anderson elevated to the status of great literature, suggesting that not only European literature but also (non-Jewish) American writing has influenced Hebrew literature

Smallness as strategy

By many measures, Amos Oz is a world author. He is known internationally for his political writings, which advocate for moderation above all, as well as for his fiction, which has been translated to over forty languages in fifty countries and has earned him prestigious honors from France, Germany, Spain, the Czech Republic, South Korea, and more. The proliferation of awards following the publication of his magisterial literary autobiography, *Sipur al ahava ve-hoshekh* (*A Tale of Love and Darkness*, 2005), indicates the importance of that text in positioning Oz as a world author. In China, for example, it was deemed one of the ten best books of 2007 and, according to the Institute for the Translation of Hebrew Literature, became the first modern Hebrew work to be included in a Chinese textbook.[1] The flow of Oz's works through such global networks, their translation into dozens of languages, and their dynamic participation in widespread literary milieus – through integration in school curricula from China to Sweden, for example – exemplify David Damrosch's designation of world literature as largely a function of wide circulation and active presence.[2] Oz's worldliness is also in evidence in his influences, which are well-known to include not only Hebrew forebears such as Yosef Hayim Brenner and Mikha Yosef Berdyczewski but also authors of "great books," including, for example, Leo Tolstoy, Anton Chekhov, and Gustav Flaubert.[3] The breadth of his reading allowed Oz to feel at home in a wider world despite his rootedness in a distinctly Israeli political, poetic, and spatial territory. His participation in a global economic network of publishing, translation, and prize culture has established Oz internationally and, to the chagrin or delight of his compatriots, anointed him as Israel's cultural representative.[4]

We might associate this far-reaching impact with *largeness*, for example that of epic poetry or of the novel, both genres that are considered central to the idea of world literature.[5] Indeed, *A Tale of Love and Darkness* is just under 600 pages long, and one of the reasons it resonates so widely is that it juxtaposes Oz's intimate life story with the biography of Israel as it came into being during his boyhood. The tale it tells is simultaneously private and historical, small and large.[6] But Oz was by no means committed solely to such vast novelistic enterprises. In his lifetime, he published several collections of essays on politics and literature and twenty works of fiction, including short stories, novellas, and a dozen novels. Like other Israeli authors, such as David Grossman and A. B. Yehoshua, he began his literary career with the publication of short stories and later became known mostly for his novels and, in the realm of nonfiction, for his political and autobiographical writings. Almost half a century would pass between the publication of his first work of fiction, the collection of short stories titled *Artzot ha-tan* (*Where the Jackals Howl*, 1965), and his next collection of short stories, *Tmunot mi-hayey ha-kfar* (*Scenes from Village Life*, 2009). His next publication, *Bein haverim* (*Between Friends*, 2012), is also a collection of short stories. In the last decade of his life, he published a single novel, *Ha-bsora al-pi Yehuda* (*Judas*, 2014). Oz's return to the short story toward the end of his life, after a hiatus of several decades, suggests that the genre served as more than a stepping stone to the novelistic greatness that would follow *Where the Jackals Howl*.

How might we productively situate the question of the small in the context of an internationally recognized author such as Amos Oz? Bearing in mind several manifestations of the small or the local manifested in genre, characterization, and particular narrative devices, I propose that "smallness" served Oz as a strategy and helped him thematize ideas central to his fiction as a whole. Smallness, in my reading, structures a broader reconceptualization of Oz's crystallization as an author, as I show by reading his short story collections together with a work he has repeatedly named as an important influence, the short-story cycle *Winesburg, Ohio* (1919), by the American author Sherwood Anderson (1876–1941). Anderson, though today not considered a great author outside of literary and academic circles in the United States, exerted an outsized influence on authors like William Faulkner, Ernest Hemingway, John Steinbeck, and Virginia Woolf, among others. While some critics have assessed both Anderson's minor form and his preoccupation with the small town as retrograde and antimodern, others read it as a function of "provincial postmodernism," in the words of Clarence Lindsay. For Anderson, Lindsay argues, Americanness was "burdened with contriving identities ... that expose the fictiveness of the world," a process that "was rehearsed again and again with peculiar intensity in small midwestern towns."[7] Understanding Anderson's representation of small-town America indicates how the most local narratives transcend their own boundaries and helps illuminate critical aspects of Oz's short stories.

In this essay, I argue that only by acknowledging Oz's profound debt to Anderson can we comprehend the greatness of the generic and thematic smallness of *Where the Jackals Howl* and later short story collections. More broadly, I suggest that it is not only European literature (Hebrew and non-Hebrew) that has influenced Hebrew literature in the second half of the twentieth century but also (non-Jewish) American literature that has left an indelible mark.[8] I begin by considering Amos Oz's narrative of authorial creation and the place he reserves in it for Sherwood Anderson's influence. I then highlight a number of ways the short stories by Anderson and Oz intersect or parallel each other, arguing that the parallels are far more profound than Oz indicates in his discussion of Anderson's influence. In this context, I consider the related-tale genre and the possibilities it affords. I also briefly address the correspondences and differences between the small place in Israel and that of the small town in the United States. Most critically, I examine the Andersonian grotesque as a key narrative device adapted by Oz. My point is not merely to make a claim of influence, which Oz has acknowledged. Rather, I want to propose the comparison of Oz and Anderson as a case study of how specific concepts fundamental to the American literary imagination of the twentieth century are amenable to and even indispensable for the modern Hebrew literary representation of Israeli people and places. Paradoxically, both Oz's literary modernism and his status as a "world author" are shaped by the context of the small, the provincial, and the exceedingly local that Sherwood Anderson elevated to the status of great literature.

"Where you are is the center of the world": the genesis of Amos Oz

The best-known narrative of transformation regarding Amos Oz is that of his metamorphosis from Amos Klausner of Jerusalem to Amoz Oz of Kibbutz Hulda. At the age of fifteen, Oz made a decisive break with the melancholic, cerebral world of his parents and the legacy of his famous uncle Joseph Klausner, a choice that reflected his intellectual autonomy and his burgeoning ideological commitment to Labor Zionism. Dramatic as it was, though, Oz's turn to the kibbutz and to the concept of Hebrew strength indicated by the very name he took up, *oz*, is by no means the only significant event in his coming-of-age. Soon after he arrives in the kibbutz, another narrative of rebirth starts to take shape. It's a story Oz has told many times in interviews and, memorably, in *A Tale of Love and Darkness*, where he elaborates on the love of books that persisted at Hulda despite his initial, mistaken conviction that intellectual pursuit was at odds with the ethos of the kibbutz. He recalls having taken up writing again, "when no one was looking, feeling ashamed of myself, feeling base and worthless, full of self-loathing: surely I hadn't left Jerusalem for the kibbutz to write poems and stories but to be reborn, to turn my back on the piles of books."[9] He soon realizes that he had misunderstood the nature of the place he now called home; agricultural labor and ideological commitment at Hulda thrived alongside reading, writing, and intellectual inquiry. This realization gave Oz permission to read and write without shame. But he would make one more crucial discovery before he could become the author we know today. Devouring the books at the kibbutz library, he begins to despair that he could never become a real writer without experiencing "the real world": "I almost gave up ... No one who lacked experience of that world could even get half a temporary permit to write stories or novels. The place of a real writer was not here but out there, in the big wide world. Until I got out and lived in a real place, there was not a hope that I could find anything to write about."[10] What was certain to Oz, in the midst of this despondency, was that Hulda was most definitely *not* a real place:

A real place: Paris, Madrid, New York, Monte Carlo, the African deserts, or the Scandinavian forests. In a pinch one could write about a country town in Russia or even a Jewish shtetl in Galicia. But here, in the kibbutz, what was there? A hen house, a barn, children's houses, committees, duty rosters, the small supplies store. Tired men and women who got up early every morning for work, argued, showered, drank tea, read a little in bed, and fell asleep exhausted before ten o'clock.[11]

Any place that was not the kibbutz, in other words, was a real place, worthy of writing. Before long, though, Oz would discover that it is precisely in its smallness, and exactly because he is *there* and not elsewhere, that the kibbutz is a subject – *the* subject – of writing.

The catalyst for this monumental discovery, which would set the course for Oz's emergence as a promising young author and, eventually, for his broader literary success, was his encounter with a slim volume of short stories published in the United States three decades earlier, Sherwood Anderson's *Winesburg, Ohio*. Oz devotes several pages of *A Tale of Love and Darkness* to describing his true birth as an author upon reading *Winesburg, Ohio*. Walking through the kibbutz, he recalls feeling "like a drunken man, . . . sobbing with awestruck joy and ecstasy: eureka!"[12] He marvels at what he learns from Anderson: "The stories in *Winesburg, Ohio* all revolved around trivial, everyday happenings, based on snatches of local gossip or on unfulfilled dreams" and filled with regular people, "types who until that night I had supposed had no place in literature .... And here, in *Winesburg, Ohio*, events and people that I was certain were far beneath the dignity of literature, below its acceptability threshold, occupied center stage."[13] Anderson's stories, best known in the United States as exemplary regional literature, upended everything Oz believed about the meaning and purpose of literature, surpassing all the seductive authors who attracted Oz to reading in the first place, and clearing the path to his own literary pursuits: "*Winesburg, Ohio* taught me what the world according to Chekhov was like even before I encountered Chekhov himself: no longer the world of Dostoevsky, Kafka, or Knut Hamsun, or that of Hemingway or Yigal Mossensohn. No more mysterious women on bridges or men with their collars turned up in smoky bars."[14] Anderson helped Oz to understand that the spatial and psychological territory of everyday life was the stuff of good writing and not its obstacle. *Winesburg, Ohio* brought about a sea change in Oz's understanding of literature and a radical transformation in his conceptualization of himself as an author. He urges us, in *Love and Darkness*, to comprehend the immensity of his discovery of *Winesburg, Ohio*:

> This modest book hit me like a Copernican revolution in reverse. Whereas Copernicus showed that our world is not the center of the universe but just one planet among others in the solar system, Sherwood Anderson opened my eyes to write about what was around me. Thanks to him I suddenly realized that the written world does not depend on Milan or London but always revolves around the hand that is writing, wherever it happens to be writing: where you are is the center of the universe.[15]

The "revolution" Oz describes upon his encounter with Anderson might surprise us. After all, for many of Oz's Hebrew literary predecessors in the first decades of the twentieth century, rural Palestine, the predominant site of the implementation of the Zionist vision, often served as a literary setting.[16] Oz himself notes that literature might be set in a Galician shtetl or a Russian country town. He even cites, in his lists of "great authors," some who produced works set in small places; Knut Hamsun, for example, wrote works set not only in urban Christiania but also in the Norwegian countryside. In other words, despite Oz's insistence, *Winesburg, Ohio*, was not the first great literary text Oz had encountered that depicted ordinary people in a small place. Clearly, it was not only the discovery that literature could be set in small places but something specific to Anderson's rendition of the small place that was particularly appealing to Oz. The Amos Oz whom the world knows today, whose narratives are set in kibbutzim, in small towns, in a wintry Jerusalem – that Amos Oz was born neither in Kerem Avraham nor in Hulda, but in Winesburg, Ohio.

The small place of Sherwood Anderson

What role does Sherwood Anderson occupy in the literary milieu of twentieth-century America? How do American readers and critics understand the fiction that acted as midwife to one of the world's most celebrated authors, situated on the other side of the globe? As Oz himself points out in *A Tale of Love and Darkness*, "In America the wonderful Sherwood Anderson, friend and contemporary of William Faulkner, was almost forgotten; only in a handful of English departments were his stories still twitching with life."[17] This is an accurate assessment but for one detail. Faulkner was not merely a "friend and contemporary" of Anderson; he was Anderson's admirer and one of several disciples, including Hemingway, Steinbeck, and others, whose literary achievements would come to overshadow those of their mentor. It's a small but critical detail, because it indicates Anderson's impact on twentieth-century American literature.

Like Oz, Anderson experienced a life-changing moment that marked his rebirth as the author he was destined to become. After the untimely death of his mother – another parallel to Oz's life – the nineteen-year-old Anderson left his hometown of Clyde, Ohio (the model for the fictional Winesburg, population: 2,500) for the allure of Chicago. He eventually made a comfortable big-city life for himself, acquiring a position at an advertising agency and later heading his own sales operation in Elyria, Ohio, where he lived with his wife and their three children. Yet his impulse to write infringed on the capitalistic contentedness of his life until finally he suffered a nervous breakdown in 1912, an event to which he would return repeatedly in interviews and writings. A few months later, he left his family and his business in Elyria and returned to Chicago, cultivating the myth of his own literary rebirth: "shedding the chrysalis of the businessman, Sherwood Anderson the artist took flight," in the words of John W. Crowley.[18] It may well be that, as Crowley asserts, the myth bears only a general resemblance to what really happened, which was messier and more difficult than the story would suggest; the refinement of the stories that would make up *Winesburg, Ohio*, Crowley points out, would arrive "only after a period of imaginative struggle."[19] Nevertheless, the moment Anderson stopped dictating to his secretary mid-sentence and walked out of his office for four days of wandering aimlessly through the countryside clearly marked a new phase in his life as a writer.

Almost immediately following the publication of *Winesburg, Ohio*, it came to be seen as an exemplar of the Midwestern "Revolt from the Village," a critical paradigm that haunts the text to this day. "The Revolt from the Village" is the title of an influential 1921 essay by Carl Van Doren, the literary editor of *The Nation* and a professor of English at Columbia University. The essay outlines how America's decades-long veneration of the village as a privileged literary site had been recently toppled by "a cadre of literary truth-tellers," in Jon K. Lauck's words.[20] These authors, maintained Van Doren, shattered the idealized image of the village and presented its realities, exposing "closeted skeletons, secrets, sexual escapades, degeneracy," and other unsightly attributes.[21] Van Doren famously conceptualized this exposé as a collective insurrection of a group of seminal American authors including Sherwood Anderson, F. Scott Fitzgerald, Edgar Lee Masters, and Sinclair Lewis. For generations of readers and scholars who would take Van Doren's cue, the village or small town in American literature was the site of hypocrisy, unsightliness, and irrelevance. The "Revolt from the Village" was a subversive collective artistic act that would pave the way from dreary boredom to experimental creativity, from vacuity to substance, from provincialism to modernism.[22] Lauck's study of Midwestern regionalism, published in 2017, laments that the "assumption that the Midwest was 'culturally impoverished' and the critical focus on cultural rebellion have persisted in recent decades."[23] The contemporary recuperation of Anderson and his work is part of a larger attempt to combat the notion that Midwestern authors were disowning the culture of the small towns whence they came.

"The Revolt from the Village" thesis is deeply embedded in the American cultural imagination, continuing to undergird our understanding of the small place as it is represented in literature. The problem with this widespread narrative, as Lauck and a handful of other critics have recently insisted, is that it "functioned and still functions as a set of blinders, blocking out and distorting significant parts of the past."[24] It fails to consider the cultural, intellectual, and historical context of these writers and their works, and it subscribes to a facile reification of "the supposed rebels."[25] Perhaps the most troubling aspect of the revolt thesis, however, is that it promotes an understanding of certain texts, including *Winesburg, Ohio*, as rejecting the Midwest and the American small town, when those texts actually engage in a far more complex – and often affectionate – representation of the place and its people. Anderson himself, commenting on the revolt thesis, dismisses the idea that he participated in any revolt, and confirms his admiration for the small American town.[26] In light of all this, literary critics have slowly begun to reappropriate Anderson and other Midwestern American authors from the revolt thesis. Lauck and others seek to situate the Midwest, the American small town, and associated authors within theoretical frameworks that acknowledge the complexity of their works and of their relationship to the small places represented in their fiction.[27]

Though the influence of the revolt thesis has diminished, it is worth noting that Van Doren and others helped draw attention to *Winesburg* through its propagation. Even absent the seduction of a subversive motive, though, *Winesburg, Ohio* positioned Anderson on the American literary map and attracted admirers and imitators. Today, even among Anderson's sympathetic readers, *Winesburg, Ohio* is considered his masterpiece. No other work of fiction he published would reach its heights. Anderson today occupies a liminal place in American literature: *Winesburg* established him as a trailblazer and influenced those who would come to be known as the greatest American authors of the century, but as a book it is modest, quiet, unassuming. Further, his identification as a regional author situated him at a geographic remove from the great literary centers of Chicago and, especially, New York, where the only acceptable way to stomach regional literature was to conceptualize it in terms of revolt. Today in the United States, Anderson's name is unfamiliar to many outside specialized literary milieus, as Amos Oz noted. "Unfortunately," laments Lindsay, "we have lost

Sherwood Anderson as a major American writer."[28] Though he continues to be anthologized, analyzed, and admired by certain readers and critics as integral to twentieth-century American literature, Anderson remains a minor author, destined to inhabit the margins he wrote about so evocatively.

Small stories: the related-tale format

Unlike the American critics who subscribed to the revolt thesis to help pave the way to American modernism, Oz had no reason to read Anderson's small-town stories as a radical rejection of the small town. Indeed, as Oz recalls, the great epiphany effected by reading Anderson was that any place could be the setting and subject of literature. The small town as Anderson presented it, Oz understood, was not a place to be disowned but rather a setting for the greatest human dramas, stories of light as well as of darkness. The permission Anderson granted Oz to write about the small place, though, was by no means his only contribution to Oz's writing. Beyond setting, Anderson profoundly impacted Oz's engagement with genre, his mode of characterization, and his development of specific narrative strategies. This multifarious, far-reaching influence is productively conceptualized in terms of smallness, or, in the words of Lindsay, "the value of littleness," a subject about which Anderson "is very nearly obsessive."[29] I want to emphasize, though, that, while it is clear that Oz's engagement with smallness in various forms clearly takes its cue from Anderson, Oz's adaptation of these ideas yields something new and distinctly well-suited to the Israeli places and people in his stories.

As we have seen, short story collections open and close Oz's bibliography. All are set in small places – two in a kibbutz, and one in a "pioneering village" – and share certain themes and devices.[30] Notably, all three of these collections employ the related-tale format, a genre that was popularized by Anderson and continues to be associated with him and with subsequent American authors who used it. The related-tale format, sometimes called a composite novel or short-story cycle or sequence, has "only one essential characteristic," as Susan Mann asserts: "the stories are both self-sufficient and interrelated."[31] They are often set in the same place and time and feature overlapping or adjacent plots; a primary character in one story might recede to the background of another, while a secondary character might become prominent. In his classic study, Forrest Ingram defines the story cycle as "a set of stories so linked to one another that the reader's experience of each one is modified by his experience of the others."[32] Many critics identify something distinctly – though not solely – American in the genre, recognizing in it the same "coexistence of fusion and fragmentation," in Rolf Lundén's words, that defines Americanness itself.[33] Though associated with modernism, the genre predates the novel and can even be traced to ancient narrative, as James Nagel and others have pointed out.[34]

Anderson's use of the related-tale format in *Winesburg, Ohio*, provides "one of the earliest examples of an important American genre," writes Crowley. Identifying well-known authors such as Jean Toomer, Hemingway, and Faulkner who utilized this genre after Anderson's publication of *Winesburg*, Crowley describes their texts as "collections of short fictions, often centered on a recurring character, that work synergistically, adding up to more than the sum of their parts despite their lacking the narrative coherence of a novel."[35] Lindsay understands the genre as exemplary of Anderson's "radical experiment in form," asserting that "our discipline's inadequate nomenclature for this particular form – portmanteau novel, short-story sequence, community narrative, related-tale novel – does not do justice to the form's far-reaching newness, its especial compatibility with the modernist or postmodernist aspects of American experience."[36] Struggling to find a way to address and engage with the related-tale format, critics have failed "to come to grips with the form's implications," argues Lindsay.[37]

For Oz, however, the genre was one of the most striking qualities of Anderson's writing. In his ecstatic recollection of reading *Winesburg, Ohio*, Oz elaborates on this feature: "The whole of *Winesburg, Ohio* was a string of stories and episodes that grew out of each other and were connected to each other, particularly because they all took place in a single, poor, godforsaken provincial town ... The stories were also connected to each other because the characters slipped from story to story: what had been central characters in one story reappeared as secondary, background characters in another."[38] The related-tale format is radical because it incorporates elements of the short story as well as those of the novel, while beholden to the limitations of neither. The related-tale format is also distinctly democratic, allowing for diverse voices and viewpoints, even if those are collected or narrated by a singular entity. It is precisely because the form hosts so many seemingly incompatible perspectives and contradictions that it lends itself so well to American stories, as Lindsay points out: "The related-tale format, with all the contradictions inherent in this form – the novel that isn't a novel, the emerging bildungsroman contradicted by counternarratives, the sense of community established by all sorts of devices up against the fragmented community established by all sorts of devices – is perfectly suited for conveying the central paradox of American experience: the common thing about Americans is their conviction of uncommonness."[39] If uncommonness is one way to describe the American penchant for individualism, then Lindsay's observation points to the challenge faced by American authors who attempt to portray characters who fracture the same national collective that depends on them for its existence. This tension emerges as a defining characteristic of the genre, as Michelle Pacht emphasizes: "the short story cycle can express both the plight of an individual and the fate of a community through its very structure."[40] J. Gerald Kennedy takes this notion further, arguing that the "structural dynamic of connection and disconnection" inherent to the related-tale format results in "an insistently paradoxical semblance of community."[41]

In Oz's Israeli context, the related-tale format – a genre Pacht describes as "particularly well suited to the inhabitants of a new and growing nation" – assumes a crucial role: it helps him humanize the small places that served as a model for the Zionist enterprise.[42] Critics lauded Anderson for an imagined "Revolt from the Village," glossing over his lyrical descriptions of Winesburg and its surroundings and his sympathy for some of his acutely-suffering characters; they interpreted his revelations of the dark and unsightly aspects of small-town life not as the elevation of seemingly irrelevant characters to humanness but rather to disgust and dismissal. Like Anderson, who had to defend his affection for small towns to readers who were certain he hated them, Oz, too, had to contend with readers who read his portrayal of the dark side of the kibbutz as a denunciation rather than as a critique.[43] For Oz, the kibbutz was an imperfect but still admirable place, a place that was also an idea – a condition that was not always compatible with the lived realities of its inhabitants who were, as Oz showed again and again, merely human, subject to sometimes destructive human desires.[44] An extensive body of scholarship attests to the centrality of the kibbutz in the Israeli imagination; one of the more comprehensive and elucidating investigations in this vein is Ranen Omer-Sherman's monograph *Imagining the Kibbutz*, which asserts that "the kibbutz serves as a stage for [Oz's] critique not merely of the utopian imagination but of the entire Zionist nationalist endeavor as well."[45] My focus here not only on the kibbutz but on small "Zionist places" more broadly considers how smallness informs the representation of collective forces.[46]

In Oz's first collection, the related-tale format is not as beholden to the kibbutz as explicitly as Anderson's is to Winesburg. In *Winesburg, Ohio*, the only story to take place outside of Winesburg follows a character to Chicago. In *Where the Jackals Howl*, most of the stories are set on the kibbutz, but one takes place on an army base, another in Jerusalem; the final story in the collection takes place in the desert and is set in biblical times. Yet the key themes of the collection, those ideas that are integral to Oz's investigation of the kibbutz, link the stories: questions of belonging and estrangement; sexual transgression as a function of the limitations of collective rhetoric; transgenerational disjunctures. Even the stories that are not bound together by the setting of the kibbutz are in dialogue with one another regarding these overarching themes, and the kibbutz itself is the place against which the reader reads the other places in the collection. The later collections cleave more closely to the shared setting and characters: in *Scenes from Village Life*, all but the final story take place in Tel Ilan; all the stories of *Between Friends* are set in Kibbutz Yekhat.

The kibbutz in which many of Oz's short stories are set differs in important ways from Anderson's small town. While Anderson writes about a type of place that was revered in nineteenth-century America as the site of American authenticity, it is, by the early twentieth century, a place in transition, falling out of favor for its perceived stultifying effect on American culture: industrialization hovers, big cities beckon, alienation and stagnation threaten. The kibbutz of the 1950s in a sense signifies a transition in the opposite direction: a return to the land away from industrialized urban places, vigorous renewal, passionate ideological commitment to collective life. Yet challenges similar to those Anderson depicts in the small town make their way to Oz's kibbutzim, as well; there, too, the collective cannot protect people from their own humanity, and occasionally actively undermines it. *Scenes from Village Life* departs from the kibbutz proper and is set in a small town, but its pioneering history is ideologically significant. Despite the differences in the small places they portray, Oz, like Anderson, is interested in the paradoxes and tensions between these historical moments of transition – in the stories that don't quite fit, in the people who are both in and out, in the place that is both beautiful and ugly. Furthermore, they both share a fascination with the failure of the collective and the ensuing crisis of a self that finds itself unmoored – whether the collective is conceptualized as falling apart or still coming into being.

The related-tale format affords the flexibility these authors require, inviting different voices to tell their tales, courting contradiction as the closest approximation to fragile communal dynamics, and empowering narrators who must navigate constantly shifting focal points. The related-tale format resists wholeness by suggesting that more stories, more perspectives can be layered on; it is a cumulative form, always open – unlike the "unrelated" short story, which looks to smallness to reach a distilled, autonomous completeness, or the novel, the inheritor of the epic poem. The related-tale format, as Lindsay argues, "is a form rising out of and congenial to small-town living," largely owing to the narrator's necessarily intimate familiarity with the people whose stories he tells.[47] The largeness at which the related-tale format gestures can only be reached through a multitude of small stories that intersect, overlap, and compete with one another.

A key characteristic of the related-tale format, one that correlates with the contradictions and multiplicities of the genre, is its disruption of narrative. For the reader of the book of related tales, disruption is an important part of the reading process. Describing his own engagement with the format as a close reader of Anderson's stories, Lindsay writes, "I must sometimes interrupt my attention to the text at hand and involve other stories, for that is the nature of this particular form and of Anderson's art."[48] That is, the related-tale format by definition encompasses disruption, upsets its own linearity and continuity, invites ruptures and invasions of some stories and characters by others, and allows readers to participate in the act of narration by inviting them "behind the scenes," so to speak, of stories, by making them privy to other perspectives. Though the reader's role may suggest wholeness, this is but "a partial and problematic view," cautions Kennedy, a mere "semblance of community" typified by "mutual estrangement" and "textual divisions."[49] The disruption effected by the related-tale format structurally mimics the disruptions thematized in stories by both authors. Human nature, in both texts, disrupts narratives of national, ideological, religious, or filial absolutism or purity, exposing a fundamental tension between stasis and disruption in the small place – between staying, associated with both stability and stagnation, and leaving, associated with both upheaval and emancipation. As in *Winesburg, Ohio*, in Oz's short stories the disruptive encounter with truths creates the conditions for fiction.

The grotesque: big truths in small places

One of Anderson's most far-reaching innovations in *Winesburg, Ohio* is his crystallization of a distinctly American grotesque, a figure defined by a particular engagement with truth. Initially entitled The Book of the Grotesque, the collection opens with a story of the same name, considered by most critics to function as a prelude to subsequent stories. "The Book of the Grotesque" introduces the figure of the grotesque and offers a partial, somewhat cryptic definition of the concept, bedeviling Anderson's critics for decades and spawning a host of interpretations regarding the nature of the grotesque and its function in the collection and beyond. Before delving into the details of this important figure and concept, I want to underscore that the overarching characteristic of the grotesque as presented by Anderson is that it mediates between the concrete, mundane, everyday business of living in a small place, with all its specific features, on the one hand, and the truths that transcend those particularities, on the other; between individual identity and social or collective identity. Though the grotesque has inhabited European arts and culture for centuries, Anderson's modification and adaptation of the figure for the midwestern American milieu produces a distinctive type that differs substantively from its nineteenth-century Russian and European forebears – Anderson's American grotesque is more psychological, more interiorized, more mundane, less fantastic, and shaped by distinctly American social and cultural forces. For Amos Oz, his professed influence by Russian authors notwithstanding – and Russian authors of the nineteenth century were seminal in the production of the grotesque – the Andersonian grotesque becomes a defining figure. It is the figure of the grotesque that helps both Anderson and Oz confront the complexity of the small place whose residents grapple with big ideas. The grotesque becomes one of the most important features in Oz's writing, beginning with *Where the Jackals Howl* and evident, to some degree, in all his short stories.

"The Book of the Grotesque" opens with a character identified as "the writer, an old man with a white mustache."[50] The writer is emphatically elderly; "his body was old and not of much use any more, but something inside him was altogether young. He was like a pregnant woman, only that the thing inside him was not a baby but a youth. No, it wasn't a youth, it was a woman, young, and wearing a coat of mail like a knight."[51] As the writer lies in bed, "figures began to appear before his eyes. He imagined the young indescribable thing within himself was driving a long procession of figures before his eyes."[52] These figures, the narrator explains, "were all grotesques. All of the men and women the writer had ever known had become grotesques."[53] The youthful thing within the writer has a dual function: she directs the grotesques who pass before his eyes; and she prevents the writer himself from becoming a grotesque. "It was the young thing inside him that saved the old man," says the narrator at the end of the story.[54] The vital, feminine force within him allows him both to recognize the grotesquerie of others and to elude their fate.

But what, exactly, are the characteristics of the grotesques? And what is it that transforms these other people into grotesques? Finally, what are the role of the author and the function of fiction vis-à-vis the grotesque? Perhaps the best-known historian of the grotesque is Wolfgang Kayser, who traces the phenomenon from one designating a deviant individual, "a freak in a normal world," in Robert Dunne's words, to its late nineteenth-century designation of a world that itself instigates grotesquerie.[55] The emphasis is no longer on "the grotesque subject-as-deviant but on modern society's role as either inducing grotesqueness or being grotesque itself."[56] Particularly in the hands of Russian authors like Gogol and Dostoevsky, the grotesque is increasingly understood as a function of a society that adversely affects the individual not only physically but also psychologically.

Anderson is identified with – indeed, considered a progenitor of – a distinctively American grotesque, which takes its cue from nineteenth-century fiction but since the early twentieth century has taken on a life of its own. James Schevill identifies two strains of American grotesque. One, which he attributes specifically to Anderson, emerges from what he calls a "grotesque version of Christianity": "The American evangelical tradition is often so fanatic in its religious intensities and obsessions that it would put Christ to shame if he could see his hardshell to say nothing of hardsell imitators. In our frenetic attempt to conquer the west, tame the land, subdue and eliminate the Indians, we put the stern zealot-Christ to work. Thus we achieved often a grotesque version of Christianity."[57] The second source he identifies as nourishing the American grotesque relates to individualism, materialism, and capitalism. As the nineteenth century transitioned into the twentieth, "throughout the country the connection between the individual and the community became distorted. Today we struggle with the contradiction of a democracy founded on agrarian frontier ideals that persist doggedly amidst the realities of a secret technology that runs our country."[58] Schevill's identification of Anderson's grotesque with American social and cultural particularities is crucial; it would be

54 AMOS OZ'S TWO PENS

impossible to transpose, intact, Anderson's grotesque to another national or cultural context. His adaptation of the figure acknowledges its power as social commentary, but also indicates a resistance to the idea of a universal, human idea of truth that erases specificity and turns a blind eye to historical context. Reading the American grotesques of Winesburg, Ohio as a function of "unchanging truth" rather than acknowledging their "particular, historically determinate condition" is itself grotesque, argues Chad Trevitte: "nothing could be more 'grotesque' than to see in this parable a timeless, metaphysical idea of 'the human condition.'"[59] The American grotesque, as Anderson constructed it, is rooted in its time and place.

It is not difficult to see how such a figure might be alluring for an author like Oz, who was, in the 1960s, in the midst of forging not only his own idiom of fiction but also very much aware of himself as contributing to a relatively new national literature. The particularities and peculiarities of Americanness help to think about the particularities and peculiarities of Israel. Where Americans had a "stern zealot-Christ" to help "conquer the west, tame the land, subdue and eliminate the Indians," Israelis had the cult of A. D. Gordon and Ben-Gurion to help conquer the desert, tame the land, subdue the Palestinians. And where Americans were reinscribing independence as materialism and failing to reconcile it with an idealized but faltering agrarianism, Israelis were succumbing to individual desires at odds with the idealized but faltering collectivity of the rural kibbutz. America of the 1920s and 1930s was, without a doubt, very different from Israel in the 1950s and 1960s. Clearly, though, certain parallels are compelling and lend themselves to a productive analysis of Oz's adaptation of the Andersonian American grotesque.

In Oz's story "Singing," in *Scenes from Village Life*, the narrator, a guest among many in the home of friends hosting a communal singing evening, reflects on those around him: "Inside everyone, I thought, there is the child they once were. In some you can see that it's still a living child; others carry around a dead child inside them."[60] In this story, the dead child is not only figurative but also literal, referring to the sixteen-year-old son of his hosts, who had died by suicide years before. The narrator's observation in this story recalls the passage from "The Book of the Grotesque" in which the narrator struggles to describe the "altogether young" thing inside the writer. While Anderson's youthful thing within calls the writer's attention to the grotesques, allowing the writer to tell their stories, Oz's child, sometimes alive and others not, inhabits everyone, indicating the degree of grotesquerie to any astute observer. In Anderson's conceptualization, the writer and the writing process are central to the recognition of the grotesques as well as to the writer's own evasion of their fate. The fact that the writer "had spent all of his life writing and was filled with words" might have caused his own transformation into a grotesque; yet we are told that "it was the young thing inside him that saved the old man," the selfsame thing that directed the grotesques before his eyes.[61] The writing that exposes the grotesque can both subdue and catalyze the author's transformation into such a figure.

Where is the author in Oz's version? What role does writing play in his adaptation of the grotesque? We encounter a few writers in Oz's stories. Geula writes poetry in "Nomad and Viper." In *Scenes from Village Life*, Adel, the shy young Arab student in "Digging," is writing a book comparing life in a Jewish village to life in an Arab village, while the woman whose shed he inhabits, Rachel Franco, writes the memories of her father, a curmudgeonly former MK. In "Lost," the narrator recalls a famous writer, Eldad

Rubin, who was born and raised in Tel Ilan, where he "wrote long novels about the Holocaust."[62] None of these writers plays a role comparable to the writer in Anderson's "Book of the Grotesque," whose narrative is set apart from the stories it helps to frame.

One strange story, however, may provide a clue as to Oz's rendering of the connection between the Andersonian grotesque and writing. "In a Faraway Place at Another Time," the final story in *Scenes from Village Life*, is the only one in the collection that does not take place in Tel Ilan. Set in an unnamed village and unspecified historical period, it departs from the mostly realistic orientation of the rest of the stories and their peaceful village setting, depicting instead a place that is horrific, swampy, toxic, and decaying, and whose inhabitants suffer from mental and physical deficiencies "because they all interbreed."[63] A narrator describes the nightmarish village: "A sweetish smell of decay spreads among our huts . . . . Our homes are full of flying and crawling insects."[64] The use of the first-person plural suggests the narrator's identification with the villagers he describes, a strategy that Oz uses to powerful effect in *Where the Jackals Howl* in particular. Here, though, the first-person plural is swiftly replaced, for the rest of the story, by a clear-cut division: the narrator reverts to the first-person singular and refers to those he describes in the third person, highlighting his otherness: "I was sent here twenty or twenty-five years ago by the Office for Underdeveloped Regions, and I still go out every evening at twilight to spray the swamp with disinfectant; I administer quinine, carbolic acid, sulfur, skin ointments and antiparasitic drugs to the suspicious locals; I encourage a hygienic and abstinent lifestyle and distribute chlorine and DDT."[65] Acting as "pharmacist, teacher, notary, arbitrator, nurse, archivist, go-between and mediator," the narrator was formerly respected by the odious locals but senses a change: "I have to admit to myself that I have no power left. My authority is dwindling."[66] The political shifts beyond the village do nothing to improve things there, the population is "in terminal decline," children are born of debauchery only to die immediately, and fleas "as big as a coin" gorge on people's blood.[67] The narrator composes memoranda to governor after governor, for naught. Years pass, and the narrator himself begins to succumb to the deplorable conditions he was supposed to help eradicate:

> My intellect is waning along with my desires. I can no longer find enough light within myself. The thinking reed is becoming empty of thoughts . . . . There is moss growing on my bedding and damp rot has invaded the walls. All my books are going moldy. The covers crumble away and fall off. I have nothing left, and I can barely distinguish between one day and the next, between spring and autumn, between one year and the next. . . . So I am gradually turning my back on everything around me, and in fact on myself as well.[68]

Could this solitary man, having finally internalized the moral and physical chaos around him, be the failed counterpart of Anderson's writer? What might this bizarre final story in *Scenes from Village Life* have to add to the quiet stories about fractures in the ordered world of Tel Ilan? A long view of this final story might suggest that the narrator's self-described role as "pharmacist, teacher, notary, arbitrator, nurse, archivist, go-between and mediator" may be associated with the Israeli writer – particularly the vocal, influential kind of writer that Oz himself was. The narrator's diminishing authority and the locals' growing disdain and disrespect for him, too, can be interpreted as a representation of the changing role of the author in an Israel increasingly hostile to the moderation and reason for which Oz advocated throughout his life. Such an interpretation literalizes

Kennedy's theorization of the related-tale format as reflecting the writer's estrangement from his audience: the characters "comprise an imaginary confederacy ... gathered to create the semblance of community in the face of the storyteller's irrevocable separation from a living audience."[69]

The single departure from the recognizable Israeli setting of the other stories in the collection, "In a Faraway Place at Another Time" depicts grotesquerie in the extreme. The story ends with an old gravedigger appealing to the other villagers to stop chattering about a mysterious, healthy stranger who appears and wordlessly disappears: "Words won't help. Another hot day is beginning and it's time to go to work. Whoever can work, let him work, put up or shut up. And whoever can't work anymore, let him die. And that's all there is to it."[70] Exaggerating the tensions, transgressions, and impulses of collective life in a village evacuated of its history, the story adds a recognizably Ozian dimension to Anderson's grotesque: chaos encroaches on order, and the nurse-archivist-mediator can do nothing to stop it, finally giving in to its force. Meanwhile, the distorted expression of the veneration for labor, together with the caricatured swampiness of the village, suggests a perversion of the history of the Zionist project. This story, which closes the collection, exemplifies the power of the related-tale format: radically departing from the rest of the stories, its inclusion in the collection nevertheless urges readers to consider it within that context.

I would like to return now to Anderson's "The Book of the Grotesque," to look more closely at the narrator's description of the grotesques. "All of the men and women the writer had ever known had become grotesques," proclaims the narrator while describing the figures who appear to the writer. He is quick to point out, though, that the "grotesques were not all horrible. Some were amusing, some almost beautiful." The writer watches the grotesques for an hour and then, "although it was a painful thing to do, he crept out of bed and began to write," intending to describe the impression made by some of the grotesques. The book he produced, says the narrator, "had one central thought that is very strange and has always remained with me." He describes it as an origin myth or a creation tale, which we might consider as a compelling counterpart to the apocalyptic final story in Oz's *Scenes from Village Life*:

> That in the beginning when the world was young there were a great many thoughts but no such thing as a truth. Man made the truths himself and each truth was a composite of a great many vague thoughts. All about in the world were the truths and they were all beautiful.
>
> The old man had listed hundreds of truths in his book. I will not try to tell you all of them. There was the truth of virginity and the truth of passion, the truth of wealth and of poverty, of thrift and of profligacy, or carelessness and abandon. Hundreds and hundreds were the truths and they were all beautiful.
>
> And then the people came along. Each as he appeared snatched up one of the truths and some who were quite strong snatched up a dozen of them.
>
> It was the truths that made the people grotesques. The old man had quite an elaborate theory concerning the matter. It was his notion that the moment one of the people took one of the truths to himself, called it his truth, and tried to live his life by it, he became a grotesque and the truth he embraced became a falsehood.[71]

These sparse lines are all Anderson offers by way of defining the grotesque that structures the characterizations in *Winesburg, Ohio*. In the century that has passed since the publication of Anderson's collection, critics have proposed various interpretations of this passage. For Dunne, the grotesque is mobilized to point to the postmodern "inefficacy of language" suggested by the rest of the passage.[72] Trevitte understands the grotesque as expressing the tension between the individual and the collective, the part and the whole; for him, the power of the grotesque lies in its capacity to illuminate "the tale itself as a curiously discordant, or grotesque, mode of 'storytelling,'" and thus to indicate "the necessity as well as the impossibility of storytelling as a vehicle of holistic experience in modern America."[73] Central to this interpretation are processes of commercial exchange and the way these shape American selfhood. The people in the story have experienced "absolute self-alienation with regard to individual identity," he asserts. "The zealous desire of the people to 'acquire truth' entails both an attempt to *overcome* this alienated relationship as well as a perverse *perpetuation* of it ... . By identifying themselves with the objectified truths they seize upon, the people appear to model their very selfhood on commercial exchange."[74] Schevill considers Anderson's grotesque against the backdrop of, on the one hand, the fanaticism of evangelical Christianity and, on the other, the hypocrisy of a society that idealizes agrarian individuality while subscribing to market capitalism: "Anderson's real insight ... is to show how *American Grotesque* masquerades as a rigid defense of truth."[75] Irving Howe reads the grotesques in *Winesburg* as signifying a "deformity," a metaphysical state of loneliness; he, too, maintains that there is something specifically American both about their loneliness and about its implications. These figures "whose humanity has been outraged" indicate that "beneath the exteriors of our life the deformed exert dominion, that the seeming health of our state derives from a deep malignancy."[76] The rotting grotesques who inhabit the pages of *Winesburg* suggest, Howe argues, that it is "a buried ruin of a once vigorous society."[77]

All of these interpretations contribute something to our understanding of Anderson's grotesque, but none can lay claim to definitive resolution. Rather than try to arrive at a singular understanding of the grotesque – which, as several critics have pointed out, would in itself reduce "The Book of the Grotesque" to grotesquerie – we are better served by conceptualizing the grotesque as a state of tension between conflicting forces, from the most interiorized impulses, desires, and anxieties to larger collective and ideological failures. The grotesque clearly has something to do with the dynamic between the individual and the collective; with the way people engage with truths; with the encounter with modernity; with the danger of absolutism.

In Anderson's hands, the small town is the only possible backdrop for the grotesques and the tensions they encompass, because of the place of the small town in the collective American imagination. By 1919, there was nothing new about alienation and anxiety in the city; indeed, alienation was supposed to be the purview of the city. Alienation in a small town went against the way America defined itself. Schevill's articulation of the American grotesque is forceful because he emphasizes the hypocrisy behind the official valorization of agrarian life at a time when the country was willingly capitulating to the seductions of capital and technology. Thomas Yingling also addresses Anderson's role in confronting this hypocrisy: "*Winesburg* renders problematic a long tradition of cultural fantasy that equates labor on the land with a completely unalienated existence."[78]

A similar cultural fantasy characterized Labor Zionism; Yingling's statement is as applicable to the Israeli context as to the American one it critiques. In Oz's kibbutz as in Anderson's small town, laboring or worn-out bodies can house alienated souls. The small-town setting is a defining factor of the Andersonian grotesque, then, not because the small town itself was deadening but because it could showcase, vividly and at close range, how the promises of American collective identity had failed individuals. Anderson's critique of this situation is also an expression of compassion for the small town and its people, some of whom have been the victims of forces beyond their control and others who have brought their fate upon themselves. In these ways, Anderson's grotesque is the arbiter of big truths in small towns.

Two salient examples can illustrate key features of the grotesque in *Winesburg, Ohio*. Wing Biddlebaum, we are told in Anderson's story "Hands," was only forty years old but looked sixty-five. He "talked much with his hands. The slender expressive fingers, forever active, forever striving to conceal themselves in his pockets or behind his back, came forth and became the piston rods of his machinery of expression. The story of Wing Biddlebaum is a story of hands .... The hands alarmed their owner."[79] The hands have a life of their own, independent of the one to whose body they are attached. The comparison of the hands to machine components establishes them as an element of an industrialized society; the description of Wing Biddlebaum as the "owner" of the hands confirms this association. Wing Biddlebaum is famous for his hands, but the fame is based on the commodification of the hands that had allowed him to pick "as high as a hundred and forty quarts of strawberries in a day," figuratively amputating the hands from the man. The narrator tells us that "Winesburg was proud of the hands of Wing Biddlebaum in the same spirit in which it was proud of Banker White's new stone house and Wesly Moyer's bay stallion, Tony Tip, that had won the two-fifteen trot at the fall races in Cleveland."[80] A few pages into the story, we learn that Wing Biddlebaum, formerly Adolph Myers of an unnamed town in Pennsylvania, had been a sensitive schoolteacher wrongly accused of "unspeakable things" and driven out of town by a lynch-mob. The hands that had previously busied themselves "caressing the shoulders of the boys [and] playing about the tousled heads ... to carry a dream into the young minds" had been his undoing in Pennsylvania, where an angry father shouted "I'll teach you to put your hands on my boy, you beast," while beating him with his fists.[81] In Winesburg, where Wing Biddlebaum had lived alone for twenty years, his hands elicited not "hideous accusations" but pride for their capacity to pick strawberries.[82] The hands come to define Wing Biddlebaum and his relations with his fellow townspeople both in Pennsylvania and in Winesburg; finally, they define him as a whole, becoming exaggerated and caricatured expressions of the man.

The story "Godliness" introduces us to another memorable grotesque, Jesse Bentley, a deeply religious man who had left his family farm at eighteen to become a Presbyterian minister and was called back to run the farm after all his brothers were killed in the Civil War. "Jesse Bentley was a fanatic," asserts the narrator. "He was a man born out of his time and place and for this he suffered and made others suffer."[83] Full of vitality, Jesse nurtures a passionate faith, and eventually starts "to think of himself as an extraordinary man, one set apart from his fellows."[84] He becomes so preoccupied with himself that he fails to realize that his wife is working herself to death, and, later, that his obsession with God frightens his grandson. Like Wing Biddlebaum, he looks older than his age: at fifty-five, he looks like he is seventy. Where Wing Biddlebaum has aged prematurely as a consequence of harboring within him the secret of terrifying violence meted out for a crime he did not commit, Jesse Bentley is consumed by a "greedy thing in him" that drives him to buy and cultivate more and more land and to invest in a great many new machines."[85] Both men have a place in Winesburg, each through his contribution to the town's economy. But though they are part of the town, they are not *of* the town; both are alone, striving in vain for a redemption that will somehow expiate their isolation, inscribe them in a story less lonely and seemingly insignificant than their own, and both fail. "Hands" ends with Wing Biddlebaum picking up crumbs from the floor following his modest supper: "the kneeling figure looked like a priest engaged in some service of the church. The nervous expressive fingers, flashing in and out of the light, might well have been mistaken for the fingers of the devotee going swiftly through decade after decade of his rosary."[86] Jesse Bentley, hungry for divine recognition, takes his grandson David to the woods, where he intends to offer a lamb in sacrifice to God; but David, struck by terror, flees, turning only to aim his slingshot at his knife-wielding grandfather, a trembling David to his grandfather's grotesque Goliath. As different as these men are, their absolutism – Wing Biddlebaum's fear and Jesse Bentley's greed, both inscribed in religious terms – distorts the love each man feels.

Winesburg, Ohio hosts diverse expressions of the grotesque. Unfulfilled women and awkward men who are painfully aware that they don't belong in the town; people who have given up on their own dreams and live on the fumes of others' potential; silent sons and desperate mothers; boys and men who are too gentle, too silent, too different: all try in vain to articulate their desires or their losses to others in a town they experience by turns as desolate or lovely, indifferent or inspiring. Each of them must contend with a life that has been taken over by a distorted truth – truths that, as the narrator explains in "The Book of the Grotesque," have become falsehoods. It is fiction itself, as the narrator suggests, that becomes the site of collectivity, binding together the inhabitants of Winesburg through a network of psychological and emotional currents that reinscribe the meaning of the small town.

Oz's short story collections, too, feature a variety of grotesque characters whose lives, loosely sutured together by fiction, are inextricably entangled with the small place they inhabit. In *Where the Jackals Howl*, the grotesque emerges, in some characters, through overzealous adherence to Zionist ideology; in others, it is a consequence of resentment or pain elicited by exclusion from the Zionist collective. In the title story, the repulsive Matityahu Damkov reveals a dark secret and upends the life of the daughter he seduced; in "The Way of the Wind," the admired Shimshon Sheinbaum drives his perpetually disappointing son to his death; In "A Hollow Stone," Batya Pinski, the widow of a respected pioneer who left his family behind to fight and die in the Spanish Civil War, isolates herself in her room and finds meaning only in her futile determination to publish her late husband's writings so that she can forge a dedication to herself.

Scenes from Village Life and *Between Friends*, published decades after Oz's first collection, persist in their depictions of grotesques. In Tel Ilan, history is scrubbed from the buildings and streets and replaced by gourmet restaurants, art galleries, and fashionable boutiques; people carry within them private tragedies – unwanted abortions, stillbirths, suicide, loneliness. While in *Winesburg, Ohio*, these private tragedies play out against the backdrop of a town surrounded by a changing society, *Scenes from Village Life* portrays the transition as fully underway, and invites the reader to witness the deterioration of the pioneers, the structures, and the farmlands of a formative period of Israeli history, and their replacement by intensely isolated and pained individuals overseeing passively the end of an era. Pesach Kedem, the elderly former Knesset member in "Digging," is preoccupied by perceived betrayals of comrades long dead. Eighty-six years old, "gnarled and sinewy" with "a hunched back," he refuses to relinquish the past. He pretends to forget the names of contemporary political leaders, "just as the world had forgotten him. He, however, had forgotten nothing: he remembered the tiniest details of every insult, resented every wrong that had been done to him two and a half generations earlier, kept a mental note of every weakness shown by his opponents, every opportunistic vote in the Knesset, every glib lie ever uttered in committee, every disgrace brought on themselves by his comrades of forty years ago."[87] Occasionally, visitors stop by the house Pesach shares with Rachel, the widowed daughter who cares for him, inspiring fresh expressions of his disgust: "he firmly believed that he and his daughter were enough company for each other, and they had no desire for unnecessary visits from strangers, whose motives were dubious [. . . .] He was of the opinion that these days everybody's intentions were self-centered."[88] Embittered, angry, and mired in self-imposed isolation, Pesach has driven the truths he embraced to distortion, a literal embodiment of the origin story Anderson's narrator tells in "The Book of the Grotesque." Every night, Pesach hears digging sounds from the direction of the house's foundation and complains to his daughter that the Arab student, Adel, is planning a takeover of their home; Rachel does not hear the digging, but Adel does. Observing that "Rachel did not believe in her father's nocturnal imaginings or Adel's dreams," the narrator suggests that she, too, may be a grotesque, her "anger and impatience" blinding her to the events taking place beneath her very feet.[89] In the midst of the father's excessive remembering and the daughter's willful forgetting, it is Adel – who not only writes about the village but also weeds, restores, and revives it – who weathers the distortion of truth and resists grotesquerie.

Between Friends takes us back again to the time and place reminiscent of Oz's first collection, a kibbutz in the second decade of statehood. As in *Scenes from Village Life*, this collection pits human impulses and desires against the ideals designed to regulate them, and a tension between leaving and staying underlies almost all the characters' narratives. The first story in *Between Friends*, "The King of Norway," introduces readers to Zvi Provizor, a fifty-five-year-old bachelor who "loved to transmit bad news: earthquakes, plane crashes, buildings collapsing on their occupants, fires, and floods."[90] Though most of the kibbutz members, who nickname him the Angel of Death, avoid him, a relationship develops between Zvi and a younger widow named Luna Blank. "Why do you take all the sorrows of the world on your shoulders?" she asks him. He replies that our helplessness in the face of cruelty obliges us "to at least acknowledge it."[91] When Luna, moved by his sensitivity to others' suffering, tries to deepen their intimacy, he recoils and begins avoiding her: "he had begun to feel that their relationship was heading toward a disastrous place where he did not want to go, a place that repulsed him."[92] Luna eventually leaves the kibbutz for a new beginning in America, and Zvi continues in his solitary role as the chronicler of the world's tragedies.

In the collection's final story, "Esperanto," a Dutch kibbutz member, Martin Vandenberg, a vegetarian and heavy smoker known among his peers as an ideological purist, lies dying from cancer. Like Zvi Provizor, he has never missed a day of work; like

Zvi, he never marries and shuns human intimacy, rejecting the institution of family "because a family unit, by its very definition, creates an unnecessary barrier between itself and society."[93] He eschews the ownership of even basic private possessions because they "take over the soul and enslave it," and looks forward to the abolition of money and borders.[94] In the spirit of this utopian "international, pacifist brotherhood," he had taught Esperanto in Rotterdam as a young man.[95] As his lungs rapidly deteriorate and his breathing becomes increasingly labored, he laments what he considers to be the inevitable decline of the kibbutz as a new generation takes over that of the pioneers: "In another twenty or thirty years, kibbutzim would become nothing more than well-kept garden communities populated by homeowners driven by material pleasures."[96] The truth by which he lives his life is a variation on the one that drives Zvi; their uncompromising compassion defines and distinguishes them even as it ensures their aloneness.

The story and the collection as a whole end with Martin's funeral, attended only by the kibbutz members since no one knows whether he has family; Zvi Provizor, who had enrolled in Martin's Esperanto lessons, is among those who shovel earth into the grave. Though the funeral scene brings together several characters who, in the preceding stories, had experienced isolation or exclusion in the kibbutz, in coming together they manage to overcome, at least momentarily, the sadness with which they privately contend. Roni Shindlin, the kibbutz comedian who had dubbed Martin "the Ghandi of Kibbutz Yekhat," remarks, "It's a real shame he's gone. There aren't many people like him left."[97] Martin's ideological zeal, considered excessive in his lifetime, in his death is recast as inspiring and admirable. The "warm feelings" among the mourners suggest a coming to terms with the passing of an era more than rejection of its principles or panic at their decline.[98] They also indicate that the new generation, though it may not adhere to ideals with the same fiery passion as the old, finds value and truth in the way they lived their lives.[99]

Specific choices, small moments, lifelong habits: the conditions that breed or reflect the grotesque vary among Oz's short story collections, but all three maintain its fundamental preoccupation with aloneness in a collective setting. *Between Friends* departs from the almost monstrous grotesques of *Where the Jackals Howl* and also from the tragic figures of *Scenes from Village Life*. *Between Friends* – notably set not in a village but in a kibbutz much like the one Oz first represented half a century earlier – nurtures a note of quiet, moderate hope. It confirms Oz's observation in his essay "The Kibbutz at the Present Time" that the social system of the kibbutz is "the least bad, the least unkind" that he had encountered.[100] As in *Winesburg, Ohio*, the structure of characters' relations with the small place they inhabit is paradoxical, encompassing comfort and pain, beauty and ugliness, kindness and cruelty, companionship and isolation. Oz never condemns the kibbutz, as Anderson never condemns the small town; they embrace these places even as they recognize the horrors they can impose. The grotesque is a figure eminently suited to host these contradictions, and the small place its most organic environment. As they diminish in the face of urban anonymity and the glittering promise of capitalism, the small places associated in Israel and America with the idea of the national collective are ground zero of the grotesque for both Oz and Anderson.

***

The small town as a complex, unromanticized site of poignant human drama is at the heart of Anderson's greatness. Illuminating the grotesque aspect of the teachers, ministers, and farmers of Winesburg, Anderson defies stereotypes of American authenticity that rely on an assumption of the small town as an idealized space of wholeness and contentedness. While these figures indicate deep psychical wounds perpetuated by the peculiar spatiality of the small American town, they point not to its rejection. Rather, the grotesques signify the human impulse to find meaning and to acquire truth – bound up in the accouterments of religious and industrial fervor, in social norms and expectations, and in a particularly American way of being in the world. The grotesque figure's intimate connection to the small town is one manifestation of the power of smallness. Another is Anderson's use of the related-tale format, a structural expression of the individual stories that create narratives of collective existence even as they disrupt and fragment these narratives. The related-tale format indicates the failures and lacunae of community even as it points to its possibilities.

Oz's affinity to these vehicles of smallness, from his earliest writings to his final ones, suggests the significant, ongoing influence that Anderson exerted on Oz's writing. More broadly, it exposes compelling commonalities between America and Israel, as characters navigate private challenges against a backdrop of collective life in transition. As such, Oz's short stories chart an American presence in Israeli literature, aligning him alongside Anderson as well as his literary heirs. Aside from the persistent association of A. B. Yehoshua with William Faulkner, links between (non-Jewish) American and Israeli literature have been investigated minimally.[101] Oz's attraction to a distinctly Andersonian smallness – featuring interior lives, rural places, and geographical and atmospheric details of a local American milieu that parallels those of Oz's Israel in distinctive ways – suggests that there is more to be said about the American influence on Hebrew literature.

Notes

1. "Amos Oz," *Institute for the Translation of Hebrew Literature.*
2. This is a key idea undergirding Damrosch's seminal study. Noting that world literature encompasses "literary works that circulate beyond their culture of origin, either in translation or in their original language," he specifies that "a work only has an *effective* life as world literature whenever, and wherever, it is actively present within a literary system beyond that of its original culture" (*What is World Literature*, 4).
3. See Holtzman, for example, on Oz's position as Berdyczewski's "most prominent heir" ("Strange Fire," 145). Other examples of scholarship comparing Oz to European authors (Hebrew and non-Hebrew) include: Aschkenasy, "Women and the Double"; Ginzburg, "Madame Bovary"; Sham, "El ha-yeled ha-zeh hitpalalti?"; Govrin, "Ha-mishpaha ha-sifrutit." Asked about his influences in an interview printed in *Voices of Israel*, Oz lists the Hebrew writers Berdyczewski, Brenner, and S. Y. Agnon and the Russian writers Tolstoy, Chekhov, and Fyodor Dostoevsky. He relegates American literature to a third tier that includes Herman Melville and Sherwood Anderson.
4. Despite Oz's status in Israel as a highly regarded bestselling author, critics have pointed out for decades the disjuncture between the idea of Oz as the cultural representative of Israel, on one hand, and the limited scope of Israeliness typical of his works, on the other. Oz is more concerned with men and masculinity than with women; with European Jews than with Mizrahim or Palestinian Israelis; with the kibbutz and Israel's "salt of the earth" than with the far more numerous populations in cities or development towns. As such, some consider Oz to have perpetuated a romanticized portrait of Israel that, by excluding or stereotyping certain people, parallels their marginalization by Israel more broadly. Relatedly, critics reading Oz in a postcolonial vein have taken him to task for his consistent commitment

to a Zionism they equate with colonialism. On women in Oz's works, see: Abramovich, "Woman-Centered Examination" and "Sexual Objectification"; Aschkenasy, "Women and the Double"; Ben-Dov, "Amos Oz's Artistic Credo"; Gertz, "Amos Oz and Izhak Ben Ner"; Fuchs, "Amos Oz's Treacherous Helpmate" and "Beast Within"; Wheatley, "It is the Hunter"; Zilberman, "Zehut nashit be-tokh zehut gavrit." On "others" in Oz's works, see: Loshitzky, "From Orientalist Discourse"; Khoury, "Rethinking the Nakba"; Amende, "Man with Such an Appearance"; Shimony, "Mizrahi Body." For a postcolonial critique, see: Laor, "Sipur al ahava ve-hoshekh" and "Hayey ha-min shel kohot ha-bitahon"; and Piterberg, "Literature of Settler Societies."

5. Wai Chee Dimock argues for a reclassification of world literature on the basis of genre, proposing epic poetry and the novel as "the durable threads that bind together the entire species [of world literature]" ("Genre as World-System," 90). For a compelling theorization of a "modern epic" as a "supercanonical" world text, see Franco Moretti, *Modern Epic*, 4.

6. It's worth noting that Eran Kaplan and others have commented on *Love and Darkness* as a text that casts Oz and his family in a minor light; though he integrates his family's narrative into the larger story of Israel, he represents his parents as marginalized because of their diasporic proclivities and his father's right-leaning politics. Long before the publication of *Love and Darkness*, Hanan Hever identifies a similar tendency already in the early story "Nomad and Viper," which he proposes as an exemplar of "minority discourse of a national majority" (Hever, "Minority Discourse").

7. Lindsay, *Such a Rare Thing*, 23.

8. This claim differs substantively from those advanced by other studies addressing the interaction between Hebrew and American literature and culture, which are concerned primarily with encounters and representations that are historically or biographically motivated. Thus, for example, Alan Mintz and Michael Weingrad have published on Hebrew writing in America; Mintz has also explored the translation and reception of Hebrew literature in the U.S.; Andrew Furman has examined American-Jewish literary representations of Israel; Emily Miller Budick has made a case for comparative readings of Israeli and American-Jewish literatures. In 1997, a special issue of *Shofar* titled "Israel and America: Cross-Cultural Encounters and the Literary Imagination" focused on literature as a "point of contact or exchange for Israeli and American Jews" (Sokoloff, "Israel and America," 3). The articles included consider literary depictions of the American-Jewish understanding of Israel, Anglophone Israeli literature, Orthodox Jewish literature in Israel and America, the presence of American popular culture in Israel, and American-Jewish struggles with identity in Israel. While these studies and others offer important insights regarding Hebrew/American literary relations, I posit that considering the role of American literature beyond Jewish texts and contexts can enrich our understanding of the development of Hebrew literature.

9. Oz, *Love and Darkness*, 487. All citations from Oz's works are from the English translations.

10. Ibid., 489.

11. Ibid.

12. Ibid., 491.

13. Ibid.

14. Ibid., 493.

15. Ibid.

16. In 1911, the Hebrew author Yosef Haim Brenner wrote what would become a highly influential essay, "Ha-zhaner ha-eretzisraeli ve-avizarehu" [The Land of Israel Genre and Its Devices]. Brenner acknowledges a link between the setting and subject of Hebrew literature produced in Ottoman Palestine at that time, and observes different modes of engagement and representation with it. Critiquing what he terms the "Land of Israel Genre" as a narrow reflection of nationalist ideology, he distinguishes between such works and an "anti-Genre" poetics that brings the local and the universal into fruitful, complex dialogue.

17. Oz, *Love and Darkness*, 493.

18. Crowley, "Introduction," 8.

19. Ibid., 9.
20. Lauck, *From Warm Center*, 12.
21. Ibid.
22. Since Van Doren deemed a positive regard for the local as incompatible with modernism, he interpreted the localism of Anderson and other authors as a repudiation of provincialism. Others, however, who understood the nexus of the local and modernism differently, developed a vibrant discourse on the subject in the U.S. at around the same time that Van Doren published his essay. Associated with figures such as the philosopher John Dewey and the poet William Carlos Williams, this discourse emphasized the significance of the local in American modernist art and literature as far more than a counterpoint for modernist cosmopolitanism; indeed, the local was conceptualized as the ground of modernism itself. "Williams," notes Eric B. White, "consistently viewed the local as a dynamic crucible of modern experience. In this sense, Williams's investment in local culture was essential to his literary modernism, not a paradoxical quirk of it" (*William Carlos Williams*, 8). White makes clear, though, that Williams's localism, defined partly by interaction with artistic forces abroad, partook in a broader transcontinental circulation and exchange of ideas.
23. Lauck, *From Warm Center*, 13.
24. Ibid., 14.
25. Ibid., 15.
26. Lauck argues that Anderson understood "how his work had been misused... and explained that his goal was to explore the inner life of the Midwest, not to attack the region" (*From Warm Center*, 28). Like many of his Midwestern contemporaries, Anderson was concerned "about the detachment from place, the growing rootlessness in the nation, the rise of technology," and other developments; the small town, despite its flaws, signified a crumbling bulwark against this transition (Ibid., 27).
27. Lauck's highly visible and much discussed book, *From Warm Center to Ragged Edge*, has been called a "manifesto" for its efforts to recuperate Anderson and other authors specifically from the revolt thesis (Kern, Review, 80). Numerous other scholars reject the revolt thesis implicitly or bypass it altogether, offering innovative theoretical approaches to Anderson that revise prevalent perspectives. Among recent examples, see: Colton, "Metafiction"; Oler, "Shadowy Figure"; Yerkes, "Strange Fevers."
28. Lindsay, *Such a Rare Thing*, xxi.
29. Ibid., 2.
30. Much of Oz's fiction, including not only short stories but also novels, is set in small places. *Makom aher* (*Elsewhere, Perhaps*, 1966) and *Menuha nekhona* (*A Perfect Peace*, 1982) take place on a kibbutz; *Al tagidi laila* (*Don't Call It Night*, 1994) is set in a small development town in the desert; *Pit'om be-omek ha-ya'ar* (*Suddenly in the Depths of the Forest*, 2005) takes place in a small village.
31. Mann, *Short Story Cycle*, 15.
32. Ingram, *Representative Short Story Cycles*, 13.
33. Lundén, *United Stories of America*, 123.
34. See Nagel, *Contemporary American*; see also Dunne and Morris, *The Composite Novel*. For more on the related-tale format, see: Luscher, "Short Story Sequence"; Mann, *Short Story Cycle*; Pacht, *Subversive Storyteller*; Ingram, *Representative Short Story Cycles*; Lundén, *United Stories of America*; and Kennedy, "From Anderson's *Winesburg*."
35. Crowley, "Introduction," 14–15.
36. Lindsay, *Such a Rare Thing*, xxiv.
37. Ibid.
38. Oz, *Love and Darkness*, 491.
39. Lindsay, *Such a Rare Thing*, xx.
40. Pacht, *Subversive Storyteller*, 1.
41. Kennedy, "From Anderson's *Winesburg*," 195.
42. Pacht, *Subversive Storyteller*, 3.

43. Citing an event held at Kibbutz Mishmar Ha-Emek in honor of *Where the Jackals Howl*, Holtzman notes "the surprise and indignation that members of the kibbutzim felt in response to the book." He elaborates on the sentiment expressed by Ya'akov Hazan, the leader of Ha-Shomer Ha-Tza'ir and Mapam, that the book failed to offer "a positive or at least a balanced portrayal of kibbutz life" and indeed had "distorted" its reality ("Strange Fire," 149).

44. Oz concludes a 1968 essay on the kibbutz by proclaiming: "it is the least bad place I have ever seen. And the most daring effort" ("Thoughts on the Kibbutz," 124).

45. Omer-Sherman, *Imagining the Kibbutz*, 70. Studies on the kibbutz in Hebrew culture abound. See, for example: Gertz, "With the Face to the Future"; Omer-Sherman, *Imagining the Kibbutz*; Milner, "Agitated Orders"; Keshet, "Kibbutz Fiction and Yishuv Society"; Halamish and Zameret, *Ha-kibutz*.

46. In *Place and Ideology*, I show that spatiality in Oz's novels illuminates the concept of "Zionist places," defined as "spaces that have been constructed or designed in the service of Zionist ideology" (Grumberg, *Place and Ideology*, 26).

47. Lindsay, *Such a Rare Thing*, 17. This observation confirms what Oz has said about the literary benefits of small places. "People sometimes ask me... if Hulda isn't too small for me," he has recounted. "Here I know a very large number of people, about three hundred. I know them at close range. ... If I lived in London, Tel Aviv, Paris, I could never get to know three hundred people so intimately" (Oz, "Kibbutz at the Present," 127–28).

48. Lindsay, *Such a Rare Thing*, xxiii.

49. Kennedy, "From Anderson's *Winesburg*," 196.

50. Anderson, *Winesburg*, 21.

51. Ibid., 22.

52. Ibid.

53. Ibid.

54. Ibid., 24.

55. Dunne, *New Book*, 1.

56. Ibid., 2.

57. Schevill, "Notes on the Grotesque," 231.

58. Ibid.

59. Trevitte, "Fate of Storytelling," 70.

60. Oz, *Scenes from Village Life*, 166.

61. Anderson, *Winesburg*, 24.

62. Oz, *Scenes from Village Life*, 86.

63. Ibid., 177.

64. Ibid.

65. Ibid.

66. Ibid., 177–78.

67. Ibid., 179.

68. Ibid., 180–81.

69. Kennedy, "From Anderson's *Winesburg*," 195.

70. Ibid., 182.

71. Anderson, *Winesburg*, 23–24.

72. Dunne, *New Book*, 43.

73. Trevitte, "Fate of Storytelling," 58–59.

74. Ibid., 68–69.

75. Schevill, "Notes on the Grotesque," 232.

76. Howe, "Book of the Grotesque," 200.

77. Ibid., 201.

78. Yingling, "*Winesburg, Ohio*," 111.

79. Anderson, *Winesburg*, 28.

80. Ibid., 29.

81. Ibid., 31, 32.

82. Ibid., 32.
83. Ibid., 67.
84. Ibid., 69.
85. Ibid., 81, 98.
86. Ibid., 34.
87. Oz, *Scenes from Village Life*, 42.
88. Ibid., 49.
89. Ibid., 70.
90. Oz, *Between Friends*, 3.
91. Ibid., 9.
92. Ibid., 13.
93. Ibid., 159.
94. Ibid.
95. Ibid., 157.
96. Ibid., 166.
97. Ibid., 178.
98. Ibid.
99. Nurith Gertz writes that in *Between Friends* "Oz aims to link traces of the past with the possibility of new, ethical, and humane relationships" ("With the Face to the Future," 95). She compares Oz's depiction of the kibbutz in that collection to Benjamin's *Angelus Novus*: it moves "towards the future" even as his gaze remains fixed on "the debris of the past" (Ibid., 94).
100. Oz, "Kibbutz at the Present," 128.
101. See note 8 above.

Disclosure statement

No potential conflict of interest was reported by the author.

Bibliography

Abramovich, D. "The Sexual Objectification of the Oz Women." *Australian Journal of Jewish Studies* 16 (2002): 5–15.

Abramovich, D. "A Woman-Centered Examination of the Heroines in the Stories of Amos Oz." *Women in Judaism: A Multidisciplinary Journal* 6 (2009): 2.

Amende, K. "'A Man with Such an Appearance Was Capable of Anything': Imaginary Rape and the Violent 'Other' in Faulkner's 'Dry September' and Oz's 'Nomad and Viper'." *The Faulkner Journal* 25, no. 2 (2010): 9–22. doi:10.1353/fau.2010.0001.

"Amos Oz." Institute for the Translation of Hebrew Literature. http://www.ithl.org.il/page_13793

Anderson, S. *Winesburg, Ohio*. New York: Penguin Books, 1992.

Aschkenasy, N. "Women and the Double in Modern Hebrew Literature: Berdichewsky-Agnon, Oz-Yehoshua." *Prooftexts* 8, no. 1 (1988): 113–128.

Ben-Dov, N. "Amos Oz's Artistic Credo in *To Know A Woman*." *Bulletin of Higher Hebrew Education* 5-6 (1992-1993): 42–46.

Brenner, Y. H. "Ha-zhaner ha-eretz-israeli ve-avizarehu [The Land of Israel Genre and Its Devices]." In *Kol Kitvey Y. H. Brener* [The Collected Works of Y. H. Brenner] edited by M. Z. Volfovski, 569–578. Vol. 3.Tel- Aviv: Hakibbutz Hameuchad, 1967.

Budick, E. M., ed. *Ideology and Jewish Identity in Israeli and American Literature*. Albany: State University of New York Press, 2001.

Cohen, J. *Voices of Israel: Essays on and Interviews with Yehuda Amichai, A. B. Yehoshua, T. Carmi, Aharon Appelfeld, and Amos Oz*. Albany: State University of New York Press, 1990.

Colton, A. "Metafiction, Literary History, and the Limits of Industrial Society in *Winesburg, Ohio*." *Studies in American Fiction* 45, no. 1 (2018): 61–89. doi:10.1353/saf.2018.0003.

Crowley, J. W. "Introduction." In *New Essays on Winesburg, Ohio*, edited by J. W. Crowley, 1–26. Cambridge: Cambridge University Press, 1990.

Damrosch, D. *What Is World Literature?* Princeton: Princeton University Press, 2003.

Dimock, W.-C. "Genre as World-System: Epic and Novel on Four Continents." *Narrative* 14, no. 1 (2006): 85–101. doi:10.1353/nar.2005.0025.

Dunn, M., and A. Morris. *The Composite Novel: The Short Story Cycle in Transition*. Boston: Twayne, 1995.

Dunne, R. *A New Book of the Grotesques: Contemporary Approaches to Sherwood Anderson's Early Fiction*. Kent, Ohio: Kent State University Press, 2005.

Fuchs, E. "The Beast Within: Women in Amos Oz's Early Fiction." *Modern Judaism* 4, no. 3 (1984): 311–321. doi:10.1093/mj/4.3.311.

Fuchs, E. "Amos Oz's Treacherous Helpmate: Toward a Feminist Critique of His Fiction." *Literature East and West* 26 (1990): 149–160.

Furman, A. *Israel through the Jewish-American Imagination: A Survey of Jewish-American Literature on Israel, 1928-1995*. Albany: State University of New York Press, 1997.

Gertz, N. "Amos Oz and Izhak Ben Ner: The Image of Woman in Literary Works, and as Transvalued in Film Adaptations." In *Israeli Writers Consider the 'Outsider'*, edited by L. Yudkin, 57–81. Rutherford, NJ: Farleigh Dickinson University Press, 1993.

Gertz, N. "With a Face to the Future: The Kibbutz in Recent Literary Works." *Journal of Israeli History* 34, no. 1 (2015): 93–107. Also in Hebrew: "Ha-kibbutz u-mal'akh ha-historiya [the kibbutz and the angel of history]." In *Ish ha-Negev: sefer Ze'ev Tzahor* [Man of the Negev: A book for Ze'ev Tzahor], edited by Dvora Hacohen and Anita Shapira, 215-30. Tel Aviv: Hakibbutz Hameuchad, 2017. doi:10.1080/13531042.2015.1014204.

Ginzburg, M. P. "Madame Bovary bi-Yerushalayim" [Madame Bovary in Jerusalem]. *Zehuyot* 3, (2012/13): 33–44.

Gniadek, M. "The Art of Becoming: Sherwood Anderson, Frank Sargeson and the Grotesque Aesthetic." *Journal of New Zealand Literature* 23, no. 2 (2005): 21–35.

Govrin, N. "Ha-mishpaha ha-sifrutit shel Amos Oz" [Amos Oz's literary family]. *Gag* 24, (2011): 151–166.

Grumberg, K. *Place and Ideology in Contemporary Hebrew Literature*. Syracuse: Syracuse University Press, 2011.

Halamish, A., and Z. Zameret, eds. *Ha-kibbutz: me'ah ha-shanim ha-rishonot* [The Kibbutz: The First Hundred Years]. Jerusalem: Yad Ben-Zvi, 2010.

Hever, H. "Minority Discourse of a National Majority: Israeli Fiction of the Early Sixties." *Prooftexts* 10, no. 1 (1990): 129–147.

Holtzman, A. "Strange Fire and Secret Thunder: Between Micha Josef Berdyczewski and Amos Oz." *Prooftexts* 15 (1995): 145–162.

Howe, I. "The Book of the Grotesque." In *The Grotesque*, edited by H. Bloom, 199–208. New York: Infobase Publishing, 2009.

Ingram, F. L. *Representative Short Story Cycles of the Twentieth Century: Studies in a Literary Genre*. The Hague and Paris: Mouton, 1971.

Kaplan, E. "Amos Oz's *A Tale of Love and Darkness* and the Sabra Myth." *Jewish Social Studies* 14, no. 1 (2007): 119–143.

Kennedy, J. G. "From Anderson's *Winesburg* to Carver's *Cathedral*: The Short Story Sequence and the Semblance of Community." In *Modern American Short Story Sequences*, edited by J. Gerald Kennedy, 194–216. Cambridge: Cambridge University Press, 1995.

Kern, K. F. "Review of *from Warm Center to Ragged Edge: The Erosion of Midwestern Literary and Historical Regionalism, 1920–1965*, by Jon K. Lauck." *Ohio History* 125, no. 2 (2018): 78–80. doi:10.1353/ohh.2018.0021.

Keshet, S. "Kibbutz Fiction and Yishuv Society on the Eve of Statehood: The Ma'agalot (Circles) Affair of 1945." *Journal of Israeli History* 31, no. 1 (2012): 147–165. doi:10.1080/13531042.2012.660383.

Khoury, E. "Rethinking the Nakba." *Critical Inquiry* 38, no. 2 (2012): 250–266. doi:10.1086/662741.

Laor. 1995/96. "Hayey ha-min shel kohot ha-bitahon: al gufanyuto shel ha-yisraeli ha-yafeh ve-ha-bithoni etzel Amos Oz" [The sex life of the security forces: on the corporeality of the beautiful military Israeli in Amos Oz]. In *Anu kotvim otakh moledet*, 76–104. Tel Aviv: Hakibbutz Hameuchad.

Laor, Y. "Sipur al ahava ve-hoshekh: ta'amula, narkisizem, ve-ha-ma'arav" [A Tale of Love and Darkness: propaganda, narcissism, and the west]. *Pithon Peh* 3, (2007): 77–108.

Lauck, J. *From Warm Center to Ragged Edge: The Erosion of Midwestern Literary and Historical Regionalism, 1920-1965*. Iowa City: University of Iowa Press, 2017.

Lindsay, C. *Such a Rare Thing: The Art of Sherwood Anderson's Winesburg, Ohio*. Kent, Ohio: Kent State University Press, 2009.

Loshitzky, Y. "From Orientalist Discourse to Family Melodrama: Oz and Volman's *My Michael*." *Edebiyat* 5, no. 1 (1994): 99–123.

Lundén, R. *The United Stories of America: Studies in the Short Story Composite*. Amsterdam and Atlanta: Rodopi, 1999.

Luscher, R. M. "The Short Story Sequence: An Open Book." In *Short Story Theory at a Crossroads*, edited by S. Lohafer and J. E. Clarey, 148–167. Baton Rouge: Louisiana State University Press, 1989.

Mann, S. *The Short Story Cycle: A Genre Companion and Reference Guide*. New York: Greenwood, 1989.

Milner, I. "Agitated Orders: Early Kibbutz Literature as a Site of Turmoil." In *One Hundred Years of Kibbutz Life: A Century of Crises and Reinvention*, edited by M. Palgi and S. Reinharz, 159–172. New Brunswick: Transaction, 2011.

Mintz, A. *Sanctuary in the Wilderness: A Critical Introduction to American Hebrew Poetry*. Palo Alto: Stanford University Press, 2011.

Mintz, A. L., ed. *Hebrew in America: Perspectives and Prospects*. Detroit: Wayne State University Press, 1993.

Mintz, A. L. *Translating Israel: Contemporary Hebrew Literature and Its Reception in America*. Syracuse: Syracuse University Press, 2001.

Moretti, F. *Modern Epic: The World System from Goethe to García Márquez*. New York: Verso, 1996.

Nagel, J. *The Contemporary American Short-Story Cycle: The Ethnic Resonance of Genre*. Baton Rouge: Louisiana State University Press, 2001.

Oler, A. "Sherwood Anderson's 'Shadowy Figure': Rural Masculinity in the Modernizing Midwest." In *Queering the Countryside: New Frontiers in Rural Queer Studies*, edited by M. L. Gray, C. R. Johnson, and B. J. Gilley, 69–87. New York: New York University Press, 2016.

Omer-Sherman. *Imagining the Kibbutz: Visions of Utopia in Literature and Film*. University Park, PA: Pennsylvania State University Press, 2015.

Oz, A. "The Kibbutz at the Present Time." In *Under This Blazing Light*, edited by N. de Lange, 125–132. Cambridge: Cambridge University Press, 1996.

Oz, A. *A Tale of Love and Darkness*. Translated by Nicholas de Lange. New York: Harcourt, 2004.

Oz, A. *Scenes from Village Life*. Translated by Nicholas de Lange. New York: Mariner Books, 2012.

Oz, A. *Where the Jackals Howl*. Translated by Nicholas de Lange and Philip Simpson. New York: Mariner Books, 2012.

Oz, A. *Between Friends*. Translated by Sondra Silverston. New York: Mariner Books, 2014.

Pacht, M. *The Subversive Storyteller: The Short Story Cycle and the Politics of Identity in America*. Newcastle: Cambridge Scholars, 2009.

Piterberg, G. "Literature of Settler Societies: Albert Camus, S. Yizhar and Amos Oz." *Settler Colonial Studies* 1, no. 2 (2011): 1–52. doi:10.1080/2201473X.2011.10648811.

Schevill, J. "Notes on the Grotesque: Anderson, Brecht, and Williams." *Twentieth Century Literature* 23, no. 2 (1977): 229–238. doi:10.2307/441342.

Shaham, C. "El ha-yeled ha-ze hitpalalti? 'Ga'agu'im' me'et Amos Oz u-'mi-kan u-mi-kan' me'et Y. H. Brener" [To this boy I prayed? 'Longings' by Amos Oz and 'From Here and There' by Y. H. Brenner]. *Iyunim bi-tkumat Yisrael* 9, (1998/99): 476–489.

Shimony, B. "The Mizrahi Body in War Literature." *Israel Studies* 23, no. 1 (2018): 129–151. doi:10.2979/israelstudies.23.1.07.

Sokoloff, N. "Israel and America: Cross-Cultural Encounters and the Literary Imagination: Introduction." *Shofar* 16, no. 2 (1997): 1–7. doi:10.1353/sho.1997.0120.

Trevitte, C. "Sherwood Anderson's 'The Book of the Grotesque' and the Fate of Storytelling in Modern America." *Genre* XL, no. 1–2 (2007): 57–79. doi:10.1215/00166928-40-1-2-57.

Weingrad, M. *American Hebrew Literature: Writing Jewish National Identity in the United States.* Syracuse: Syracuse University Press, 2011.

Wheatley, N. "'It Is the Hunter and You are the Harpooned Dolphin': Memory, Writing, and Medusa – Amos Oz and His Women." *Jewish Quarterly Review* 100, no. 4 (2010): 631–648.

White, E. B. "William Carlos Williams and the Local." In *The Cambridge Companion to William Carlos Williams*, edited by C. MacGowan, 8–23. New York: Cambridge University Press, 2016.

Yerkes, A. C. "'Strange Fevers, Burning Within': The Neurology of *Winesburg, Ohio.*" *Philosophy and Literature* 35, no. 2 (2011): 199–215. doi:10.1353/phl.2011.0027.

Yingling, T. "*Winesburg, Ohio* and the End of Collective Experience." In *New Essays on Winesburg, Ohio*, edited by J. W. Crowley, 99–128. Cambridge: Cambridge University Press, 1990.

Zilberman, D. "Zehut nashit be-tokh zehut gavrit be-tokh" [A feminine identity within a masculine identity within]. *Iton* 77, no. 144–145 (1991/92): 40–41.

The American Oz: Notes on translation and reception

Omri Asscher ⓘD

ABSTRACT
This article offers a discussion of Amos Oz's early translation and reception history in the American literary scene. The article pays particular attention to Oz's double capacity as novelist and political commentator, and how it may have contributed to the unique role quickly assigned to him in American public and intellectual discourse. Against the backdrop of the formative social and political context of the 1970s, the article suggests some defining traits of the transformation, and ultimately the reduction, of the Israeli Oz into the American Oz. Oz's works were largely perceived through an allegorical-political framework or pigeonholed as portrayals of the national psyche, while Oz himself was assigned the role of spokesman for the Israeli Left. Oz was actively involved in shaping his political persona and nonfiction repertoire in English, mainly through his (non-)selection of essays for translation, and his interviews and topical commentary in the American press. These, the article shows, were sometimes moderated for the English-speaking audience, diluting the more forceful political criticism the novelist had presented to his Hebrew readers, and abating the description of aspects of Israeli reality that drew his ire.

Amos Oz was, emphatically, not only an *Israeli* novelist and public intellectual. As regularly noted by his interviewers and critics in any language in the past decades, the renowned author had been translated into over forty languages and well-received worldwide.[1] Oz's passing in December 2018 was noted by newspapers in China and Turkey, Poland and Argentina, Egypt and Australia; in the United States alone, the *New York Times, Los Angeles Times, Washington Post, Chicago Tribune*, and Jewish venues such as the *Forward, Tablet, Moment, Jewish Week*, among many others, devoted a eulogistic article to the writer's death. Often proclaimed as Israel's most translated novelist, Oz's international stature as a writer and political commentator was an integral part of his literary and intellectual figure, both in terms of how he was perceived and in terms of the dissemination and reception of his work.

Despite this, little scholarly attention has been given to Oz's reception in different countries and languages. Articles have touched on the dissemination of Hebrew literature around the globe,[2] and a few book chapters and book-length studies dealt with the translation and critical reception of Hebrew literature in the United States more generally.[3] There were also some discussions by Oz's translators into Russian, German, and Romanian of their work.[4] Yet no essays, up to date, were specifically devoted to examining Oz's cross-cultural reception, for all its discursive, institutional, economic, and societal aspects, in the nearly fifty countries in which his work has appeared. A particularly notable lacunae is the absence of studies of Oz's translation and reception in North America. Among the many scholarly works on Oz's literary and political production published in English, the academic lingua franca of our time, only a few took note of the potential shifts inherent in the cross-cultural, cross-linguistic transfer of the original writings. However, as abundantly demonstrated by translation scholars in recent decades, the translation of an author into a different language should not imply an unproblematic form of transparent equivalence across cultures, presuming the existence of some "universal" version of that author. Sociologists of reception such as Wendy Griswold, Tamar Liebes, and Elihu Katz have also effectively described variation in textual and other forms of interpretation along national-cultural lines.[5] In other words, apart from the Israeli Amos Oz there are also a Polish Oz, a Spanish Oz, a Russian Oz, a German Oz, a Chinese Oz, and an Arabic Oz, among others.

The present article concentrates on the American Oz, touching on the writer's reception and mediation in what has arguably been the most dominant literary field, surely with reference to World Literature circulation, in the second half of the twentieth and beginning of the twenty-first century; and, at the same time, the major center of world Jewry, and Jewish readership, other than Israel. The American scene is of particular interest also because it was, as this article shows, the main cultural domain outside Israel in which Oz was actively engaged over the years, dedicating much energy to influencing how his persona and politics were shaped and received.

The reception of a translated author, particularly one as iconic as Oz, is a multifaceted process. In recent decades, the focus of translation studies has shifted from the linguistic and stylistic aspects of the translated text to the individual and institutional actors involved in mediating, managing, and regulating the text's social and ideological meanings.[6] Scholars have worked to examine the various effects of these socially-governed activities, based on the widely-accepted premise that, in the words of translation theorist Lawrence Venuti, "[e]very step in the translation process – from selecting a foreign text to implementing a translation strategy to editing, reviewing and reading the translation – is mediated by the diverse values, beliefs, and representations that circulate in the translating language, always in some hierarchical order."[7]

Recent discussions on literary reception complement Venuti's position by acknowledging the extent to which authors' intentions may also constraint reception dynamics and "have a role in readers' interpretative processes of making sense of creative works."[8] This is pertinent in a case such as ours, in which the translated author has developed a visible presence in the receiving culture, actively representing his persona and views on the American scene through interviews and political commentary – and, unlike most Israeli novelists, also collaborating with his English translators. As conceptualized by translation theorist André Lefevere, translation is in itself a form of "rewriting," on a par with these interventions by the author, and other phenomena of textual production by publishers, editors, reviewers and professors ("introductions, notes, commentary accompanying the translation, articles on it"[9]), all of which should be taken into account in understanding the reception of translated literature. Lefevere thus broadens our scope of inquiry to any kind of reframing or "adaptation of a work of literature to a different audience, with the intention of influencing the way in which that audience reads the work."[10] The importance of these channels of mediation cannot be overemphasized. Together they create in the receiving culture a sprawling body of knowledge and images pertaining to the translated author and Israeli literature more generally. They are, as Lefevere reminds us, "the original to the great majority of people who are only tangentially exposed to literature. Indeed, it would hardly be an exaggeration to say that this kind of reader is influenced by literature precisely through [these] refractions, and little else."[11]

The present article accepts these premises and follows this line of scrutiny. It aims to take a preliminary step toward a broader discussion of Oz's reception in the United States, focusing on Oz's appearance on the scene in the 1970s. The article concentrates on ideological aspects of Oz's reception in these formative years, identifying some defining traits of the transformation, and ultimately the reduction, of the Israeli Oz into the American Oz. It begins by outlining the early history of Oz's publication, translation, and reception on the American scene, noting how Oz's double capacity as a novelist and political commentator had contributed to the unique role quickly assigned to him in American public and intellectual discourse. It then suggests that Oz's works were largely perceived through an allegorical-political framework or pigeonholed as portrayals of the national psyche, while Oz himself was cast as a leading spokesman of the Israeli Left. Next, the article describes Oz's own role in actively shaping his political persona and nonfiction repertoire in the English language, mainly through his (non-)selection of essays for translation and his interviews and topical commentary in the American press. These mediations, the article argues, had a largely moderating effect: they watered-down important instances of Oz's political commentary for the English-speaking audience, removing some of the writer's more forceful political self-criticism. Taken together, then, these two tendencies imply that while the writer and his works were often pegged as emblematic of a critical leftist prism on Israel, Oz's political criticism was in fact diluted for his American readers.

This outline makes no claims to be exhaustive – not in terms of the channels of mediation discussed, nor in terms of the discussions themselves. Because of the limitations of space, I chose to concentrate on findings that exemplify most clearly the entanglement of the literary and the political in Oz's American persona. These channels of mediation are also helpful in demonstrating how shifts in Oz's American repertoire were determined both dependently and independently of Oz himself – how some were more controlled by the novelist while others were beholden to other forces. Finally, as my discussions are grounded in the literary, journalistic and academic settings of the United States, they do not claim to pertain to the mediations of Oz's English-language writings in Great Britain, South Africa, Canada, and Australia, which represent different cultural and political environments and may involve different dynamics of reception. Studies of Oz's reception in these English-language countries could make for fruitful comparisons in future research.

Early publication and reception history

Oz's first novel to appear in the United States was *My Michael*, translated into English by Nicholas de Lange in collaboration with the author. A modest beginning, it was published by Lancer Books, a relatively minor publishing house, in 1970.[12] Two years later, *My Michael* was acquired and reprinted by Harcourt, Brace, and Jovanovich – a major commercial publishing house and thereafter Oz's regular American publisher – a republication that quickly solidified Oz's reputation. Within three years, *Elsewhere, Perhaps* (1973), *Touch the Water, Touch the Wind* (1974), and *Unto Death* (1975) appeared in English translation.[13] Oz had been translated and published regularly ever since, as typical only to the most popular of international authors in the United States. Most of his novels were published soon after their original publication in Hebrew, and some works, like the coauthored 2012 essay *Jews and Words*, came out in English even before the Hebrew.[14] While exact sales data are unavailable, the number of reprints and paperback editions to each of Oz's works, some by major houses such as Knopf and Bantam Books, stand out among translated Israeli authors in America, attesting to the writer's ongoing popularity.[15] Oz differed from most Israeli novelists who preceded him in English translation in two other respects: he dealt regularly, and from the starting point, with a commercial (rather than Jewish or academic) American publisher; and he had never been represented by the Institute for the Translation of Hebrew Literature, but rather by a private agency.[16]

Oz's reception on the American literary scene was enthusiastic and relatively swift. The first major piece to introduce the writer to an English-speaking audience was an essay by influential scholar and critic (and later Bible translator) Robert Alter, published in *Commentary* magazine in 1969, before *My Michael* appeared in English.[17] With the publication of *My Michael*, however, Oz's reputation quickly spread beyond the Jewish intellectual sphere to the major American magazines and literary supplements. Within a few months in 1972, the novel was reviewed in the *New York Review of Books* (twice), *New York Times Book Review* (twice), *Chicago Tribune, Time, Saturday Review*, among others. Apart from Alter (who also wrote the first review in the *New York Times*), reviewers of Oz's first few books included influential Jewish and non-Jewish literary critics and writers such as Richard Locke, Christopher Lehmann-Haupt, Paul Zweig, Thomas R. Edwards, Joseph McElroy, John Bayley, Alfred Kazin, Morris Dickstein, and Anatole Broyard.[18] For three consecutive years, a different novel by Oz appeared on the *New York Times Book Review* annual or bi-annual list of notable titles: first, *My Michael* in the 1972 mid-year selection; then, in the Christmas Issue list of "Noteworthy Titles," with *Elsewhere, Perhaps* in 1973, and *Touch the Water, Touch the Wind* in 1974.[19] The attention the young Oz received from literary critics did not wane but continued well beyond the 1970s. In Yuval Amit's collected data on reviews of Israeli works in English-language newspapers, journals, and literary magazines between 1980 and 2003, one finds that Oz had the largest number of reviews (97) among Israeli writers by a far margin; most other translated Israeli writers had a total of fewer than five reviews.[20] With his regular publication history and wide critical recognition, Oz may be said to have paved the way for subsequent Israeli authors – especially during the heyday of Israeli literature on the American publishing scene in the 1970s and 1980s.[21] – even more than S. Y. Agnon's Nobel Prize in 1966. At the same time, his own central status and visibility remained unparalleled.

It would be wrong to underestimate the role of Oz's regular translator, Nicholas de Lange, in establishing and maintaining the writer's standing in the English language. The two first met in 1969, during Oz's stay at Oxford as a visiting fellow. An ordained reform Rabbi, and professor of Hebrew and Jewish studies at Cambridge University, de Lange is an author himself (mainly of scholarly works on Hellenistic and Byzantine Judaism) and translator of medieval Hebrew poetry. For their close collaboration on *My Michael*, de Lange went to live in Hulda, Oz's kibbutz, and the two reportedly worked together on the translation up to sixteen hours a day.[22] In later years, the collaboration was less intense and carried out mainly through correspondence. Still, throughout his entire literary career, Oz enjoyed a uniquely enduring author-translator relationship with de Lange, who continued to translate all but one of Oz's fifteen works of fiction for adults in English, from 1970 to 2014. De Lange's translations have been repeatedly praised for their richness, eloquence, and idiomaticity; his translation of *A Tale of Love and Darkness* was a finalist for the Man Booker International Prize in 2007, his translation of *Judas* short-listed for the same prestigious prize in 2017. Some commentators even suggested that Oz's works gained stylistically from their translation into English.[23] As for Oz's nonfiction, de Lange translated the collection of essays *Under This Blazing Light* (1995), while earlier and later works of political commentary and literary criticism, and two of Oz's three young adult books, were rendered by other translators and published by various publishers.[24] Finally, the importance of Oz's English translations lies not only in introducing the author to the world's major literary market, thus playing a decisive role in the writer's international dissemination, but also in that they served as the actual source text for some of Oz's translations into more "minor" languages such as Bulgarian, Danish, Finnish, Greek, Hungarian, Japanese, Korean, Norwegian, Polish, Romanian, and Slovak, and, in one or two of his books, even into languages such as German, Italian, Mandarin, and Spanish.[25]

A probe into the Israeli psyche

The usefulness of studying Oz's American reception extends well beyond the realm of literary criticism. This is not only because Oz was translated so much more than most of his contemporaries and elicited discussion and debate so regularly on the American scene for nearly fifty years. It is also because of what is arguably the defining aspect of his reception: the prevailing tendency of critics, across a wide range of newspapers, magazines, and ideological orientations, to read Oz's works as carrying a *representative* quality as a probe into Israeli life and culture. From *My Michael* onwards, Oz's works in translation were repeatedly framed as offering a precious key for unlocking the mysteries of the Israeli psyche.

This kind of reading should not be seen as self-evident. Oz's novels involve a suggestive tension between the political and apolitical, as well as strains between a humanistic Left-leaning tradition and chauvinistic and Orientalist undercurrents.[26] His works move delicately between the nationally and culturally specific and more existential-universal aspects of human experience. *My Michael*, with its nuanced mapping of the private life of its estranged female protagonist, feeling trapped in her stale marriage and having very particular sexual fantasies, some of which, however, resonate with Arab-Israeli tensions and orientalist tropes, is a case in point. Enticing for Israeli critics, these characteristics of Oz's writings provided much fertile ground for analysis and debate of what his works represent, as evident in the many competing, clashing interpretations of his works.

The tendency of American reviewers to frame Oz's works as a probe into the Israeli national psyche was evident from the outset; once *My Michael* appeared on the scene, it was assigned with broad allegorical intentions. These assumptions took on the most generalized form in short summaries of the novel: the *New York Times*, for instance, recommended it as "a novel that illumines a nation's private soul"; *Publishers Weekly* declared that the book gives American readers "insight into the makeup of modern Israel."[27] The interpretive lens that was adopted in longer reviews variegated in terms of its conceptions and emphases, as well as its profundity and degree of nuance. Still, most critics shared an idea of the characters as a national symbol, an attempt at a representation of collective consciousness. For Thomas Edwards of the *New York Review of Books*, the character of Michael, a "steady, patient, good-natured but not witty or imaginative man," performs a symbolic function as his "achievement of a professional career vaguely parallels the consolidation of the Israeli state."[28] The female protagonist Hannah Gonen in turn was seen by critics to represent a disillusioned, dark side of Israeli consciousness, "an interior life which Israel had not had time for, which it had paid no heed to, an interior life that contained a secret bond to the Asiatic world beyond its border."[29]

National-allegorical readings could lead to sweeping conclusions about the implications of Oz's novel. For A. T. Baker of *Time* magazine, Oz meant to imply that "the passion that animated the early founders of Zion has cooled. The new passionate people are the Arab fedayeen, and in some small dark recess of the national psyche, the Israelis are jealous."[30] For Richard Locke of the *New York Times*, too, "the political implications are not hard to unravel: Amos Oz is suggesting that in her heart Israel is going mad dreaming of Arabs, while on the surface emotionally stunted 'new Israelis' are going about their nation's business cut off from self and history."[31] This is not to say that all allegorical interpretations were overly simplistic, but only to point to a dominant tendency among reviewers to assign a primarily national-political meaning to Oz's novel. Consequently, the few readings that resisted this framing, such as Robert Alter's review "An Apolitical Israeli" in the *New York Times* in May 1972, almost had to assume a polemical tone. Alter, as Alan Mintz later suggested, "must have been aware of how widely the novel was being read along these [allegorical-political] lines," as his review makes a point of explicitly counteracting that approach.[32]

The political-allegorical prism remained dominant in the reception of Oz's later works in translation. "One of Oz's chief concerns is clearly the nature of Israeli society," William Novak asserted about *Elsewhere, Perhaps* in the progressive weekly *The Nation* in 1973, noting that the novel "is an engaging story, but more important, it illuminates the character of a nation that represents a new phenomenon in the history of the Jews and of the world."[33] Along similar lines, historian and Herzl biographer Norman Kotker generalizes his interpretive assumptions regarding *The Hill of Evil Counsel*, in a 1978 article in *The Nation*: "Oz's book, a collection of three interrelated stories, is in essence about Zionism, that astonishing phenomenon"; and writer and publicist Morris Dickstein asserted in the *New York Times* that the collection was "an indirect comment on Israel's status as a nation."[34] In a later interview with de Lange, Oz's translator expressed skepticism about particularistic readings of Oz's works, stating his belief that Oz is "a writer with universal values. And, you know, a great deal about Amos Oz is not locked into Israel or the Jewish people. I think it's extremely universal, and that's what readers all around the world have found." De Lange expressed the feeling that by translating Oz's work, he is, in fact, "unlocking its inherent universality," and concluded by saying he believed that Oz felt so too.[35]

Still, many reviewers tended to peg the implications of Oz's narratives and characters in a particularistic, national framework of interpretation. "In a sense, Amos Oz has no alternative in his novels but to tell us what it means to be an Israeli," leading British critic John Bayley declared in his review of *The Hill of Evil Counsel* for the *New York Review of Books* in 1978. "Unlike much ethnic writing his does not seek to masquerade as *Weltliteratur*. It is Jewish literature acquiescing amusedly in its new militantly provincial status. [...] Oz accepts the obligation to tell us what it means to be an Israeli."[36] These and other reviews in the 1970s anticipated literary discourse on Oz in English over the coming years, as critics continued to assume the novelist's intention and ability to illuminate the "national psyche," "Israeli consciousness," among others. It is worth noting that this kind of framing was not atypical in approaches to translated Israeli works as a whole, where literature was sometimes generalized as metonymic for Israeli culture and society. Still, it was especially evident in literary debates on Oz. Moreover, the influence of this discourse should not be understated. Through its extensive circulation, it reached a wide audience, constituting a relatively effortless and accessible way for American (Jewish and non-Jewish) readers to stay updated on Israeli literature and culture. It could indeed be argued that the magazines and literary supplements of American newspapers may have instilled in readers some of the decisive images of the books and their meanings.

Oz as a political spokesman

Within a few years of his appearance on the American scene, Oz was already deemed representative not only as a literary figure but also as a public intellectual of the Israeli Left. In some major newspapers, such as the *New York Times* and *Los Angeles Times*, the novelist was mentioned in a piece on Israeli current affairs even before any of his translated novels had been reviewed.[37] In July 1970, the *New York Times* provided a platform for left-wing academic and publicist Amnon Rubinstein, a future member of the Knesset from the progressive Meretz Party, to survey the recent revival of leftist critique on the Israeli scene. Rubinstein suggested that "the deepest and most significant expression of dissent is to be found not in the mass media, but in contemporary Israeli literature. There one can find the most stirring, controversial and soul-searching words written on the Arab-Jewish conflict."[38] Among the young generation of Israeli writers, Rubinstein noted the influential works of Amos Oz and A. B. Yehoshua, which had not yet appeared in English translation. During the next few years, in parallel to the reception of his first translated novels, articles published across different magazines and newspapers, in Jewish and general venues alike, marked the young generation of Israeli authors, led by Oz, as the principal voices challenging the institutional hegemony in post-1967 Israeli politics and culture.[39]

Not unlike in Israel, Oz's social-political activism and eloquent public commentary increased his overall visibility as a novelist – giving his American readers and reviewers the feeling that they hold a key to a better understanding of Israeli society. The writer was often mentioned among the leading figures in the leftist camp, as in the *New York Times* 1972 reports on protests surrounding the denied return of Palestinian villagers of Ikrit and Biram to their expropriated land, a *Washington Post* piece from April 1973 on the growing resistance to politics among the country's youth, or a *Jewish Week* piece on leftist demonstrations against establishing a Jewish settlement near Nablus in August 1974.[40] In a kind of self-nurturing pattern, the mention of Oz's name in political sections, interviews, news items, and the like guaranteed that the connection between Oz and the Left would catch readers' attention. This is encapsulated in a *St. Louis Jewish Light* review of *The Hill of Evil Counsel*, which concluded a discussion of the novellas' narratives and stylistic features by reverting abruptly to Oz's recent political commentary in *Time* magazine on the conflict and summarizing: "Oz is an articulate spokesman for a generation that has grown up with Israel and lived with the uncertainty of combat while yearning for the order that comes with peace. He is a dove, living in a constant state of war."[41] Oz himself was instrumental in shaping his image in American culture, as a willing interviewee on the Israeli-Arab conflict and international politics in American newspapers from 1973 onwards (as elaborated below). The mention of his literary work in tandem with his political activism and of his political persona in reviews of his translated novels made his "representativeness," his perceived metonymy with Israeli thought and culture, arguably even more pronounced.

Oz would not have acquired his status on the American scene had his writing not been powerfully appealing, his translations not talentedly done. That said, there is no shortage of engaging novelists of various languages and cultures who did not enjoy the same degree of visibility as Oz did upon translation into English. As in many cases of literary reception, the historically contingent social and political terms of literary transfer played an important role – influencing everything from the author's moral reputation to the translation strategies of his works. It is, therefore, useful to identify the historical moment of Oz's appearance on the American scene, when his reputation began to be forged. The particularities of his reception did not happen in a historical vacuum. The issues that defined that period raised the currency of Oz's voice and made it highly politically relevant, contributing to the appeal and evolvement of his literary and intellectual persona in America. These same issues would indeed remain pertinent to the author's American reception for years to come.

The first half of the 1970s saw the convergence of several highly significant trends in this respect. In these years, the relationship between Israel and the United States was increasingly cemented as an integral part of the American political and cultural repertoire.[42] The role assigned to Israel in an American public discourse still highly defined by Cold War sensitivities fueled feelings of fascination and affinity with the small state, which built upon deep-seated religious structures in American Protestantism, and only grew with Israel's high visibility in world politics after the 1967 Six Day War.[43] American Jews in particular identified strongly with Israel. Against the backdrop of the ethnic revival and rise of multiculturalism of the 1960s and 1970s, many in the American Jewish community had already been shifting from universal forms of self-perception toward what political scientist Michael Barnett has described as a more particular, "tribalistic" approach to Jewish identity.[44] American Jews' identification with Israel thus infused, even as it was influenced by, the community's cultural needs at the time. This identification reached its zenith after 1967, as Israel became the main ingredient of their Jewish identity, sometimes referred to as American Jewry's "civil religion."[45]

Oz's persona had a strong appeal for the American Jewish readership in these circumstances. Even his physical appearance played a role. As leading journalist and editor of the *New Yorker* David Remnick would later recall, in Oz's early years, "reviewers and readers routinely commented on his rugged, emblematic looks. [...] Dressed in rumpled chinos and a work shirt, Oz became part of the mid-century Zionist iconography: the novelist-kibbutznik, the Sabra of political conscience."[46] Indeed, aside from Oz's visibility in the abovementioned general channels of reception, the 1970s saw the writer receive a prize from the B'nai B'rith's Commission on Adult Jewish Education for literary works dealing with Jewish life; be invited to read from his writings at various Jewish community centers and synagogues in America; beginning to be taught in university courses, against the backdrop of the heightened interest in and disciplinary rise of Jewish Studies; have his works reviewed in Jewish organs such as the *Detroit Jewish News, Hadassah Magazine, St. Louis Jewish Light,* among others; and, more generally, have his books found "in the glass display cases of synagogue gift shops."[47]

At the same time, this trend coincided with the rise of the New Left in intellectual circles that had become increasingly critical of Israeli policy.[48] Through the mid-1970s, with the growing influence of a volatile Middle East on American life (i.e., the 1973 oil crisis), mainstream American commentary on Israel shifted too. The earlier admiration of Israel as a militarily committed citizen-soldier society turned into the perceived need to "reform" Israel and move the country, as put by historian Shaul Mitelpunkt, from "the futility of reliance on military solutions" to the "path of diplomacy."[49] Public debate on each of these cultural and political trends separately, and the convergence of all of them together, created an environment that put Oz's voice in high demand. The majority of American Jews had been largely progressive, Left-leaning, pluralistically religious; the cultural-political trends elaborated above touched them directly, and increasingly so. Against this backdrop, and as internal strains in Israeli society over the fate of the occupied territories exacerbated, and Israeli wrongdoings toward the Palestinian population drew more and more attention in the American press, Oz was sometimes assigned – in Jewish and general venues alike – the role of unofficial "spokesman" for an Israeli liberal humanism. He was interviewed on the conflict in the Labor Zionist organ *Jewish Frontier* in 1974, and by New York intellectual Irving Howe in an issue of the Left-wing *Dissent Magazine* titled "Middle East: Peace or War?" in 1975.[50] By the 1982 Lebanon War, Oz had acquired a privileged status and become, in Mitelpunkt's words, an "almost a mandatory interviewee for foreign visitors."[51] Oz conveyed to American readers the Israeli Left's skepticism and apprehension about the war, which he stressed was being fought, for the first time in Israel's history, "without a wide national consensus."[52] At the same time, interwoven in his sharp critique of the great human and moral cost of Israel's invasion of Lebanon was a reminder for his English-language audience of the idealistic historical roots of socialist Zionism.[53]

The inclination in American progressive circles to place the major share of the blame in the unresolved conflict between Israel and the Palestinians on Israel only intensified the need of American Jews for an eloquent voice of the Zionist Left. In a deeper sense, turning to this voice could also be a means to defend the way American Jews were themselves perceived in the society in which they live, as the moral profile of Israel, the Jewish state, reflected on their own.

The curation of Oz in university courses

Oz's pragmatic, "Jewishly" knowledgeable rhetoric for the Zionist Left was not always conceived separately from his fiction. Rather, the novelist's political commentary often served as a comparative frame of reference for reviewers' interpretations of the troubled Israeli protagonists in Oz's novels, and may have even contributed to the tendency to read his works as allegorical. In fact, this framing could be found not only in literary debates but also in the representation of the writer's works in syllabi of courses taught in American universities. Here, too, the curricula-building conventions of humanities courses, together with the effect of Oz's dual persona as popular author and political commentator, seemed to make it difficult to treat the output of his "two pens" – the literary and the political – truly independently.

In the North American academic setting, courses on modern Hebrew literature have been historically housed in departments of Near Eastern Studies or Near Eastern Languages and Cultures, or in Comparative Literature departments. A comprehensive database of course syllabi from the 1970s is, unfortunately, unavailable. Nonetheless, we can appreciate how Oz's versatile and multifaceted fictional and non-fictional works were framed by the courses in which they were taught in later years, based on a survey of syllabi used by nearly twenty professors of Israeli literature in North American universities from the mid-1980s to the early 2000s.[54] As the survey shows, the expectation of "curating" and squeezing Israeli literature and culture into one semester of teaching or less, required college professors to represent broad stylistic trends and social themes with particular literary works. Most often, for limitations of time and pedagogical demands, preference was given to short stories that, in some way or other, were reductively framed to represent a slice of Israeli social reality. This could be found more generally in Ethnic American literary studies, and may not have been particularly unique to teaching literature in the American context of Jewish Studies or, since the mid-1980s, Israel Studies.[55] As a consequence, and unlike in literature departments in Israel, many of the courses that included works by Oz were quite general in scope, with titles such as "Introduction to Israeli culture," "modern Hebrew literature in translation," or "Israeli fiction in translation." Other courses, somewhat more focused in scope, were organized around a certain theme, like "War and Peace in Israeli literature," "Israeli literature and culture in conflict," "Topics in Modern Hebrew Literature: From Shtetl to Kibbutz: The Quest for New Identities."

While Oz has been represented by a variegated selection of stories and novels, one does find particular works that appeared more often in American syllabi. The two most recurring works by Oz to be used in these syllabi were the short stories "Before his time" and "Way of the Wind." In both stories, a father-son relationship epitomizes the tension between the founding generation of Zionist pioneers and the ideologically or otherwise disheartened younger generation. In both cases, the sons die in grotesque or cruel military circumstances: in "Before his Time," the son is killed in a failed military excursion, his corpse soon after devoured by jackals; in "Way of the Wind," the son, trying to win his father's love by performing a trick with his parachute, gets entangled in high wire and electrocuted. The stories represent the sacrificial role thrust on the sons' generation, even as Oz explores, in Anatole Broyard's words, "the emotional life of people who exist in a constant state of crisis."[56] The protagonists of the Zionist endeavor, in these and other stories by Oz, are predestined to fail in their attempt to build a structured, stable moral world and to rationally and productively find meaning in their individual and national life. The two stories thus allow, perhaps even encourage, a national allegorical reading.

The predicament of Oz's protagonists in the stories, however, is more complex and no less existentially defined. Primeval, irrational powers, represented externally by the Arabs and jackals (or "the dispossessed-turned-Jackal," in novelist A. G. Mojtabai's words), but always also lurking from within, determine the protagonists' fate. Moreover, the struggle between mythic, psychic powers in these two stories "is concretized in the hostility between bull and jackal, in the war between Israel and her Arab neighbors, and more." Yet, these powers are also inextricably bound, as Oz presents a "world in which struggle and reconciliation go hand-in-hand, a world in which an object is described as its complete opposite, on the one hand, and on the other hand, sworn enemies are brothers in the soul."[57] As a result, there is a suggestive tension between an understanding of the haunted psyche and symbolic fate of Oz's protagonists as stemming from the universal, existential, "human condition," or rather from the particular, historically contingent Jewish-Israeli condition.

This tension, which also applies to *My Michael* that appeared in many of the syllabi, has indeed been mirrored in the critical reception of Oz's works in contentious literary debates and scholarly research, in Hebrew as well as in English. In the North American setting, however, the framework of courses essentially dealing with Israeli culture and identity implies that the stories were framed and interpreted in class first and foremost as testimonies to and explorations of Israeli-Jewish identity and *social reality*. That is, the understanding of Oz was done primarily through the "particularistic," "realistic" lens. Some of the titles for the separate classes in which Oz's stories were taught ("Post State Reality: The Individual Voice"; "Israeli Literature and the Quest for National Identity"; "The 1948 War of Independence and Its Aftermath"; "The Kibbutz," among others) strengthen this hypothesis, as does the other most frequently taught piece by Oz included in the syllabi, "Thank God for his daily blessings" – a short quasi-reportage excerpt from *In the Land of Israel* on an ultra-Orthodox enclave in early 1980s Jerusalem, in which Oz describes and reflects on the reclusive world of this non-Zionist community and the challenge it poses to the existence of a secular state.[58]

The works that were selected to represent Oz in these university courses attest to his contribution to the Hebrew literary tradition, yet they are a small fraction of the writer's oeuvre and necessarily only part of a broader, much more complex picture. The sieve of American university curriculum follows a certain logic and reflects certain emphases. At least before the 2000s, we do not find Oz being read to the same extent in literature courses that center on more "universal" social or psychological themes such as gender, ethnic tensions, or childhood. Above all, the frame of reference for approaching Oz and his works in American universities was influenced by preoccupation with the "big issues" of the Israeli-Palestinian conflict, the history of Zionism, and modern Jewish identity. This is not to suggest that Oz's fiction was never discussed and taught in terms of his treatment of marriage life, adolescents, women, or ethnicity, among other themes, but only that the broader political categories of Jewish identity, and their manifestation in the social reality of Israel, seem to have been much more dominant in shaping the representation, classification, and interpretation of Oz's work. In this regard, university courses parallel the reception dynamics that we have seen in other areas of American literary discourse. They further demonstrate the entanglement of the literary and the political in Oz's American persona, and exemplify how this entanglement contributed to the American engagement with his oeuvre as a probe into the Israeli psyche.

Self-representation in the American press

Aside from Oz's critical reception, a sometimes overlooked aspect of mediation has been the portrayals and images of Israeli life and politics offered by the novelist himself in interviews and news items. Wide-reaching topical articles that either featured Oz or quoted him appeared almost every year during the 1970s, making Oz the most interviewed and quoted Israeli writer in the American press. Conscious of his role, Oz took an active part in mediating images of Israel, the Israel-Palestine political situation, and international politics to the American readership of major newspapers such as the *New York Times* and *Los Angeles Times*, among others.[59] The writer was also interviewed in the *Boston Globe* and *Wall Street Journal*, which rarely, if at all, published reviews of translated Hebrew literature, making these accounts the readers' main encounter with the connection between literary figures and politics in Israel.[60]

These frequent media appearances contributed much to Oz's reputation as Israel's voice abroad. However, the writer's sharp critique of Israeli policies in the post-Six Day War years in Hebrew-language newspapers, and the ways he expressed himself in the English-language press, reveal considerable gaps. They imply that Oz perceived himself as filling a somewhat "ambassadorial" role vis-à-vis American audiences at the time. Habitually introduced by reporters and critics as a member of the Peace Now movement and fierce progressive critic of the Israeli government's attitude toward the Palestinian refugees and of the budding occupation, the early Oz often chose to curb his critique of Israel in American reviews or to counterbalance it with criticism of the United Nations, the West, the Arab countries, or the Palestinian leadership. Indeed, Oz's oft-quoted sober, critical appraisals of Israeli discourse and politics in the years following the Six Day War were, if not altogether missing in his 1970s commentary for American readers, at least less prominent than his "outward" criticism – in conservative- and liberal-leaning newspapers alike. The following report from February 1974 in the *Wall Street Journal* is a case in point. In it, Oz makes a brief reference to the Israeli-Palestinian situation by noting that "the stupid, idiotic leadership" of the Palestinians "does not change the fact that they have a case in this conflict."[61] This half-hearted endorsement was followed by a sarcastic comment on what Oz perceived to be the biased international treatment of Israel. Oz even implies a deep-rooted antisemitism of the nations of the world, which he ties with anti-Israelism:

> "In a sense, it's just back to normal," says Amos Oz. "The 30 or 40 years of relative sympathy for Israel and understanding of Zionism is a very short episode in Jewish history [...] there had been an episode, perhaps thanks to Hitler, when very many non-Jews sympathized with the Jewish people, its vision, its suffering, its heroic attempt to reconstruct itself. Now it's probably gone."[62]

Admitting that the Palestinians "have a case" in the conflict was thus not only qualified by Oz's negative description of their leadership but is also secondary, in length and emphasis, to his sweeping accusation of the nations of the world. Examining Oz's commentary on Israeli policy published in the Israeli press in the mid-1970s, and surely the late-1970s, reveals a harsher, more self-critical orientation (albeit one that ascribes much responsibility for the unresolved conflict to the Palestinian leadership).[63] Conversely, when quoted in a political column in the *Boston Globe* after the 1973 Yom Kippur War, Oz chiefly bemoaned what he saw as the habitual hostility of the world toward Israel:

> They were against us back in 1967 when we attacked first. They're against us now when our enemy attacked first. They're against us whether we're good guys or bad guys.[64]

The balance between "internal" and "outward" criticism is almost a photographic negative of the parallel balance in Oz's articles in Hebrew. This is particularly evident when topical commentary served Oz to weigh in on international politics as well, inasmuch as they had a bearing on Israel. In 1974, one year after the Yom Kippur War, Oz referred to East-West tensions in world politics in the *Los Angeles Times*, warning the Western world of the threat of Arab countries that have become "drunk with power." Against the backdrop of worldwide critique of Israel in the context of the Oil Crisis, and the willingness to allow the Palestinian Liberation Organization and its leader Yasser Arafat to appear before the United Nations, Oz generalized that

> The situation now is not that Israel is a kind of nuisance that gets America into trouble with the Arabs. It goes far beyond that. This coalition of oil-producing countries, Communist countries and Third World countries is headed not only for the destruction of Israel, it is trying to bring Western Civilization to its knees. [...] The Arabs right now are the spearhead of the campaign. They are drunk with power that goes with control of energy resources, but it is the Western World as a whole at which this coalition is aiming.[65]

In all of the political items above, as well as in Oz's bemoaning American foreign relations with Persian Gulf countries or criticizing the hostility of Arab countries and biased approach of the United Nations in a number of other reports these years in the *New York Times, Chicago Tribune*, and *Baltimore Sun*,[66] the proportion between Oz's self-critical remarks on Israel and his defensive political rhetoric weighs toward the latter. This stands out in comparison not only to Oz's contemporaneous commentary published in Hebrew but also to English-language statements of A. B. Yehoshua, another leading Israeli author who was introduced in the American press of the 1970s as a spokesman for the Israeli Left (though on a much smaller scale than Oz).[67] In some of Yehoshua's political commentary from that decade, one finds an almost antithetical approach to the role of the Israeli intellectual in American public discourse, as Yehoshua admonished Israeli policy harshly and without feeling the need to counterbalance the implied blame for the situation.[68] In contrast, as we have seen, Oz perceived his American role in the 1970s in a rather ambassadorial and guarded manner, keeping his harsher critique "in house."

Filters of translation

From the late 1960s through the 1970s, Oz published in Hebrew some of his more important pieces of political commentary. A selection of these essays, together with a number of literary and autobiographical essays from this time, was published in Israel in 1979 by Sifriyat Po'alim as *Be-or ha-tkhelet ha-aza* to form the writer's first major collection of essays. Unlike later nonfictions by Oz – e.g., *In the land of Israel* (1983 [orig. 1983]), *The Slopes of Lebanon* (1989 [orig. 1987]) – the compilation was not translated in proximity to the original Hebrew publication; the English edition, *Under this Blazing Light*, appeared in Nicholas de Lange's translation only in 1995, against the backdrop of a radically different political climate. Significantly, several fundamental changes were introduced by Oz "behind the scenes," in the selection of material for translation and interferences in the actual translation.

As noted in the front matter of the book, the English translation had "benefited from Amos Oz's cooperation," who had also made the preliminary selection of eighteen of the original thirty-six essays of the Hebrew edition, and added as an introduction an expanded version of an article that appeared in *Time* magazine in September 1993.[69] The introduction discusses the Israeli-Palestinian conflict in light of the recent break-through in the "labors of peacemaking" (the peace talks with the PLO that would lead to the Oslo Accords) while offering a short discussion of the historical roots of the conflict and an abbreviated history of Zionism.[70] It is, in effect, an article of political commentary. Serving as the new threshold to the collection, it places the whole book in a more topical political framework than the original 1979 Hebrew edition. In the English edition, the various nonpolitical essays that form the bulk of the book – about Hebrew literature, the kibbutz, Oz's childhood, etc. – become more emphatically embedded in the story of national Jewish revival (they are also not separated into thematic sections, unlike the original Hebrew collection). In the last paragraph of the introduction, which is also the first of the introduction to relate to anything other than the conflict, Oz proclaims the "revival of the Hebrew language and its literature" to be "the most certain achievement of Zionism."[71] The various essays are thus re-contextualized historically and politically in a more structured way than in the introduction-less Hebrew collection.

The proportion of Oz's selection from each thematic section of the Hebrew edition adds nuance to this framing and defines its character. The Hebrew edition is divided into four sections: reflections on Hebrew literature; contemporary political commentary (1967–1978); musings on socialism and the kibbutz; and some autobiographical vign-ettes. Oz selected for the English edition six out of ten of the literary essays, all six kibbutz pieces, and four out of five of the autobiographical reflections – but only two out of fifteen of the topical political articles. Left out of the political section are, among others, an article published two months after the Six Day War, in which Oz rebukes Moshe Dayan's withdrawal from the formula of exchanging territories for peace. The article blasts the ex-general's nationalistic pathos, particularly his description of the Israeli need for "living space," which reminds Oz of Nazi propaganda. Also omitted from the English edition is an essay that dissects the controversy that arose over the broadcasting on Israeli public television of the adaptation of *Khirbet Khizeh*, S. Yizhar's canonical short story that describes the expulsion of Palestinians from their village by an Israeli department in the 1948 War of Independence. Yet another omitted essay castigates the orientalist rhetoric used by Jewish settlers of Hebron in their altercation with the Israeli government in 1968; here, Oz draws parallels between the settlers and European colonizers of previous centuries. These and a few other essays that offer a forceful critique of post-1967 Israeli euphoria and creeping acceptance of territorial expanse and occupation are thus left out of the English edition. Conversely, all six pieces on the kibbutz are kept in the English edition, perhaps in anticipation of readers' lingering fascination with the famed Israeli socialist institution and on account of its favorable ethical connotations.

Very rarely, one also finds interference in the actual translation. Such a case is found in the following sentence from the essay "The Meaning of Homeland," in which the original Hebrew reads (in this citation and those that follow, phrases omitted in the English translation are included but indicated by, and material added in the English translation is indicated by [**boldface in brackets**]): "And that is the tragedy: the mutual understanding [between Israelis and Palestinians] *does* exist. We want to exist as a nation, as a State of Jews. [**They do not want that state.**]"[72] A less common adjustment in English translations of Oz's essays, this textual shift refines and somewhat "liberalizes" an awkward formulation, moderating the source text's nationalistic overtones and generalization about the wishes of the Palestinian people.

The most dominant strain of Oz's political commentary, in both the Hebrew and English editions, is the writer's criticism of tendencies he sees as typical to the political Left and Right to over-simplify the conflict, which he famously framed as a "tragic clash between right and right."[73] Oz does not relinquish the standard socialist Zionist narrative yet acknowledges the existence of a just, competing Palestinian claim for self-determination, and repeatedly suggests that only "some unsatisfactory, inconsistent compromise"[74] could bring a solution that is the least of all possible evils for both sides. The non-translation of most of Oz's articles on current events, however, dilutes the topical commentary in which the writer's prophetic criticism of the post-Six Day War settlement project, and his castigation of growing ethnocratic tendencies in Israeli society, is at its fiercest. Taken together with the added introduction, the English edition thus, on the one hand, confines Oz's social, literary, and autobiographical essays within a national-political framework, yet on the other hand and at the same time leaves out some of Oz's poignant political critique – the very critique that made Oz's reputation as a leading voice of the Israeli Left.

A final shift in the English edition worth noting has little to do with the conflict and was most likely done with Oz's Jewish audience in mind. In the original essays, Oz uses the word *Golah* or *Galut* [exile/diaspora] several times in various ways, mainly as a pejorative adjective or as an objective reference to a Jewish historical reality that nonetheless carries disparaging connotations. The English translation sometimes avoids these connotations by using a less generalized denotation than "golah/diaspora," thus skirting the deep-rooted Zionist conception of diaspora life as deplorable. This is found, for instance, in the translation of Oz's description of major Hebrew modernist, Y. H. Brenner: "Brenner was ostensibly a [**miserable**] Jew straight from the squalor of the [**ghetto**]."[75] Elsewhere in the same essay, Oz goes on to muse on "those bent and broken men that we know so well from Brenner's stories" who have permeated the works of later generations of Hebrew literature – "The whole unheroic rogues' gallery which seized Hebrew literature two generations ago and more, and which remained there ever since, pulling faces and broadcasting various [**old-world**] complaints as if nothing had changed in the meantime, the State, the army, the European basketball cup and so on."[76]

In another essay, one of the two political articles that were selected for translation, Oz discusses the meaning of Jewish sovereignty and suggests that "Independence does not mean that 'nobody will tell us what to do' (but we, 'with God's help,' will finally tell others what to do). No, independence means that we are capable of achieving and in danger of losing, that we risk bringing disaster on our own heads if we do not make proper use of our independence. And that is the real difference. That is the thing which the Jewish people never possessed in all its [**wanderings**], even in its most agreeable and secure [**interludes**]. And here it does possess it."[77] Each of the described shifts creates a more palatable formulation for Oz's English-speaking Jewish audience. Whereas the writer's original usage of *galut/golah* may obliquely apply to *contemporary* Jewish communities of Western countries as well, the English substitutions of "miserable," "ghetto," "old-world," "wanderings," and "interludes" are more contingent and expressive than clearly denotative, and less likely to be read as pertaining to today's Western Jewish reader.

As I have shown elsewhere, ideological interferences in the English translations of Israeli fiction in the 1950s through the 1980s reflect a similar preoccupation with Israel-diaspora tensions and the moral implications of the Israeli-Palestinian conflict.[78] The findings pertain, inter alia, to two novels by Oz: *Elsewhere, Perhaps* (1973 [orig. 1966], translated by Nicholas de Lange), and *Perfect Peace* (1985 [orig. 1982], the only Oz novel not translated by de Lange, but by the American-Israeli writer and essayist, and important English-Hebrew translator, Hillel Halkin). Some of the passages omitted in the translation of these novels had originally depicted a volatile, violent element in the consciousness of its Israeli characters, obliquely stemming from the militarization of an Israeli society in a state of war, or a repressed sense of guilt over the destruction of Palestinian villages in Israel's war of independence.[79] Gone with the omissions in the English translation are the author's implied criticism for these described instances of Israeli aggression and the individual and collective guilt this criticism intimated.

Unlike in the selection of essays for *Under this Blazing Light*, it is hard to tell what role Oz played in the ideological interferences in the actual translation of his novels. The Amos Oz Archive at Ben-Gurion University does not hold the original drafts of the translations. In personal correspondence in 2015, de Lange related that he could not recall if it had been the publisher or Oz himself who suggested the cuts in *Elsewhere, Perhaps*.[80] In a more recent interview, de Lange stressed that he did not have "any opinion about Amos Oz's political views. I am a translator, and I'm really not involved or interested in Israeli politics."[81] De Lange further expressed his translation ethos of impartiality: "[i]t is not my job to pass judgement on the opinions expressed in the book. It is not my job to impose myself on the text. It's not my job to get involved in the politics. It is my job to translate what's put in front of me."[82] Halkin, in turn, described his close collaboration with Oz on the translation's final draft, recalling that Oz came to stay at his house for a week of intense work.[83] According to Halkin, Oz not only played an integral role in the translation process but also introduced changes to the text in later phases together with the editor of his American publisher, most of which Halkin highly disapproved of. In correspondence with Oz in 2015, the novelist reported that he remembered nothing of the revisions, done so long ago, but that in any case, his copy-editing considerations were never political.[84] In an interview done in 1986, Oz touched on the topic of translation shortly by expressing opposition to a stylistically domesticating approach to translation. He added, with reference to *A Perfect Peace*, that Halkin "is a good translator, but it may be that he and I are philosophically divided over the art of translation."[85]

Was this indeed only a split over the art of translation? Unlike de Lange, Halkin never shied away from expressing his politics on Israel and the Jewish world, and had been clearly more politically conservative than Oz.[86] It seems, however, that the two differed here above all else over Halkin's stylistically domesticating orientation that contrasted Oz's preference for an "adequate" or even "foreignizing" translation: where Halkin preferred to adjust, appropriate or localize cultural references for the sake of fluency, Oz favored leaving the original formulations intact, even at the price of a certain strangeness of style or meaning for the English-language reader.[87] Thirty years later, in a lecture delivered at the 2017 annual conference of the Israel Translators Association, Oz mentioned such changes introduced by the editor of the American publication of his 2004 *A Tale of Love and Darkness*, of which he did not approve but were carried out nonetheless.

Based on my correspondence with the author and his translators, and given the prevalent copyediting conventions for translation in English-language publishing,[88] it seems safe to suggest that any *ideological-political* interferences in Oz's text – inasmuch as they can be separated from stylistic or esthetic considerations – were introduced by the editors of the translation rather than by the author or translators themselves. Nonetheless, it also seems reasonable that Oz may have been able to veto such interferences, if he were aware of them, had he insisted on doing so. Sadly, Oz did not bequeath us with his translation drafts, without which these remain speculations, educated guesses which admittedly can never be verified. Whoever may be responsible for the shifts in translation, and whatever the extent of Oz's own participation in them, in the case of *Elsewhere, Perhaps* and *A Perfect Peace*, as in the selection of essays for *Under This Blazing Light*, they resulted in a more palatable depiction of Israeli moral ambiguity for English-language audiences.

Conclusion

"There is considerable evidence," literary scholar Robert Alter wrote of Israeli novelists Amos Oz, A. B. Yehoshua and Aharon Appelfeld in 1991, "of a group of [American] readers who eagerly follow these writers book after book, trying to make out the course of their development, remembering their past achievements, relishing their individual literary methods and their distinctive vision."[89] Perhaps no Israeli author fits that description better than Oz, whose popularity and symbolic capital – especially with an American Jewish readership – sparked interest in Israeli literature and greatly contributed to its presence in American newspapers and literary supplements in the 1970s and 1980s. Along these lines, Alter's description of readers who turn to Israeli literature to find "an acutely sensitive and subtle seismograph for the spiritual and political life that cannot be equaled by the cruder gauge of journalistic report and analysis"[90] seems to apply to Oz's American reception more than that of any other Israeli writer.

Not unlike Saul Bellow and Philip Roth's response to similar tendencies in American Jewish literary criticism, Oz himself strongly opposed the implication of being read as representative of or key to Israeli-Jewish consciousness or social life. "I never regarded myself as a representative," he noted in an interview in the Jewish online magazine *Tablet* in 2013. "I'm a storyteller, not a representative. Whether my stories and my novels reflect a certain Israeli reality or not is not for me to judge, but I am not in the business of representing. I'm not a sociologist."[91] Whether justifiably or not, the representative role was nonetheless persistently attached to Oz since he first appeared on the American scene. This, as I have argued above, makes the study of his reception in American culture all the more significant. The ways in which Oz's literary works and political commentary were mediated and received tells us a great deal about the exposure and responses of the American readership not only to these particular texts, but also to what the novelist was seen to stand for more broadly. And as we have seen here with regard to the selection of Oz's essays for translation, the interferences in the translations themselves, the writer's political commentary in major American newspapers, and the representation of his works in course syllabi, the American Oz indeed differed, sometimes sharply, from the Israeli Oz. These mediations, found in disparate but related areas of culture, were often governed by similar dynamics: a narrower allegorical framing, focused on the national and political, was applied to Oz's persona and works in translation, even as some of the writer's more forceful political self-criticism was subdued.

The present article concentrates mainly on the 1970s – arguably, the formative decade of Oz's international career. Whether the dynamics that characterized these years persisted to the same degree in later years is a matter for future research. What can nonetheless be generalized is that the reductive framing that has been characteristic of Oz's early reception in American culture was a complicated, multifaceted product. It was borne out of Oz's own inclinations as much as it was shaped by factors that had little to do with him. It reflected "particularistic" viewpoints, such as Oz's own leftist Zionist ideology and the internal needs of the American Jewish community, and also spoke to broader cultural trends, such as universities' curricula-building conventions. In these respects, the American Oz may indeed be considered a representative case of World Literature. When writers from "minor" literary cultures enter a major literary field via translation, they often become, for a complex variety of reasons, more narrowly defined as emblems of their national culture and politics. This has surely been the case in the American reception of other major figures from Israeli culture and art. But even in this context, Oz seems to stands out in particular for his famed "two pens" as a novelist and an active public intellectual. This double capacity of his added to the interdependence between the reception of Oz's literary and political writings, and fed into the ambiguity already inherent in his novels and short stories between a more Israel-centered inter-pretation and a more existential, universal one; between a more allegorical national exegesis and a more gender/ethnicity/psychoanalytic-oriented one.

The curbing of Oz's forceful political criticism also reflects the convergence of the writer's own agency, as a careful spokesman for the Israeli Left, and broader factors such as the ideological appeal his position held for American Jews. The pressing need of American Jews for a humanistic voice to emerge from Israel still had some discernible boundaries. For the liberal mainstream, and surely in the 1970s, this voice could be deemed acceptable as long as it was not *too* critical, or considered too far left.[92] Oz, too, had preferred to stay within certain confines when switching to English, balancing his rebuke of Israeli governments' disregard for Palestinian rights with a passionate, unequi-vocal apologia for Zionism and a sharp critique of the New Left. This convergence indeed points to some common ideological needs and a shared self-perception of (at least considerable parts of) the two major Jewish communities in Israel and North America. This is not to say that the decidedly secular, sometimes diaspora-negating Oz did not pose a challenge for his liberal Jewish readership in the United States. As I have shown elsewhere, Oz's secular conception of Hebrew language and culture, and his stance on Jewish life in the diaspora, sometimes elicited American moderation, adjustment, or dispute.[93] However, even when his thought generated disagreement in American circles, it was always treated as an important *Jewish* point of reference, provoking serious debate. Ultimately, Oz's unique status, emanating from the entangled historical and ideological factors discussed in this paper, played an undeniable role. It provided a sound box to the charisma of his writing, and the often superb English renderings of his works, to form the lasting imprint that the Israeli intellectual left on his American audience.

Notes

1. For a list of the forty-six countries where Oz's translations were published, and the various languages in which each of his books was published, see the Amos Oz Archive: https://in. bgu.ac.il/heksherim/Archives/Pages/amos-oz-archive.aspx. Accessed: November 26, 2020.
2. Halevi-Wise and Gottesman, "Hebrew Literature in the 'World Republic of Letters'."
3. Mintz, *Translating Israel*; Asscher, *Reading Israel, Reading America*.
4. Radutsky, "Nigun rusi"; Achlama, "Mehapsim shidukh"; Braster, "Ketsev ha-tirgum." See also Nicholas de Lange's eulogistic piece, "Amos Oz's reading voice was beautiful. Translating his books was a marvellously fulfilling experience" in the *Jewish Chronicle*, January 3, 2019. https://www.thejc.com/culture/features/amos-oz-s-reading-voice-was-beautiful-1.477933. De Lange touches shortly on his experience as Oz's regular translator into English. Accessed: November 30, 2020.
5. Griswold, "The Fabrication of Meaning"; Liebes and Katz, *The Export of Meaning*.
6. Wolf, "Emergence of a sociology of translation"; Snell-Hornby, "The turns of Translation Studies."
7. Venuti, *The Translator's Invisibility*, 266.
8. Childress and Friedkin, "Cultural Reception and Production," 50.
9. Lefevere, "Mother Courage's Cucumbers," 216.
10. Ibid., 205.
11. Ibid., 216.
12. *My Michael* was Oz's third book in Hebrew. The short-lived paperback publisher Lancer Books (1961–1973) published a variety of genres, but specialized in science fiction and fantasy. Its two founders were Walter Zacharius and Irwin Stein. Zacharius was an active member of several Jewish organizations, and served as chair of the United Jewish Appeal.
13. One of the two novellas in *Unto Death*, "Crusade," first appeared in the UK-based *Jewish Quarterly* and American *Commentary* in 1971. It was in fact the first work of Oz de Lange translated.
14. Oz's first novel in Hebrew (1966), *Makom aher* (*Elsewhere, Perhaps*), appeared in English in 1973. The fact the American publisher caught up with his earlier *Be-arzot ha-tan* (*Where the Jackals Howl*, 1965) only in 1981 stems from the American commercial aversion to short story collections.
15. As explained by Mintz, sales figures are unattainable as they are regarded as proprietary information, and publishers are not willing to disclose them for various reasons. Mintz, *Translating Israel*, 249.
16. Amit, "Yitsu shel tarbut Yisraelit," 32–33.
17. Alter, "New Israeli Fiction." The article also discusses A. B. Yehoshua's rise on the Israeli literary scene with his first two volumes of short stories.
18. Robert Alter, "An Apolitical Israeli," *New York Times*, May 21, 1972, BR5; Richard Locke, "An Israeli Madame Bovary," *New York Times*, May 25, 1972, 43; Thomas R. Edwards, "News from Elsewhere," *New York Review of Books*, October 5, 1972; Christopher Lehmann-Haupt, "Books of the Times: Amos Oz's Initial Promise," *New York Times*, November 14,

1973, 43; Paul Zweig, "Life and Sex in a Kibbutz and on a Campus," *New York Times*, November 18, 1973, 418; Alfred Kazin, "Beyond the Promised Land," *Saturday Review*, November 2, 1974, 38; Joseph McElroy, "Unto Death," *New York Times*, October 26, 1975, BR4; Morris Dickstein, "In the Beginning," *New York Times*, May 28, 1978, BR2; John Bayley, "Pioneers and Phantoms", *New York Review of Books*, July 20, 1978; Anatole Broyard, "Books: People in Crises," New York Times, May 22, 1981, C24.

19. *New York Times Book Review*, "A selection of recent titles," June 4, 1972, 12; "1973: A selection of noteworthy titles", December 2, 1973, 525; "1974: A selection of noteworthy titles", December 1, 1974, 459.

20. Amit, "Yitsu shel tarbut Yisraelit," 219–220. Amit includes other English-speaking countries in his count, but they account for a relatively small number of the reviews and do not change the big picture.

21. Alter, "The Rise and the Rise."

22. De Lange, "Amos Oz's reading voice was beautiful." The collaboration is noted on the front matter of some of the books.

23. Ruby Namdar, "The Wizard of Words and the Baggy Monster: Rereading Amos Oz's *A Tale of Love and Darkness*," *Jewish Review of Books*, Fall 2020.

24. Translators include Maurie Goldberg-Bartura, Penelope Farmer, Barbara Harshav, and Sondra Silverston. Apart from Harcourt, Brace and Jovanovich, publishers include Harper & Row, Vintage, Cambridge University Press, and Princeton University Press. Most of these books, too, appeared in several printings.

25. Personal correspondence with Nicholas de Lange, October 23, 2020. See also: "Amos Oz" in Ohio State University's online Modern Hebrew Literature: A Bio-bibliographical lexicon, which specifies the source language for many of the translations: https://library.osu.edu/projects/hebrew-lexicon/00397.php. Accessed: November 30, 2020.For a useful discussion of the circulation of "minor" literatures and languages in world literature, see: Heilbron, "Towards a Sociology of Translation"; Brems et al, "The Transnational Trajectories of Dutch Literature as a Minor Literature."

26. Oppenheimer, *Me'ever la-gader*, 202–211.

27. *Publishers Weekly*, "My Michael," March 20, 1972, 60; *New York Times*, June 11, 1972, BR37.

28. Thomas Edwards, "News from Elsewhere" *New York Review of Books*, vol. 19 no. 5, October 5, 1972.

29. Paul Zweig, "Life and Sex in a Kibbutz and on a Campus", *The New York Times*, November 18, 1973, 418.

30. Quoted in Mintz, *Translating Israel*, 29. The original review was published on July 3, 1972.

31. Richard Locke, "An Israeli Madame Bovary," *The New York Times*, May 25, 1972, 43.

32. Mintz, *Translating Israel*, 30.

33. William Novak, "Kibbutz Life: An Insider's View," *The Nation*, September 7, 1974, 188.

34. Norman Kotker, "Living in history," *The Nation*, May 20, 1978, 606; Morris Dickstein, "In the Beginning," *The New York Times*, May 28, 1978, BR2.

35. Pollack, "Guide to the Land of Oz." 2009 interview with de Lange, on the Posen Foundation's Secular Culture and Ideas blog: http://www.jbooks.com/secularculture/Pollak.htm. Accessed: November 30, 2020.

36. John Bayley "Pioneers and Phantoms," *New York Review of Books*, July 20, 1978.

37. *Los Angeles Times*, December 7, 1972, 59; "Israeli Novelist to Speak Friday," *Los Angeles Times*, December 1, 1974, 103.

38. Amnon Rubinstein, "And Now in Israel, a Fluttering of Doves," *New York Times*, July 26, 1970, 159.

39. Apart from the *New York Times, Los Angeles Times*, and *Chicago Tribune*, such reports appeared in local newspapers in Iowa, Missouri, Montana, Kansas City, Florida, and Texas, among others (independent pieces or reprints from the major newspapers); see, for instance, "Israel," *Tampa Bay Times* (Florida), May 6, 1973, 14A; Nicholas Shuman, "Bullhorn at Israel's Ear," *The Billings Gazette* (Montana), February 22, 1976, 57; Robert Donovan, "Arab Oil Power Influences U. N," *Austin American Statesman* (Texas), December 8, 1974, 79.

40. Henry Kamm, "Village Issue Shows Rift in Israelis' Outlook," *New York Times*, August 20, 1972, 3; Amos Elon, *New York Times*, October 22, 1972, SM44; Eric Silver, "Israeli Youth Scorn Politics, Reject Forefathers' Zionism," *Washington Post*, April 2, 1973, A3; "Nablus Debate Stirs Clash at Sharon's Farm," *Jewish Week*, August 10, 1974, 13.

41. Dale Singer, "The Hill of Evil Counsel," *St. Louis Jewish Light*, July 15, 1978, 7.

42. Grose, *Israel in the Mind of America*.

43. Mart, *Eye on Israel*. McAlister, *Epic Encounters*.

44. Barnett, *The Star and the Stripes*.

45. Liebman, *Pressure without Sanctions*.

46. David Remnick, "The Spirit Level," *The New Yorker*, November 1, 2004.

47. Alter, "The Rise and the Rise," 6; "Two Authors, One Israeli, Get B'nai B'rith Awards." *The New York Times*, February 20, 1973, 41; see, for instance, Oz's reading at the Modern Orthodox Beth Israel Synagogue in Omaha, Nebraska, on February 1973 (*The Jewish Press*, February 2, 1973, 7); discussion of "conflicting rights of Israelis and Palestinians to a homeland in the Middle East," at the Reform-affiliated University Synagogue in Los Angeles, on December 1974 (*Los Angeles Times*, December 1, 1974, 34); and reading at the 92nd Street Young Men's and Young Women's Hebrew Association in New York, on May 1978 (*New York Times*, May 15, 1978, 18). For a university course in UC, Berkeley in 1970 that relates to Oz, see: Alter, "America and Israel: Literary and Intellectual Trends." The course was documented and published in a booklet by the Hadassah Education Department. See also: Baskin, "Jewish Studies in North American Colleges and Universities."

48. Shapira, "Israeli Perceptions of Anti-Semitism," 251–253.

49. Mitelpunkt, *Israel in the American Mind*, 179.

50. "A Talk with Amos Oz", *Jewish Frontier*, New York, January 1974, vol. 41, no. 1, 17–22; Howe, Irving "Peace in the Middle East? A Conversation between Amos Oz and Irving Howe," *Dissent Magazine*, New York, Spring 1975.

51. See, for instance, in Terence Smith, "6 who saw perilous birth assess State of Israel, 25," *New York Times*, May 5, 1973, 8; Mitelpunkt, *Israel in the American Mind*, 302.

52. Timothy McNulty, "Conflict Hits Home as Never Before: Israelis Fear Lebanon Is Their Vietnam," *Chicago Tribune*, June 28, 1982. Quoted in Mitelpunkt, *Israel in the American Mind*, 302.

53. Amos Oz, "Has Israel Altered Its Vision?" *New York Times Magazine*, July 11, 1982.

54. The request for syllabi was distributed based on the member network of the National Association of Professors of Hebrew in 2009–2010. Syllabi were also taken from Yudkin, *Selected Syllabi*, and from professors' online repositories. It is worth noting that unlike the teaching of other Israeli writers, which required professors to rely on English-language anthologies (that often represent each writer with one story) for material for their courses, Oz's publication history in English meant that professors could teach practically any of his works they wanted.

55. Douglas, *A Genealogy of Literary Multiculturalism*, 320, 339. For an influential critique of the selective formation of ethnic American literary canons in the academy, see Palumbo-Liu, *The Ethnic Canon*.

56. Anatole Broyard, "People in Crises," *New York Times*, May 22, 1981, C24.

57. Balaban, "Language and Reality in the Prose of Amos Oz," 86.

58. Oz, *In the Land of Israel*, 1-24.

59. Robert J. Donovan, "The Arab-Communist-Third-World threat," *Los Angeles Times*, December 2, 1974, C7; Herbert Mitgang, "The Stones of Jerusalem," *New York Times*, August 19, 1975, 33.

60. Joseph Kraft, "The New Crisis of Zionism," *Boston Globe*, November 8, 1973, 55; James Ring Adams, "Israel's Second Thoughts on the War," *Wall Street Journal* February 4, 1974, 10.

61. Ibid.

62. Ibid.

63. Gan, "Ad Mavet." See also, Amos Oz, "Shalosh teguvot be-yamim terufim" [Three responses in distressing times], *Davar*, January 5 1973, 12; Aharon Peri'el, "Amos Oz be-kenes ha-tsionut

ha-acheret: avodat elilim be-kipot serugot" [Amos Oz in a conference of a different kind of Zionism: Idolatry with knitted kippot], *Ma'ariv*, October 3, 1977, 3; among others.

64. Joseph Kraft, "The New Crisis of Zionism," *Boston Globe*, November 8, 1973, 55.
65. Robert J. Donovan, "The Arab-Communist-Third-World Threat," *Los Angeles Times*, December 2, 1974, C7.
66. Herbert Mitgang, "The Stones of Jerusalem," *New York Times*, August 19, 1975, 33; Jonathan Broder, "Israeli Victory Cursed Blessing," *Chicago Tribune*, June 5, 1977, 8; Michael Parks, "Israel Differs from Founders' Expectations," *Baltimore Sun*, May 8, 1978, A1.
67. Amnon Rubinstein, "And Now in Israel, a Fluttering of Doves," *New York Times*, July 26, 1970, 159; Amos Elon, "The Mood: Self-Confidence and a Subdued Sadness," *New York Times*, May 6, 1973, 315; Bernard Avishai, "The Arts in Israel: Rebirth," *Vogue* 169, no. 5 (May 1979): 291.
68. See, for instance, Yehoshua's scathing criticism in two reports in the *New York Times*: Victor Perera, "A letter from Israel," May 5, 1974, SM21, SM24, SM30, SM37; Anthony Lewis, "Corruption of power," April 19, 1979, A23.
69. Oz, *Under this Blazing Light*, xi.
70. Ibid, 10.
71. Ibid, 11.
72. Compare: *Be-or ha-tkhelet ha-aza*, 81; with *Under this Blazing Light*, 92. The Hebrew reads: "hem rotsim li-shlol me-itanu ma'amad shel uma u-le-hantsiah et arviyuta shel ha-arets ha-zot."
73. Ibid, 10.
74. Ibid, 95.
75. Compare: *Be-or ha-tkhelet ha-aza*, 37; with *Under this Blazing Light*, 53.
76. Compare: *Be-or ha-tkhelet ha-aza*, 41; with *Under this Blazing Light*, 59.
77. Compare: *Be-or ha-tkhelet ha-aza*, 156; with *Under this Blazing Light*, 112.
78. Asscher, *Reading Israel, Reading America*, 73–79, 88–93, 104–108, 118–122, 213.
79. Ibid., 75–76, 77–78, 91–93.
80. Nicholas de Lange, personal correspondence, June 22, 2015.
81. "Professor Nicholas de Lange, Linguist of the Month of July 2017", https://www.le-mot-juste -en-anglais.com/2000/07/professeur-nicholas-de-lange-linguist-of-the-month-of-july -2017.html. Accessed: November 30, 2020.
82. Ibid.
83. Hillel Halkin, personal correspondence, June 21, 2015.
84. Amos Oz, personal correspondence, June 29, 2015.
85. Cohen, *Voices of Israel*, 190.
86. See, for instance: "An Exchange on Zionism", *New York Review of Books* 25, no. 5 (April 6, 1978), 38; and, more obliquely, in his recent biography of founder of Revisionist Zionism: *Jabotinsky: A Life*.
87. Hillel Halkin, personal correspondence, June 21, 2015. Compare Halkin's approach, as discussed in Cutter's essay on his translation of Agnon's *A Simple Story*, "Rendering Galicia for America," with Oz's discussion of translation in Cohen, *Voices of Israel*:"[t]ranslation should avoid any attempt to neutralize the characters. There is no point in making a Sephardic Jew speak like a black person from the South of the United States even though the temptation is there, or vice versa. A Faulknerian black should never speak in the Hebrew version of a Faulkner novel like a North African Jew. Time and again, I have had disagreements with my translators about issues such as 'a cup of tea' or 'a glass of tea.' They normally tend, as an immediate response, to translate 'a glass of tea with milk' into the obvious English term, 'a cup of tea,' which is officially correct for the British. Otherwise, it is lemon tea. I therefore normally insist that the translation, at the cost of sounding peculiar, odd or even outlandish sometimes, or clumsy, that where the circumstances require, it ought to remain 'a glass of tea with milk' rather than 'a cup of tea.' That is what I mean by avoiding the temptation to neutralize the characters." (189).

88. The guidebook *Translation in Practice*, published following a symposium of English translators and editors on literary translation held in 2008, provides a peek behind the scenes of the publishing world that lends support to the assumption that the "cushioning" of critical aspects of the texts occurred on the editorial level. See: Paul, *Translation in Practice*, 59, 63.
89. Alter mentions sales that constitute "a respectable presence" (without however substantiating this with actual numbers), large audiences that come to public readings, and commentary made by critics on the oeuvre as a whole, to attest to a "real following" developed by the major Israeli writers in America. See: Alter, "The Rise and the Rise," 5.
90. Ibid.
91. Vox Tablet, "Amos Oz Still Dreams of Life on the Kibbutz," September 23, 2013. http://elmundo sefarad.wikidot.com/amos-oz-still-dreams-of-life-on-the-kibbutz. Accessed: November 30, 2020.
92. In reference to the plight of Palestinian refugees, which may be extended to other thorny issues of Israeli political and historical ethics, historian David Myers writes that "misinformation and denial . . . have been more pronounced in the Diaspora [than in Israel]," adding, "Conformity was and remains a prominent value among Diaspora supporters of the State of Israel." Myers, *Between Jew and Arab*, 11.
93. For a compelling recent example, see: Gordon, "Does anybody still need Judaism?" For a discussion of Oz's approach to Jewish culture in the diaspora, see Asscher, *Reading Israel, Reading America*, 175–176.

Acknowledgments

The author would like to thank Arie Dubnov, the editor of this special issue, and the two anonymous reviewers, for their useful and constructive comments on earlier drafts of this article.

Disclosure statement

No potential conflict of interest was reported by the author(s).

ORCID

Omri Asscher (iD) http://orcid.org/0000-0002-3891-8058

Bibliography

Achlama, R. "Mehapsim shidukh le-Fima: Al tirgum yetsirotav shel Amos Oz le-Germanit" [Looking for a Match for Fima: On the Translation of Amos Oz's Works into German]." In *Sefer Amos Oz* [The Amos Oz Book], edited by A. Komem and Y. Ben-Mordechai, 157–159. Beer Sheva: Ben-Gurion Publishing Press, 2000.

Alter, R. "New Israeli Fiction." *Commentary* 47, no. 6 (1969): 59–66.

Alter, R. *America and Israel: Literary and Intellectual Trends.* New York: Hadassah Education Department, 1970.

Alter, R. "The Rise and the Rise in the United States." *Modern Hebrew Literature* 7 (1991): 5–7.

Amit, Y. "Yitsu shel tarbut Yisra'elit: Pe'ulatam shel mosadot rishmiyim be-tirgum sifrut me-Ivrit le-Anglit [The Export of Israeli Culture: The Role of Formal Institutions in the Translation of Hebrew Literature to English]." PhD diss., Tel Aviv University, 2008.

Asscher, O. "A Case for an Integrated Approach to the Mediation of National Literature." *Translation and Interpreting Studies* 12, no. 1 (2017): 24–48. doi:10.1075/tis.12.1.02ass.

Asscher, O. *Reading Israel, Reading America: The Politics of Translation between Jews.* Stanford, CA: Stanford University Press, 2019.

Balaban, A. "Language and Reality in the Prose of Amos Oz." *Modern Language Studies* 20, no. 2 (1990): 79–97. doi:10.2307/3194829.

Baskin, J. "Jewish Studies in North American Colleges and Universities: Yesterday, Today, and Tomorrow." *Shofar: An Interdisciplinary Journal of Jewish Studies* 32, no. 4 (2014): 9–26. doi:10.1353/sho.2014.0047.

Beebee, T. O., Ed. *German Literature as World Literature.* New York: Bloomsbury Publishing, 2014.

Braster, M. "Ketsev ha-tirgum, tirgum ha-ketsev: Al tirgum ha-roman *Al Tagidi Layla* le-Romanit [The Rhythm of Translation, the Translation of Rhythm: On the Translation of *Don't Call It Night* into Romanian]." In *Sefer Amos Oz [The Amos Oz Book],* edited by A. Komem and Y. Ben-Mordechai, 161–167. Beer Sheva: Ben-Gurion Publishing Press, 2000.

Brems, E., T. Feldmann, O. Réthelyi, and T. Kalmthout. "The Transnational Trajectories of Dutch Literature as A Minor Literature: A View from World Literature and Translation Studies." *Dutch Crossing* 44, no. 2 (2020): 125–135. doi:10.1080/03096564.2020.1747005.

Casanova, P. *The World Republic of Letters.* Cambridge, MA: Harvard University Press, 2004.

Childress, C., and N. Friedkin. "Cultural Reception and Production: The Social Construction of Meaning in Book Clubs." *American Sociological Review* 77, no. 1 (2012): 45–68. doi:10.1177/0003122411428153.

Cohen, J. *Voices of Israel: Essays on and Interviews with Yehuda Amichai, A. B. Yehoshua, T. Carmi, Aharon Appelfeld, and Amos Oz.* Albany, NY: SUNY Press, 2012.

Cutter, W. "Rendering Galicia for America: On Hillel Halkin's Translation of Sippur Pashut." *Prooftexts* 7, no. 1 (1987): 73–87.

Damrosch, D. *What is World Literature?* Princeton, NJ: Princeton University Press, 2018.

Douglas, C. *A Genealogy of Literary Multiculturalism.* Ithaca, NY: Cornell University Press, 2009.

Fuchs, E. "The Beast Within: Women in Amos Oz's Early Fiction." *Modern Judaism* 4, no. 3 (1984): 311–321. doi:10.1093/mj/4.3.311.

Fuchs, E. "Amos Oz's Treacherous Helpmate: Toward a Feminist Critique of His Fiction." *Literature East and West* 26 (1990): 149–160.

Gan, A. "Ad Mavet,' 'Al sheven ahim be-tsel totahim': Oz ve-Levin ke-neviei tokheha anti-euphoriyim [Amos Oz and Hanoch Levin as Anti-Euphoric Prophets of Rebuke]." *Israel 1967-1977, Iyyunim Bi-tekumat Yisrael* 11, (2017): 334–359 thematic series.

Gordon, D. "Does Anybody Still Need Judaism?" *History and Theory* 57, no. 1 (2018): 149–165. doi:10.1111/hith.12051.

Griswold, W. "The Fabrication of Meaning: Literary Interpretation in the United States, Great Britain, and the West Indies." *American Journal of Sociology* 92, no. 5 (1987): 1077–17. doi:10.1086/228628.

Halevi-Wise, Y., and M. Gottesman. "Hebrew Literature in the 'World Republic of Letters': Translation and Reception, 1918–2018." *Israel Studies Review* 33, no. 2 (2018): 1–25. doi:10.3167/isr.2018.330202.

Heilbron, J. "Towards a Sociology of Translation: Book Translations as a Cultural World-system." *European Journal of Social Theory* 2, no. 4 (1999): 429–444.

Laor, Y. *Tsad Ma'arav* [Facing West]. Tel Aviv: Afik, 2017.

Lefevere, A. "Mother Courage's Cucumbers: Text, System and Refraction in a Theory of Literature." In *Translation Studies Reader*, edited by L. Venuti, 203–219. London: Routledge, 2012.

Lefevere, A. *Translation, Rewriting, and the Manipulation of Literary Fame*. London: Routledge, 2017.

Liebes, T., and K. Elihu. *The Export of Meaning: Cross-Cultural Readings of Dallas*. New York: Oxford University Press, 1990.

McAlister, M. *Epic Encounters: Culture, Media, and US Interests in the Middle East since 1945*. Berkeley and Los Angeles: University of California Press, 2005.

Michelle, M. *Eye on Israel: How America Came to View Israel as an Ally*. Albany, NY: SUNY Press, 2006.

Mintz, A. *Translating Israel: Contemporary Hebrew Literature and Its Reception in America*. Syracuse, NY: Syracuse University Press, 2001.

Mishani, D. *Be-khol ha-inyan ha-mizrahi yesh eize absurd* [There Is Something Absurd about the Whole Mizrahi Thing]. Tel Aviv: Am Oved, 2006.

Mitelpunkt, S. *Israel in the American Mind: The Cultural Politics of US-Israeli Relations, 1958-1988*. Cambridge, UK: Cambridge University Press, 2018.

Myers, D. *Between Jew and Arab: The Lost Voice of Simon Rawidowicz*. Waltham, Mass.: Brandeis University Press, 2006.

Omer-Sherman, R. "Zionism and the Disenchanted: The Plight of the Citizen-Soldier in Amos Oz's *A Perfect Peace*." *Middle Eastern Literatures* 8, no. 1 (2005): 53–71. doi:10.1080/1366616042000309184.

Oppenheimer, Y. *Me'ever la-gader: Yitsug ha-aravim ba-siporet ha-Ivrit ve-ha-Yisraelit, 1906-2005* [Barriers: The Representation of the Arab in Hebrew and Israeli Fiction, 1906-2005]. Tel Aviv: Am Oved, 2008.

Oz, A. *Menuha nekhona* [A Perfect Peace]. Tel Aviv: Am Oved, 1982.

Oz, A. *In the Land of Israel*. New York: Harcourt, 1983.

Oz, A. *A Perfect Peace*. New York: Harcourt Brace Jovanovich, 1985.

Oz, A. *Be-or ha-tkhelet ha-aza* [Under This Blazing Light]. Jerusalem: Keter, 1990 [1979].

Oz, A. *Under This Blazing Light*. Cambridge: Cambridge University Press, 1996.

Palumbo-Liu, D., ed. *The Ethnic Canon: Histories, Institutions, and Interventions*. Minneapolis: University of Minnesota Press, 1995.

Paul, G. *Translation in Practice: A Symposium*. Champaign and London: Dalkey Archive Press, 2009.

Radutsky, V. "'Nigun rusi': Hebetim ahadim be-tirgym yetsirotav shel Amos Oz le-Ivrit ['Russian Melody': Aspects of Translating Amos Oz's Works into Russian]." In *Sefer Amos Oz* [The Amos Oz Book], edited by A. Komem and Y. Ben-Mordechai, 169–173. Beer Sheva: Ben-Gurion Publishing Press, 2000.

Shaked, G. "Judaism in Translation: Thoughts on the Alexandria Hypothesis." In *Hebrew in America: Perspectives and Prospects*, edited by A. Mintz, 277–295. Detroit, MI: Wayne State University Press, 1993.

Shapira, A. "Israeli Perceptions of Anti-Semitism and Anti-Zionism." *Journal of Israeli History* 25, no. 1 (2006): 245–266. doi:10.1080/13531040500503013.

Snell-Hornby, M. "The Turns of Translation Studies." In *Handbook of Translation Studies*, edited by Y. Gambier and L. von Doorslaer, 366–370. Vol. 1. Philadelphia: John Benjamins, 2010.

Venuti, L. *The Translator's Invisibility: A History*. second ed. London: Routledge, 2012.

Wolf, M. "Introduction: The Emergence of a Sociology of Translation." In *Constructing a Sociology of Translation*, edited by M. Wolf and A. Fukari, 1–36. Philadelphia: John Benjamins, 2007.

Yudkin, L. I., ed. *Modern Hebrew Literature in English Translation: Papers, Selected Syllabi and Bibliographies*. New York: Markus Wiener Pub, 1987.

Amos Oz: A humanist in the darkness

David Ohana

ABSTRACT

The article examines Amos Oz's political and social outlook through four topoi that constitute his books, articles and correspondence: The first concerns his dialectics with Israel's Mediterranean character, from his affinity to Albert Camus to his treatment of Ashdod as a metaphor for Mediterraneanism; the second is the Zionist-crusader analogy in the literature and poetry of his contemporaries, and particularly A. B. Yehoshua and Dahlia Ravikovitch; the third topic is Oz's oppositionality to the political actualization of messianism on the gamut from Ben-Gurion to "Gush Emunim"; and the fourth issue relates to Oz's controversy with what I have branded as "Canaanite Messianism," namely those who promote expansionism toward Greater Israel. Together, these combined perspectives unfold Oz's humanist vision on the future of the State of Israel.

In an old photograph of the members of the kindergarten on Zephaniah Street in Kerem Avraham, Jerusalem, the children in the photo look happy. The Second World War had ended shortly before it was taken, and three years later, the British soldiers would leave and the new state would be founded. To paraphrase a poem by Yehuda Amichai, God took pity on Pnina's kindergarten children, some of whom became famous: e.g. the philosopher Avishai Margalit and the physicist and cancer researcher Itzhak Kelson. In the picture of the children, Oddeda appeared as well, the little girl whom Amos Klausner (later Oz) was in love with. Unlike the children of the elitist Rehavia kindergarten run by Yigael Yadin's mother, the children from "Pnina's Kindergarten" represented a mosaic of diasporas, ideologies and religious and secular families. These children would eventually seek an independent collective identity. The journalist Danny Rubinstein said that the children of the kindergarten may have left Keren Avraham, but Keren Avraham never left them.

Amos Oz's first public appearance after the publication of his book *A Tale of Love and Darkness* took place at Midreshet Ben-Gurion in Sde Boker at the end of 2002. It is not known why he chose that site for the unofficial launching of the novel. Perhaps it was because the primeval desert landscape and Nahal Zin, which could be seen from the Midrasha, were the absolute opposite of the Jerusalem alleyways described in the autobiography. Perhaps in that way he expressed his opposition to (and perhaps a late rapprochement with) Ben-Gurion, the ideological rival both of his old Revisionist home and his new home, Hulda, the kibbutz of the supporters of Pinhas Lavon and Levi Eshkol, the latter of whom Oz loved and has shown personal affection to due to his warm personality, especially considering that his political adversary, David Ben-Gurion, was a hard man. When he arrived at the Midrasha from nearby Arad, he was pale and nervous, openly fearful of how his most personal novel will be received. In order to pass the time until his appearance, we discussed Albert Camus, the lyrical prose-writer we both admired, and my book about him entitled *Humanist in the Sun*. When his fears were allayed, he wrote the following dedication to me: "From the humanist in the sun of Arad to the humanist in the sun of Sde Boker."

Oz, Camus and the Mediterranean

There are many points in common between the Algerian-French writer and the Israeli one. The scars that marked their childhoods and the sources of their productivity were the death in battle of Camus's father Louis Auguste at the beginning of the First World War and the suicide of Fania Klausner, Amos's mother. It is not surprising that they both needed personal and literary maturity in order to confront these formative experiences. *The First Man* was Camus's last book, the manuscript of which was discovered at the site of the motor-accident in which he was killed.[1] The hero of the novel stood at his father's grave, on which were inscribed the dates 1885–1914. The son now had to run his life on his own.[2] This is how young Amos Oz also felt when he decided to join Kibbutz Hulda after his mother's death. The passion of Camus and young Oz is shown in their desire, determination and ability to fashion their lives with their own hands.

Good-looking, talented, admired at home and abroad, they were not content to bask in their literary reputations but were courageous intellectuals who strode against the current to such an extent that they were called traitors by fascist groups in their respective countries. At a time when most of the French people accepted passively the shame of Nazi occupation, Camus risked his life as the editor of the underground journal *Combat*. Although Oz was not in danger of his life in his country, his grandson, in his funeral oration for his grandfather, related that the latter had had checked the tires of his car every morning to see if they were punctured. It is possible that Oz intended his novel *Judas* to be about himself when he presented a different version of Judas Iscariot, Jesus's betrayer. "We are all Judas Iscariot,"[3] admitted one of the characters in the novel. The works of Camus and Oz as a whole, both the fictional and the political, are directed against the violence expressed in nationalism, extremism, racism, and religious and ideological fundamentalism, and in this way they created what may be called a "Mediterranean humanism" which they shared with other Mediterranean writers and thinkers such as Albert Memmi, Edmond Jabès, Primo Levi, Jorge Semprún, Neguib Mahfouz, Orhan Pamuk, and, in Israel, A.B. Yehoshua, Emile Habibi and others. They share an opposition to violence, integral nationalism, dictatorship, and ideological radicalism, an anti-racism stemming from their tolerance of the "other" and their acceptance of the foreign and the different, a multicultural outlook that foreshadows postmodernist discourse, and an affirmation of dialogue as a form of human activity. They valued the warm, unmediated contact of dialogue between peoples and cultures. Rather than dreaming of a "new man" they considered the problems of existing human beings in Mediterranean societies.[4]

Israeli literature has only recently opened a window to the Mediterranean. Oz took an interesting path to the Mediterranean, although originally he did not want to go there. As a young writer of the school of Micha Yosef Berdichevsky (1865–1921), he believed that vital, creative powers were the main thing, and not the local form which was seen as sentimental and provincial. But he later depicted contemporary Israeli society as one with typical Mediterranean qualities: warm of heart and temperament, hedonistic, life-loving and emotional. Oz thought that Israel would continue to develop as a Mediterranean society if its conflict with its neighbors is resolved. In *In the Land of Israel* (1983), he saw Ashdod as a metaphor for the Mediterranean profile being created before his eyes:

> And what is, at best, the city of Ashdod. A pretty city and to my mind a good one, this Ashdod. And she is all we have that is our own. Even in culture and in literature: Ashdod. All those who secretly long for the charms of Paris or Vienna, for the Jewish shtetl, or for heavenly Jerusalem: do not cut loose from those longings – for what are we without our longings? – but let's remember that Ashdod is what there is. And she is not quite the grandiose fulfillment of the vision of the prophets and of the dream of generations; not quite a world premiere, but simply a city on a human scale. If only we try to look at her with a calm eye, we will surely not be shamed or disappointed. Ashdod is a city on a human scale on the Mediterranean coast. And from her we shall see what will flower when peace and a little repose finally come. Patience, I say. There is no shortcut.[5]

Oz looked at Ashdod with resignation, with the sadness of a houseowner whose dream has evaporated like the dreams of those socialist world reformers, the fathers of the kibbutz. He thought that Israel was becoming more like Greece than like Germany, more like the south of France than like Poland. The Israelis, he believed, were more suited to a film by Fellini than to one by Ingmar Bergman. He saw "Mediterranean-ness" not as an ideological term but as the characterization of the shared space of people from Morocco and Eastern Europe, a non-fundamentalist space and an open society. Miron Benvenisti considered some of the Israeli intellectuals who advocated the Mediterranean Option as people who preferred the "Mediterranean Cruise" over the Middle East,[6] an esthetical escape from the Arabs, the bloody conflict, to Marseille and the Piraeus. The Architect Sharon Rotbard continued the critique offered by Benvenisti, seeing the Mediterranean Option as "the ultimate place of escape."[7] However, despite the justified critique, Oz dedicated his entire political and intellectual career to the Israeli-Palestinian conflict. One would be hard-pressed to find, in the articles or books wrote about politics, without an explicit, central reference to the conflict. For him Mediterraneanism was not a pure ideology, as it was for Canaanites Adia Horon and Yonatan Ratosh, but the real space where Israel belongs.

Oz admitted that it took him some time to come to terms with the region – not in terms of his ancestral tradition, but in terms of the character of the people. He realized that Israel was slowly becoming a Mediterranean country and that might be a good thing. According to Oz, "Then I asked myself if I like it or not – although I had some hesitations, it was in contradiction to I actually discovered, yes: I do like it."[8] Not that he prefers it, not that he regarded it as superior to something else – he just liked it. "I felt more at home in Ashdod, in Tel Aviv, in Haifa, or in Arad, which is not by the Mediterranean, than I feel in the north of Europe. I like it this way. I find myself more at home. In the next phase I was asking myself: why not?" He went on to say:

My question is not how Israel should fit into the neighborhood. My question is: how the Israeli sense of identity and everyday life is evolving into what I describe as Mediterranean: secular, pluralistic, middle class, noisy etc. [...] I am not an ideologist. I don't think the Mediterranean option is a model, a goal or a purpose. [...] I don't know where the Middle East is going, maybe it is becoming more and more fundamentalist, which in my vocabulary means less and less Mediterranean. It is not that I like the Mediterranean reality because it is a good bridge to Syria and Iraq. I like it, because I like it, because it suits me, my temper, my way of life and my essentially secular, pluralistic and tolerant perspective.[9]

Oz surprisingly began his novel *The Same Sea* (1998) with the following description of its hero-anti-hero: "Not far from the sea, in Amirim Street, lives Mr. Albert Danon. He likes olives and salty cheese."[10] This is not a romantic opening or a fanfare, but just sea, olives and cheese. This poetic novel takes place close to the Mediterranean: not in Jerusalem or in Hulda but in Bat-Yam and Tel-Aviv – though also in Tibet. It is not surprising that critics compared *The Same Sea* to Natan Alterman's *Summer Festival* which also took place in a Mediterranean town, Jaffa. Among the contemporary Israeli characters depicted by Oz, bereft of dreams and living an everyday existence, there are some who reflect the sea, and there is even a "Mediterranean philosophy": "The sea took, the sea gave; the sea gives, the sea takes." And as if all this was not enough, Oz's "repentance" toward the Mediterranean was expressed as a gesture of homage to Camus in the form of a poem-chapter, "Exile and Kingdom" (*Exile and Kingdom* was also the title of a book by Camus). This suggests a closeness, admirable though late, to Camus, the lyrical prosaist of the Mediterranean.

Colonialism was a subject that preoccupied both Camus and Oz. In the former, the problem was complex and proved to be insoluble as he wavered between the difficult alternatives of his original homeland, Algeria, and his adoptive country, France.[11] And Oz, for his part, decided on the fourth day of the Six-Day War that the state had to renounce the idea of a complete homeland as it would involve a colonialist occupation like the medieval precedent of the crusades. If the Mediterranean metaphor suggested dialog and good neighborly relations between east and west, the crusades were a metaphor for cultural and military colonialist domination, for the rule of one people and civilization over another, for confrontation between east and west and perpetual conflict.

Oz and the Crusaders

The "colonialist" discourse is not a new one, and its metaphor, the Zionist-Crusaders analogy, has been disproved by Zionist historians. The Zionist acquisitions in the 1948 war, they wrote, were gained without military or political assistance from foreign states and so it does not resemble any colonialist movement.[12] However, there are other experts, such as Ziad Asali and Amin Maalouf, who reject the Zionist position.[13] Zionism was not a religious movement but a national movement which saw the return to Zion as the modern expression of a people that wished to forge its collective destiny through a return to its historical sources. The Israelis created a rejuvenated homeland and established an identity between a large part of the people and their soil, developed settlement, science and technology, achieved a clear national identity with a culture, language and creativity of its own, and succeeded in maintaining a democratic existence (within the "Green Line", except within East Jerusalem) under the most trying conditions there can be for a democracy – a protracted military conflict. Most important of all, the

Israelis never felt strangers in their country, did not apologize for their national existence but saw it as the historical realization of a universal right supported by international recognition and not as an original sin.

Oz's ideas on the crusaders were preceded by many scholars and thinkers. Prominent molders of Israeli culture, and especially the writers of the "generation of the founding of the State" – A.B. Yehoshua, Dalia Ravikovitch and Oz himself[14] – each wrote a major and significant work dealing directly or in a veiled manner with the Zionist-crusader analogy. Yitzhak Shalev, Dan Tzalka, and Yovel Shimoni all dealt with the subject of the crusaders.[15]

A.B. Yehoshua's story *Facing the Forests* first appeared in 1963 in the journal *Keshet*.[16] The text, in its plain sense, concerns a tired student writing a doctoral dissertation on the crusades. He works for a living as a forest guard, warning of approaching fires. The other major character is an Arab whose tongue was cut out in the war, who watches over the forests that were planted on the ruins of his village by the Jewish National Fund and prepares to set fire to them. The hidden meaning of the text is of course that it is a radical allegory of the Israeli-Arab dispute, to which the crusader episode forms a background. Is the subject of the student's dissertation – the crusaders – an incidental choice on Yehoshua's part? The crusader metaphor hints of course at this foreign element: the Israeli who watches over the forests of the Jewish people, who surveys the house of Israel.

The student was distracted from the subject of the crusaders by his fear of a forest fire. The past and the present interpenetrated one another. It was the first hint of a connection between the crusades, which represent that which is dark and alien, and the fire which the Arab was to create in the forest like a desperate complaint and battle-cry against the alien Israelis who had taken control of his land. A relationship which was a non-relationship developed between the student-watchman and the mute Arab. The student "tells him about the fervour, about the cruelty, about Jews committing suicide, about the children's crusade [...]. The Arab listens with mounting tension and is filled with hate [...] He wishes to say that this was his house." The story ends with a great forest fire. The encroaching end hinted at finally happens. The student abandoned his cases of research-material and saved the Arab's home. The forest went up in flames and also the watch-tower. The fire also spread to his room: the books were burnt to cinders.

There is an intrinsic connection between *Facing the Forests* and *Ad mavet* (Unto Death, 1971),[17] perhaps Amos Oz's best story, which appeared three years after the Six-Day War.[18] This was a historical novella about the journey of some Christian crusaders to Palestine, led by the nobleman Gerôme de Touron and his faithful servant Claude the crooked-shouldered. On the first, Jewish level, the novella reveals the roots of the extermination of the Jews in the twentieth century in the persecution of the Jews in the crusades, which perhaps is an allegory of the Holocaust. Oz lays bare underground, mythical currents of Jewish-Christian relations and skillfully depicts the "crucifixion" of the Jews by the Gentiles. The cruelty of the crusaders toward the "other" in Europe, the Jews, turns inward and becomes self-hatred.

In Oz's story, the Jews were suspected of infesting the crusaders' convoy. Claude the crooked-shouldered perceived that the evil forces of darkness, sent by the Jews to engulf them, proceeded from their own ranks. The Jews wanted to possess the bodies and souls of the Christians. The crusader convoy imagined that they had been placed under siege by an invisible body that drove them insane. A "Jew" hid among them within the camp and caused madness, slander, murder. The demon was apparently within the nobleman, and that is what caused the failure of the expedition. The nobleman committed suicide, for only through a suicide – like that of Otto Weininger, the proclaimed Jewish-Austrian thinker, at the beginning of the twentieth century – could he rid himself of his Jewishness.

In an interview, Oz explained the relationship of this story to Saul Tchernichovsky and his poem "Baruch of Magenza" (from Mainz):

> In that poem there are also crusaders, but there they are depicted from the outside. Just look at what they did to us! I, on the other hand, try to depict them from within. It is not the history that interests me, but the crusades as a universal phenomenon. In order to understand it, I as a writer had to dress myself up as one of the crusaders. The fear, the hatred, the alienation are a universal phenomenon, of which hatred of the Jews was only one aspect. For me, therefore, it was easier from a psychological point of view to speak with the voice of Baruch of Magenza, with the voices of the victims of hatred, but less interesting than to speak with the voice of Claude the crooked-shouldered.[19]

At the height of the Holocaust, Saul Tchernichovsky published his Vermisa Ballads – "The Rabbi's Daughter and Mother," "The Rabbi's Beautiful Daughter," and "The Rabbi's Daughter and the Wolf" – in which the crusaders were depicted as cruelly massacring the Jews like the Nazis of their time.[20] In these ballads, the poet continued to deal with the subjects he treated in "The Slaughtered of Taormina," which was a reaction to the rise of the Nazis. The literary scholar Chaya Schaham pointed out that Y. L. Baruch's ballad "Birkat ha-mazon" (Grace after Meals), written in memory of Simon Dubnow, equated the crusader persecutors with the Nazi murderers. In "Rehovot ha-nahar" (Paths of the River) (1951), and especially in the poem "Lament for the Whole House of Israel," Uri Zvi Greenberg also saw a direct affinity between the persecutions of 1091, the expulsion from Spain, and the Modern Pogroms.[21] In the collective memory, Tchernichovsky's poem "Baruch of Magenza" (1902) is undoubtedly the most impressive poetic expression of the crusader pogrom. The ballad is the confession of a Jewish father who in his madness killed his two daughters, set fire to a monastery, and looked happily at the burning town, the scene of his revenge.

Oz's story depicts in a few different layers the theme of the crusaders. He even describes with a shred of sympathy the crusader anti-hero, a description that reminds the reader the poem of Dahlia Ravikovitch, "The Horns of Hattin", in which she feels pity for the crusaders that are away from their home:

> With morning, strange ships were espied in the sea,
> prow and stern of primeval allure.
> In the eleventh century the crusader companies sailed forth,
> kings and a mixed throng.
> Arks of gold and booty rolled into the ports,
> ships of gold,
> expanses of gold
> ignited by the sun with wondrous fires,
> a forest ablaze.
> With the flashing of the sun and the heaving of the waves
> their hearts were drawn to Byzantium.
> How cruel and simple the crusaders were!
> They plundered all . . . [22]

After Saladin's victory at the battle of Hattin (1187), the third crusade set out in two directions: one, over the sea under the leadership of the kings of France and England, and the other overland under the leadership of the Holy Roman Emperor.[23] Ravikovitch's poem describes the sea-voyage, and thus the crusade is associated with the voyage of Jason and the Argonauts to capture the golden fleece, which is compared to the Kingdom of Jerusalem. In the myth of the Odyssey there were special ships similar to the ships of the Vikings, who were venturesome like the crusaders. The crusader sea-robbers are depicted as the bearers of apollonian wisdom, after the fashion of Nietzsche's analysis in *The Birth of Tragedy*: a wisdom concerning form, structure and a sense for the beautiful. But Christian compassion, in whose name they came to preach, turned into violence and it gave way to madness and simpleminded cruelty. The Christians soon surrendered to the Muslims under Saladin, "who passed sentence on them at the Horns of Hattin." He restored the world to the scales of righteousness: finally righteousness triumphed, as is suggested by the name (the title Salah ed-Din – Saladin – resembles the Hebrew for "imposing justice"). In the poem, Ravikovitch effects a switching of roles: contrary to Jewish tradition, which warns that mercy to the cruel is liable to lead to cruelty to the merciful, the poetess shows sympathy for the crusaders far from their homes, exposed to dangers and bereft of glory.

Oz's interpretation is of course in opposition to Yitzhak Shalev's nationalistic outlook expressed in his poem "Crusaders" (1975)[24]:

> I saw Godfrey de Bouillon
> And Robert of Flanders
> And Robert of Normandy,
> Tancred, and Raymond de Saint Gilles
> And all the men-in-arms.
> Said Raymond to Tancred the fearless,
> "It looks like we burned the whole community
> In a single synagogue,
> And all that escaped the fire
> Were slaughtered.
> And now, see,
> Their flag is on the fortress
> And ours has been lowered."
> And Robert of Flanders, to Godfrey he said:
> "What remains, brother,
> Of all thy kingdom?
> Only a castle laid waste,
> Ruined apses,
> Blue-eyed babes
> In an Arab village
> And blond hair, here and there."

At the beginning of the Second Intifada in the West Bank in the year 2000 Oz published an article in the *New York Times*, in which he put his finger on the salient point: the choice was between images and myths on the one hand and historical reconciliation on the other. Oz describes Yasser Arafat's return from the failed Camp David summit in 2000 which accelerated the process toward the Second Intifada, as follows:

The whole Gaza Strip is covered with flags and slogans proclaiming the Palestinian Saladin. Welcome home, Saladin of our era! is written on the walls.

In silence, astounded, I watch, and I can't help reminding myself that the original Saladin promised the Arab people that he would not make pacts with the infidels: he would massacre them and throw them in the sea. I see Mr. Arafat dressed in his grey-green combat uniform. It's an Arafat clothed like Che Guevara and treated like Saladin: my heart breaks [...] The Palestinians must choose if they want a new Saladin, or to really work for peace.[25]

On the same subject, Oz turned (in Hebrew) to the Palestinians in the name of the Israeli peace camp: "The supporters of peace in Israel will make an effective contribution to peace if we – we precisely – say to our Palestinian counterparts: the demand for an agreement to implement the right of return to Israel accompanied by a 'Saladin' atmosphere, sending the Israelis to drink the sea – all this increases suspicion and fear exactly at the critical moment when there is an urgent need for an emotional breakthrough of the kind effected by Sadat. The question to be addressed to our Palestinian counterparts is: is it Arafat the Nobel prizewinner or Arafat as Saladin?"[26] At a meeting of Israeli intellectuals and Palestinians in July 2001, Oz once again located the point of inception of the Al-Aqsa intifada: the welcome which Arafat received on his return from America where he had demanded the right of return. He was received with the greeting, "Welcome home, Saladin!"

One finds that whenever Oz referred to the Palestinians before 1967, there was a recognition that despite the historical injustice incurred by their expulsion and the troubled conscience that resulted, the clock could not be turned back. But one injustice did not justify another, and there was therefore no need to annex the West Bank and set up the Greater Land of Israel. The conquest of West Bank on the contrary provided a golden opportunity to repair the disaster that befall the Palestinians in 1948 (*Nakba*) to some degree. And thus, from the Six-Day War until his death, he did not waver from his demand for two states for two peoples. He decided that 1967 was dialectically a revision of 1948.

It is interesting, here, to see what Yehoshua, Ravikovitch and Oz wrote concerning the crusader episode. Unlike Yehoshua and Ravikovitch, who already before the Six-Day War saw a resemblance between the crusaders and Zionists, Oz suggested this analogy only three years after the war in the volume *Unto Death*. Loud messianic and colonialist voices from religious Zionists and some Laborites that were heard after the war spoke with admiration of the crusader precedent. Although he did not say this in so many words, Oz thought that the Zionist pioneers bore no resemblance to the crusaders because the latter came to defeat the Muslims and rule over the whole land in accordance with the ideas of the medieval Christianity. The desire to rule over the whole land and create a second injustice toward the Palestinians, Oz thought, brought us close to the crusader precedent. And thus he came to the conclusion that neither side should receive the whole legacy, which should be divided.

Whereas the Israelis examined here translate the crusader anxiety into literary metaphors like the arson of a forest of the Jewish National Fund in A.B. Yehoshua, the return of the swamps in Meir Shalev or the wailing of jackals in Amos Oz, the Palestinians do not feel themselves to be potential victims but actual victims of the Israeli "crusaders," who pay the price for the progress of Zionism by the burial of what happened before. The Palestinians ask themselves if the strata covered over by the process of destruction and creation still exist and can facilitate their redemption. Are there orchards still blossoming beneath the car-parks? Many post-Zionists see the Israeli place in terms of the redemption envisaged by Walter Benjamin, and they allot themselves the task of telling the tale of the defeated and the losers, brushing history against the grain and sticking pins in the Zionist-crusader narrative, which they describe in a reversed form: The historical crusaders were defeated and disappeared; the metaphorical crusaders – the Zionists – were victorious, and the Palestinians of today are swept under the carpet of history.[27] The post-Zionist see this a Pyrrhic victory. For them, the defeat is yet to come (in a "crusader" way), and the historical example serves as a warning.

There were several levels to Oz's depiction of the crusader episode. First, his description of the fundamentalist zealotry of the Christian crusaders on their way to the Holy Land, the outstanding feature of which was their insane frenzy in destroying entire Jewish communities; second, his refutation of the Zionist-crusader analogy, whose rationale was the de-legitimization of Zionism by its enemies even before the occupation of the territories of the West Bank in 1967, an attempt that was repeated at the time of the second intifada in the year 2000; third, a warning to the Israeli settlers that in their colonies in the occupied territories they may come to resemble the crusaders of the Middle Ages. The settlers perhaps exemplify the dystopia warned of in "Unto Death," suggesting that the Israelis after the Six-Day War became modern crusaders through an act of self-transformation involving cruelty, self-destructiveness and decadence. The Israelis in the occupied territories, like the crusaders, have a state from which they set forth which finances and sustains them, a state they can return to. This is contrary to the ethos of the State of Israel which arose in Europe "out of nothing" and burned its bridges to it.

This complexity was reflected in his answer to his interviewer Helit Yeshurun, a famous Israeli critic and translator, in 1988 explaining his attraction to the crusader episode: "I seem to have been fascinated all my life by the crusades, by fire and snow, by operatic death, by great gestures of self-immolation. That seems to be my Revisionist genes. And as long as I have the strength, I will oppose it, I will spew it out, I will struggle against it politically and I will depict it in stories. I will also depict what it leads to."[28]

Oz and messianism

Why was Oz so preoccupied with the crusaders, the crucifixion and the cross? He was fascinated by both the dark and the light sides of Christianity: He warned against the Christian zealots, the Crusaders, but admired the personality of their Messiah, Jesus of Nazareth. In *A Tale of Love and Darkness*, he spoke of his uncle, Professor Joseph Klausner, the Israeli historian who wrote a research book on Jesus. His uncle told little Amos to read the New Testament and see that Jesus the Jew had an outstandingly Jewish morality. In the tale, Oz says of his uncle's attitude to Jesus: "[...] that Jesus was born and died a Jew, and never intended to found a new religion. Moreover, he considered him to be 'the Jewish moralist *par excellence*'[...]".[29] In his last novel *Judas* (2014) one can see his sympathy with the character of Jesus: "[...] Jesus' humanity, the warm, infectious love that he radiated all around him, that mixture of simplicity, humility, endearing humor, and intimacy with everyone – together with the moral insight, the elevated vision, the poignant beauty of his parables, and the charm of his glorious gospel [...]"[30]

In 2000, Oz said in his article, "Jesus's Deputy Comes to Jerusalem" (in the book, *Actually, There Are Two Wars Here*), that "Rabbi Jesus was not holy and not a prophet but simply a rabbi, meaning teacher, and in fact Jesus was an unorthodox Jewish teacher. Jesus was clearly not a Christian."[31] He declared that:

> [...] My Jesus is not superhuman or subhuman but painfully human [...] I sometimes call him Rabbi Jesus, an epithet that some of the Christians concerned with him and some of the Jews concerned with him are a bit surprised to hear, although that is just what his first disciples called him – a rabbi. [...] who wanted to bring Judaism back to what he saw as its pure origins, and he perhaps wanted to bring it to what he saw as its logical conclusion. He never set foot – and could not have set foot – in a church. He did not make the sign of the cross, and did not bow down to any image or any figure even once at any time in his life. In contemporary terms, one could perhaps say that he lived as a Jew who sought to improve the world and improve our heritage and died as a Jew who refused to go with the current [...][32]

There was also the work of the historian David Flusser, who claimed that Jesus the Galilean was Jewish, and the Jewish interest in Jesus was shared by thinkers, historians and writers such as Haim Hazzaz, Zalman Shneur, Yehezkel Kaufmann, Marin Buber and others.[33] Of all of these, Oz was most influenced by his uncle, the historian and literary critic, who thought that Jews were no longer afraid of Christianity.

Although Oz's description of his uncle Joseph in his autobiographical novel was satirical and slightly derisive, he appears to have been the most inspiring figure in his nephew's life. Among Klausner's works on Jesus of Nazareth and the Jewish Messiah, his book *The Messianic Idea in Israel* stands out like a beacon.[34] The Jerusalem historian described pre-exilic Judaism as an outstanding combination of national uniqueness and universal aspiration, hope of messianic redemption and desire for social justice. Oz described him as an enlightened liberal nationalist of a nineteenth-century kind, a product of the Enlightenment, romanticism and the springtime of nations.[35] And certainly, the Gospel according to Uncle Joseph conformed to the idea of "messianic peoples" which had developed universal visions and which existed in European nations in the nineteenth century. Prominent among them were, for example, Mazzini's vision of the Third Rome in Italy and Adam Mickiewicz's idea of Poland as the Christ among the nations. Similarly, Zionism was not content to be selfish and provincial but had aspirations for the whole of humanity.

The young socialist of Kibbutz Hulda was far from the revisionist nationalism of his uncle. He too worked all his life on the polarity of Judaism and humanism, on locating the place of Israel in the world. The child from Kerem Avraham that Amos Oz had been became an observer of the house of Israel in the original sense one finds in the Book of Ezekiel in which the intention of the observer was to give a universal meaning to his particular vision. In *Jews and Words* (2014), Oz and his daughter Fania Oz-Salzberger claimed that the Jewish culture, in its constant exchanges with other cultures, is a great river of giving and a great river of taking.[36]

If his uncle stressed the messianic mission of Judaism, his grandmother bequeathed to her grandson an awareness of the difference between Jews and Christians with regard to the Messiah. The Jews believe that the Messiah has yet to come, the Christians believe he was here once and will come again. This controversy, she said, had brought us a great deal of hatred and anger. Why should we not both simply wait and see what will happen?[37]

But patience is not at present a prized commodity. Religious zealotry like that of the present-day crusaders and other political zealotries were Oz's reason for writing *Dear*

Zealots (2017). In *Dear Zealots*, Oz claims to be an expert on Comparative Fanaticism. Already in *How to Cure a Fanatic* (2011) he wrote: "I have called myself an expert on comparative fanaticism. That is no joke. If you ever hear of a school or university starting a department of comparative zealotry, I am applying for a teaching post. As a former Jerusalemite, as a reformed zealot, I feel I'm fully qualified for the job."[38] According to Oz, he learned what zealotry is when he was exposed in his youth to the political messianism of his uncle Joseph Klausner. On August 15, 1929, a group of Revisionist marched to the Western wall in Jerusalem in protest. They were associated with the Committee for the Western Wall, whose founder was Joseph Klausner. The Arabs perceived the march as an attempt to lay claim to the territory of the Temple Mount (Haram al-Sharif in the Muslim tradition) and reacted with violence all across the land. Ten years before Oz was born, this was the inception of the violent national dispute between the Arabs and the Jews. For Oz, the messianism of his uncle Klausner became a model of political zealotry. No wonder that later in his life Gush Emunim, as a contemporary national-religious-messianic movement, became his prime political rival, the nemesis against whom his political intellectual activity was directed (although he participated in many left-winged oriented demonstrations in Israel).[39]

This book and his final lecture at Tel-Aviv University, "The full account has not yet been settled," (2018) are destined to be his political will and testament.[40] Although the messianic idea is not necessarily combined with zealotry, in certain conditions zealotry and messianism fit one another like hand and glove. In the nineteenth century, messianic political movements from both the right and left declared that they were the oracles of history, the vanguards of a nation or a class, and they therefore had the right and duty to move history forward and to discard anything that stood in the way.

The works of the historian Jacob Talmon also showed destruction to be the other side of redemption, an apocalyptic ruin out of which a righteous and reformed world was supposed to emerge. This problem did not become actual until the birth of Zionism. But Oz discerned a time-bomb in the combination of the messianic idea with the notion of the rebirth of the nation.

In 1986, in a review of Lova Eliav's book *New Heart, New Spirit*, Oz claimed that Zionist society was a future-oriented society; as one of its anthems states, "Yesterday is gone and far behind us/But tomorrow still lies far ahead."[41] The Bible, a source of inspiration for innovators and reformers during the "good years" of the Zionist revolution, was becoming, according to Oz, an authorization for stagnation, for objection to change, for abstention from the present, and for adoption of a backward-facing mental stance. Zionism, continued Oz, has always incorporated a sort of dialectical tension between profound longing for the long-lost beauty of yesteryear and burning ambition to turn over an entirely new leaf in Israel. In matters both great and small that tension persisted between the urge to re-create and the urge to innovate; the names given by early Zionists to their children, their settlements, and their books bear witness to this covert struggle. In the biblical words "renew our days as of old" (Lamentations 5:21), which became a popular Zionist slogan, this dialectic can be seen quite clearly. There can be no renewal without our days as of old. This dialectical move is almost the entire Zionist sensibility in a nutshell.[42]

For thousands of years, Oz explained, the Jews lived outside history, even in opposition to history. History was a "game" considered fit for Gentiles only, and no good Jew would dream of dirtying his hands with it. The Jews were supposed to live in humility, willingly accepting their sufferings, until the coming of the Messiah – like a bunch of disaster victims lying at the foot of a mountain and waiting for the tornado to pass. History, it was thought, would go away; eventually it would come to an end. Afterward, the Messiah would come and take the Jews, in his miraculous chariot, back to the glorious past, to the days of the Temple and the Kingdoms of Israel, and even farther back, to the Garden of Eden. All the Jews had to do was to keep themselves pure, avoid sin, bow their heads, and wait. As long as, alas, they were still surrounded by history, they could have only one temporal goal: to survive. To get through history unscathed. Not to try to change it; not to try to shape its course; and, heaven forbid, not to be so impertinent before the Creator as to attempt to take history into their own hands. Oz maintains that the Jews thought for thousands of years that history is something through which one must suffer, like a protracted illness, and from which to emerge on the other side – right into the days of the Messiah, whose coming would cancel all history, restore them to their homeland, and bring them full redemption.[43] The intent of Zionism, concluded Oz, was to smash that passive attitude. The revolt involved in so doing was by no means easy. To break up the long wait for the Messiah, and to take an active role in shaping the historical and political future.

In *Jews and Words*, Oz said that the return of the Jews to Zion, which was seen by the secular mentality as the coming of the Messiah, was regarded by many people as the end of exilic history, the end of history as such and the final release from the extra-temporality of exile. Zionist thinkers used the messianic metaphor extensively – redemption without the person of the Messiah – and this typified many of their utopian dreams. Indeed, Oz considered the Zionists a family:

> From the beginning, Zionism was a family name and not a first name. Various people sang, "We came to the country to build it and be built by it," and we had all kinds of different programs in mind. There were people who came to the Land of Israel because they cherished the dream of reviving the kingdom of David and Solomon. There were people who came to implement the humanistic tradition of Judaism: that is to say, to create an advanced western social-democratic welfare state. There were people who came to the Land of Israel to create a Marxist paradise. There were people who came to live here quietly and await the Messiah.[44]

An obsession with the Messiah has awakened, almost simultaneously, in various corners of the believers' camp. Disciples of the rabbis Kook – father and son – imagined they heard the stirrings of the Messiah in the roar of the tanks during the Six-Day War.[45] If widespread sectors of the religious community believe that the Messiah is at the gate, then no compromise is possible and there is, from their point of view, no room for tolerance and forbearance.[46] Through most of history, the Jews have usually adopted two spiritual reference points: the distant, glorious past and some sort of distant messianic future. The present and the immediate future were almost always viewed as a "vale of tears," whose tribulations could be bemoaned but not acted upon; accordingly, it was considered pointless to spend too much emotional energy on them. It was assumed that when the Messiah came he would bring about the exalted future – thus renewing the marvelous past and at the same time dissipating the troubles of the present.[47]

Oz stressed the fact that the modern return to Zion, the building of the moshavot (the first places to be settled in Palestine by the Zionists), the kibbutzim and the towns "did not come about through the Messiah but through a secular, pragmatic, modern political movement."[48] He saw the claim of the disciples of the Rabbis Kook that the secular pioneers were instruments of divine providence without knowing it, as a great insult. According to this view, they were really only "The Messiah's Mule." (a common phrase in Hebrew which refers to the redundancy of the means by which the Messiah will use to come to the fore) Oz identified the problem with these messianists: "For some of them, this state is only a 'husk,' or, at most, 'defective'".[49] These messianists assert that democracy is a foreign implant to the Jewish tradition and that Israeli Jews should not want it, and instead they should strive for a renewal of the Judaic Kingdom of old in a form of a monarchy. Oz further claimed that to impose "Jewish character," as the religious call it, through coercion or legislation – "any attempt to hasten the coming of the Messiah through the tanks of the Israel Defense Forces" – only deepens the rupture.[50] He warned of a situation "in which the messianic zealots would succeed in destroying the mosques on the Temple Mount and building the Temple in place of them [...]." He said this would be a catastrophe like the catastrophe brought about by zealots in the past. He feared a political theology perpetuating a conflict between enemy and friend, like that of Carl Schmitt: "There are quite a few who think that, as important that the territories are to us, it is more important that the eternal conflict should remain eternal." Nevertheless, one must distinguish between Oz's political views and his acceptance of the existence of the Israeli society to which he felt he belonged: "I feel good about being the citizen of a state in which there are eight and a half million prime ministers, eight and a half million prophets and eight and a half million Messiahs. Each one of us has a personal formula for redemption, or at least for a solution."[51]

In this context Talmon argued that "Gush Emunim" [Bloc of the Faithful][52] – the movement of the national-religious settlers during the 1970s – were the "new Sabbatians." After 1967, Talmon declared: "I am very afraid of the time when we sober up and experience Sabbatian disillusionment with all that it involves." Exactly ten years later, in the 1980s, Talmon wrote to the Israeli prime minister Menachem Begin: "Is it an escape into a world of mythological thought patterns and emotions whose classical example may be found in Sabbatianism?"[53] When Gershom Scholem was asked about Talmon's letter, he replied: "I think he is quite right in saying that the use of religious ideas is a most harmful and senseless thing in politics."[54] With regard to Ben-Gurion's messianic rhetoric, Scholem said: "He [Ben-Gurion] used the term 'messianism' no less than the people of the religious camp, who perhaps really believed in 'the beginning of redemption'."[55] Oz too thought that some of the new immigrants to Israel (during the first years of the state) indeed tended to see in Ben-Gurion a Messiah.[56] In Scholem's opinion, the failure of messianism in the seventeenth century invalidates the idea of a figure of flesh and blood as a Messiah. Ben-Gurion's secular and universal messianism was directed toward the State of Israel, while the messianism of Gush Emunim focused on the land of Israel.

Messianic faith as such did not trouble Oz, only when it became a political theology and political zealotry. After the Six-Day War, he came to the conclusion that quite a number of Israelis really and truly believe that the war signified the coming about of redemption. Although the neo-messianism of Gush Emunim was religious, according to Oz its intellectual roots were already to be found in Berdichevsky, one of Oz's Hebrew progenitors, who declared that "Zionism is the continuation of messianism."[57] From

Herzl, who was a messianic figure, to Ben-Gurion, who was known for preaching a secular and universal messianism, two messianic terms are applicable: "Promethean," whereby modern secular man builds himself and his world by himself, and "transcendental," whereby non-human and a-historical forces fashion his life.[58] Oz thought that secular Zionism harnessed for its benefit religious-messianic sources of energy, but it incidentally transpired that this use of messianic and redemptive rhetoric came at a high price. He declared that anyone who translates the messianic idea into the present is guilty, in Jewish terms, of false messianism. Oz prefer to remain without a Messiah and without redemption.

Oz and Canaanism

The present manifestation of the messianic idea in Israel is what I call "Canaanite messianism."[59] This ideology, which after 1967 exchanged the holy trinity of traditional religious nationalism – Torah, people, land – for a territorial messianism of the Gush Emunim variety, places the land at the head of a new order of preferences: land, people, Torah. The writer Haim Be'er called the members of Gush Emunim, who believe in this nativistic messianism, "phylactery-wearing Canaanites."[60] Or in the words of the historian Anita Shapira, who wrote in the context of Baruch Kurzweil, the renowned literary critic: "[Kurzweil] denied the growth-potential of a new species of religious Cannanism which today is very present among the settler communities."[61] Also, the historian of education Rachel Alboim-Dror is of the opinion that Canaanism exposed the basic problems of Zionism, whose imprint could also be found in the national-religious movements, from the religious youth movement Bnei Akiva to Gush Emunim.[62]

This Canaanite-Hebrew option also has an perpetual presence in the Israeli consciousness. Since the early 1940s when the activities of the "Committee for the Formation of Hebrew Youth" began, and the manifesto "Letter to Hebrew Youth" was published, the secular-radical option has formed part of the range of possibilities of the Israeli discourse. Canaanism was the boldest cultural and political challenge – at least in literary and intellectual-political circles – to Zionism, Judaism and Israelism in its known form. Yonatan Ratosh, the poet and founder of the Canaanite Group, offered a total alternative that would sever Israelism from Judaism and adopt only the elements of geographical affiliation.[63] The place – the Semitic space – would replace the "Place," the Jewish God; there would be a "Hebraization" of the peoples of the area who were "lacking nationality" and a complete severance from exilic Jewish history. Was Canaanism an attempt at an Israelization of the French national model that defines itself as a synthesis of territory and language? In opposition to this exclusivity of secular Canaanism, Oz wrote:

> Admittedly, it would be foolish to deny the religious experience that lies at the root of Jewish independence. Even the first founders of the new Land of Israel, who broke out of the straitjacket of religion and revolted against it, brought to their Tolstoyan or Marxist or nationalist enthusiasm a religious temperament, whether Hasidic or messianic or reverential. [...]

> But the experience that has taken shape and grown in the Land of Israel in the last two or three generations has already begun to develop a new appearance of its own: the main thing is neither liberation from the ancestral heritage nor the restoration of old-time Judaism, but the liberation of the Jews.[64]

What were the sources of Oz's anti-Canaanite outlook? The Israeli orthodox cultural critic Baruch Kurzweil (1907–1972) would probably have seen him, as he saw S. Yizhar, as a Hebrew, secular, nativistic "spoiled fruit" who descended from the school of thought of Berdichevsky and the *Tsa'irim*, desecrators of traditional Judaism, forerunners of the Canaanites and pavers of the way to secular Zionism. Kurzweil's first attack on the Canaanite ideology was not aimed at Yonatan Ratosh and his group but took place in January 1948 against the Israeli journalist Uri Avneri's intellectual circle and their provocative journal. The Canaanites held that it is the nativistic and linguistic factors that govern the national consciousness. The territory and the language were both essential, not merely instrumental. They were not ideologically marginal but had considerable sociological potential, and in April 1949 the philosopher Samuel Hugo Bergman declared that the Canaanites expressed "clearly and unhesitatingly what others feel and experience timidly and halfheartedly."[65]

What in fact was the Canaanite idea? Its main point was nativistic Israeli nationhood, the geographical conception that it was the territory that defined the national identity of a country's inhabitants. It was not ethnicity or biology that created a nation, but the physical space and a common language, which obliterated differences and formed a national melting-pot. It was the space that created national significance.

There was apparently a Canaanite potential in the young Oz: a Revisionist home, a secular outlook, an affinity for Berdichevsky and not Ahad Ha-Am, an attraction to the local and the native, the centrality of the Hebrew language, and contribution to the journal *Keshet*, edited by Aharon Amir, which he saw as the leading journal in Israel. But Oz completely rejected the Canaanite idea:

> The question of our attitude to the Arab population provided from the very beginning the meeting-point for two extreme and opposed trends of thought: revisionist nationalism and "Canaanism" (which, incidentally, had grown up on the soil of Revisionism). Many years before the surprising and ironical meeting of Uri Zvi Greenberg and Aharon Amir in the "Committee for the Greater Land of Israel," the "Canaanites" and the nationalists had met in their common view of the Arabs as the reincarnation of the ancient Canaanites, Amorites, Ammonites, Amalekites, Jebusites and Girgashites. Both the romantics and the counter-romantics wanted to paint the present in the colours of the biblical period. Admittedly, their conclusions were opposed: the Revisionists dreamed of a holy war against the tribes of Canaan, the direct continuation of the wars of Joshua, David and Alexander Jannaeus, "revenging the spilt blood of Thy servants"; the "Canaanites," on the other hand, dreamed of returning in order to be restored to the bosom of the Semitic ethnos and the magical oriental paganism from which we had been uprooted thousands of years ago by namby-pamby "phylactery Judaism," fatally tainted by Yiddishkeit.[66]

Oz ridiculed the "childish side" of Gush Emunim and thought that there was no such thing as "being reborn." He did not accept the Canaanite idea of a distinction between the Hebrew "nation" in the land of Israel (and in the region as a whole) and the Jewish "flock" (community) abroad. Zionism, which included Oz, sought to connect Jewish history, with all its vicissitudes, to its point of departure. The land of Israel was the "metaphorical womb" of Jewish history. But he rejected the ideas of those who said that exile was an absence, a "negative" of the authenticity and Jewish fulfillment which could only be obtained in the land of Israel. Oz refused to see exile as a sickness and nativism as a cure, unlike his friend A. B. Yehoshua, who saw Zionism as "the name of a cure for a certain kind of Jewish sickness called exile."[67]

Oz was not a nativist or a diaspora intellectual. He remained to his last day neither a crusader nor a Canaanite, not messianic or exilic, but a Mediterranean Jew, a patriotic Israeli who lovingly stuck pins into his country, an anguished lover of his people and his land who never for a moment regretted his Zionist ideology. But unlike the Canaanite "Nimrod" who was fashioned from a single material, Nubian sandstone, Oz was composed of many strata, masses and masses of crusader and Canaanite and messianic levels and fascinating affinities both with Berdichevsky at the start of his career and with Ahad Ha-Am, who founded the monthly journal *Ha-Shiloah* edited by his Revisionist uncle, the historian who wandered between messianism and the Jewish Jesus. Like Berdichevsky and Brenner, Ahad Ha-Am and Klausner, Oz did not want Israel to be like Albania or Sparta, but promoted the "added value" of the people of the book, proud among the nations of its Jewish legacy and Hebrew culture. In his last books, he built with his words a palace to the glory of the national identity, a "linguistic Judaism," textual and intellectual, extending as far as the books of the prophets. He linked up with an ancient genealogy, and said that his allies on the journey toward human justice and peace are Amos the prophet and Ahad Ha-Am the essayist, not Rabbi Abraham Hacohen Kook.[68] His parents gave him the name of the prophet of the eighth century BCE, the first one whose prophecies were written down, who dwelt in Tekoa and was known for his chastisement of the wealthy members of the kingdom of Israel in Samaria, the "cows of Bashan." Little Amos of Kerem Avraham, the youth from Kibbutz Hulda, who documented a hundred years of nativism and immigration to his old-new country, was also the writer and intellectual, the voice of the conscience of Israel among the nations.

Notes

1. Camus, *The First Man*.
2. Ohana, *Albert Camus and the Critique of Violence*.
3. Oz, *Judas*.
4. Ohana, "Mediterranean Humanism."
5. Oz, *In the Land of Israel*, 241.
6. Miron Benvenisti, "Namal yam-tikhoni kozev [Deceptive Mediterranean Port]," *Haaretz*, March 21, 1996.
7. Rothbard, *White City, Black City*.
8. Alexandra Nocke, Interview with Amos Oz, April 2, 2003. Private correspondence.
9. See also, Ibid.; Idem., *The Place of the Mediterranean*.
10. Oz, *The Same Sea*, 1.
11. Bartfeld and Ohana, "Albert Camus: Parcours Méditerranéens."
12. Shapira and Wiskind-Elper, "Politics and Collective Memory."
13. Asali, "Zionists Studies of the Crusader Movement"; and Maalouf, *The Crusaders through Arab Eyes*.
14. Here I will briefly analyze works of Yehoshua, Oz and Ravikovitch. Further elaboration on the history of the Zionist-Crusader analogy, see: Ohana, *The Origins of Israeli Mythology*.
15. Shalev, *Parashat Gabriel Tirosh*; Zalka, "Ba-derekh le-Haleb"; and Shimoni, *Ma'of ha-yona*.
16. Yehoshua, "Mul ha-ye'arot," 122–92.
17. Oz, *Unto Death*.
18. Ibid.
19. Naomi Golkind, Interview with Amos Oz, *Ha-Tzofe*, May 29, 1981.
20. Bassok, *Le-yofi nisgav libo er*.
21. Greenberg, *Ha-gavrut ha-ola*.

22. Ravikovitch, *Kol Hashirim ad ko,* 133–4; See an illuminating interpretation in: Tikotzky, *Dahlia Ravikovitch.*
23. The full name of Saladin is: An-Nasir Salah ad-Din Yusuf ibn Ayyub, however, in European literature he is often called "Saladin" and in spoken Arabic as well as in Hebrew sometimes is called "Salah ad-Din". Here I will use the two interchangeably.
24. Shalev, "Tzalbanim," 43–44.
25. Oz, "The Specter of Saladin," *The New York Times,* July 28, 2000.
26. Oz, "Falestin tzrikha li-vhor [Palestine Must Choose]," *Yediot Aharonot,* August 8, 2000.
27. Benvenisti, *Sacred Landscape.*
28. Yeshurun, *Eikh asita et ze?,* 189–228.
29. Oz, *A Tale of Love and Darkness,* 58.
30. Oz, *Judas,* 149.
31. Oz, "Netzigo shel Yeshu megi'a le-Yerushalaim [Jesus's Deputy comes to Jerusalem]," *Be-etzem yesh kan shtei milhamot,* 65.
32. Ibid., 64–65.
33. Flusser, *Yeshu*; see also Rosenzweig's discussion in "Atheistic Theology," could reveal an interesting analogy between the discussions of the Protestant theologians in the 19th century and the discussions of the Israeli scholars concerning the character of Jesus, and especially the tendency to demythologize the Messiah, to view Jesus as a human being.
34. Klausner, *The Messianic Idea in Israel.*
35. Oz on Joseph Klausner, see especially: *A Tale of Love and Darkness,* 58.
36. Oz and Oz-Salzberger, *Jews and Words.*
37. Oz, *Dear Zealots,* 44.
38. Oz, *How to Cure a Zealot,* 49; Thirty-three years before the publication of *Dear Zealots,* in a fascinating meeting that has not been previously recorded with the Dominican Father and philosopher Marcel Dubois, Oz went up to him and said, "I once said ironically that the first university in the world that opened a department of comparative zealotry should turn to me and ask me to be the first professor. I think I am qualified. Forgive me my lack of modesty. I am acquainted with zealotry. It is perhaps my luck that I have experienced more than one zealotry. After you have experienced two, you are inoculated." Apart from the anecdotal interest, one can already see in the young Oz his mature outlook concerning political zealotry. I wish to thank Professor Avraham Shapira for bringing this conversation to my notice. "A Conversation between Amoz Oz and Marcel Dubois," Avraham Shapira's private archives.
39. Oz, *How to Cure a Zealot.*
40. Oz, "Kol ha-hesbon od lo nigmar [Until All Accounts Have Been Settled]," Lecture at the Tel-Aviv University, June 3, 2018.
41. *Oz, Me-moradot ha-Levanon,* 196.
42. Ibid., 196–7.
43. Ibid., 197–8.
44. Oz, *Kol ha-tikvot,* 10–11.
45. *Oz, Me-moradot ha-Levanon,* 116.
46. Ibid., 117.
47. Ibid., 195.
48. Oz, *Dear Zealots,* 82.
49. Ibid., 89.
50. Ibid., 96.
51. Oz, *Dear Zealots,* 131.
52. Dov Schwartz, *Religious Zionism*; Aran, *Kookism.*
53. Jacob L. Talmon, "Dmuta shel Yisrael be-tfutzot ha-olam [Israel's Image in the World]," address by Talmon at the *Ma'ariv* symposium, January 9, 1970.
54. Howe, "Interview with Gershom Scholem."
55. Zeev Gallili, "Meshihiyut, tziyonut, ve-anarkhiya ba-lashon," 58.
56. Oz and Salzberger-Oz, *Jews and Words,* 177.

57. Brinker, *Ha-safrut ha-ivrit.*
58. Ohana, *The Intellectual Origins of Modernity*, London 2019.
59. Ohana, "The Israeli Identity and the Canaanite Option."
60. Haim Be'er, "Gush Emunim: 'Can'anim' ha-menihim tefillin [Gush Emunim: Canaanites who Wear Phylacteries]," *Davar*, October 15, 1982.
61. Shapira, "Le'an halkha shlilat ha-galut?" 22.
62. Ya'akovi, *Eretz ahat ve-shnei amim ba*, 104.
63. Diamond, *Homeland or Holy Land?*
64. Oz, *Under this Blazing Light*, 85.
65. Samuel Hugo Bergman, "Al itzuv dmut ha-uma be-medinateynu [On the Formation of the Nation's Character in Our State]," *Ha-Poel Ha-Tzair*, vols. 26–27, April 10, 1949.
66. Oz, *Under this Blazing Light*, 88.
67. Yehoshua, "Be-khol zot mahapekha [Nevertheless, A Revolution]," 59.
68. See note 36 above.

Disclosure statement

No potential conflict of interest was reported by the author(s).

Bibliography

Aran, G. *Kookism: Shorshei Gush Emunim, trabut ha-mitnahalim, teologia tzionit, meshihiyut be-zmanenu* [The Roots of the Bloc of the Faithful, Settlers' Sub-Culture, Zionist Theology, Current Messianism]. Jerusalem: Carmel, 2013.
Asali, Z. J. "Zionists Studies of the Crusader Movement." *Arab Studies Quarterly* 14, no. 1 (1992): 45–59.
Bartfeld, F., and D. Ohana. "Special Issue on 'Albert Camus: Parcours Méditerranéens'." *Perspectives* 5 (1998).
Bassok, I. *Le-yofi nisgav libo er, Shaul Tchernichovsky – haim* [His Heart Awake to Sublime Beauty, Shaul Tchernichovsky – A Life]. Jerusalem: Carmel, 2017.
Benvenisti, M. *Sacred Landscape: The Buried History of the Holy Land since 1948*. Translated by Maxine Kaufman-Lacusta. Berkeley: University of California Press, 2000.
Brinker, M. *Ha-safrut ha-ivrit ke-safrut eropeit* [Hebrew Literature as European Literature]. Jerusalem: Carmel, 2016.
Camus, A. *The First Man*. Translated by David Hapgood. New York: Vintage, 1996.
Diamond, J. S. *Homeland or Holy Land? The Canaanite Critique of Israel*. Bloomington: Indiana University Press, 1986.
Flusser, D. *Yeshu* [Jesus]. Jerusalem: Magnes and Dvir, 2009.
Gallili, Z. "Meshihiyut, tziyonut, ve-anarkhiya ba-lashon: Divu'ah al ha'azanato: Ze'ev Gallili. [Messianism, Zionism and Linguistic Anarchy]." In *Retzifut ve-mered: Gershom Scholem ba-omer u-ve-siah* [Continuity and Rebellion: Gershom Scholem in Speech and Dialogue], edited by A. Shapira, 56–64. Tel-Aviv: Am Oved, 1993.
Greenberg, U. T. *Ha-gavrut ha-ola* [The Rising Masculinity]. Tel-Aviv: Sadan, 1926.

Howe, I. "Interview with Gershom Scholem: 'The Only Thing in My Life I Have Never Doubted Is the Existence of God'." *Present Tense* 8, no. 1 (1980): 53–57.

Klausner, J. *The Messianic Idea in Israel From its Beginning to the Completion of the Mishnah.* Translated by W. F. Stinespring. New York: Macmillan Company, 1955.

Maalouf, A. *The Crusaders through Arab Eyes.* Translated by Jon Rothschild. New York: Schocken Books, 1984.

Nocke, A. *The Place of the Mediterranean in Modern Israeli Identity.* Leiden: Brill, 2009.

Ohana, D. "Mediterranean Humanism." *Mediterranean Historical Review* 18, no. 1 (2010): 59–75.

Ohana, D. *The Origins of Israeli Mythology: Neither Canaanites nor Crusaders.* New York & Cambridge: Cambridge University Press, 2012.

Ohana, D. "The Israeli Identity and the Canaanite Option." In *The Gift of the Land and the Fate of the Canaanites in Jewish Thought,* edited by K. Berthelot, J. David, and M. Hirshman, 311–351. Oxford: Oxford University Press, 2014.

Ohana, D. *Albert Camus and the Critique of Violence.* Brighton: Sussex Academic Press, 2016.

Ohana, D. *The Intellectual Origins of Modernity.* London: Routledge, 2019.

Oz, A. *Unto Death: Crusade and Late Love.* Translated by Nicholas de Lange. Boston: Mariner Books, 1978.

Oz, A. *In the Land of Israel.* translation Maurie Goldberg-Bartura. London: Flamingo, 1983.

Oz, A. *Me-moradot ha-Levanon: Ma'amarim ve-reshimot Amos Oz* [From the Slopes of Lebanon: Articles and Essays by Amos Oz]. Tel-Aviv: Am Oved, 1987.

Oz, A. *Under This Blazing Light: Essays.* Translated by Nicholas de Lange. Cambridge: Cambridge University Press, 1995.

Oz, A. *Kol ha-tikvot: Mahshavot al zehot Yisraelit* [All of Our Hopes: Thoughts on Israeli Identity]. Jerusalem: Keter, 1998.

Oz, A. *Be-etzem yesh kan shtei milhamot* [But These are Two Different Wars]. Jerusalem: Keter, 2002.

Oz, A. *The Same Sea.* Translated by Nicholas de Lange. New York: Mariner Books, 2002.

Oz, A. *A Tale of Love and Darkness.* Translated by Nicholas de Lange. Orlando: Harcourt, 2005.

Oz, A. *Judas.* Translated by Nicholas de Lange. Boston: Houghton Mifflin Harcourt, 2016.

Oz, A. *Dear Zealots: Letters from a Divide Land.* Translated from the Hebrew by Jessica Cohen. Boston: Houghton Mifflin Harcourt, 2018.

Oz, A., and F. Oz-Salzberger. *Jews and Words.* New Haven: Yale University Press, 2012.

Ravikovitch, D. *Kol Hashirim ad ko* [All the Songs Thus Far]. Tel-Aviv: Ha-Kibbutz Ha-Meuhad, 1995.

Rosenzweig, F. "Atheistic Theology." In *Philosophical and Theological Writings,* Translated and edited with notes and commentary by Paul W. Franks and Michael L. Morgan, 10–24. Indianapolis: Hackett Publishing, 2000.

Rotbard, S. *Ir Levana, Ir Shehora* [White City, Black City]. Tel-Aviv: Babel, 2005.

Schwartz, D. *Religious Zionism: History and Ideology.* Boston: Academic Studies Press, 2008.

Shalev, I. *Parashat Gabriel Tirosh.* Tel-Aviv: Am Oved, 1964.

Shalev, I. "Zalbanim [Crusaders]." In *Shikaron Zahav – Shirim* [Golden Drunkenness – Poems], edited by I. Shalev, 43–44. Tel Aviv: A. Levin-Epstein, 1975.

Shapira, A. "Le'an halkha shlilat ha-galut? [What Happened to the Negation of Exile?]." *Alpaim* 25 (2003): 54–59.

Shapira, A., and O. Wiskind-Elper. "Politics and Collective Memory: The Debate over the 'New Historians' in Israel." *History & Memory* 7, no. 1 (1995): 9–40.

Shimoni, Y. *Ma'of ha-yona* [Flight of the Dove]. Tel-Aviv: Am Oved, 1990.

Tikotzky, G. *Dalia Ravikovitch: Ba-haim u-va-safrut* [Dalia Ravikovitch: In Life and in Literature]. Haifa: Haifa University Press, 2016.

Ya'akovi, D. *Eretz ahat ve-shnei amim ba* [One Land, Two Peoples]. Jerusalem: Magnes, 1999.

Yehoshua, A. B. "Mul ha-ye'arot [Facing the Forests]." In *Ad horef 1974 – mivhar* [Till Winter 1974 – A Selection], edited by A. B. Yehoshua, 122–192. Tel-Aviv: Ha-Kibbutz Ha-Me'uhad, 1974.

Yehoshua, A. B. "Be-khol zot mahapekha [Nevertheless, A Revolution]." In *Shoresh ha-dvarim: Iyun mehudash be-she'elot am ve-hevra* [The Heart of the Matter- Redefining Social and National Issues], edited by R. Rosenthal, 58–70. Jerusalem: Keter, 2005.

Yeshurun, H. *Eikh asita et ze? Ra'ayonot "hadarim"* [How Did You Do It? Interviews with Poets]. Tel-Aviv: Ha-Sifriya Ha-Hadasha, 2016.

Zalka, D. "Ba-derekh le-Haleb [On the Road to Aleppo]." In *11 sipurim* [Eleven Stories], edited by E. Hirsch, 173–181. Tel-Aviv: Hargol, 2004.

"Now we shall reveal a little secret" first person plural and lyrical fluidity in the works of Amos Oz

Vered Karti Shemtov

ABSTRACT

Throughout his career, Amos Oz explored different kinds of narrations that would enable him to capture both the story of individuals and the voices of the collective. The stories often presented a tension between the first person singular and the first person plural narration. In *A Tale of Love and Darkness*, Oz finally found a harmonious and comfortable way to speak and write in what I define as his "fluid I-Us" voice. I argue that a key to understanding the new and poetic I of *A Tale of Love and Darkness* is the 1999 book *The Same Sea*, which preceded the memoir. This book was the first fictional work by Oz to include his biographical self. In this book, Oz experimented with prose poetry, and with the narrative possibilities that the lyrical "I" can introduce into his work.

The Fluid "I-Us"

> I write novels for the same reasons I dream: I have to dream. I have no choice. And I have to write novels. I have no choice. Novels for me have never been a political vehicle. I want to make a statement I write an article.
>
> —Amos Oz, "One Pen I Use to Tell Stories"[1]

Novels might not have been a political vehicle for Amos Oz, but they were also not a reflection of his own private dreams. "I bring up the evil spirits and record the trauma, the fantasies, the lunacies of Israeli Jews, natives and those from Central and Eastern Europe," he said in 1978. "I deal with their ambitions and the powder box of self-denial and self-hatred."[2] If for Freud creative writers turn dreams and fantasies into public artifacts, in the books of Amos Oz sometimes the opposite takes place. The dreams of the collective become a personal fantasy. This is the case especially in Oz's 2002 bestselling memoir, *A Tale of Love and Darkness*, which tells the story not only of his own family but also of the Zionist dream and the establishment of Israel from his perspective.[3] In interviews about the book, Oz presented time and again the similarities between his own story and the story of the country. "Look, I am a sage," he said to Bill Thompson in 2014; "being an Israeli of my age is the exact equivalent of being a 356 year old American, because I saw the Boston Tea Party of Israel with my own eyes, I knew personally the George Washingtons and Abraham

Lincolns of Israel, every single person whose image is printed on our bills, our money notes, I knew personally."[4] Ranen Omer-Sherman writes that Oz became the Israeli everyman. His biography allowed him to have "an intimate understanding of the movement of Israeli society from a collectivist ethos to a socially critical and finally to an increasingly Americanized, and, hence, individualistic culture. The novelist's rebellion against his father's religious Jerusalem household when he was only fifteen mirrors the path taken by many of his rebellious characters and reflects the tension between the individual and the collective which has informed his oeuvre ever since."[5]

Amos Oz didn't want people to read his books as "gossip" or as personal stories. "My work is the result of photosynthesis, not photography," he said.[6] He insisted that *A Tale of Love and Darkness* is a tale and not a memoir, and he devoted an entire chapter (chapter 5) to giving instructions to the reader on how to read and how not to read the book, insisting that the book should not be read as a story of his personal life. In an agitated tone, the narrator of the book compares "the bad reader" to "a psychopathic lover" who strips off his victim's (the writer) skin, impatiently removes the flesh, dismantles her skeleton, and then, when the reader is pulverizing her bones between his crude yellow teeth, "he finally attains his satisfaction: that's that. Now I'm really, really inside. I've arrived."[7] The good reader, on the other hand, understands that the real distance to be covered is not the gap between the text and the writer but the gap between the text and the reader. The chapter, which was removed from the English and other translations of the book, expresses the author's discomfort with being exposed, with "letting the reader in," and with writing about himself. Oz felt much more at ease talking about the gap between the text and the Zionist story than about the gap between the text and his own private life. And indeed, this connection between the family's story and the story of the state (rather than the family story and his inner world) was at the center of his many book tour speeches and the many interviews he gave about the book. Some of these lectures even had the title "Israel: A Tale of Love and Darkness," creating the connection between his own story and the story of Israel. Nevertheless, after many years of arguing for a clear division between his "two pens," one for fiction and one for essays, Oz now was ready, as he said, to "[erase] the lines between confession and fiction, between fact and fiction, because I no longer believe in these lines."[8] In the last two decades of his life, he often spoke in one voice that openly combined the storyteller with the essayist, the biographical with the political. He talked about memories of buying cheese or of visiting an Arab family as junctions in which the personal and the political met and as ways of explaining and reflecting on his childhood as well as on the history of Israel.

Many excellent studies were written about the connection between writing the narrative of the self/country in Oz's memoir. Some of these studies look at how this work redefined his voice as a writer and his image. Eran Kaplan writes that the memoir

> Signaled a shift in the image of Oz, who captured in the public imagination both in and out of Israel the essence of the classic Sabra. The book is at once the personal and private account of a family tragedy and a vivid and rich historical account of the emergence of the new state. As such, it reveals both Oz's personal history and the history of his generation. He emerges from *Tale of Love and Darkness* as a native-born Israeli whose environment and cultural background were shaped as much by Jerusalem of the 1930s and 1940s as by Europe of the previous century. He is not a self-assured kibbutznik but a frail, pale child who, with

his father, fails miserably in an attempt to grow plants in his backyard and who finds comfort in books.[9]

Kaplan argues that Oz, in his memoir, tells the story not of a hegemonic Zionist group but rather of one group among many others that compete in an ever-expanding cultural arena. And like many of the other groups that have claimed a voice in the Israeli public sphere over the past two decades and have placed trauma and loss at the core of their collective identity (Mizrahim, Orthodox Jews), Oz does the same to his social milieu (urban Ashkenazim). The loss of Europe and the trauma of the existential threat posed by the 1948 War of Independence becomes the core of his group's identity. The Zionist ideal of the negation of the past is replaced by an attempt to recover a (personal as well as collective) traumatic past.[10]

Karen Grumberg writes about the trauma through the concept of being haunted and argues that in *A Tale of Love and Darkness* Oz writes about his mother for the first time. His mother, she writes, "haunts her son through her absence in life as in death [...] Oz uses the personal life-story to convey a broader narrative: the story of Israel, intricately entwined with his own."[11] Thus, even if Oz, as Anita Shapira argues, re-affirms the Zionist story in his memoir[12] he does it in a new and much more personal way, and in a voice that is different from the one he used at the beginning of his career.

Oz explained the shift in psychological terms: "for many years there was anger and forgetfulness and censorship. I didn't discuss my former life with my new family, with my wife and children. I didn't discuss [it] with my friends. I did not discuss them with anyone."[13] He argued that he was able to open up because the distance of time allowed him to look back, with a new kind of compassion, to the time when his parents were as old as his children were when he was writing *A Tale of Love and Darkness*.[14] But since the memoir is also a story of the Zionist dream and the establishment of the state, this same perspective allowed Oz to look with compassion not only at his past but also at the past of the "Israeli Jews, natives and those from Central and Eastern Europe." After the criticism of the New Historians and the post-Zionism discourse, looking at the past of the country with compassion required thinking about his story/Israel's story as marginal. In an essay published in *Haaretz* right after Oz's memoir was republished in Hebrew, Avirama Golan asked, "Is his story our story?" She argued:

> The power of *A Tale of Love and Darkness* lies, among other things, in how Oz uses the multicultural legitimization of the marginal narrative to strengthen the mainstream narrative (or what used to be mainstream). Nationalist movements need literature to tell their history. When the movement achieves its goal, the storytellers are accused of being "enlisted" and sent back to the storeroom of history. Zionism, during the pre-state period and the early years of Israeli sovereignty, had some excellent storytellers. The best of them, including Oz himself, were able to walk the narrow tightrope between passionate affiliation and the Diaspora approach of watching critically from the sidelines (and this is one of the things that made his stories so appealing, this inner conflict within the consensus). But the Zionist narrative lost its legitimacy with dizzying speed, Being attacked by the "New Historians," cultural researchers, sociologists, literary critics, and extra-parliamentary entities, left and right. The linkage of postmodernism and post-Zionism, along with the seduction of multiculturalism, inflicted considerable damage. [...] What *A Tale of Love and Darkness* did was to free Zionism from its musty corner, allow it to cough up all the dust, and encourage it to sing out again, loud and clear. [...] That is why so many people wrote to Oz (700 [...]), some of them acting on an urge to tell their story. On the surface, it

would seem that Oz has done a great thing. In practice, however, the danger of nostalgia looms.[15]

This kind of nostalgia for the personal and the collective past, Golan concludes, "paints the sins of the past in a rosy hue, making it impossible to look at them with eyes wide open." Golan's perspective can explain many of the literary choices in the memoir. Maybe most notably, it explains the exposition. *A Tale of Love and Darkness* opens not with Oz's first memory – this we get much later in the book – but with a description of Israel in the 1940s that places Oz and his family at the margins of the city and of the Zionist dream: "I was born and bred in a tiny, low-ceilinged ground-floor apartment. My parents slept on a sofa bed that filled their room. [...] their bedroom also served as study, library, dining room, and living room" (1).[16] the narrator tells us. His house was at the edge of the city, and the "Jerusalem my parents looked up to lay far from the area where we lived: it was in leafy Rehavia with its gardens and its strains of piano music." Jerusalem was also far from the pioneers: "the pioneers lived beyond our horizon, in Galilee, Sharon, and the Valleys. Tough, warmhearted, though of course silent and thoughtful, young men, and strapping, straightforward, self-disciplined young women." And it was far from Tel Aviv: "over the hills and far away, the city of Tel Aviv was also an exciting place, from which came the newspapers, rumors of theater, opera, ballet, and cabaret, as well as modern art, party politics, echoes of stormy debates, and indistinct snatches of gossip" (6–10). Every detail of the setting places the story at the margins.

The fragility of life is also presented in the first chapter of the book when the speaker asks the reader to show compassion for the Jews in Israel in the 1940s: "our lives hung by a thread. I realize now that they were not at all sure they would really talk again [with their relatives], this might be the last time, who knew what would happen, there could be riots, a pogrom, a blood bath, the Arabs might rise up and slaughter the lot of us, there might be a war, a terrible disaster, after all, Hitler's tanks had almost reached our doorstep from two directions, North Africa and the Caucasus, who knew what else awaited us?" (15). Writing with nostalgia for both the personal and the collective past, with compassion for the darkness, the marginality, and the fragility of his individual characters and of the community ("our lives hung by a tread") made it possible for Oz to say "us," "our," "we," and to use the first-person plural in a harmonious way, without his old conflict between the individual and the community and without the sharp criticism of the past that had become so common in Israel at the time of writing the memoir.[17]

I would like to argue that finding this harmony between past and present and between "I" and "we" is a major development in Oz's poetics. Throughout his career, Oz wrote in what I define as a fluid "I-We" or "I-Us" voice. I am using here the terminology of Gender Studies to speak not of the fluidity between gender pronouns but of the fluidity between the first-person singular and the first-person plural. It is in this voice that Oz narrated his short stories, his kibbutz stories, some of his political work, and his prophetic essays. The different books and the different genres allowed him to express the varying degrees of conflict that existed within the personal-collective experience. In *A Tale of Love and Darkness* Oz finally found a harmonious and comfortable way to speak and write in his fluid "I-Us" voice, and this allowed him to erase the lines between biography and fiction and between the personal and the political. Using the notion of fluidity to speak about Oz's narration will allow us to understand the development of his poetic "I" and to go beyond the convincing but partial claims that it was nostalgia and compassion for the older generation or a recognition of the personal and collective traumas that allowed Oz to write his story as the story of the birth of the state. My claim here is that a key to understanding the new and poetic I of *A Tale of Love and Darkness* is the 1999 book *The Same Sea* that preceded the memoir. It was also the first fictional work by Oz to include his biographical self. In this book, Oz experimented with a new genre and with a new type of fictional subjectivity. I argue, then, that in addition to the many psychological and historical circumstances that allowed Oz to write his memoir, it was also the discovery of a new poetic subjectivity that made it possible for him to be intimate and impersonal, and to write his story as if it was "our story."

The Polyphonic I, an Orgy of One

> I wrote this book with everything I have. Language, music, structure—everything that I have . . . . This is the closest book I've written. Close to me, close to what I always wanted . . . . I went as far as I could.
>
> —Amos Oz, about *The Same Sea*[18]

Amos Oz's book *The Same Sea* is often overlooked as a minor book although Oz himself described it as his favorite work and as the only book that he would return to and reread.[19] The book was overshadowed by the publication of Oz's celebrated memoir and received relatively less attention despite its centrality and importance to the development of Oz's poetics. As Oz himself said, this book "opened a few things for the next book,"[20] not in the sense of being an introduction to the memoir but, as I argue, in terms of the narrative possibilities it introduced into his work. I ascribe these openings to the experimentations with the lyric form. While many of Oz's books have rich and poetic language, *The Same Sea* is his only attempt to write prose poetry.

From the poetic form Oz took the musicality, intertextuality (which is extremely common in Hebrew poetry), minimalism (telling a story, describing an image, and/or creating effects with only a few words), and the lyrical I, especially as it is defined by Helen Vendler in her *Soul Says*:

> If the normal home of selfhood is the novel, which ideally allows many aspects of the self, under several forms, to expatiate and take substance, then the normal home of the "soul" is the lyric, where the human being becomes a set of warring passions independent of time and space. It is generally thought that the lyric is the genre of "here" and "now," and it is true that these index words govern the lyric moment. But insofar as the typical lyrics exist only here and now, it exists nowhere, since life as it is lived is always bracketed with a there and then. Selves come with a history: souls are independent of time and space.[21]

The "lyrical I," according to Vendler, is the speech of the soul. The interaction of the "soul" and the "self" within a single person is, she writes, one of the great themes of lyrics. The "lyrical I" creates the illusion of an intimate connection between the biographical I and the lyrical one, but, at the same time, the abstraction and detachment from a certain here and now allow the reader to enter the poem and make it his or her own speech. Jacques Derrida talks in similar terms about lyrical abstraction and the body:

A poem, I never sign(s) it. The other sign(s). The I is only at the coming of this desire: to learn by heart. Stretched, tendered forth to the point of subsuming its own support, thus without external support, without substance, without subject, absolute of writing in (it)self, *the 'by heart' let's itself be elected beyond the body, sex, mouth, and eyes; it erases the borders, slips through the hands, you can barely hear it but it teaches us the heart* (my emphasis).[22]

As Vendler argues, the writer, speaker, and reader become one only as far as they share universal emotions, values, and impressions. The abstraction of the lyrical poem creates the illusion of "big" topics that are relevant to all of us (love, loss, desire, death, etc.). "The traditional lyric," she writes, "desires a stripping-away of the details associated with the socially specified self in order to reach its desired all-purpose abstraction." Vendler does not necessarily assume unity of voice: "when soul speaks," she writes, "it speaks with a number of voices." But, she argues, *the voices in the lyric are represented not by characters, as is in the novel or drama, but by the changing registers of the diction, contrastive rhymes, and varieties of tone*" (my emphasis). Vendler and Derrida are fundamentally different scholars but, in this case, they are both writing within a long history of thinking about the "lyrical I" as being "overheard," as a speech of the soul or the heart that is addressed to no one but that is meant to be heard by someone who is just as abstract as the "I."[23]

The lyrical line, then, can easily flip between being read as representing the biographical I and as representing an everyman, between being the speech of the speaker and that of the reader who recites it (erasing the borders and flowing from the heart of the writer to that of the reader), and it can shift between being a moment of truth and intimacy and being a fictional speech. I see the ability to contain these fluid movements, this flow between states, as defining the lyrical voice. I argue that it is in this definition of the lyric that Oz found his new "I-You," or "I-Us." Oz wrote the initial versions of *The Same Sea* away from Israel, in the mountains of Cyprus, with a view to the sea: *the same sea* that borders Israel. In Cyprus, he was free from the here and now. The original plan was to write a novel, but Oz found himself writing notes in verse, and the verses turned into the prose-poem novel.[24] In these notes in verse, Oz found his lyrical I. The lyrical I allowed him to enter the book as his biographical self and to let himself be "overheard." The lyrical allowed him to bring into his work reflections about his past and to do it within the safety of abstraction. He could say "I" as the subject of the poetry of love, death, loss, longing, and other universal human experiences.

To clarify, I do not assume that lyrical speech is universal. In a previous paper on lyrics and hybridization I demonstrated how lyrical voices are always connected to a here and now, they are specific and have contexts, and they are addressed to certain kinds of readers. However, the lyric can create the illusion of a flow between the biographical and the anonymous, between speaker and reader, so when a song or a poem says, "can I compare thee to a summer's day?" or "the art of losing isn't hard to master," we can "erase the borders" of the specific bodies and read it as a speech of hearts and souls. This kind of lyrical reading, which is a feature of the text itself but also of our reading conventions, allowed Oz to use an "I" that is personal yet abstract, individual yet collective, and freed his work from the distance between the autobiographical and the fictional.[25]

The combination of poetry and prose, of lyric and fiction, in *The Same Sea* created a meeting between the poetic I and the dialogism and polyphony of prose. The voices in the book are represented by characters, but they are also created through what Vendler defined as "the changing registers of the diction, contrastive rhymes, and varieties of tone."[26] The poem "A Bird," for example, begins with the narrator introducing us to the character of Nadia Danon:

A bird

Nadia Danon. Not long before she died a bird

on a branch woke her.

At four in the morning, before it was light, narimi

narimi said the bird.

What will I be when I'm dead? A sound or a scent

or neither. I've started a mat.

I may still finish it. Dr. Pinto

is optimistic: the situation is stable. The left one

is a little less good. The right one is fine. The X-rays are clear. See

for yourself: no secondaries here.

At four in the morning, before it is light, Nadia Danon

begins to remember. Ewes' milk cheese. A glass of wine.

A bunch of grapes. A scent of slow evening on the Cretan hills,

the taste of cold water, the whispering of pines, the shadow

of the mountains spreading over the plain, narimi

narimi the bird sang there. I'll sit here and sew.

I'll be finished by morning. (Oz, *The Same Sea*, 12)

While some of the musicality of the prose poem is lost in English, the translation still conveys the soft tone and diction of Nadia Danon's unique voice. The combination of the prosaic and the lyrical, of the storytelling and the singing, is especially interesting here. We shift from being told about Nadia to witnessing her in a very intimate moment. Nadia is alone, it is four in the morning, the lyrical songbird is there with her, and we "overhear" the bird as well as Nadia's private conversation with herself right before her death. The short segments create what I define as "a lyrical suspense," a pause between reading in order to find out "what's next" in the linear narrative and reading with the conventions of the lyric. The text calls here for reading each short segment as meaningful, as symbolic. In this case, they are reflections on how prosaic death is ("The right one is fine. The X-rays are clear") and how lyrical life could be ("the taste of cold water, the whispering of pines"). At the end of this piece, the biographical author joins Nadia in a duet to describe the mountains – the pines, the grapes, the evening on the hill – which are at once the scenery of the place in which Oz writes and a memorable space for Nadia. We hear Nadia and Oz through their lyrical speeches, or to use Vendler's term, we hear what their souls say. This musical duet can be read as voices controlled by the speaker/narrator who quotes them but also as freeing Nadia's speech and placing it side by side with that of the author, as two voices singing in unison with the narrator.

The voices of Oz and his characters meet not only in moments of indirect speech. The narration in *The Same Sea* is unusual in its ability to create hybrid voices and fluidity between souls and minds: all the characters know everything about each other (they are all omnipresent). It is a "world of full transparency" to use Oz's own words, where everyone is naked. In interviews about the book Oz often referred to it as "an orgy":

> Ideally, those people in *The Same Sea* are not only in the same room together all the time even when they are far away, they are in the same bed together most of the time in their minds. So I haven't written a novel, I wrote an orgy. But it is set in a way that should remind us all that even on the slopes of an erupting volcano, there still may be everyday life. There still may be desire and loneliness and longing and death and desolation.[27]

In many of the prose poems in the novel, the lyrical storyteller enters the story, "joins the orgy," and interacts with the characters directly. On the one hand, the author is the collective (the sum of all the voices in the book; they all exist together in his mind), but on the other, he is also a voice within the collective. This creates a complex shift between the "I" and the "we" of the novel. The narrator "drops in" for half a glass of wine with his character Albert or gets a phone call from Bettine, another character. In the prose poem "Magnificat," for example, the writer takes his characters outside to the garden: "delightedly leaving the desk and going off to work in the garden, although it is not even six, the fictional Narrator, the whole/cast of characters, the implied author, the early-rising writer, and I." In the garden, they meet Oz's daughter Fania, his son, his grandchildren, and his wife, who calls them back in for a snack. The lines between the biographical and the fictional self are erased, but the lyrical balancing between the biographical and abstractions is carefully preserved. "Magnificat" is followed by the prose poem "Where Am I?," in which the narrator refers to Oz in the third person, speaking about his process of writing but also about being a writer in general, about being absent and present, about creating and erasing. The biographical shifts into the abstract notion of writing:

> Why do we never see you anywhere, they say to him, why
>
> do you bury yourself in that hole, they say, far away from your friends,
>
> with no parties, no nights out, no fun, you ought to get out,
>
> see people, clock in, show your face, at least give some signs
>
> of life. Forget it, he says to them, I get up at five o'clock have a coffee
>
> and by the time I have erased and written six or seven lines
>
> the day's already over and evening is falling to erase (*The Same Sea*, 149).

The prosaic and minor conversation between the author and the "they" (friends? colleagues? family?) becomes universal. In the poetic form, it is no longer merely a scene in the middle of a story but a reflection on the title "Where Am I?" (where is the fictional narrator, the implied author, the real author) and on "what is writing?" In "Adagio" we move fully to a lyrical abstraction and get to "pick," or "overhear," the poet's/narrator's intimate conversation with himself:

Night after night

the wind whirls and blows over forests and hills. It whirls

continually. And blows. Not thinking and not appealing.

Only you, dust and humors, all night long you write

and erase, looking for a reason, a way to correct. (*The Same Sea*, 162)

It is thought that Oz finds his harmonious I-We, this balance between intimacy and abstraction, through the poetic-prosaic "lovemaking" between the characters and the writer, between the external world and the internal world. It is through this kind of writing that he can finally feel compassion and empathy even toward the "villain" of the story, and it is in this space of I-We that Oz feels comfortable, for the first time, in writing directly about his most intimate pains and memories: the struggle with his mother's death, the difficulties of being "an outsider" in the kibbutz, and much more.[28] For the first time in his long career as a writer, Oz focused both on creating a fictional world and on telling his own story. From this place, the distance was not far to writing a memoir in which he was able to bring the people who populated his childhood to his desk and to write, with them, *A Tale of Love and Darkness*.

Oz's new lyrical I-We freed him from the "We" and "Us" of Israel and from the type of first-person plural that was, directly and indirectly, part of all his previous works. Yitzhak La'or argues that in *The Same Sea* Oz's mastery of free indirect speech

allows him to effect a continuous movement between his narrator and his characters. Free indirect speech plays a major role in modern Hebrew prose, partly because it is an aestheticized (civilized, liberal) means of choking off the Other's voice, leaving him or her the right to speak only on the condition that the "I" has the final say. Yet, when Oz [in *The Same Sea*] speaks to himself about himself, for the first time in his long public career, he sounds more sincere than he ever has in an interview or a public discussion. [...] Every personal story was always in a way a story about "us," the Zionist "dream," or the Zionist nightmare.[29]

Oz returned to the Zionist dream in *A Tale of Love and Darkness*, but now he was able to take with him what he learned from the prose poem: the ability to be personal, to speak to himself and about himself, to interact from within with his characters, to be part of a collective in a more harmonious, compassionate, and sincere way. He used all of that not to sing within an existing choir, and not to record the voices of the tribe, but to rewrite the story, to rewrite the past, and to affect how we will remember it in the future. The new personal-collective persona not only expressed Oz's internal state as a writer at this point in his life but also became a very powerful tool for influencing the way the Zionist story can be perceived and remembered with compassion.

The influence of *The Same Sea* on Oz's work goes beyond the writing of the memoir. His 2012 collection of stories *Between Friends* is a lyrical rewriting of his old kibbutz. Literary critics often compared Oz's earlier and later kibbutz stories. I would like to examine this comparison here from the perspective of the fluidity of the I-We or I-Us and as a demonstration of the shift between the first-person plural in Oz's works before and after *The Same Sea.*

First-Person Plural: From Reciting to Reclaiming Narratives

> all night long you write
>
> and erase, looking for a reason, a way to correct.
>
> —Amos Oz, *The Same Sea*, 162

Narrator types are usually divided into the unreliable and the trustworthy, the limited and the omniscient. Accordingly, they are likely to be expressed in the first-person singular or the third person. First-person plural narration in prose is relatively rare. We don't expect a group to tell us a story together in unison. After all, how can a collective tell the same story unless they are reciting a memorized text? "Modern readers," as Laura Miller writes

> find collective first-person narrators unsettling; the contemporary mind keeps searching for the familiarity of an individual point of view, since it seems impossible that a group could think and feel, let alone act, as one. The ancient Greeks believed otherwise. Their drama, which is the root of our novel, emerged from the dithyramb, a hymn to the god Dionysus, originally recited in unison by 50 men, a collective voice that survived in the form of the Greek chorus. You could say that the history of Western literature so far has been a journey from the first-person plural to the first-person singular, the signature voice of our time. The solitary first-person narrator – confessional, idiosyncratic, often unreliable – is the choice of novelists ranging from Vladimir Nabokov to Philip Roth in some of their most celebrated works.[30]

First-person plural narration tends to create an impression of a constructed identity. Brian Richardson finds this form to have great potential for expressing social minds. In his study of the use of "We" and "They" in English literature, Richardson concludes that "the relative rarity of their use heightens their ability to highlight idiosyncratic styles and foreground their difference from the autonomous individual consciousness frequently associated with the rise of the novel in England."[31] "We" narration stands out and calls our attention to the tension between the individual and the community, and between the community and our own values as readers.

A famous and interesting case that is often presented as an example of narrating the social mind is the collective voice of the town of Jefferson in William Faulkner's "A Rose to Emily." Tara Shea Nesbit's list of some of the notable examples of the use of the first-person plural includes the nineteenth-century novella *The Nigger of the Narcissus* by Joseph Conrad, the mid-twentieth-century novel *This Way for the Gas, Ladies and Gentlemen* by Tadeusz Borowski, Jeffrey Eugenides's novel *The Virgin Suicides*, and more recent works such as Joshua Ferris's *Then We Came to an End*, Jon McGregor's *Even the Dogs*, Kate Walbert's *Our Kind*, Julie Otsuka's *The Buddha in the Attic*, Justin Torres's *We the Animals*, and Chang-Rae Lee's *On Such a Full Sea.* In many of the first-person plural novels, as Nesbit writes, the "we" "creates an in-group that pushes against an out-group." In the contemporary first-person plural we also see the rise of new dilemmas such as "how does one create one's self in relation to the groups we are a part of? Where do our loyalties lie? What gets lost, and what is gained by group membership? This sense of social responsibility and selfhood, as well as uncertainty about how to act on such feelings, describes, in part," according to Nesbit, "our contemporary moment."[32]

For Amos Oz, the tensions between belonging and loyalty and between responsibility and ethics were part of his writing from the initial first-person plural stories he published. Oz grew up in an environment with little use of "I statements," especially when it came to the feelings of individuals. He writes in his memoir about

> how hard it was for them—for everyone, not just my parents—to express private feelings. They had no difficulty at all expressing communal feelings—they were emotional people, and they knew how to talk. Oh, how they could talk! They were capable of conversing for hours on end in excited tones about Nietzsche, Stalin, Freud, Jabotinsky, giving it everything they had, shedding tears of pathos, arguing in a singsong, about colonialism, anti-Semitism, justice, the "agrarian question," the "woman question," "art versus life," but the moment they tried to give voice to a private feeling, what came out was something tense, dry, even frightened, the result of generation upon generation of repression and negation. A double negation in fact, two sets of brakes, as bourgeois European manners reinforced the constraints of the religious Jewish community. Virtually everything was "forbidden" or "not done" or "not very nice."

In their private moments they never spoke Hebrew to each other. Perhaps in their most private moments they did not speak at all. They said nothing. Everything was overshadowed by the fear of appearing or sounding ridiculous. (*Tale*, 18–19)

When he was fourteen, Oz moved from his parents' house to a kibbutz. Here, too, individualism was not celebrated. Yael Ne'eman, a contemporary author who wrote about the kibbutz in a book entitled *We Were the Future*, describes her childhood experiences with phrases such as "we dreamed," "we wanted to," "we were afraid," or "we were ill." In an interview, she explained that unlike people who lived outside the kibbutz, she has almost no memory of a moment in which she was alone.[33] According to Ne'eman, it was hard to say "I" in a way that would mean something completely different from "we."

After living in his parents' household, in midcentury Jerusalem, in the socialist environment of the kibbutz, and in the collective atmosphere in Israel at the time, it is not surprising that Oz was reluctant to speak directly about his biographical self. Oz's early stories and novels about the kibbutz are known for their use of the first-person plural. In these books, the first-person plural often serves as the voice of the collective consciousness, especially when it comes to judgments and opinions. "Now we shall reveal a little secret," Oz's narrator tells us in the first pages of his 1966 book *Elsewhere, Perhaps* that contacts have been maintained between Reuven Harish and Mrs. X. "[…] our opinion is that these relations can be read in different ways, from warm affection to cool indifference."[34] Speaking in unison can remind the reader of the voice and role of the Greek chorus in ancient Greek theater. The chorus represented the voice of the social values and expectations, and it commented on the characters' actions during the performance of the plays. In an interview about his book *Elsewhere, Perhaps* Oz said that he "wanted to tell the story of an entire community from the point of view of a Greek chorus. The 'we' of that novel is the voice of the crowd."[35]

Christopher Lehmann-Haupt finds in this kind of narration, not Greek roots, but a Jewish voice:

126   AMOS OZ'S TWO PENS

> What *Elsewhere, Perhaps* eventually reveals is interesting. It is decidedly not what it appears to be at first: a straight-faced slice of kibbutz life told in imitation of the traditional Yiddish narrative voice of the invisible community gossip, who, begging your pardon, knows everything and tells all. No, although the quote by the narrator appears initially to be the genial voice of tradition ("Now let us look toward the fields of crops all around the kibbutz. A heart-warming sight"), it soon becomes apparent that it is kidding us. It knows perfectly well we will scoff at Reuven Harish's verses. For the story it is about to tell is compounded of nothing but ironies.[36]

As Lehmann-Haupt argues here, the values and sentiments that Oz's first-person plural narrator expresses are being mocked and questioned by the author. Oz creates gaps between the voice of the group and the implied judgment of the readers. The ironies and parodies of the chorus are not there to place the narrator outside the group. Thus, Oz does not create an opposition between the individual and the community. He constructs an "I-We" voice that is conflicted and which contains the uneasy feeling of struggling with a group's perspective and values without necessarily stepping outside the group. Irony was, for Oz, a way to create double meanings and signal to the reader that the author does not identify with the speaker and that the "we" narrator is not reliable.

A classic example of this in Oz's early work is the 1963 story "Nomads and Vipers." The story opens with several paragraphs that describe the nomad tribe that moved close to the kibbutz. The nomads are the out-group, the "they," and the members of the kibbutz are the "we" in the story (especially the young members):

> You [the Hebrew text uses the second-person singular here] might imagine that the nomads' incursion enriched our heat-prostrated nights with a dimension of poetry. This may have been the case for some of our unattached girls. But we cannot refrain from mentioning a whole string of prosaic, indeed anesthetic disturbances, such as hoof-and-mouth disease, crop damage, and an epidemic of petty thefts. The hoof-and-mouth disease came out of the desert, carried by their livestock, which had never been subjected to any proper medical inspection. Although we took various early precautions, the virus infected our sheep and cattle. [...] We are not the kind to take such things lying down. We are no believers in forbearance or vegetarianism, this is especially true of our younger men.[37]

The plural form of narration stands out especially when it is juxtaposed to the second-person singular address to the reader. The narrator invites the reader into the group of young men, turning the reader into "one of them" and suggesting that any reasonable person would see things in the same way as the young men of the kibbutz. The narrator is subjecting the reader to "literary" peer pressure, expecting him to be part of the collective view. But Oz discredits his "first-person plural" narrator and works against him/them. The narrator's views are clearly immoral and he loses our trust. At some point, the narration shifts to first-person singular and offers a questionable justification for the violent acts of the kibbutz men against the nomads. After telling us in a plural form about a beating of one of the nomads, the narrator says:

> Decency constrains me not to dwell in detail on certain isolated and exceptional acts of reprisal conducted by some of the youngsters whose patience had expired, such as cattle rustling, stoning a nomad boy. Or beating one of the shepherds senseless. I must state clearly that the shepherd in question had an infuriatingly sly face. [...] A man with such an appearance was capable of anything ("Nomads and Vipers," 23).

The racist descriptions of the nomads, the cruelty of the kibbutz men, and the horrifying justification made by the narrator present an extremely critical picture of the group. Oz went out of his way here to describe the coercive and dangerous power of thinking with and as a group. The descriptions of the nomads are full of fear, contempt, and hate for the Other. There is a clear dissonance between the values that are expressed by the group and the implicit values of the story. To discredit the narration even further, the narrator becomes omnipresent and tells us about an encounter between Ge'ula, his female friend, and one of the nomads, an encounter in which he didn't participate. Thus, while the speaker tries to convince us to identify with the "we" of the group of young men, the author makes sure that we will distance ourselves from their values. At a critical moment in the story, the narrator distinguishes himself from the young men and is reluctant to participate in a revenge attack on the nomads. When the men of the kibbutz discuss the attack, the narrator tells us that he received permission to speak and that he joined the elder members in opposing the "lynch mob." But later, when the young men decide to go on the attack anyway and the narrator decides to join them although he felt that he had no voice: "After a moment's hesitation I rose and followed them. I did not share their views, but I, too [...] had been deprived of the right to speak" (37–38). At this point, the narration turns back to the first-person plural, and the story ends with the following description:

> We were carrying short, thick sticks. Excitement was dilating our pupils. And the blood was drumming in our temples.

> Far away in the darkened orchards stood somber, dust-laden, cypresses swaying to and fro with a gentle religious fervor. She [Ge'ula] felt tired, and that was why she did not come to see us off. But her fingers caressed the dust, and her face was very calm and almost beautiful.

These lines exemplify the complicated narration of the story and the shifts from a limited first-person singular, to the first-person plural, and to an omnipresent "we" that can enter Ge'ula's feelings and thoughts. The narrator here is clearly not the group but the I-We, the individual who defines himself as part of the group, who tries to understand who he is and who others are while thinking of himself and others as part of a joint unit, especially when it comes to the values "we" hold and the stories "we" tell. The focus on an encounter that is hearsay calls into question the ability of a group to tell stories together and warns us against taking actions that are based on the narratives of an "in-group" versus an "out-group."

"Nomads and Vipers" includes anger, violence, and tension not only between "us" and "them" but also between "I" and "we." At the center is the question of ethics: balancing the sense of social responsibility and selfhood without focusing on an individual and without breaking the collective voice.

Oz returned to the kibbutz in *Between Friends* but this time not as a struggle between the individual and a collective notion of the self but in order, possibly, to find a way to "erase and correct," narratives about the place and rewrite them in his new voice. The story "Father" from this collection tells us about Moshe, a Sephardic boy:

> Moshe Yashar was a boarder at our Kibbutz. He was brought to us by a welfare worker: his mother died when he was seven and when his father fell ill. [...] He quickly learned to walk

around barefoot and dress as we did, in shorts and singlet. We signed him up for the art club and the current-events group. [...] But there was always something of an outsider about him: when we went on nocturnal forays to the food storeroom to scavenge treats for a sumptuous midnight feast, he never came with us. After school, when we all went to work and then to our parents' house for the evening, Moshe remained alone in his room, doing homework, or went to the clubhouse where, with his glasses sliding down his nose, he would read all the newspapers from beginning to end (*Between Friends, 60*).

The "we" of the story describes with curiosity Moshe's "different" behaviors and routines. We learn, for example, that he spoke to the girls as if there was "something marvelous about the mere fact that they were girls" (62). The story's "we" watches Moshe with interest and with very little judgment or mocking. The "we" narration seems to be curious about Moshe's ability to be an individual and to think differently. The story includes comments by the older kibbutz members. The older crowd, especially the teacher, take on the role of educating the new Sephardic boy and shaping his identity:

Rivka said, "We have to encourage him to break off contact with them. They will pull him back."

David said, "When we came to this country, we simply left our parents behind. We cut them out of our lives at a stroke and that was that."

[...]

David said: "On the whole, I have a very optimistic view of the Sephardim. We'll have to invest a great deal in them, but the investment will pay off. In another generation or two, they'll be just like us." (63)

While the kibbutz members expected Moshe to become more like them and believed that their own kind of life was ideologically better, they nevertheless viewed the Sephardim with compassion as being from another time and age. There is no malicious or violent pressure, none of the disgust and revulsion expressed in "Nomads and Vipers" when confronted by otherness and no reflection of the frustration and anger experienced by marginalized communities. The kibbutz is not a melting pot but a mold, and its expectations of uniformity are presented here as done with good intentions by people who think in ways that are just not acceptable in today's world.

The story slowly shifts from the collective voice to Moshe's own point of view. We learn about Moshe's reflections on his teacher, on his group, and on socialism. Moshe, we are told, has read Karl Marx, and while he does not challenge his teacher's views about the text, he questions the arguments in his own private moments. He finds the collectiveness described in *We Die Alone* by David Howarth to be a more appealing way to think of the collective and concludes that more affection is needed, and not necessarily more ideology (64–65).

The story also tells us about Moshe's empathy for the chickens:

after all, no two chickens are or ever have been exactly alike. They all look the same to us, but they are actually different from one another the same way people are, since the creation of the world, no two identical creatures have ever been born. Moshe had already decided to become vegetarian one day, maybe even vegan, but he had to postpone his decision because being vegan among the kibbutz boys would not be easy. Even without being vegetarian, he had to work hard day and night to seem like everyone else here. He had to keep his feelings to himself. Pretend (68).

Through Moshe the story places individuality and socialism side by side as two ways of living. When Moshe gets permission to visit his father, the story abandons the first-person plural, and we learn about the trip through an omniscient narrator that follows fully Moshe's point of view. The father does not recognize his son because of his illness but also because Moshe has changed, and the guard at the hospital comments about Moshe's decision to take his hat off. The uniformity requirement is thus presented as the expectation of any community and not only the kibbutz. "Father" then becomes a story of coming of age but not necessarily in the 1950s as much as in our contemporary world, in which stories place at the center questions such as "how does one create one's self in relation to the groups we are a part of? Where do our loyalties lie? What gets lost, and what is gained by group membership?"[38] And is it possible to immerse oneself in a new group? Becoming part of the group of boys from the kibbutz is presented here as a choice. Moshe ponders that choice throughout his trip to his father, thinking, "how good it was to be part of them," and then wondering "would he become one of them someday? He yearned for that day but was afraid of it too, and he also knew in his heart of hearts that it would never come." The story ends with Moshe choosing to be one of them but with the realization that "it would never happen" (83). We are left with the question of why this will not happen. Is it because the group will not accept him as one of their own, or because Moshe is an individual who was and is not shaped by one community and does not think in a collective first-person plural? Whatever the answer might be, the story with its complex narration describes a group mentality and an individual perspective as interwoven.[39]

However, Moshe can be seen as becoming part of this community merely by being included in the collection of stories about a kibbutz. The book as a whole does not reflect the "we" of the kibbutz but tells its stories through lonely individuals and their interactions with each other and with the community. It is a portrayal of how a community is created by individuals whose lives are interwoven. Some of the characters appear in several stories, which turns the book into a hybrid between a short stories collection and a novel. *Between Friends*, as Ben Lawrence argues, "is a series of almost musical set pieces, duets and trios, about relationships that (almost) inevitably go awry."[40] The shifting points of view, the changing narration, and the juxtaposition of individual stories that paint a picture only when they are carefully placed together turn the book into an exploration of community and identity. Oz's stories have some biographical seeds. Oz himself moved to a kibbutz as a teenager and lost his mother. But he shifts the focus in the stories and in the interviews from the biographical to the universal, talking about the book a reflection on the kibbutz, on Israel, and on the human condition and in general.

In its retelling of the collective narrative through marginal, lost, lonely, confused members of the kibbutz, this view stands out from the background of numerous criticisms of the kibbutz and the Zionist project. The narrator's voice is one of reconciliation and acceptance and not of rage. Mistakes are forgiven or at least seen with compassion.

The search for a harmonious individual-collective form and voice is a deep need and desire that underlies Oz's late work. The meeting between lyrical and prosaic narration in *The Same Sea* allowed Oz to find a literary voice that represented his comfort in speaking from the position of a fluid I-Us. To say that Oz shifted from a national voice to an individual one would be to miss seeing the complexities of his use of pronouns from his early work to his last writings. Erasing the boundaries in his later work between storytelling and political perspectives, between speaker and narrator, between fact and fiction, between the lyrical and the prosaic was a powerful new tool employed by Oz to speak about politics and to write his fictional work. As I demonstrated in the first section of this essay, Oz's lectures after the publication of *The Same Sea* often combined arguments and storytelling. The danger in this new kind of writing was that his literature can be viewed as prophetic, and as "a way to correct" the Zionist narrative.

Oz's reconciliation with his own past came at a time when Israel's political system started pushing a new form of localism and nationalism. *A Tale of Love and Darkness* became one of the seminal texts of the post-post-Zionist era. that was comforting and unifying. Unlike the memoir, *Between Friends* deliberately moved away from the writing of "our story." The two pens of Oz joined in a new way, one that is even closer to *The Same Sea* than the memoir was. The political and prophetic pen tries to correct the discourse and make it more empathetic, and the poetic pen tries to get away from the "here and now" and sketch pictures that reflect the human condition. I believe that Oz managed in *Between Friends* to fully erase the artificial division between the collective and the personal, the fictional and the factual, and to sustain a delicate balance between the prosaic and the poetic. This may indeed be one of Oz's greatest achievements in mastering lyrical fluidity and lyrical suspensions in prose.

Notes

1. Laura Marlowe, "Amos Oz: One Pen I Use to Tell Stories, the Other to Tell the Government to Go to Hell," *Irish Times*, June 14, 2014. https://www.irishtimes.com/culture/books/amos-oz-one-pen-i-use-to-tell-stories-the-other-to-tell-the-government-to-go-to-hell-1.1830079. Accessed November 12, 2020.
2. Thomas Lansky, "Amos Oz, Conjurer of the Tribe," *New York Times*, May 19, 1978, https://www.nytimes.com/1978/05/19/archives/publishing-amos-oz-conjurer-of-the-tribe.html?module=inline. Accessed November 12, 2020.
3. On the exceptional popularity of the book see: Schwartz, "Nikhnasta le-armon mekhushaf," 188.
4. Amos Oz in conversation with Bill Thompson for "Eye on Books," 2014.
5. Omer-Sherman, "A Disgrace to the Map of Israel," 99.
6. Lasky, "Amos Oz."
7. It is interesting to compare this with an interview Oz gave in 1993 on the *Charlie Rose* show. Oz then shifted away from seeing himself as the conjurer of the tribe and argues that his fiction is about individuals. When Charlie Rose asked him if he writes about Israel or about specific characters, he said, "Definitely about characters. I am no sociologist. I never attempt to encapsulate the whole country or different sections of the country even though – " Charlie Rose then interrupted Oz and asked, "You're not a voice for your homeland?" To this Oz answered, "Well, I do in my essays. Not necessarily for my homeland. On a lucky day I manage to be a voice for myself and for people who share my views." What remained consistent until the publication of *The Same Sea* is the exclusion of the biographical "I" from the fictional work. See "Prolific Israeli Author Amos Oz Introduces His Latest Book, *Fima*," Charlie Rose interviews Amos Oz, November 23, 1993, https://charlierose.com/videos/28704. Accessed November 12, 2020.
8. Amos Oz, "Israel: A Tale of Love and Darkness," lecture at Stanford University, published on July 11, 2014, https://www.youtube.com/watch?v=aegK_iDp6xs. Accessed November 12, 2020.It is interesting to compare this statement with an interview from 1991 where Oz said, "I write prose. I aim at truth, not facts, and I am old enough to know the difference between

facts and truth." Jay Parini, "The Land of Oz," April 14, 1991, http://movies2.nytimes.com/books/97/10/26/home/oz-land.html. Accessed November 12, 2020.

9. Kaplan, "Amos Oz's 'A Tale of Love and Darkness,'" 120.
10. Ibid.
11. Grumberg, "Of Sons and (M)others," 377.
12. Shapira, "Ha-siper ha-tsiyoni shel Amos Oz," 164.
13. Oz, "Israel: A Tale of Love and Darkness," 33:40.
14. Oz, "Israel: A Tale of Love and Darkness." Regarding personal stories that become political, see, for example, the first 40 min of the lecture.
15. Avirama Golan, "Haim ha-sipur shelo hu ha-sipur shelanu?" [Is His Story Our Story?], *Haaretz*, August 28, 2005, https://www.haaretz.co.il/literature/1.1040323. Accessed November 23, 2020.
16. All quotes from the book will appear in text.
17. The "Us" and "we" of Oz, as I demonstrated at the beginning of the paper, was presented by him and seen by others (especially outside of Israel) as representing the story of Israel. But to clarify, I am not claiming that there is one unified Zionist story. Oz's story reflects what he sees as a collective, as "us." As Uri Margolis writes, "'we' does not designate multiple 'I's, but rather an individual 'we'-sayer, together with one or more co-utterers and/or hearers and/or others, all of whom belong to the reference class of this 'we'." Margolin, "Telling our story," 115.
18. This quotation was used by the publisher in the marketing of the English translation of the book online. See, e.g., https://www.amazon.com/Same-Sea-Amos-Oz/dp/B00A1A7BEM.
19. Interview with Amos Oz, "*One Book: The Same Sea*," February 19, 2019,https://www.ynet.co.il/articles/0,7340,L-5465926,00.html.https://castbox.fm/episode/-ספר-אחד-עמוס-עוז עוז-עמוס-אחד-ספר-id1449284-id130322961?country=us. Accessed November 14, 2020.
20. Ibid.
21. Vendler, *Soul Says*, 1–8.
22. From "Che cos'è la poesia," 223–37.
23. "The lyric poet normally pretends to be talking to himself or to someone else: a spirit of nature, a Muse, a personal friend, a lover, a god, a personified abstraction. [..] The poet, so to speak, turns his back on his listeners." Culler, "Reading Lyric," 99.
24. Interview with Amos Oz, "One Book: The Same Sea."
25. See Shemtov, "Metrical Hybridization."
26. For Oz, characters were extremely important and so was narration. When talking about his writing process, Oz said that he often starts a new book by thinking about a character. He walks "pregnant" with this character for a while, imagining how he or she functions and feels in different daily situations. See interview with Amos Oz, "One Book: The Same Sea."
27. Elizabeth Farnsworth, PBS interview with Amos Oz, "Coping with Conflict: Israeli Author Amos Oz," January 23, 2002, https://www.pbs.org/newshour/show/coping-with-conflict-israeli-author-amos-oz. Accessed November 23, 2020.
28. In one of the prose poems in *The Same Sea* a character by the name of Dita suggests to him: Why don't you try and see it my way for a moment: I'm twenty-six and you'll soon be sixty, a middle-aged orphan who goes knocking on women's doorsand guess what he's come to beg for. The fact that before my parentswere even born your mother called you Amek isn't a life sentence. It'shigh time you gave her the push. Just the way she chucked you. Let herwander round her forests at night without you. Let her find herselfsome other sucker. It's true that it's not easy to ditch your own mother, so whydon't you stick her in some other scene, not in a forest, let's say in a lake:cast her as the Loch Ness monster, which as everyone knows may bedown there or may not exist, but one thing is certain, whatever you see orthink you see on the surface isn't the monster, it's just a hoax or an illusion (134).
29. Yitzhak Laor, "It's Wild. It's New. It Turns Men On," *London Review of Books* 23, no. 18 (September 20, 2001), https://www.lrb.co.uk/v23/n18/contents. Accessed November 23, 2020.

30. Laura Miller, "The Last Word: We the Characters," *New York Times*, April 18, 2004. www.nytimes.com/2004/04/18/books/the-last-word-we-the-characters.html. Accessed November 23, 2020.
31. Richardson, "Representing Social Minds,"212.
32. Tara Shea Nesbit, "We Can Do a Lot: The Rise of First-Person Plural Narration,"*Guardian*, May 14, 2014, https://www.theguardian.com/books/booksblog/2014/may/14/first-personal-plural-narration-novels-stories. Accessed November 23, 2020. On this topic see also: Maxey, "The Rise of the 'We' Narrator in Modern American Fiction."
33. Sifriat Ha-Kore Ha-Ivri, "Reayon im Yael Ne'eman, hayeenu ha-atid, yalduta be-Kibbutz Yehiam,,"November 1, 2016, https://www.hebrewreader.com/ראיון-עם-יעל-נאמן-היינו-העתיד/. Accessed November 23, 2020.
34. Oz, *Elsewhere, Perhaps*, 6.
35. Parini, "Land of Oz."
36. Christopher Lehmann-Haupt, "Books of the Time," *New York Times*, November 14, 1973, http://movies2.nytimes.com/books/97/10/26/home/oz-elsewhere.html. Accessed November 23, 2020.
37. Oz, "Nomad and Vipers," 22.
38. Nesbit, "We Can Do a Lot."
39. I am grateful to Hannah Naveh, who gave a talk on "Father" in my class. I am sure that my own reading was implicitly influenced by her insightful talk.
40. Ben Lawrence, "*Between Friends* by Amos Oz: review," *Telegraph*, April 29, 2013,https://www.telegraph.co.uk/culture/books/10021555/Between-Friends-by-Amos-Oz-review.html. Accessed November 23, 2020.

Disclosure statement

No potential conflict of interest was reported by the author(s).

Bibliography

Derrida, Jacque. "Che cos'è la poesia?" [What is Poetry]. In *A Derrida Reader: Between the Blinds*, edited and translated by Peggy Kamuf. 221–237. New York: Columbia University Press, 1991.
Grumberg, K. "Of Sons and (M)others: The Spectropoetics of Exile in Autobiographical Writing by Amos Oz and Albert Cohen." *Prooftexts* 30, no. 3 (2010): 373–401.
Jonathan, C. "Reading Lyric." *Yale French Studies* 69 (1985): 98–106.
Kaplan, E. "Amos Oz's 'A Tale of Love and Darkness' and the Sabra Myth." *Jewish Social Studies* 14, no. 1 (2007): 119–143.
Margolin, U. "Telling Our Story: On 'We' Literary Narratives." *Language and Literature* 5, no. 2 (1996): 115–133. doi:10.1177/096394709600500203.
Maxey, R. "The Rise of the "We" Narrator in Modern American Fiction." *European Journal of American Studies* 10, no. 2 (2015): 1–15. http://journals.openedition.org/ejas/11068.
Omer-Sherman, R. "A Disgrace to the Map of Israel': The Wilderness Journey of the Citizen-Soldier in Amos Oz's 'A Perfect Peace." *Journal of Modern Literature* 27, no. 3 (2004): 97–114.

Oz, A. *Elsewhere, Perhaps. Translated by Nicholas De Lange.* Boston and New York: Mariner Books, 1986.

Oz, A. *The Same Sea. Translated by Nicholas De Lange.* Orlando: Harcourt, 2002.

Oz, A. *A Tale of Love and Darkness. Translated by Nicholas De Lange.* Orlando: Harcourt, 2004.

Oz, A. "Nomad and Vipers." In *Where the Jackals Howl and Other Stories*, edited by N. de Lange, 20–38. Boston and New York: Mariner Books, 2012.

Oz, A. *Between Friends. Translated by Sondra Silverston.* Boston: Houghton Mifflin Harcourt, 2013.

Richardson, B. "Representing Social Minds: 'We' and 'They' Narratives, Natural and Unnatural." *Narrative* 23, no. 2 (2015): 200–212. doi:10.1353/nar.2015.0008.

Schwartz, Y. "Nikhnasta le-armon mekhushaf ve-shihrartah oto me-ha-kishuf: Al sipur al ahavah ve-hoshekh ke-sefer pulhan." [You've Entered an Enchanted Castle and You've Freed It from Its Spell: On A Tale of Love and Darkness as A Cult Book]. *Israel* 7 (2005): 173–209.

Shapira, A. "Ha-siper ha-tsiyoni shel Amos Oz." *Israel* 7 (2005): 163–171.

Shemtov, V. K. "Metrical Hybridization: Prosodic Ambiguities as a Form of Social Dialogue." *Poetics Today* 22, no. 1 (2001): 65–87.

Vendler, H. *Soul Says: On Recent Poetry.* Cambridge: Belknap Press, 1995.

"Like a cow that gave birth to a seagull": Amos Oz, Yoel Hoffmann and the birth of *The Same Sea*

Neta Stahl

ABSTRACT

This article examines Oz's novel *The Same Sea* (1999) and argues that it marks the novelist's attempt to join a new phase in Israeli literature. Comparing *The Same Sea* to two novels by Yoel Hoffmann, one of the most famous representatives of this phase, the article sheds light on Oz's struggle to balance between the writing norms that helped establish his status as "the shaman of the tribe" and the new norms, associated with Israeli postmodernism.

Introduction

In his last radio interview, Amos Oz likened himself to "a cow that gave birth to a seagull," the "seagull" being his novel *Oto ha-yam* [*The Same Sea*, 1999].[1] Twenty years after the publication of *The Same Sea* and a few months before his death, he echoed a sentiment shared by many readers, critics, and scholars. *The Same Sea* was not only strikingly different from Oz's previous novels; it is also patently different from the novels that followed it. The last fact is surprising especially given Oz's disclosure in his last interview that *The Same Sea* is his favorite amongst his works and the only one which he likes to re-read.[2] This article will try to explain this conundrum: what brought Oz to write a novel that he himself viewed as an anomaly, and if he liked it so much, why was it such a singular episode in his long and successful literary career?[3] In other words, how come it did not mark a turn in his path as an author? I am going to show that at least part of the answer can be found in Oz's metaphor of a cow that gave birth to a seagull, although I would argue that it is only in retrospect that Oz looked at his novel in such terms.

The distinctiveness of the novel can be noticed already in its appearance. The novel's lines are short and appear in a format similar to that of poetry, divided into short sections that are each titled and not clearly connected to the following section. Many of the sections are versed or even rhymed, at times sporadically and at times throughout the entire section. The fully rhymed sections appear in symmetric stanzas and resemble a typical poem. The narrative of the novel is not easy to follow. Its temporality is non-linear and it moves back and forth between different times, locations, characters, and streams of consciousness. There are also seemingly fantastical episodes, including conversations between the author and his characters who comment on the author's work and publicist articles.

For anyone who is familiar with Oz's novels, the description above might sound surprising. Indeed, as Nurith Gertz shows in her 1980 monograph on Oz, he was always looking for what Gertz calls "compromise formulas" (nus'haot pesharah) between new literary norms and the literary and political systems in Israel which are more conservative in nature. According to Gertz, Oz's prose "combined new and old norms and this is how it reduced the sharpness of the literary rebellion" that he and his peers were leading.[4] This middle-of-the -road approach, or double stance, in Gertz's words, was also crucial to Oz's attempt to appeal both to a general audience[5] and to the academic milieu.[6] Gertz designates a few such compromise formulas, but for our discussion, the most important is the one that attempts to avoid a complete break with the realism of the earlier literary generation, known as "The Palmach generation," by using symbolism that maintains the lines of reality but subordinates them to abstractions.[7] In the 1970s, the symbolism of Oz (and A.B. Yehoshua) was criticized in the name of a new realistic norm that prioritized detailed descriptions of reality over symbolic abstractions.[8] Oz's language soon adjusted to the new literary norm that called for the language of the novelist to realistically reflect the way his characters speak. Yet, even here, according to Gertz, Oz first kept with the two conflicting norms at the same time; higher, archaic language was used for thoughts and dreams and everyday spoken Hebrew was used for conversations among the characters. He later fully shifted to the new norm of spoken language and this norm has mainly dominated his prose ever since.[9]

In his book *Pulhan ha-sofer ve-dat ha-medina* (2011), Yigal Schwartz argues that in order for an author to play a certain role in the literary-cultural scene of his era, he needs to join in a certain way to a complex of contents and forms relevant to the expectations of his readers. This "joining" is done, according to Schwartz, with the intention of the author.[10] Schwartz asserts that in the case of Oz, the wish – even the sense of mission – to function as the "shaman of the tribe" (mekhashef ha-shevet)[11] had to be grounded in the habitat of his work. He had to join the mainstream of modern Hebrew literature and to mark a new junction, his junction.[12]

Indeed, Oz clearly did exactly that when he first joined the Israeli cultural and literary scene in his early twenties and as Gertz showed adapted his writing, with a clear sense of awareness, to the new literary norm that called for realism, a norm which emerged from academia. In this article I argue that *The Same Sea* should be understood as Oz's attempt to "join in" again, this time to a literary and cultural scene that in the late 1990s was already at its next juncture, to continue Schwartz's metaphor, a juncture that many viewed as a sort of rebellion against the realism of Oz and his generation. In the late 1980s, a set of new literary norms emerged in the Israeli academic and cultural discourse, and *The Same Sea*, I would argue, should be understood as Oz's reaction to these new norms.

One of the most prominent representatives, of these new norms is the author and professor of Japanese philosophy and literature, Yoel Hoffmann (1937-). Despite their closeness in age and other biographical similarities (both lost their mother in their childhoods; both spent part of their childhood away from their family, Oz in a kibbutz and Hoffmann in an orphanage; both were university professors and chose to settle in a peripheral part of Israel, Oz in Arad and Hoffmann in Ma'alot), in terms of public persona the two writers could not be farther apart. Oz was a public figure, speaking and writing in various media and always welcoming the opportunity to discuss his literary work as well as his political views. He saw himself as having a public role, not as a politician but as a sort of a moral leader. Hoffmann, on the other hand, has been avoiding public exposure almost religiously. He refuses to grant interviews of any kind and does not give public lectures.[13] It is no wonder that there are only a handful of photos of him available in the public domain. Unlike Oz, he remains an enigma, sharing biographical anecdotes in his novels while blocking any attempt to access the novelist behind them.[14]

It is therefore quite surprising to find some clear similarities between Oz's *The Same Sea* and Hoffmann's first two novels, *Bernhard* (1989) and *Christus shel dagim* (*The Christ of Fish*, 1991). In what follows, I will argue that these similarities in plotlines, style, and structure can help us understand Oz's (temporary) break with realism. Moreover, a comparison between the works also sheds light on the differences between them, and these differences will help us understand the ways in which Oz attempted to join the new phase in Israeli culture, a phase that is often referred to as "Israeli postmodernism."

Between the postmodernist and the "shaman of the tribe"

The term "postmodernism" refers to an intellectual mode of discourse across various fields[15] that emerged in the middle of the twentieth century and evolved throughout its second half.[16] In an attempt to characterize this mode, the Egyptian-American scholar Ihab Hassan used the term "indeterminacy" which in literature, according to Hassan, means questioning "our ideas of author, audience, reading, writing, book, genre, critical theory, and of literature itself."[17] Hassan's 1971 attempt to define postmodernism aimed at understanding it as a departure from modernism and at the same time to define it on its own terms, using its many and sometimes contradicting characteristics. When, more than a decade later, writers such as Yoel Hoffmann, Orly Castel-Bloom, David Grossman, Meir Shalev, Itamar Levy, and Ronit Matalon published their first works, their prose-fiction was met with a similar sense of a new era but one that would not easily lend itself to traditional categorization. In the early 1990s, the term "postmodernism" was used in reference to these writers and they were hailed as demarcating a new phase in the history of Israeli literature.[18]

Indeed, the appearance of Hoffmann's *Bernhard* and *The Christ of Fish* was celebrated in the Israeli literary scene as the beginning of a new era. Gershon Shaked described Hoffmann as "quintessentially postmodernist," an author whose novels' structure is fragmentary in the extreme, creating the sense that "something is being suppressed or left unsaid or otherwise cannot be rendered articulate."[19] Shaked argues that in his novels Hoffmann no longer depends on the thematic or stylistic conventions of the 1960s and that *The Christ of Fish* represents a wholly new departure in Hebrew fiction.[20] Shaked designates this departure as a "revolution in form"[21] as well as an intellectual challenge to readers due to its allusiveness.[22] Similarly, Nili Gold, in her article on Hoffmann's first novel, *Bernhard*, argues that Hoffmann, who came from the academic world, brought with him an innovative postmodernistic voice, previously unfamiliar to the Israeli reader. Gold explains that Hoffmann offered not only a revolution in form and genre but also "a demand for reflection that blends Far-Eastern with Western philosophy, minimalist aesthetics with uncontrolled imagination, 'tender murmurings of heart' with rationalism, educated awareness with mystical trance."[23] In a 1995 article Schwartz designates Hoffmann as the most extreme and subversive among the generation of writers that Schwartz calls "the generation after"; the "before" being the "state generation."[24] Avraham Balaban called this group of writers "the other wave" (ha-gal ha-aher),[25] following Shaked's title of a book on the writers of the 1950s-1960s, *A New Wave in Hebrew Prose* (1974).[26]

Clearly, what stands out in the attempts to characterize Hoffmann's first two novels is the view that they open a new era in Israeli literature,[27] pushing aside the kind of novels and novelists that dominated it in the previous decades. Oz and A.B. Yehoshua are the best-known novelists among the writers of the previous decades, and together they often stand as representatives of the literature that the "other wave," or the postmodernist novelists, wrote against. Indeed, in a chapter on postmodernism in Israeli literature, David Gurevitz chooses the works of Oz and Hoffmann to demonstrate the differences between the modern and the postmodern Israeli novel.[28]

It is no wonder, then, that when *The Same Sea* was published, it was received with great surprise. Avner Holtzman was probably the first to review the book, and indeed he described it as "a great and exciting surprise," arguing that in the last years prior to the appearance of *The Same Sea*, Oz's novels seemed to lose energy and that the new novel represents a shift from a sort of a deadend that he has reached in his writing.[29] Other scholars described the novel as marking Oz's turn to postmodernism. For example, Talia Horwitz, in an article from 1999, and Chaya Schacham, in a chapter from her 2004 book, identify the novel as postmodernist in nature. Horwitz details the postmodernist features of the novel: its mixing of genres; meta-poetic orientation; return to the past as a source of inspiration; discourse between the reader, the author, and character; featuring an open ending; and the blending of imagination and reality.[30] Shacham sees in the novel a clear embrace of the postmodernist spirit in its total fragmentism, the nonhierarchical order of sections with different generic natures (sometimes even within one section), the nonhierarchical voices, the blurring of the boundaries between the real and the imagined, the use of bricolage by mixing various linguistic styles from different periods and social class regiments, the exposure of the mechanism of writing, an open ending and a rich intertextuality. In the second part of her chapter, Schacham maps and analyzes the various allusions and intertextual references in *The Same Sea*.[31] Ruth Kartun-Blum likens the novel to "poetry at its best" and attributes this quality to the language, the musicality and the general effect of the words.[32] Like Horwitz and Schacham, Kartun-Blum finds in the novel rich intertextual relations, and she defines it as a variation on the Menippean satire in its collagist nature that mixes genres and forms of speech. The adoption of the Menippean genre allows Oz, according to Kartun-Blum, to connect to the past and at the same time to write a new and surprisingly contemporary novel that breaks the lines between various genres, between history and imagination, the distant and the nearby, the serious and the amusing.[33]

Scholars then found in Oz's *The Same Sea* similar features to the ones they found in Hoffmann's work, not only insofar as the novel was categorized as postmodernist, but also in its resemblance to poetry, its musicality, and even some of its specific allusions, such as the allusion to New Testament characters. All were found in Hoffmann's first two novels, the first of which was published ten years before Oz's *The Same Sea*. As in the case of Hoffmann, scholars found autobiographical aspects in Oz's novel and some connected them to the choice to write in a prose-poetry format and style.[34]

The fact that Oz's poetic-prose work was celebrated as a postmodernistic novel is not surprising, of course, but what might surprise us is that none of these scholars mentioned the similarity to Hoffmann's work. This is all the more surprising given the fact that by the time *The Same Sea* was published, Hoffmann had already published four novels in the poetic-prose mode, distinguishing himself not only from the previous generation of writers but also from his fellow postmodernist novelists, none of whom wrote in such a unique format.

The Same Sea and Hoffmann's novels share a similar format of unconnected fragments and short sections, each of which can be read individually. In both cases, the authors often pay close attention to the musicality of their text, to its rhythm and style, and this attention dictates, in turn, similar attention on the part of the readers. Importantly, in both Hoffmann's novels and The Same Sea, metonymic and metaphoric depictions dominate the texts and the norms of linear plot are broken in favor of a more seemingly sporadic, sometimes associative order of narration. Both authors tend to expose the process of writing and to pose as sharing their deliberations about plotlines with the readers. They even use a similar metaphor for the act of narration, borrowed from the visual arts: Hoffmann refers to it as drawing while Oz in The Same Sea describes it in terms of embroidering. Thus, at the end of a fragment titled "Synopsis" in which he indeed summarizes the main plots of the novel, Oz writes:

> This embroider resembles the pattern in the curtain at the Greek necromancer's, who died and left in his place a crow-woman. She has no living soul and her embroider gives a foretaste of the worm. And so a certain shadow falls over this story too.[35]

And Hoffmann writes in The Christ of Fish:

> When you think of Frau Stier you must
> draw a picture that is both careful and
> crude at one and the same time (like a
> Chinese drawing. Not a line too many).[36]

For both, then, the story is compared to a delicate craft. Surprisingly, there are even similarities in terms of themes. Hoffmann in Bernhard, and Oz in The Same Sea, place at the center of the novel an aged man whose wife recently died, and both novels follow the attempts of the new widower to adjust to his new reality.

In the novel Bernhard, the protagonist, Bernhard, is a German immigrant in mandatory Palestine whose wife, Paula, died shortly after they arrived in the new land. The novel is divided into numbered fragments which appear in seemingly arbitrary order, each on a different page, and in which the only connection between one fragment to the next is an isolated line that appears at the bottom of each page and is also the first line in the following fragment. Bernhard's story is told, then, in a non-linear and fragmented way, and the narrative itself is mostly combined of Bernhard's thoughts and daily routine which includes encounters with other characters; his friends Gustav, Herzog, and Elvira; and his memories of his wife, his childhood, and in particular his parents. In the background of this narrative there is an additional historical narrative that takes place in Europe and is mostly represented by the news report of Hitler's military advances in Europe.

The Same Sea tells the story of Albert Danon, whose wife, Nadia, died recently, and whose son, Rico, is leaving him for a long trip to Tibet. Albert finds some sort of comfort in the company of his son's wife, Dita, to whom he is shamefully and secretly attracted while leading an affair with a woman his age, named Bettine. Meanwhile, Dita is hoping to sell a script that she wrote to a producer named Dubi Dumbrov who tries to manipulate her into handing him all of her money and at the same time falls in love with the protagonist of her script. Dita also has a sexual relationship with Gigi Ben Gal. Albert's dead wife accompanies both Albert's and Rico's thoughts, and the story of her childhood, first marriage, and death is told as well. Additional characters are Miriam, a prostitute whom Rico meets in his trip, and the carpenter who made the author's desk, the same desk that serves the author, namely Oz himself, when he is writing the novel. Oz also integrates into his novel the story of his parents, reflections on his early steps in writing poetry, and the description of his daily work on the novel in his home in Arad.[37]

As one can see from the above descriptions, both novels, despite their seemingly non-hierarchical plot, do have one central leading theme, which is the death of a wife. In the case of *The Same Sea*, this loss is paralleled and at times countered by Rico's struggle with his own sense of loss. This sense of orphan-hood stands at the center of *The Christ of Fish* (as well as Hoffmann's novella "Katchen"), which is narrated in the first person by the now-adult man who lost his mother at birth, his father dying a few years later. The boy's caregiver is his aunt and her friends, all of whom are old immigrants from central Europe. *The Christ of Fish* describes the daily routine of the characters that surround the narrator, as he recalls them from his memory, leading to his reflections on memory, its representation, and the sense of loss it brings. The overarching theme of Oz's *The Same Sea* and Hoffmann's first two novels is, then, loss and, accordingly, memory and the passing of time.

For the sake of comparison, let us look at how the two novelists describe each of their respective protagonist's thoughts about the death of his wife. Here is a fragment from Hoffmann's *Bernhard*:

> When Bernhard opens his eyes and
> Sees a strange ceiling, he remembers Paula's death.
> Because of the daylight it seems to him for a mo
> ment that Paula is where she is ought to be. But when
> he sees her in his mind's eye (he thinks: "Earth fills
> her mouth"), his heart is fit to break. He looks at his
> face in the mirror and thinks: "Everything happens
> but once. And this moment too (Paula is dead and
> Bernhard, in his pajamas, on Prophets Street) will
> not come again." He tries to picture to himself a
> world without Bernhard, but always finds himself
> hiding near the edge of the picture. Visions of the
> world, Bernhard thinks, are only visions in my
> mind.[38]

And here is a similar situation in Oz's *The Same Sea*:

> Albert in the night
> on the roof her shadow, a slow shadow,
> a shadow that is gradually leaving me.
> Indoors it is bad. Outside
> it is dark. The bedroom at night
> feels lower.[39]

Both widowers are depicted lying on their back in their bedroom looking up, one in the night looking at the ceiling and the other in the morning looking at the roof. For each, the situation is a reminder of his dead wife and her absence. The bedroom setting serves in the novels as a metonymy for the inner world of their protagonists. The visual reflections – Bernard's face in the mirror in Hoffmann's case and the shadows in the bedroom in Oz's – are metaphors for the ghost-like memory of the dead wife, representing the widower's own self-reflection. The process of coming to terms with the wife's death is thus depicted in both scenes as involving questions about the gap between her actual departure from the world and the sense of her presence in the room, which represents her presence in the mind of the mourning husband.

However, we can also detect some clear differences between the two scenes: Oz's symmetric rhyming (which is not directly reflected in the translation) and his short sentences, which include short, matter-of-fact observations, are meant to depict the raw, almost childish state of mind of his protagonist. Hoffmann gives the reader a deeper sense of Bernhard's thoughts. This difference is also indicative of the different characters that the two authors depict. Hoffmann's Bernhard is an intellectual, whose thoughts about his own loss take him toward the metaphysical. For Oz, similar spatial metaphors serve to depict a much more simple-minded protagonist. The two characters share perhaps a similar loss, and both are agonizing over it, but their ways of grieving are very different.

This difference between the two protagonists mirrors a wider difference between the two novels. While Hoffmann's novel aims at the metaphysical, Oz's novel gives the impression that despite the sad reality it depicts, it is also meant to entertain its readers, even to charm them. This wider difference suggests that Oz, in his attempt to shift to a new set of norms, chose to apply once again what Gertz called in her 1980 monograph "compromise formulas."

As in the 1970s, here, too, it seems that Oz was careful to embrace the new and elitist norms of the academic and literary circles, while at the same time aiming to maintain his wider, more general readership. While he writes a unique novel in terms of format and narration, his characters are simple, everyday people. As Holtzman pointed out, the plot itself, though rich with characters and plotlines, is not complicated or hard to follow.[40] Unlike in Hoffmann's novel, in Oz's narrative there is a lot of action that occurs outside of the characters' minds, as is evident from the above summary of each novel's plot. Indeed, when Oz was asked what the novel is about, his answer was that it is about life and death, love and desire, about people and what they want.[41] The last words are in fact a quotation from Nathan Zach's poem "An Opening For a Poem" from 1966.[42] We can see in the fact that Oz quotes Zach when he describes his novel another indication that the topic of Oz's new novel remains in line with the literary norms that the two introduced in the 1960s and 1970s. Zach led a parallel revolt against the older generation style, albeit in poetry, and Oz's quotation indicates that he still holds on to the literary norms that both he and Zach held decades before he wrote *The Same Sea*.

If we get back to the difference in the poetics of Oz and Hoffmann, we will notice that even when compared to Hoffmann's less philosophically oriented and more poetically tightened novel, *The Christ of Fish*, *The Same Sea* is more symmetric in its rhyming and rhythm. It is also easier to access in terms of its narrative. For example, both novelists integrate into their narrative catalog-like lists, a technique that is associated with the post modernistic norm of a nonhierarchical, collagist depiction of reality. However, they apply this norm in very different ways. Here is how it appears in fragment 49 of *The Christ of Fish*:

> . . . all the things that the heart forgets:
> seaweed, for instance, on the shore
> at Tel Aviv. Baklava. The Book
> of Nehemiah. Stomach Juices. In ver
> ted commas. Buckles. Cooking recipes.
> Flickering lights. Parcelation maps.

Panes of glass. Bicycle tires. A
Drawing of an arrow and two hearts (or
Of two arrows and a heart) and names
like: "Kurt".

And here is an example from *The Same Sea*:

Rico David was always reading. He thought the world
was in a bad way. The shelves are covered with piles of his books,
pamphlets, paper, publications, on all sorts
of wrongs: black studies, women's studies,
lesbians and gays, child abuse, drugs, race,
rain forests, the hole in the ozone layer, not to mention injustice
in the Middle East.[43]

The two lists have very different goals: Oz's is meant to give us a sense of Rico's interests and to portray him, perhaps with a humoristic, even ridiculing tone, as an Israeli liberal leftist young man. Hoffmann, on the other hand, uses a list of materialistic objects to depict the abstract and mysterious nature of memory. It is of course paradoxical in nature, as it includes under the category of things that the "heart forgets" objects that the narrator in fact remembers, or at least recalls when he lists them. Hoffmann's list is indeed a collage: placing together objects that normally have nothing in common and do not seem to be naturally associated with one another. Oz's list, by contrast, is very predictable and intentionally so: it is meant to portray a typical, even stereotypical character. The list in Oz's case serves as a code familiar to both the readers and the author and in a sense functions as a signal to the readers, that the author knows that they know what he is talking about.

The readers of Hoffmann's work rarely experience such a sense of familiarity with his characters. The author, who was born in Romania to a family with a strong affinity to Austro-Hungarian culture, often tells the story of new immigrants and his characters reside in the periphery of Israeli society and, in some cases, outside of Israel altogether. Such is the case of Yosef, who escapes from Poland to Germany after his wife was murdered in a pogrom. His life with his young son in the days leading up to their murder by a young Nazi is depicted in Hoffmann's early novella "The Book of Josef" (Sefer Yosef, 1989). Yosef and his son, Yingale, are remote from the life and culture of Hoffmann's readers, a distance that is reflected not only in the narrative but also in the fact that Hoffmann integrates their Yiddish language in the Hebrew text, placing at the side of the page a translation into Hebrew of the words that he is well aware most of his readers are not familiar with. In both *Bernhard* and *The Christ of Fish* he uses the same technique, and there too the protagonists are all but typical Israeli characters. New immigrants from central Europe, they still speak in their European languages and maintain the cultural and intellectual lives that they brought with them to Palestine, rarely attempting to integrate into the Zionist society. This choice often reflects Hoffmann's critique of the Zionist culture, that Oz, despite his critique, took part in constructing. In *The Same Sea*, Oz chooses to tell the story of people who live in the outskirts of this culture, but when depicting himself – the real-life author – his admiration of the land and the Zionist ideal of "making the desert bloom" are echoed in the long descriptions of the early mornings in his town of Arad, where the author celebrates his deep connection to the land by staring at the desert or toiling in his garden.[44]

Similarly, Hoffmann and Oz employ a wide net of allusions that aims at what we can call "high culture": Classical music, Biblical and New Testament figures and themes and various poets and prose writers. However, most of Oz's allusions are to texts and figures that many of his readers would easily recognize, such as the frequent allusions to King David, The Song of Songs, and Ecclesiastes. As many scholars have noticed, he often alludes to famous Hebrew poets, the most dominant among them being Nathan Alterman, whose "A Summer Festivity" (Hagigat Kayitz) is one of the main intertexts in the novel.[45] Hoffmann on the other hand often alludes to figures and texts with which, as Shaked notes, most of his Israeli readers are not familiar.[46]

The two authors also integrate allusions into their novels in different ways. Hoffmann often centers a great deal of his text around a specific allusion and a familiarity with the text or figure that the allusion targets is required to make sense of his narrative. Oz integrates the allusions into the text in a way that makes their identification and location not essential to the reading, as Nicholas de Lange, the English translator of the novel, notes.[47] In this way, Oz can write his novel for two different audiences: the intellectual and the nonintellectual; each group can find in the text what it is looking for.

This leads me to what is perhaps the main difference between Hoffmann's novels and Oz's *The Same Sea*. In a chapter on *The Christ of Fish* in my monograph on Hoffmann, I argue that Hoffmann introduces a new and innovative model of a novel, one that challenges the norms of the realistic novel and exposes its limitations.[48] One central norm that Hoffmann breaks with in his works is the norm of causality. In *The Christ of Fish* we can see this on almost every level of the text: in the plot, the connection between the numbered fragments, and even sometimes within a single sentence. Hoffmann frustrates his readers' expectations regarding causality as the main mechanism in the reading process. Here is a typical example: "Although my uncle, Herbert Hirsch, played the harpsichord, the ship on which he sailed for Palestine ran aground."[49] The word "although" creates an expectation for a certain relation between the two parts of the sentence, but instead, the reader is left to wonder how the fact that Uncle Hirsch played the harpsichord is connected to the fact that the ship on which he sailed to Palestine ran aground. Either some law in the world of the novel, unlike a law of nature, dictates that playing music is expected to save the ship from foundering, or the author simply intended to have the reader question the rules of language itself. Either way, the result is a plot that is almost impossible to reconstruct, and the sense is that Hoffmann does not tell a story but rather investigates the nature of a story, and more specifically, the nature of the realistic novel.

Oz too, as mentioned above, does not provide his readers with a novel that is easy to read. He introduces multiple characters and plot-lines, various narrators whose identity is not always clearly exposed, a nonlinear connection between one section and another, and at times a metaphoric and metonymic language that blurs the causal relations between sentences within one section.[50] However, unlike Hoffmann, he compensates for these difficulties by not leaving unexplained almost any gap in terms of the plot, and almost anything mentioned has a reason for its being so. In other words, the causality of his various stories and their linearity, and in particular the motivations of his characters and even of the author himself, are exposed. As the author-narrator says to himself in one of the repeated episodes which depict the process of writing the novel: "Only you, dust and humors, all night long you write and erase, looking for a reason, a way to correct."[51] Concerning this desire of the author to provide an explanation, a reason is suggested in Oz's explanation in his last interview mentioned above, that "there is in this book a complete transparency."[52] This attempt to be transparent in a novel that has so many characters and plotlines is conveyed by the exposure of the process of writing. The author reflects, wonders, and then provides the reader with reasoning regarding all the characters, even the ones that seem marginal such as Dita's lover, Gigi Ben Gal, or Dubi Dumbrov, the producer who is interested in Dita's script. All these characters receive an explanation and even justification for their actions. Often this explanation occurs in the form of a meeting with the author himself. The author goes as far as to share with the readers his wondering about the fate of Nadia's first husband. This almost obsessive attempt to provide information about almost every character that is mentioned in the novel can be explained by the very same desire to explore the new norms of writing and at the same time to keep the old ones. The postmodernist norm of nonhierarchical text, which is often reflected in the absence of selectivity in the details given to the readers, dictates the plurality of characters and the attention given to all of them. At the same time, a full and detailed presentation of reality, which provides reasoning and justification for the reality that it represents, is an important characteristic of realism in general and of Oz's realism in particular.

However, there is one character in the novel whose action remains a riddle, and the author is bothered by his inability to provide a reasoning or an answer for his action. This is Elimeleh, the carpenter who commits suicide, leaving his family and the author to wonder why. The relatively longer section that deals with his story is titled "The riddle of the good carpenter who had a deep bass voice." Here, in a relatively long section and in a format of long lines typical to prose, the narrator abandons his poetic style, and his first-person narration may remind the readers of Oz's earlier (and future) style. The title of the section seems at first to refer to Elimeleh's deep bass voice that came "from a chest of modest dimensions" or to the fact that "the man was a total addict" to opera.[53] These riddles are of course only a diversion from what really bothers the author, who transitions to the voices of the carpenter's wife and daughters, whose "grief had been displaced by surprise."[54] The fact that "there was no reason" for Elimeleh's act and that there were no warning signs or note left, leave the family with many questions, and this time neither the narrator nor Oz have answers. This episode is told as an event that takes place outside of the novel, in Arad when the author visits the family during the *Shiva*. But Oz, as he does a few times throughout the novel, blends the real and the imagined. Here he does it only at the end of the section when Elimeleh's wife sends her regards to Albert, the fictional character from the novel that the author is busy writing (although the author mentions that Elimeleh died "nine years ago").[55] This addition conflicts with the realistic tone of the episode, but the latter still dominates the general impression that this one story is a real-life event that indeed happened to the real-life author.

The reality of the story of the suicide might also be more convincing than many other stories in the novel because of Oz's own biography and the fact that his mother committed suicide, leaving no note or obvious reason for her act. Years later, Oz will get back to this painful memory in his semi-autobiographic novel *A Tale of Love and Darkness*, but as previous scholars have noted, already in *The Same Sea* he integrates not only autobiographical details, but some painful memories about his parents and their relationship,[56] perhaps in an attempt to find an answer to his mother's suicide.[57] For the memories too he is eager to find reasons and provide answers. Thus, placing those real and painful memories in the imagined story, he locates them in the realm of the imagined, only to pull them back to the real by the force of, perhaps desire for or even faith in, causality.

It is this faith in causality and subsequently in realism that stands as one of the core differences between Oz and Hoffmann. In an article that appeared shortly after the publication of *The Christ of Fish*, Anat Waxman argued that Hoffmann's works present a reckoning with realism as a genre. This is how Waxman explained *The Christ of Fish*'s fragmentary nature and what she called its "playfulness."[58] I suggest that Hoffmann not only criticizes the tradition of realism, but that in *The Christ of Fish* he counters the realistic novel as a genre by presenting an alternative option.

Oz, as one of the main representatives of this genre, wrote a novel that indeed aimed at breaking with realism while, at the same time, he still believed in its power. Hoffmann mocks the realistic tendency to provide a detailed description of reality. For example, in *The Christ of Fish* he ridicules the note that his third-grade teacher wrote on his composition titled "What I saw in the market." The teacher wrote at the bottom of his assignment: "You should have written everything you can see."[59] Later in the novel, Hoffmann returns to this demand and says in regard to one of the characters in the novel that:

I want to tell you about Mr. Moskowitz
But what do I know about
Jassy and Baku and Timisoara and
Bucharest? A man should (through the power of logical analogy)
be able to know everything. It should be possible
with the correct reasoning, to infer (from the present to the past)
what Mr. Moskowitz, for instance, saw in
Constantsa, in 1926, when he was a soldier in the Romanian army, through
The window of the barracks room.[60]

He later gets back to describing Mr. Moskowitz, but instead of telling about him, he says:

No doubt about it. The light was not
so sharp in the Carpathian Mountains.
Wild goats seemed almost to blend
with the blocks of the furs of the foxes
were of one shade with the pines.
Why then be so pedantic about
distinguishing between Mr.
Moskowitz and everything else?

This is, in a way, an answer to the third-grade teacher and the demands of realism that her note represents. The teacher knows that there is no way one can write about everything that he or she sees. What she actually meant in her remark is that she misses in the composition the typical views that one sees in the market. Instead, the third grader wrote that he saw a "mongoloid man" and then continued the composition with a description of what he imagines the life of the man looks like.[61] The "mongoloid man" is of course what the child remembers from his visit to the market thanks to the man's uniqueness, but according to the teacher's norm of representation, he is not relevant to the description of the market. Furthermore, the description in the composition is speculative, and is based on what might have happened and not what the child sees. It then brings us back to the question that Hoffmann asks about his depiction of Mr. Moskowitz: why should he distinguish between Mr. Moskowitz and everything else? It is also in a sense a question that Hoffmann may have been asking writers like Oz, even when it comes to a novel in which Oz intended to break from realism. For both writers, the question of how and what to represent is important, and both share these questions in their novels, but it seems that while Hoffmann is mostly concerned with the question of representation and less with how this representation will be received, Oz cares about both. His awareness, even sensitivity, to the expectations of his readers and to storytelling as an act of communication, is at least partly the reason for the dominance of the author in the novel. Posing as one of the fictional characters yet identifying by his real name, mentioning the real names of his children and grandchildren, depicting his daily writing routine, and even portraying a scene in which the author stays in a hotel ahead of a lecture about his work (then meeting Dita who works there), he does not leave much doubt about this identification. Adopting the guise of the fictional, but clearly recognizable as the real-life author of his fiction, Oz can communicate with his readers – can explain and reason, ultimately filling with words the silences that he often mentions as crucial to his novel. His attempt at silence, which, as he mentions, was driven by advice that he received in his youth from his beloved teacher and poet, Zelda,[62] is repeatedly in tension with his eagerness to speak.

Why had not the shaman become a postmodernist?

As I have tried to show, Oz attempted in *The Same Sea* to balance the new norms of the academic elite with the old norms of realism that his general readership was used to. But unlike the 1970s, when this balance led to a complete embrace of the new norms and therefore to a new writing style, *The Same Sea* remained an isolated episode in his literary career, so much so that Oz has admitted that he does not even believe that he himself wrote the novel.[63] Soon after the novel appeared, he avowed that it scared him.[64] In retrospect, as we have seen, he compared it to a seagull. Why did the novel scare the famous writer and what caused him to change his attitude toward it? I believe that the answer to these questions can be found in Oz's desire to be the "shaman of the tribe." To guide and to comfort, the author needs to be communicative, a desire that obviously conflicts with the postmodernist norms that call for allusiveness, gaps, and ambiguity. In *The Same Sea* he aimed at balancing these norms with stories about simple people, whose reality might reflect the readers' reality. He also used a simple language and made sure that the motivations of the characters are clearly explained.

In academia the novel indeed was mostly received with excitement and even, as we have seen, with a celebration of what was viewed at the time as Oz's transition to a new style. However, Oz's old and faithful readers outside the intellectual scene did not appreciate the new style. As he acknowledged years after the publication of the novel, people thought the novel was too heavy, too weird.[65] This time it seems as if the attempts to soften the new norms and balance them with the old ones did not convince the readers. In retrospect, we might understand Oz's fear of the novel as a fear of its rejection by his old readers, and this fear was indeed realized.

An attempt to answer the question why what worked so well thirty years earlier did not work this time should consider two factors. First, now Oz was an established and well-known author, the "shaman of the tribe", the "story teller" of the nation. He was the author who almost every year provided his readers with a new novel. This time, though, the novel frustrated the generic expectations of the readers: they were looking for a story and instead the beloved author wrote something that seemed like either poetry or prose or maybe neither. The comforting, guiding, and charming powers of the shaman were not easily found in *The Same Sea*.

Second, back in the 1970s and 1980s Oz's transition to realism did not pose a great challenge for his readers. After all, Oz's previous work, characterized with heavy symbolism, was much more challenging. Now, toward the end of the millennium, the new literary trend was much more elitist and intellectually demanding in terms of the reading process. Thus, despite Oz's adjustments and attempts to soften the new norms of writing, this time the transition was viewed as aiming solely at the academic and intellectual elite.

To this we should add another aspect that Oz might have relied on in his hope to appeal to both audiences, and that is the mere esthetic beauty of the novel. Oz, it seems, believed or hoped that the beauty of the text – its poetic nature, the beautiful rhymes, the poems, the rhythm and the musicality – would be appreciated outside of academia as offering a pleasurable esthetic experience. And in case they would not, at least the readers would be able to enjoy a narrative, rich in plot and action, about people like them. But the reading of poetry demands a different kind of attention and probably more effort. Many of Oz's readers ultimately did not find the novel entertaining but rather, as he later acknowledged, heavy and hard.

This precise reaction is very common when it comes to Hoffmann's works, but while Hoffmann embraced it, and even, I believe, thrived on it, Oz found it disappointing. Oz, a modernist and realist writer at his core, was not ready to become a postmodernist writer, precisely because of his desire to communicate, to explain, to comfort and guide. The new norms that called for a text that is combined of silences, gaps, and ambiguity also required an author who was ready to accept a reaction of wonderment and even misunderstanding. The difference between Oz and Hoffmann is that Hoffmann aimed at this reaction. Oz, on the other hand, desired the understanding of all readers. This desire is clearly what pushed him to explain the novel, even years after its appearance. In one of his last lectures, in a course on medicine and literature at Tel Aviv University, he chose to speak on *The Same Sea*. In a video of the event, Oz seems eager to explain the novel to his listeners, claiming in regard to one of the scenes, which he reads from the novel, that he will explain it until everyone will leave with a clear understanding of what happened. Despite his efforts, when the students were invited to ask questions, only one student raised his hand, and asked a question about Oz's *Love and Darkness*. Indeed, in *Love and Darkness* Oz found what he seemed to miss in *The Same Sea*: a warm reception by both academia and the wider audience.

Oz's attempts at shifting to a postmodernist style conflicted, then, with one important characteristic that all the norms mentioned above share, namely, their uncompromised nature. Furthermore, postmodernist literature demanded that the writer embrace a status that was not familiar to Oz before, the status of the marginal writer. In other words, it challenged the writer in his attempt to appeal to a wider readership and conflicted with Oz's aim to be the shaman of the tribe. He had to choose one or the other, and it seems like he resorted to the older status on the account of the first. Even his 2007 novel *Rhyming Life and Death*,[66] in which he writes again about the writing process in the spirit of postmodernism, should be seen, I suggest, as neglecting the postmodernist qualities that might risk the communicative nature of the novel. Despite its seemingly blending of reality and imagination, the later novel differentiates between the two in a way that readers can easily distinguish between the reality of the frame story and the imagined narratives that its protagonist, an author himself, tells about various characters that he meets.

If *The Same Sea* marked a new phase in Oz's writing, it is not because he abandoned the realistic genre, but rather because it opened him up to new forms of realistic prose. The five books that followed *The Same Sea* can be seen as attempts to explore these various forms: from an autobiographical novel that realistically narrates his and his family life, including his mother's suicide (*Sipur al ahava va-hoshekh* (A Tale of Love and Darkness), 2002), which in *The Same Sea* he only alluded to, to his return in his *Bein haverim* (Between Friends, 2012) to the site of the kibbutz to re-tell the stories of its people, this time in a prose striped of the symbolism that characterized his kibbutz stories in his first book *Artzot ha-tan*, (Where the Jackals Howl, 1965).[67] His last novel *Judas* (Ha-besorah al-pi Yehudah, 2014), uses Sholem Asch's *The Nazarene* (1939) as one of its main intertexts. *The Nazarene*'s storyteller is a young Polish Jew who is invited to the house of an old Polish Catholic archeologist, Pan Viadomsky, to translate a Hebrew account that, as the storyteller will later learn, is the lost gospel of Judas Iscariot. While working together on the manuscript, Viadomsky shares with the storyteller his most closely-kept secret: he is the reincarnation of the hegemon Cornelius, a first-century Roman lieutenant of Pontius Pilate. As such, he was not only a witness to Jesus' death but also in charge of his execution. The storyteller himself turns out to be the reembodied soul of a young Jewish man from the first century named Yochanan, who – like Cornelius – witnessed Jesus' life and death. Oz chose to name the main protagonist of his novel Shmuel Asch, a clear allusion to the famous Yiddish novelist, and like in Asch's novel, he sets his narrative in the house of an old intellectual man from whom the young Shmuel Asch learns many details about Jesus's life and death. However, while Asch could only guess the content of The Gospel of Judas, let alone its very existence, Oz based his account on the gnostic gospel with the same title that was found in the late 1970s and that was celebrated in 2006 following the reconstruction and publication of its content. Oz not only relocates the encounter between the old and the young man to 1950s Jerusalem, but he also strips this encounter from its unrealistic elements, basing the historical revelations that he details in his fiction on historical sources. While he borrows a realistic storyline from Asch, he avoids the fantastic elements that Asch integrated to his novel and strives to make it as historically accurate.

The realistic nature of Oz's later novels is more than a return to his familiar storytelling style of the period prior to *The Same Sea*; it is in fact an exploration of the various generic and stylistic possibilities of realism as a genre. It seems that after the disappointing reception of *The Same Sea*, the author was eager to gain back his reputation as a communicative storyteller, but at the same time he looked to maintain the acceptance of the academic and the intellectual elite. This could therefore be seen as Oz's third and last phase in his long and rich literary career and here, too, he uses the same mechanism that Gertz described as "compromise formulas." Adopting a direct and communicative style of narration – typical of realism – within intellectually sophisticated, realistic literary forms, such as the historical and the autobiographical novel, he can appeal to two different audiences: the intellectual elite on the one hand and the wider audience on the other.

As to Hoffmann, the non-communicative nature of his novels indeed caused him to be read mostly in intellectual circles, and to be deemed unreadable by the wider audience. A very critical review, published in 2007, claimed that his novels are unreasonably sophisticated, and that he only appeals to a very limited and elite readership. The title of the review was "A Holy Cow Named Hoffmann."[68] I doubt that Oz was thinking about this review when he compared himself to a cow that gave birth to a seagull, but nonetheless it is telling that he chose to compare himself to a cow. In Oz's comparison, the cow is a female, nurturing and comforting domesticated animal metaphor for the author as the shaman of the tribe. Like him, she is associated with warmth, affection, and caring. The choice of the seagull as a metaphor for *The Same Sea* can be understood, then, as Oz's retrospective view of *The Same Sea* as a beautiful and delicate bird. The beauty of the novel in Oz's view was missed because of the surprise that it was born of an author whose role for so many decades was to nurture and guide. Toward the end of his life, it seemed like Oz was bothered by the fact that the novel did not gain the attention it deserved. In both his last public lecture and his last radio interview, he chose to focus on *The Same Sea*, and perhaps to signal to his readers that in fact he would have liked the novel to be seen as an important part of his legacy. Indeed, in the novel, his semi-fictional narrator remarks self-ironically that "It wouldn't be a bad thing to leave behind ... a few lines worthy of the name." It might not be surprising, in light of what I have shown in this article, that this sentence appears in a fragment titled: "And what is hiding behind the story?" I therefore would conclude this article with these lines and some others, as an homage to Oz's attempt both to explain what is hiding behind the story and his wish that the lines of *The Same Sea* will be remembered as an integral part of his literary legacy:

> We go and we come, we see and we want until it is time to shut up and leave. And then silence. Born in Jerusalem lives in Arad looked around him and wanted this and that. Since he was a child he has heard, impatiently, time and again from Auntie Sonya. A woman who suffers, that we should be happy with what we have. We should always count our blessings. Now he finds himself quite close to this way of thinking. Whatever is here, the moon and the breeze, the glass of wine, the fan, the desk lamp, Schubert in the background, and the desk itself: a carpenter who died nine years ago worked hard to make you this desk so that you would remember that you didn't start from nothing. From starlight down to olives, or soap, from a thread of shoelace, from a sheet to the autumn. It wouldn't be a bad thing to leave behind in return a few lines worthy of the name. All this is diminishing. Disintegrating. Fading. What has been is being gradually wrapped in pallor. Nadia and Rico, Dita, Albert, Stavros Evangelides the Greek who brought up the dead and then died himself. The Tibetan mountains will last for a while, as will the nights, and the sea. All the rivers flow into the sea, and the sea is silence silence silence. It's ten o'clock. Dogs are barking. Take up your pen and return to Bat Yam.[69]

Notes

1. In an interview with Maya Kosover and Sari Shavit, "Sefer ehad – Amos Oz al *Oto ha-yam*" [One Book – Amos Oz on *The Same Sea*], *Kan Tarbut*, February 20, 2018. https://www.kan.org.il/podcast/item.aspx?pid=12474. Accessed November 27, 2020.
2. Oz explained that re-reading his other work frustrates him, as he either thinks that today he could do better or that he would never be able to write as good. As to *The Same Sea*, he said that he simply enjoys reading it, perhaps because he does not entirely believe that it is his.
3. I will return at the end of the article to Oz's 2007 novel, *Rhyming Life and Death*, which is the only novel of his that shares some qualities with *The Same Sea*, but is still written in the same style and structure as the rest of his corpus.
4. Gertz, *Amos Oz: Monographia*, 16.
5. Gertz designates this audience as the members of the Kibbutzim. See: ibid., 16.
6. Ibid., 16.
7. Ibid., 16.
8. Ibid., 40-41.

9. Ibid., 42.

10. Schwartz, *Pulhan ha-sofer*, 47.

11. Oz himself defined his role in Israeli society as that of an author who functions as "The shaman of the tribe", the man who tells stories around the fire and through them gives his people a source of comfort, guidance and healing. On Oz as the shaman of the tribe, see: Zilberman, *Mekhashef ha-shevet*.

12. Schwartz, *Pulhan ha-sofer*, 47.

13. In 1988, following the publication of Hoffmann's first collection of stories *Sefer Yosef* (The Book of Joseph), Yigal Serna published in *Yediot Ahronot* an article that tried to introduce the author by interviewing Hoffmann's students and giving a short biographical summary of his life. In an article that was published in *Akhbar ha-ir* in 2010, following the publication of Hoffmann's last novel, *Matzavei ruah* (Moods), Shai Greenberg attempted to answer some of the questions about Hoffmann's private life that Serna has left unanswered, but without much success. Greenberg's article ended up documenting Hoffmann's great efforts to guard his privacy, expressing frustration and at the same time a sort of admiration for the author's success in shielding himself from the public. See: Yigal Serna, "Yoel Hoffmann," *Yediot achronot, shiv'a yamim*, January 1, 1988, 34-35, and Shai Greenberg, "De-Hoffmanizia," *Akhbar ha-ir*, April 15, 2020. https://www.haaretz.co.il/gallery/art/1.3313284. Accessed November 27, 2020.

14. Two of his works, a 1988 story and a novel that was published in 2007, are called *Curriculum Vitae*. However, they hardly grant a real access to the actual author behind them.

15. Nuyen, "The Role of Rhetorical Devices in Postmodernist Discourse."

16. "Postmodernism," https://www.pbs.org/faithandreason/gengloss/index-frame.html, retrieved November 28, 2020.

17. Hassan, *The Dismemberment of Orpheus*, 15.

18. Throughout the 1990s other writers such as Yitzhak Laor, Avraham Hefner, Gafi Amir, Gadi Taub, and Etgar Keret joined this new trend.

19. Shaked, *Modern Hebrew Fiction*, 235. Shaked refers the reader to Conner, *Postmodernist Culture*.

20. Shaked, *Modern Hebrew Fiction*, 236.

21. Shaked, "Afelah tahat ha-shemesh," 46.

22. See note 20 above.

23. Scharf Gold, "Bernhardt's Journey," 272.

24. Schwartz, "Hebrew Prose: The Generation After," 7-8.

25. Balaban, *Gal aher*.

26. Shaked, *Gal hadash*.

27. Together with Orly Castel-Bloom. See for example, Shiffman, "Orly Castel Bloom and Yoel Hoffmann."

28. Gurevitch, *Postmodernism*. Gurevitch focuses on Oz's *Ha-matzav ha-shelishi* (*Fima*), in which, according to Chaya Shacham, Oz already started his journey into postmodernist writing. See: "Bein Bat Yam le-Xanadu," 235. See also: Horwitz, "Oto ha-yam," 102.

29. Holtzman, "Be-karov bein shishim," 190. First appeared in *Yediot achronot*, December 11, 1998.

30. Horowitz, "Oto ha-yam," 104-112.

31. Schacham, "Bein Bat Yam le-Xanadu," 175-182.

32. Kartun-Blum, "Ha hipus ahar halaltit ha-em," 175.

33. Ibid., 177.

34. See for example: Yosef Oren, "Zore'a shirim be-dim'a" [Seeding Poems with Tears], *Makor Rishon: Musaf Shabbat*, December 28, 2012. https://musaf-shabbat.com/2012/12/28/%D7%96%D7%95%D7%A8%D7%A2-%D7%A9%D7%99%D7%A8%D7%99%D7%9D-%D7%91D7%93%D7%9E%D7%A2%D7%94-%D7%99%D7%95%D7%A1%D7%A3%D7%90%D7%95%D7%A8%D7%9F/. Accessed November 30, 2020; Kartun-Blum, "Ha-hispus ahar halalit ha-em," 177.

35. Oz, *The Same Sea*, 72. I have modified the translation slightly to reflect the use of the word "rikma" in the Hebrew original, which de Lange replaced here with "pattern."

36. Hoffman, *The Christ of Fish*, 213.
37. For a discussion of the allusions to his family's roots in Europe in Oz's work, see: Ben-Dov, *Haim ktuvim*, 97-108.
38. Hoffmann, *Bernhardt*, 7.
39. Oz, *The Same Sea*, 24.
40. Holtzman, "Be-karov bein shishim," 190.
41. In an interview with Maya Kosover and Sari Shavit, *Kan Tarbut*.
42. Oz quoted these lines from Zach's poem already a few years earlier when he discussed his writing in general in a speech that he gave in Frankfurt in the ceremony for a reception of the Peace Award from the Union of German Press in October, 4, 1992. The speech was printed in his book *Kol ha-tikvot*.
43. Oz, *The Same Sea*, 3.
44. In her book *Place and Ideology in Contemporary Hebrew Literature*, Karen Grumberg deals with Oz's affinity to places such as the desert and the garden and counters this tendency with works by Hoffmann as well as Orly Castel-Bloom, Sayed Kashua, and Ronit Matalon.
45. See: Holtzman, "Be-karov bein shishim," 193; Batya Gur, "Oto ha-yam," *Ha'aretz* December 25, 1998; Ziva Shamir, "She-tehe ha-musica yam-tichonit" [Let the Music be Mediterranean], *Moznayim*, April 1999, 14-20; Kartun-Blum, "Ha-hispus ahar halalit ha-em," 176; Shacham, "Bein Bat Yam le-Xanadu," 245-6.
46. Shaked, *Modern Hebrew Fiction*, 236.
47. Oz, *The Same Sea*, translator's Note, 198.
48. Stahl, *Ha-poetica shel Yoel Hoffman*, 69-84.
49. Hoffmann, *The Christ of Fish*, 21.
50. Kartun-Blum argues that Oz replaced the use of metaphors and hyperboles that were typical to his style with lots of metonymies which shed a different light on the souls of his characters. See: Kartun Blum, "Ha-hispus ahar halalit ha-em," 180.
51. Oz, *The Same Sea*, 128.
52. In an interview with Maya Kosover and Sari Shavit.
53. Oz, *The Same Sea*, 75.
54. Ibid.
55. Ibid.
56. See also, Shacham, "Bein Bat Yam le-Xanadu," 238; Holtzman, "Be-karov bein shishim," 192; Kartun-Blum, "Ha-hispus ahar halalit ha-em," 181.
57. Oz described in many interviews his struggle with the fact that his mother did not leave any clue as to her decision to end her life.
58. Anat Waxman, "Af milah al Christus" [Not a Single Word on Christus], *Davar*, July 12, 1991.
59. Hoffmann, *The Christ of Fish*, 4-5.
60. Ibid., 80.
61. Ibid., 5.
62. Oz, *The Same Sea*, 111.
63. See note 52 above.
64. See Shacham, "Bein Bat Yam le-Xanadu," 235.
65. In an interview with Maya Kosover and Sari Shavit,
66. Oz, *Rhyming Life and Death*. Originally published as *Ha-sipur ve-ha-haruz*, Jerusalem: Keter, 2007.
67. I would like to thank Prof. Tamar Sovran for sharing with me her paper "Early and Later in the Language of Amos Oz's Kibbutz Stories" (NAPH Annual Conference, Boston, June 2019).
68. Daphna Shchori, "Para kedosha u-shma Hoffman" [A Holy Cow Named Hoffmann], *Ha'aretz Sefarim*, April 16, 2007. https://www.haaretz.co.il/literature/prose/1.1550160. Accessed November 30, 2020.
69. Oz, *The Same Sea*, 42.

Disclosure statement

No potential conflict of interest was reported by the author(s).

Bibliography

Balaban, A. *Gal aher ba-siporet ha-Ivrit: siporet Ivrit postmodernistit* [An Other Wave in Israeli Fiction: Postmodernist Israeli *Fiction*]. Jerusalem: Keter, 1995.

Ben-Dov, N. *Haim ktuvim: Al autobiyographiot safrutiot Yisraeliyot* [Written Lives: On Israeli Literary Autobiographies]. Jerusalem and Tel Aviv: Schoken, 2011.

Conner, S. *Postmodernist Culture: An Introduction to Theories of the Contemporary.* Oxford: Blackwell, 1989.

Gold, S., and N. Rachel. "Bernhardt's Journey: The Challenges of Yoel Hoffmann's Writing." *Jewish Studies Quarterly* 1, no. 3 (1993-94): 271–287.

Grumberg, K. *Place and Ideology in Contemporary Hebrew Literature.* Syracuse: Syracuse University Press, 2011.

Gurevitch, D. *Postmodernism: Tarbut ve-safrut be-sof ha-mea ha-esrim* [Postmodernism: Culture and Literature at The End of The 20th Century]. Tel Aviv: Devir, 1998.

Hassan, I. *The Dismemberment of Orpheus: Toward a Postmodern Literature.* Madison: University of Wisconsin Press, 1982.

Hoffman, Y. *The Christ of Fish* translated by Eddie Levenston. New York: New Directions, 1999.

Hoffmann, Y. *Bernhardt* translated by Alan Treister and Eddie Levenston. New York: New Directions, 1998.

Holtzman, A. "Be-karov bein shishim."[Soon to be Sixty Years Old] In *Mapat derakhim: Siporet ivrit ka-yom* [A Road Map: Hebrew Prose Today]. edited by A. Holtzman, 190–192. Tel Aviv: Ha-Kibbutz Ha-Meuhad, 2005. .

Horowitz, T. "*Oto ha-yam* le-Amos Oz ke-yetzira postmodernistit." [Amos Oz's *The Same Sea* as a Postmodern Work] *Sha'anan: Shenaton ha-mikhlala ha-datit le-hinukh* 5, (1999): 101–108.

Kartun-Blum, R. "Ha-hipus ahar halaltit ha-em." [The Search for The Mother Spaceship: On The Same Sea by Amos Oz] In *Sefer Amos Oz* [The Amos Oz Book]. edited by Y. Ben-Moredchai and A. Komam, 175–182. Be'er Sheba: Ben Gurion University Press, 2000.

Nurith, G. *Amos Oz: Monographia* [Amos Oz: A Monograph]. Tel Aviv: Sifriyat Po'alim, 1980.

Nuyen, A. T. "The Role of Rhetorical Devices in Postmodernist Discourse." *Philosophy & Rhetoric* 25, no. 2 (1992): 183–194.

Oz, A. *Kol ha-tikvot: Mahshavot al zehut Yisraelit* [All of our Hopes: Reflections on Israeli Identity]. Jerusalem: Keter, 1998.

Oz, A. *The Same Sea.* Translated by Nicholas de Lange. New York: Harcourt, 2001.

Oz, A. *Rhyming Life and Death,* Translated from Hebrew by Nicholas de Lange. London: Vintage Books, 2010.

Schwartz, Y. "Hebrew Prose: The Generation After." *Modern Hebrew Literature* 15 (1995): 6–9.

Schwartz, Y. *Pulhan ha-sofer ve-dat ha-medina* [The Cult of the Author and the State's Religion]. Or Yehuda: Kinneret, Zmora Bitan, and Dvir, 2011.

Shacham, C. "Bein Bat Yam le-Xanadu: Postmodernism, bein-textualiut, ve-parodia be-*Oto ha-yam* le-Amos Oz." [Between Bat Yam and Xanadau: Postmodernism, intertextuality, and parody in Amos Oz's *The Same Sea*] In *Krovim rehokim: Bein textualiyut maga'im u-ma'avakim be-safrut ha-Ivrit ha-hadasha* [Distant Relatives: Intertextuality, Contacts, and Contests in Modern Hebrew Literature]. edited by C. Shacham, 235–251. Be'er Sheva: Ben-Gurion University Press, 2004.

Shaked, G. *Gal hadash be-siporet h-Ivrit: Masot al siporet Yisraelit* tz'ira [A New Wave in Hebrew Literature: Essays on New Israeli Prose]. Tel Aviv: Sifriyat Po'alim, 1974.

Shaked, G. "Afelah that ha-shemesh." [Darkness under the Sun] *Politika* 40, (1991): 42–48.

Shaked, G. *Modern Hebrew Fiction*. Bloomington: Indiana University Press. 2000.

Shiffman, S. "Orly Castel Bloom and Yoel Hoffmann: On Israeli Postmodern Prose Fiction." *Hebrew Studies* 50, no. 1 (2009): 215–227. doi:10.1353/hbr.2009.0013.

Sovran, T. "Early and Later in the Language of Amos Oz's Kibbutz Stories." Talk delivered at the NAPH Annual Conference, Boston, June 2019.

Stahl, N. *Ha-poetica shel Yoel Hoffman: Kavei beriah ve-tziyurei lev* [Drawings of the Heart: The Poetics of Yoel Hoffmann]. Tel-Aviv: Resling, 2017.

Zilberman, D. *Mekhashef ha-shevet: Amos Oz – hypnoza ve-misktika be-yetzirotav* [The Shaman of The Tribe: Mystics and Hypnosis in Amos Oz's Work]. Or Yehuda: Hed Artzi, 1999.

Memory and space in the autobiographical writings of Amos Oz and Ronit Matalon

Adia Mendelson-Maoz

ABSTRACT
This article discusses the autobiographical writings of Amos Oz and Ronit Matalon and focuses on *A Tale of Love and Darkness* (2002) and *The Sound of Our Steps* (2008). Although the novels differ in terms of era, language, ethnic background, and the gender of the narrator/protagonist, the core plot of mother and child, the spatial concepts of home, garden, and land, and other shared structural elements invite comparison. This reading nevertheless pinpoints their disparity: whereas Oz's own trajectory elicits empathy, redefines the notion of personal life stories and their ideological role in Israeli society, and eventually justifies the Zionist ideology, Matalon's poetics of rupture creates unease that subverts the possibility to voice one's personal story and challenges the national narrative and its validity.

Autobiography remains a key literary genre in Modern Hebrew literature and an essential vector integrating individuals into the imagined national community. According to Leigh Gilmore, in Western literature and the history of criticism "the writers whose texts have been used as the base of an argument for what autobiography is form a set of 'exemplary' literary, political, and military men; they have been seen as singular figures capable of summing up an era in a name: Augustine, Rousseau, Franklin, Henry Adams."[1] These "exemplary" individuals are always the ambassadors of a social structure, and are considered role models for society and its ideal values and norms. In Hebrew literature, Tamar S. Hess noted that from the Haskalah period onward, from Moshe Leib Lilienblum, who "carried his autobiographical self through the hopes of the Enlightenment until he embraced the Zionist cause,"[2] Hebrew autobiographies have depicted the national (masculine) model. These autobiographies, while dealing with the life of individuals, played an important role in the renaissance of the new Hebrew culture in the nineteenth and twentieth centuries. They captured the shifting spirit and soul of Jewish and Israeli nationality, and championed the notion that "in national literatures the individual self is generally defined as both particular and universally representative."[3]

In the 1970s, Philippe Lejeune defined autobiographical writing as an "Autobiographical Pact," a contract between the reader and writer "which reflects an understanding by the reader that the author, the narrator, and the protagonist are the same person."[4] This pact is based on declared and stable concepts of identity. Many classical autobiographies describe the coming-of-age process of the protagonist toward his successful adulthood, which anchors the adult's stable identity and personality within society and nation.

However, as Leigh Gilmore has shown, Lejeune's notion that autobiography takes "a rational and representative 'I' at its center" has been challenged.[5] The development of gender, ethnic, and feminist theories in Western literature and criticism, from the 1960s onward, has led to new readings of autobiographies that examine the sociopolitical power of placing the "I" (as a woman or as a minority) as the focal point of the text. Feminist intellectuals such as Julia Kristeva (*Desire in Language*), Helene Cixous ("The Laugh of the Medusa") and Luce Irigaray (*This Sex Which Is Not One*) along with poststructuralist theorists such as Paul de Man (*Allegories of Reading*) and Roland Barthes ("The Death of the Author") have paved the way for new variants on autobiographical texts where textual gaps, silences, and incoherencies in terms of linearity and causality are not only accepted but are vaunted.[6] Today, autobiography is perceived as a literary genre that is "virtually impossible" to define, and which includes many forms and directions.[7]

In contemporary Israeli society, which, as Eran Kaplan suggests, "no longer accepts a single hegemonic group or set of images as the only representative of its collective identity,"[8] autobiography has remained a major genre whose literary contours are often indicative of the shape of modern Israeli culture.[9] Paralleling the widening fissures in efforts to consolidate a homogeneous Jewish-Israeli culture, autobiographies or autobiographic novels have taken on a variety of attributes, as exemplified in Haim Be'er's *Havalim* (The Pure Element of Time, 1998), Aharon Appelfeld's *Sipur haim* (The Story of a Life, 1999), Amos Oz's *Sipur al ahava ve-hoshekh* (A Tale of Love and Darkness, 2002), Dan Tsalka's *Sefer ha-alef bet* (Alphabet Book, 2003), and Yoram Kaniuk's *Tashah* (1948, 2010). Although most of these authors are members of the cultural Ashkenazi elite in Israel, enjoy national acclaim, and in many respects are "exemplary" individuals, they have opted to distance themselves from the national story and write autobiographies that "produc[e] marginal subjects."[10] These autobiographies focus on identities in collision and aim to (re) define the Israeli self. Several women have also written autobiographies, including Netiva Ben-Yehuda's *The Palmah Trilogy* (1981, 1985, 1991) and Alona Frankel's *Yalda* (Girl, 2004). Mizrahi autobiography appeared more recently with Shimon Balas' *Beguf rishon* (In the First Person, 2009), the first Iraqi-born novelist to publish a memoir. Female Mizrahi writers made a dramatic entry into the Israeli autobiographical scene with Ronit Matalon's *Kol tze'adenu* (The Sound of Our Steps, 2008) and Orly Castel Bloom's *Ha-roman ha-mitzri* (The Egyptian, 2015).

These examples and many others show that Israeli literary autobiographies, autobiographic novels, or auto-fiction[11] writing are, in fact, hybrid genres. They not only shun the mono-national narrative, but also upend memory, history, and the poetics of narration. These texts often engage in a "basic tension between memory and the forgotten,"[12] and constitute an "oxymoronic amalgamation" of the authentic and the fictional, the prosaic and the poetic, documentation and invention.[13]

In the fifth chapter of Amos Oz's *A Tale of Love and Darkness*, in a literary aside that was not included in the English translation, Oz (1939–2018) makes the provocative statement that "every story that I have written is autobiographical."[14] He orients his stories and novels toward an identification of the sources of the plot, the characters, and their backgrounds, and hints that autobiographical moments, thoughts, and traumas are the kernel of his narratives. He also charts out the path "good readers" should follow:

readers should not be driven by voyeurism or the search for salacious tidbits but rather by empathy, which should prompt them to compare the dark labyrinths and monsters in the story to the labyrinths and monsters in their own lives. However, Oz knew that readers would be fascinated by *A Tale of Love and Darkness*, in which he openly and intimately talks about himself in the first person, and would consider it to be a key to his entire oeuvre, the wellsprings of his talent, and his deepest motivations for writing.

These declarations in the fifth chapter ground Oz's project not only thematically but also in terms of tone. Throughout the novel, he addresses the reader directly in two voices. The first is the voice of the boy who lost his mother when he was 12, who goes through identity crises but scaffolds himself out of the trauma, thus annealing empathy. The other is the voice of the narrator as an white-authoritative-male-adult, who is not only a symbol of "ha-Israeli ha-yafe" (the nice Israeli) but also the person who nurtured it,[15] who, from this position, can explain "[...] who brought us here. Why we came here. What would have happened if we had not come here."[16] My contention is that this intermixing of empathy and authoritative voices is the core of Oz's text and has played a crucial role in its success.

Unlike Oz, Ronit Matalon (1959–2017), a Mizrahi female author, insisted that her novel *The Sound of Our Steps* was not autobiographical, to the extent of subtitling it "a novel." It describes the lives of Lucette and her three children, who live in an immigrant neighborhood near Tel-Aviv during the 1950s. Both readers and reviewers have pointed to the parallels between Matalon's text and her life.[17] A number of episodes, as well as the setting for the book, appeared in her collection of essays *Kro u-khtov* (Read and Write), which was published in 2001, where she describes her childhood and adolescence in the Ganei Tikva neighborhood, which was built in the 1950s to settle immigrants from Muslim countries (North Africa, Iraq, and Yemen) as well as Poland and Romania.[18] The descriptions of the house and its surroundings in *The Sound of Our Steps* (although not mentioned by name), the poverty and lack of basic infrastructure, and the specific references to the nearby affluent neighborhood of Savion are very similar to those found in *Read and Write*, which strongly suggest that the novel depicts this space.[19] Other similarities include the descriptions of her family members who emigrated from Cairo to Israel, and specifically the character of Matalon's father, an educated Jewish-Egyptian who wrote political articles in Hebrew, French, and Arabic (146, 294), and the portrayals of his ideological and political circle (88). In the novel, Maurice, Lucette's husband, is also a political activist dedicated to fighting the Ashkenazi establishment's discrimination of Sephardi and Mizrahi Jews, while abandoning his responsibility for his family.

Matalon does not use actual names in the novel,[20] and while she did not link the novel to her life in the Hebrew media, she admitted to the foreign press that the novel was actually about her mother and her childhood:

> I never wrote as much about my mother before *Kol tz'adenu*. I think writing about my mother changed my style of writing, my image of the world. [...] Her physical features are fragmented throughout the book. [...] I was only preoccupied with my memories.[21]

In her collection of essays, *Ad argi'ah* (Only Fleetingly, 2018), published after her death, Matalon refers to memory and autobiography and relates to the novel. She describes the beginnings of her writing as a transition from the first person to the third person (from "I" to "She") and the moment when part of herself became able to see things from the outside. When questioned as to the veracity of her stories, she admitted that she chose the "childish eagerness and ability to be in the twilight zone between imagination and reality, true and what may have been true."[22] Na'ama Tsal suggests that the epigraph of the novel, a quote from T.S. Eliot's "Four Quartets" may signal Matalon's narrating voice that merges "what might have been" and "what has been."[23]

Matalon's writing is perhaps best situated in the current literary discourse, which views autobiographical writing as a way to understand the colonial subject and give a voice to the silenced subject.[24] Gayatri Chakravorty Spivak, in "Can the Subaltern Speak?", argued that the subaltern has no history and thus cannot speak. However, in her later writings, Spivak admitted that the culture of confession and testimony is a major technique of "giving witness to oppression."[25] This is what Matalon does when she focuses on her childhood home and family. It is not a story of coming of age told from the standpoint of a successful adult, but a story that reveals an unstable identity that still has the scars of oppression. Thus, Matalon locates herself both in the first person and third person and preserves the gap between them. She constitutes a radically different persona than Oz: she does not let her reader be carried away by her narrative since she constantly instills doubt as to its reliability and relinquishes the role of the omnipotent author.

Motherhood and the trauma of immigration

The childhood memories of Oz and Matalon differ in terms of time, place, language, and context. Nevertheless, the trauma of immigration is present at the kernel of their autobiographical writing. The mother figure hovers over the narrative and exemplifies their great loss. Several spatial concepts that appear in both texts such as the home, garden, and their complex meanings, make a comparative reading possible. Contrasting with these similarities, the differences between the texts stand out even more starkly.

In her essay "Mi-hutz la-makom, be-tokh ha-zman" (Out of Place, Inside Time), Matalon writes about immigration as follows:

> Until recently, only a few writers on the fringes of society dared utter the term "immigrant" rather than the Zionist "oleh," as a subversive act of defiance. I believe that the instance in which the word "immigrant" finally and completely replaced the word "oleh" constitutes an important moment [....] Saying "oleh" rather than immigrant [...] annuls and denies the inherent wretchedness inherent to the process of immigration, and presupposes that this state is only a phase on the way towards something else; namely, absolute assimilation.[26]

Matalon is centering on the ideological clash between *aliyah* and immigration (*hagira*). The origin of the Hebrew word *aliyah* is religious: it suggests going to a holy site (such as Jerusalem) and affirming one's faith. Zionist ideology, which drew on symbols from Jewish collective memory, adapted this term and gave it the new meaning of building a national home for all the Jews. The new narrative of the Zionist *aliyah* tells the story of Jews who come to Israel out of ideological yearning, and are prepared to undergo a radical transformation that will alter their identity and create a sense of belonging to their "AltNeu" historical homeland, as Theodor Herzl so aptly put it in his 1902 book [*Altneuland: The Old New Land*]. The success of this process is grounded in the acceptance and assimilation of a new and homogeneous prototype of Israeli Jew emerging from the production and construction of the national imagination.[27]

The tension between *aliyah* and *immigration* can be formulated in a more abstract conceptual model. Homi Bhabha's distinction between the pedagogical and the performative is a useful starting point:

> The pedagogical founds its narrative authority on the tradition of the people [...]. The performative intervenes in the sovereignty of the nation's self-generation by casting a shadow between the people as "image" and its signification as a differentiating sight of Self, distinct from the Other and its Outside.[28]

From this more general perspective, *aliyah* reflects a hegemonic picture of national ideology. It forms a pedagogical narrative of Zionist thought and education that defines the successful enterprise of settling in Palestine and building a new society. The *immigration* narrative is a specific realization of this general idea. Specific individual immigration recognizes the struggle for identity, the failure of the attempt to impose a homogenous nationality, and the ensuing trauma.[29] However, must the pedagogical and the performative always point in two opposite directions?

Oz's book reveals the trauma of an entire generation whose lives were so often uprooted. His personal story is also a collective one in terms of key national moments relating to a certain time, spaces, and history.[30] Oz combines his personal story with what Michael Feige claims to be "objective history" – the hegemony of the national context,[31] so that his work demonstrates that the performative and the pedagogical (in Bhabha's terms) can operate together. This combination is what has given the novel its cult status, as Yigal Schwartz has shown.[32]

To construct his personal story, Oz's poetics emphasize a particular and concrete space, and the work breaks the linear, causal, mono-dimensional fabula by expressing a pluralized and provisional narrative. The identity of the immigrant is composed of memories constructed over a continuum of time. *A Tale of Love and Darkness* is not a one-dimensional narrative; it is interspersed with testimonies, documents, postcards, poems, notes, literary criticism, memoirs written by members of the family, old newspapers, and stories, all of which deviate from one clear voice to create a chorus. The text is constructed as a collection of episodes and there is no single answer to the question of belonging and identity which is so central to the narrative. Even though the book is autobiographical, it deliberately blurs the distinction between facts, historical truth, and fiction. His mother's stories and the spaces they suggest penetrate Oz's story and impede the act of reconstruction. This bending of time, space, and voices creates fluidity in relation to the personal story.

Oz details the intimate story of the irrevocable damage caused by his family's immigration, which eventually led to his mother's suicide. The Zionist establishment demanded that immigrants cut themselves off from their diaspora home and forget their previous identities, language, memories, and culture.[33] In reality, however, the situation was different, and Oz portrays this bluntly by showing how his parents, like many others, felt uprooted and lived in two different times and places. They lived in Israel but thought about, and longed for, Europe, "a forbidden promised land [...] far from the dusty tin roofs, the urban wasteland of the scrap iron thistles, the parched hillsides of our Jerusalem, suffocating under the weight of white-hot summer" (2).[34]

Oz's family came to Israel filled with dreams and hopes, quoting the song "all our hopes will be fulfilled/There to live in liberty, there to flourish, pure and free" (242). They underwent a painful split between what they used to be and "what they have become,"[35] between who they were, what they expected to be, and their lives in Israel. The Klausner family was part of the Russian middle-class intelligentsia that moved to Odessa and in 1933 immigrated to Israel. His father studied history and literature and hoped to become a professor of comparative literature, but ended up working for most of his life as a librarian in the Jewish National and Hebrew University Library. His mother's family belonged to the same milieu. Fania grew up in Rovno (then in Poland, today in Ukraine) and studied history and philosophy in Prague. She abandoned her academic career to go to Israel in 1934, where her parents and sister had already settled. Anita Shapira states that "the two families' move to Palestine should not have been traumatic; both families were Zionists, they had learned Hebrew in Europe and they went to Israel with their family members before the Holocaust."[36] However, the neighborhood of Kerem Abraham "suited neither of them" (288–289), and "Hebrew was still not a natural enough language, it was certainly not an intimate language, and it was hard to know what exactly came out when they spoke it" (11).

Oz's immigration story in the novel is about death and mourning, parents' love, and orphanhood. It is the story of his colorful grandmother, who was disgusted with the weather and the dirt in Israel and died after insisting on taking two hot baths a day in a vain attempt to keep clean. It is also the story of his father, whose dream of a professorship "was like a running sore in my father's soul" (123). But above all, it is the story of Oz's mother's suicide.

> What did she hope to find here, what did she find and did she not find? What did Tel-Aviv and Jerusalem look like to someone who had grown up in a mansion in Rovno and arrived straight from the Gothic beauty of Prague? [...] By the time I reached the age when my mother could have told me about her childhood and her early days in the Land, her mind was elsewhere [...] The bedtime stories she told me were peopled by giants, fairies, witches. (181-2)

Oz is fascinated by the character of his mother, who remained an unsolved mystery. In an attempt to understand her, he collects testimonies from others but also tries to recall what he remembers, her movements and words. Sonia, Fania's sister, describes their reunion when Sonia came to Israel. Fania was a few months pregnant then, but she was already "very pale and was even more silent than usual" and her "forehead seemed sort of clouded" (191). This silence and paleness also correspond to Oz's description of what he remembered. Oz recalls her hands and softness when she helped him put on his first pair of shoes (210). Later, he chronicled her activities: when she sat down, what she did, what she read. His finely-hewn portrayal of his mother underscores her mental and psychological deterioration: she immersed herself in reading "she read every evening, while I played outside [...] she also read after the supper things were washed up, she read while my father and I sat together at his desk" (264), "From morning to evening she sat in a deck chair [...] and read" (265). Later he noticed that "A slowness had started making itself felt in her movements [...] she has stopped giving private history and literature lessons" (383). Two years before she died she began to suffer from migraines and "had to cut down on the housework" (385) and "[b]y the end of the winter she had almost stopped eating" (389). She "couldn't stand the electric light. Every evening she would sit in the dark" (387) and "In the autumn, towards the end of 1951, my mother's condition took another turn for the worse. [...] she sat all day at the window counting the birds or the clouds. She sat there at night too, with her eyes wide open" (428). She gradually alienates herself from the world, as well as from her family; she stands by the window and stares outside or lies on her back "with her open eyes fixed" (383). Except for the shoes scene, when he was a baby, she is never described in relation to Oz, and her gaze is never directed toward him.

Fania tells stories of an imaginary Europe with legendary spaces inhabited by unreal characters. In his gentle description of her activities, Oz almost turns her into a character in one of her fairytales. Her weakness and remoteness and her bizarre behavior make her seem unreal in the novel, as though she were a kind of ghost. She is like an angel who could not survive in the real world: "my mother grew up surrounded by an angelic cultural vision of misty beauty whose wings were finally dashed on the hot dusty pavement of Jerusalem stone" (207).

Oz paints his parents and particularly his mother as victims of circumstance. Those who came to Israel suffered from an alienation that ruined them, but the branches of the family who stayed in Europe were exterminated in the Holocaust. This personal and historical picture nurtured a position that is often inherent to the Zionist narrative and is frequently expressed in the form of "victim-community," to use Martin Jaffe's terminology.[37] Oz's mother is the ultimate victim here, and her description as an angel or ghost is highly stirring and emotional. She is a symbol, a myth, almost a martyr, who pays the price for the national resurrection. The end of the novel narrates Fania's last hours. This is a condensed trauma for the child who lost his mother, a trauma that was known to the reader from the beginning of the novel but is actualized in the final pages when Oz calls to his mother and begs her not to kill herself. This end constitutes the closure.

Schwartz's analysis of the massive responses of readers to the novel documents the highly emotional reactions it elicited, from laughter and crying to feelings of catharsis. Above all, readers related to the text as though it were their own stories and often described their own family histories in the long letters they wrote to Oz.[38] They reacted to this personal story as though it reflected general history. Thus, even though the work ends with a very personal scene, the acknowledgment of the suffering and the empathetic reaction of this traumatic fascinating literary plot support the national endeavor and the price it demanded.

By contrast, Schwartz argues that Matalon's success is due to the fact that "Matalon adopted [...] the main survival strategy of the hegemonic establishment [...] the presentation of the personal, familial, and sectorial story of the author as if it were a collective and universal story."[39] He suggests that Matalon worked within the same hegemonic platform (as did Oz and others) and therefore deserves her place in the literary canon. However, Schwartz admits that this is only a deceptive technique that allows her to take a subversive position.

As in Oz's works, Matalon's text testifies to the trauma of immigration, and its impact on her mother's personality. She says that "Immigration, whether perceived as a temporary or chronic evil, almost always represents a state of a fracture or a wound. Not belonging is a wound,"[40] and depicts how Lucette, who grew up a "lady" (she did not work, she did not clean or cook), is defeated by the new homeland that changes her entire life, turns her into a working woman, and breaks her spirit.

The collapse of the authoritarian father figure in Israel in the 1950s and 1960s in many Mizrahi immigrant families created a vacuum and forced women to enter the public sphere. As the head of the family, fathers had the final word on everyone's affairs but were often unable to find work or support their families. The breakdown of traditional familial patterns often placed women in a new position. Not only did they continue to be responsible for cooking and caring for the whole family, but had to join the struggle to stay afloat, work outside the home, and find other ways of feeding the family and raising the children.[41] However, this shift from the domestic to the public sphere did not result in liberation from gender oppression. Rather, going to work outside the home and traveling to affluent neighborhoods did not make these women part of the hegemonic space. Most of them remained in the margins.

Matalon's text presents a finely-tuned description of her mother's appearance, job skills, attitude toward her children, life story, and relations with her husband. It starts with the sound of her mother's steps as she returns home after a long day of physical labor: "The sound of her steps: not the heels tapping, the feet dragging, the clogs clattering or soles shuffling on the path leading to the house, no" (1). Her mother's body is described as bent and lolling, with her "skirt with the broken zipper" and "her overflowing stomach" (8).

As in Oz's novel, Matalon also observes her mother, whom she sees as enigmatic. Although like Fania she sometimes escapes her hard life through fantasy and rereads Alexandre Dumas' novel *La dame aux Camélias*, which is integrated into the novel as the symbol of a heroine who sacrifices herself for love (68),[42] she is mostly very unemotional and pragmatic. Lucette never shows gentle emotions or complains but what she does not utter out loud is reflected in her body, the soles of her feet, and the palms of her hands, to which the narrator devotes long pages. Her body tells the true story that "femininity had been sacrificed to this rough place" (17). With no words and language to reflect the hardships of her life, she often takes on manly, aggressive behavior: "the shack didn't have a man in it, so she became the man" (94). When she gets back home, she checks to see whether the house is neat, and if it is less than perfect she reacts violently, smashes cups and vases, throws shoes, and strikes her children.

The violence she expresses toward the prefab and her children is also directed at her own body: "Between me and my sister stretched a train of dead children [...] 'I got rid of them, I got rid of them like kittens and ran to work' she said as if to herself" (30). The girl in the story learns that her mother did not want to have any more children and planned to "get rid of her" as she did with her previous pregnancies. She was saved by her grandmother who had a fateful dream and begs her daughter not to have an abortion. The two reach an agreement that the grandmother will raise "the girl."

However, this aggression has another facet in that the novel reveals the mother as the defender of her children. When the rabbi of Savion, where she works as a cleaning lady, wants to adopt "the girl", the mother refuses: "whatever happens, we don't do that, we don't give away our children" (138). The rabbi is the hegemonic patron who wants to "protect" the young child from an apparently unqualified (primitive) mother and life on the fringes of society.

Yochai Oppenheimer's writings about the Mizrahi body in Israeli fiction suggest that Mizrahi literature deconstructs physical identity which is often represented as a binary structure where the Ashkenazi Sabra, who is manly, strong and healthy is pitted against the diasporic Jew and his feminine, weak, and vulnerable body.[43] Matalon does not hide these defective bodies or beautify them. Organs are described intimately and intrusively by revealing every wrinkle, every lump of fat. These unflattering physical descriptions intensify the chasm in her mother's life between her former persona, the daughter of an affluent educated family from Egypt, capable of cultured conversation and activity, and her Israeli life as a down-and-out, inarticulate woman, who cleans houses. Thus, Matalon subverts the hegemonic concept of the body by her refusal to hide it and reveals the real scars of immigration.

Oz and Matalon voice the pain of their mothers and express what Cathy Caruth calls "the plea of an other who is asking to be seen and heard, this call by which the other commends us to awaken."[44] They also reveal the impact of the suffering of immigration on their lives as children who were born in Israel, thus exposing one of the primal traumas of Israeli society. However, Lucette's extreme physicality is completely unlike Fania's fantastic embodiment. Matalon courageously exposes the violence of immigration on a person who not only experienced a fractured life but has also had to confront discrimination as a Mizrahi woman. She illustrates the physical cost of her mother's survival. Unlike Oz, who describes his mother with great empathy by disclosing her sense of the impossibility of her life which eventually leads her to abandon it all, Lucette is not a lovely character or an ultimate victim. She is less gentle and not pretty: she is fat and aggressive toward her children, but stubbornly refuses to hand over her child to a foster family, whereas Fania sinks into depression and is unable to be a mother. Matalon describes an alternative to the emotional depiction nurtured by Oz. Instead of silent cooperation with the national project through the moving story of the mother as a symbol or a martyr, Matalon crushes any attempt to turn her mother into a myth. Instead of empathy, she chooses what Dominick LaCapra calls "empathic unsettlement."

Empathy is the ability to think or feel with another person and simulate the experiences of others. Since the eighteenth, and to a greater extent in the nineteenth, century empathy has been seen as one of the pillars of social behavior, and in terms of ethics, is viewed as enabling a better understanding of the suffering of others. In literature, empathy is thought to enable the reader's emotional engagement with the perspectives of others, which may encourage the growth of humanistic values.[45] However, postmodern criticism and ethics have tended to question the power of empathy and its educational effect. One of the reservations is that the concept of empathy draws on an hypothesis of universality that assumes that people have shared experiences that enable assimilation and understanding. This hypothesis does not necessarily work when literature discusses different times and cultures. People may believe that they feel or understand the other while actually appropriating others to their own self. The second reservation has to do with the emotional effect of empathy that can work in different directions while manipulating the reader.[46]

LaCapra's assessment of trauma argues that while empathy is "important in attempting to understand a traumatic event [...] it may have stylistic effects in the way one discusses or addresses certain problems."[47] LaCapra claims that empathy may tap into the pleasure principle since one of its components involves achieving empathy by reaching some kind of harmony.[48] Instead, LaCapra puts forward the concept of "empathic unsettlement," which constitutes a barrier,[49] since it allows for certain types of empathy to emerge, but still maintains distance and does not seek resolution, harmony, or closure.[50]

LaCapra's distinction suggests where Oz's and Matalon's texts diverge. Oz is telling a personal story which is also the national story and has the readers' full engagement and may generate catharsis. This catharsis is of course not necessarily negative, and in the case of Oz it is part of the artistic achievement of the novel. However, it leads the reader to validate the Zionist enterprise since it makes it clear why this suffering was inevitable, and thus enables closure. Unlike Oz, Matalon's narrative of immigration has no "happy end" or "final destination,"[51] with no saints or martyrs and no harmony. This unsettlement is the main arsenal in Matalon's strategy of confronting the teleological national story.

Home, garden, and the disputed land

When Gaston Bachelard defined the home as an individual's "corner of the world," or primary universe, he was underscoring the extent to which the home plays a crucial, powerful role in crystallizing people's thoughts, memories, and dreams.[52] The notion of "home" relates not only to a dwelling place but also to a birthplace that creates an intimate relationship between people who live together.

A person's home is the "small place" (or "a place") to use Zeli Gurevitz and Giddeon Aran's terminology and from there circles of places of belonging fan out to the neighborhood, the city, and the country. The national home, the Land of Israel, is the "big place" ("the place"). Gureviz and Aran claim that there is no continuum between "a place" and "the place," but rather a dialogue "between a contemporary, local and close reality of life and an idea,"[53] an imagined place that is a product of historical memory.[54]

The formulation of the national space was concretized in the Zionist narrative of the early twentieth century in communal settings such as the moshava and the kibbutz, but also in natural landscapes such as mountains, valleys, and orchards. This Zionist work aimed at forming a physical bond to the place, through working the land, the ability to make a living from manual labor, and infiltrating open spaces.[55] The image of the Sabra in Hebrew literature was constructed in open spaces: Alik and Uri, Moshe Shamir's characters, are never described in their homes. They are always outside, on a horse, in the yard, in the vegetable garden, in the plum orchard or the pine forests, near the irrigation channels.[56] However, this formation of the new person on the new land completely ignored the people who have long been on the land – the Palestinians.

Yigal Schwartz's examination of the Hebrew literature in the last 150 years shows that the growth of secular nationalism, as depicted in descriptions of landscapes and people's affinity to space, can be characterized as a relationship between "the engineering of man" and "the thought of space." He argues that Hebrew literature is based on a spatial momentum that stems from a "vector of passion" that channels the passion from the Diaspora to the Land of Israel but also severs emotional and mental existence from the body and corporality. Yehuda Halevi's poetization "my heart is in the East and I in the uttermost West" best manifests this trait[57] by expressing the unbridgeable gap between the heart and the body – between "a place" and "the place."

This nexus was integrated into the meta-narrative of Hebrew culture from the outset. Initially, these models constituted attempts to erase the gap between "a place" and "the place,"[58] since part of the vision of reaching the promised land was to unite the two – a vision that failed. The literature of the 1960s onwards has not only made peace with the heart/body dichotomy but has also fashioned the vector of passion into an inverted duplication of the Diaspora where we are in the East but our heart is in the West. Thus, the literature of this generation

> reflected, but even more so, designed the very essence of what it is to be an Israeli – it reversed the direction of the vector of passion that ruled Zionist literature, and thus grounded our statutes [...] at the very moment we achieved sovereignty, after two thousand years in the diaspora, as 'immigrants in our country.'[59]

Oz and Matalon chart this reverse direction of the vector of passion by unveiling the deceptiveness of the national place. They focus on alternative homes that underscore and negate the Zionistic conceptualization of space and thus expose the schism between the personal home and the national home, and between the reality of life and the ideal image. Moreover, they also bring back the Palestinians, who were removed from this formation of the Zionist place.

Oz's "structure of the scenery of the homeland lies far from the objective intended by the formulators of the Zionist ethos," Iris Milner argues,[60] in that he expropriates spaces from their national role and emphasizes their personal importance.[61] Oz's childhood home was cramped and dark. It measured no more than 30 square meters and was made up of two rooms, a sofa, a large library, and a tiny green room with a closet. A corridor apartment: "A narrow, low passage, dark and slightly curved, like an escape tunnel from a prison, linked the little kitchenette and toilet to these two small rooms" (1). The light is always pale and the windows were closed: "Through a tiny opening high up in their back walls the kitchenette and toilet peered out into a little prison yard [...] where a pale geranium planted in a dusty olive can was gradually dying for want of a single ray of sunlight." (1). The kitchen was "narrow and low as a solitary confinement cell" (261) and every evening there was a ceremony that closed off the family from the world, where "[t]he whole outside world was locked out, and inside our armored cabin [...] the whole flat was sealed off every evening and slowly sank, like a submarine, beneath the surface of the winter" (286).

Oz's childhood home is a prison. It is a closed structure that needs to be barricaded off from intruders. This is, in essence, a diasporic home, a reinforced cell located in a hostile environment, exposed to the winds, to danger, and to the voices of the outside world. In wartime, the house is used as an air-raid shelter, and the neighbors go down to the basement apartment to find protection, but Oz's story clearly shows that danger comes not only from the outside but also from the inside.

Oz's home is a metonymic for his mother and her feelings. "Even during the day the corridor was pitch black, unless you switched the light on. In the black my mother floated to and fro, unvaryingly [...] as prisoners wailed round their prison yard" (343). His mother cannot stand the light, and her feeling of imprisonment and despair are encapsulated in the space where "a thousand dark years separated everyone. Even three prisoners in a cell" (437).

Across the threshold, when the locks are removed, attempts are made to connect with the Israeli space. The tie to the Land of Israel is to the soil, and the Zionist connection to the soil means "making the desert bloom." In Oz's work, the contact with the land is reduced to a tiny yard in which the protagonists make strenuous efforts to fulfill the most important of all Zionist missions, getting a plant to emerge from the soil.

"The garden wasn't a real garden, just a smallish rectangle of trampled earth as hard as concrete, where even thistles could scarcely grow" (225). Nevertheless, father and son want to be farmers and grow a vegetable garden: "we'll make a little kibbutz in the space by the pomegranate tree, and bring forth bread from the earth by our own efforts!" (226).

Oz's father aspires to make his own "desert" bloom. Nurit Gertz points out that Oz's description hones in on the stages of agricultural effort and the continuation of the struggle as he fights the elements and the primal wilderness, while his son is entrusted with the mission of joining the charging ranks of soldiers.[62] Although the father's tenaciousness likens him to David resisting the Philistine Goliath, and "although he borrows from the library a book about gardening and vegetable growing" (232) and is eager to find a cure, the dying seedlings dry up in the yard, "the saplings bowed their heads, and once more started looking as sickly and weak as persecuted diaspora Jews, their leaves dropped, the shoots withered" (233). The attempt to revive Israeli soil fails.

Who, nevertheless, is able to make the desert bloom? The pioneers and the members of the kibbutzim, who will always be "beyond our horizon" (5). As Oz constantly states: "Somewhere, over the hills and far away. A new breed of heroic Jews was springing up" (4). While the pioneers are out of sight, Oz identifies others who know the secret of the land – the Palestinians. One example is the lavish home with its thriving yard where a "respectable European family," the El-Siluanys, live: "It was surrounded by a thick stone wall that concealed the orchard shady with vines and fruit trees. My astonished eyes looked instinctively for the tree of life and the tree of knowledge" (300). Oz sees the coveted amalgamation of the Israeli bond to the land and to European education and manners in the Arab family. There and only there do the trees of the Garden of Eden grow. However, in his efforts to impress the Palestinian children, when visiting the house with his uncle, he tries to prove to them that he is not part of a "pitiful nation, a nation of crouched scholars, weak moths flying from every shadow" (372). He loses control of an iron ball he is trying to swing by its chain, and the iron ball flies loose and crushes the foot of the family's son. Later in the novel, he continues to think about the Palestinian family listening to the radio when the United Nations' 1947 resolution is announced and imagines what happened to them during and after the War of Independence.

Oz does not ignore the Palestinians or their links to the land but adopts an orientalist gaze both in the description of the El-Siluany home and family (300–305) and toward the Arab who discovers him hiding in a clothing store, with his "warm cheek and pleasant grey stubble [. . .] like a kind-hearted, elderly carpenter, a sort of Gepetto" (332), whom he remembers with longing. They are described as warm people, close to nature, living a peaceful life with extended families and many children. The episode in the El-Siluany home with the iron ball is certainly part of Oz's acknowledgment of Jewish cruelty and insensitivity to the Palestinians and their suffering, but when he comes to formulating the Jewish-Arab conflict and interpreting it, he is drawn again to Jewish victimhood: "In the lives of individuals and of people, too, the worst conflicts are often those that break out between those who are persecuted" (330).

According to Oz, both the Jews and the Arabs suffered oppression originating in Europe that caused trauma on both sides. "When the Arabs look at us they see not a bunch of half-hysterical survivors but a new offshoot of Europe, with its colonialism, technical sophistication and exploitation, that had cleverly returned to the Middle East – in Zionist guise this time – to exploit, evict and oppress all over again" (330). When the Jews look at the Arabs they "do not see the fellow victims either, brothers in adversity, but somehow we see pogrom-making Cossacks, bloodthirsty anti-Semites, Nazis in disguise"

(330). Jews and Arabs are like siblings (Isaac and Ishmael in the Bible) who have a common abusive father but instead of uniting and amassing a common strength, they fight each other.

Oz attempted to understand the nature of the Israeli-Palestinian conflict by proposing a highly appealing psychological explanation for the behavior of the two nations. However, by positioning Jews and Arabs as two counterparts who are equal he denies the Palestinian tragedy and Israeli responsibility. Oz's discussion of the land and the conflict brings both the empathetic vision and the authoritative voice to the fore. He relates to the Jewish people as "a bunch of half-hysterical survivors" who continue to nurture their victimhood, a position which, as Raz Yosef has noted, "refrain[s] from dealing with the question of responsibility for the injustices."[63] Furthermore, he adopts the paternalistic stance of the friendly therapist advising these two nations to address their suffering as psychological distress and suggests a resolution.[64]

Unlike Oz's orientalism and paternalistic approach, Matalon's version has what Karen Grumberg has called "subversive spatiality" (200), where she uses spatial contexts to depict circumstances that are unsettling and their ensuing instability. Clearly, as Ktzia Alon and Dalya Markovich have argued, Mizrahi literature engages in a dialogue with Israel's territorial borders, and with spaces that are both geographic and cultural. The Mizrahi space – the *ma'abara*, the development town,[65] and, in Matalon's works, the immigrant neighborhood – is a space outside "the place." Authors describe life in these peripheral neighborhoods as experiences that are engraved into the immigrants' identities as well as those of their children. As Batya Shimoni comments, these spaces are "depicted in literature as choking,"[66] and undesirable but which are nevertheless inescapable.

Lucette's family's prefab was forlorn, poorly insulated, and constructed directly on the sand without a foundation. This house is a haven for the family, a place where "the law of the ways and habits of life known only to members of the household, the unspoken rules of how things were done and how they should be done, with the right rhyme, rhythm, and meter" (275). However, it is not called "home" in the novel but, instead, it is referred to as "the shack," or the "not-home," or the missing home (2–3). The disparity between "home" and "shack" makes it clear that this enclosure fails to serve as an intimate and safe space. The shack repulses protective significance.

The shack is a silent witness to all the events in the novel, and also changes with time, thus mirroring the condition of those inhabiting it. In Oz, the dark and silent room is linked to his mother's mental state. Matalon's mother is not a character in the shack; she is analogous to it: "She [the mother] herself wasn't another person, she was the shack" (27). Lucette struggles to confirm her ownership, destroying and rebuilding its interior in a desperate attempt to make it a home. Na'ama Tsal, in her study of the idea of home in Matalon's novel, maintains that "this agitation and ongoing mobility are inseparable [...] from the deep desire for stable domestic boundaries."[67] For instance, Lucette puts up wallpaper, then covers it with wooden beams, replaces carpets, turning the structure into a dynamic entity and a source of limitless possibilities. She constantly attempts to redesign the walls to feel that she belongs and that this is her home (312). As Matalon writes: "That was it – the process: she tore down and moved the walls of the shack as renewed confirmation of belonging, of home" (225).

This non-home is constantly contrasted with the mother's previous home and sense of belonging in Egypt. What remains of these experiences are the objects from her former space that she throws out and then rescues in a toxic combination of nostalgia and anger (114). Instead of stability, the house trembles from the inside, as well as from the outside, since the shack "gets lost" in wind and rain (189).

Like Oz's house, the Matalon's living quarters do not provide safety or belonging. In Oz's home, the walls are thick, like a bunker or a jail, as though the only way to survive this Land was by closing the doors and blocking out the light. In Matalon's prefab, the walls are thin and unstable, and the shack is open to the winds, as though there was no protection at all. In both novels, the mother is analogous to the home either through her remoteness in Oz or her physicality in Matalon.

Appended to the home is the garden or a dream of a garden. As in Oz's novel, the inability to grow trees and flowers takes on symbolic meaning. Matalon describes a similar defeat: the narrator illustrates at length the "non-garden" that is concurrently a source of hope and testimony to failure. In the mother's constant attempts to invent a sense of home, she tries to grow flowers by following the guidelines for an ideal garden in a horticulture book (which parallels Oz's father and the books he borrows from the library). This is her dream:

> Elgnena in place of suspended desire, her suspended desires. Elgnena as an invitation to climb a slippery mountain slope, to reach the peak, the rose garden. Elgnena as a penal colony, a forced labor camp – for her, for her fellows. Elganana as a Sanatorium. Elgenena as a natural extension of the interior (52).

As in Oz, Lucette believes that the land pleads for the Palestinians, as though only they knew the secret of the promised land. She dreams of a garden in Arabic, constantly uses the Arabic word "elgnena" to describe it, and hires a Palestinian gardener, Mustafa, to whom she can express her hopes in her first language. However, despite their joint efforts at producing a garden, the flowers die and she draws flowers instead, rather than growing them and paints roses, cyclamens, and poppies. Thus, parallel to their efforts to make the land bloom, Lucette and Mustafa drink coffee together, while Mustafa examines her painting (336).

The novel ends when Lucette decides to visit Mustafa, to see how he is doing during a curfew imposed by the Israeli military on the Occupied Territories, and persuades her son to take her to the West Bank, an unusual step by an Israeli. There she discovers the extent of his hardship and his poverty and when she looks around she sees that "the entire wall of the room was covered with the mother's flower painting," (367) on which his daughters stuck real soil and leaves and flowers, most of them already dried.

Matalon's decision to end her novel with this picture of the glued soil on the picture on the wall of Mustafa's apartment suggests a new assessment of the question of the promised land. Mustafa and Lucette shared their longing for the land they lost. They are both uprooted, and thus are not on opposite sides as in Oz's equation. Matalon does not suggest a resolution or political scheme in her novel but points to the intimate suffering of the two people. However, while Matalon creates an analogy between Mizrahi women and the Arab gardener she bluntly articulates that while the novel illustrates the marginal place of Mizrahi women and the trauma of immigration, the reader must not forget the Palestinians, the victims of the national project. In describing the Palestinian in his territory, with his wretched house (unlike the orientalist flourishing garden of the El-Siluany family before 1948 in Oz's work), Matalon inserts visible cracks in her main story of the Mizrahim by showing that behind the exclusion of the Mizrahim lies the worse fate of the Palestinians.[68]

These differences between the two novels again highlight the disparity between Oz's empathy and paternalism in his version of the conflict and Matalon's "empathic unsettlement." In Emmy Koopman's analysis of the concept of "empathic unsettlement" in the works of J.M. Coetzee, she suggested that it can provide a "fruitful 'middle ground' between a 'conventional' engaging narrative which allows readers to understand the represented Other, and disrupting techniques which make it clear that understanding the Other can never be complete."[69] This creates a "balance between disruption and engagement."[70] While Oz's authoritative version assumes it understands the Palestinians and encourages empathy for Jewish survivors, Matalon's "empathic unsettlement" breaks down any delusive empathy. By bringing the real victims of this disputed land to the fore, she eliminates any possibility for self-pity and refuses to prolong the national denial.

The photo – A portrait of the artist as a young person

A photo is assumed to be objective evidence of an experience in that its caption can confirm a story. It is an authoritative representation of the factual. To document his family's story, Oz goes through an album that survived, "studying," as Nancy Miller suggested, "the portraits of family and friends captured in these snapshots of Eastern European life before the disaster."[71]

> A battered photo album survives from Vilna days. Here is Father, with his brother David, both still at school [...] here is Grandpa Alexander [.] and here are some group photographs, perhaps a graduation class (98).

Oz looks at the pictures, wondering about the fate of each face. As the reader cannot see the pictures, they operate as a point of departure to the narrative. However, one real picture is reproduced in the book. In Chapter 59, one week before the death of Fania, she suddenly feels better and decides to take her "two men" to a restaurant. "She looked so beautiful and elegant in her navy jersey and light skirt, in her nylon stockings with a seam at the back and her high-heeled shoes" (484). Mother and son go to the Terra Sancta Building, where the Hebrew University was located at that time, to surprise Oz's father who "suddenly cheered up, and fired with enthusiasm" and "put his arms round both our shoulders" (489), feeling that "heaven is smiling on us today" (490). The idealistic picture of the loving family is destroyed a few minutes later, possibly because they overhear a tense conversation in German between two elderly women sitting at the next table. Mother turns pale and says she wants to go home, a cab is ordered, a doctor is called, and new pills are prescribed. A few days later she goes to her sister's home in Tel-Aviv, to the apartment where she commits suicide. An actual photo of Oz with his parents is however included in both the Hebrew and English editions of the novel. This is the only photo in the text. Fania is in the middle, with a smiling face, Oz's father tilts his head gently toward her shoulder and Oz the child looks straight at the camera (Figure 1).

What can we learn from this photo? In this picture, Oz is a small child, younger than he was during the scene at the restaurant, yet the insertion of the picture in this story encapsulates the story of love and darkness and his poetics.

Figure 1. Amos Oz with his father, Yehuda Arieh, and his mother, Fania. Courtesy of the Oz family.

Oz's novel presents his personal struggle for identity. Oz the child is described in the book as lonely,[72] and feels that the entire burden of his parents' aspirations is upon him: "everything they did not achieve in life, everything which was not given to them was loaded onto my shoulders by my parents" (307). This is evidenced in the photo where he stands beneath his parents in his good clothes representing the promise of the future.

After his mother's death he is "too hurt and angry" (203) to mourn her, and decides to separate himself from his parents and change his name, in an attempt to adopt the native Israeli Sabra identity. He takes on the change of identity demanded by the national ideology – an act his parents could not perform – but nevertheless describes this decision in terms of violence directed against the self. However, the text itself, with its dual gaze that authorizes both irony and criticism, is proof that the aspirations of the young Amos were impossible to achieve. "Oz had come a long way from the day he turned 14-and-a-half, the day he decided to erase his family name, to abandon his father's house, to leave Jerusalem and uproot himself to Hulda," writes Dan Laor, suggesting that Oz could only fully accept his origins, Jerusalem and his immigrant parents in this later book, many years after he "killed" his father.[73] Oz could only reveal his childhood trauma once his position and status were established.

The choice to include this picture exemplifies this idea. It shows the true story beneath Oz's Sabra image (familiar from the many photos of Oz himself) and is part of the book's cultural importance. This is especially true for the nature of the photo which is typical of people who go to a photographer's studio to have a family picture taken. It does not reveal the pain and suffering experienced by Oz's mother and family, but rather captures an instant of normativity that does not exist in the hundreds of pages of Oz's autobiography. It immortalizes a minute, a dream of love, an optimistic gaze, while emphasizing the loss. The photo was taken in the 1940s and does not show Israeli spaces. It is a diasporic photo, where the heavy clothes and the photographer's backdrop resembles many other family pictures of the 1930s and the 1940s, including pictures that were taken before the Holocaust and are a testament to family members who were murdered later. Through this image of "the lost family" that many readers are familiar with from their own photos of family members, Oz, the well-known Sabra, reveals the child he once was. This was a brave and inspiring action and accounts for the enormous attention and the emotional and empathetic reactions it received, but it cannot be separated from Oz's voice and his senior status as one of the canonical authors of Israeli literature.[74]

Unlike Oz, who came from a hegemonic-intellectual family where writing was almost a vocation and wrote this novel at the peak of his career, Matalon had to struggle to find her voice. In "Mihutz la-makom, be-tokh ha-zman" (Out of Place, Inside Time), she discusses this challenge and inquires "how does the minority, the immigrant, identify itself from within itself, in its own voice?"[75]

In contrast to Oz, whose family's aspirations were concentrated on him, a son who would fulfill the national aspirations, "the girl" in Matalon's novel is always perceived as an interruption, and she internalizes that it is better for her to disappear or be mute. She is an addition to the family, she clings to her mother and her brother and sister, she is passive, tries not to make a lot of noise, and does not express any demands, complaints, or thoughts. Her choice to write follows what bell hooks, an African-American author, feminist, and social activist describes as "talking back."[76] This constitutes the point of departure for the process of "coming to voice" as a woman who expresses "our movement from object to subject."[77] This is typical of women's autobiographies in general and the autobiographical writings of marginal women authors in particular.[78] The act of writing and the position of the writer, both of which are part of Matalon's novel, lead to a process of gazing and phrasing:

> The yearning heart, which was born with the first gaze at the first object: the pathos of the reservoir. The future, in the guise of the yearning backward gaze, was also the past and the present, a memory that I must discard if I am to preserve it (81).

Writing and gazing allow the protagonist to look at her past from a different perspective and use that knowledge to bolster her coming of age as an intellectual. This process is full of contradictions and incompleteness and thus demands a different structure. Although Matalon stated that "I tried to be a very faithful listener to my memories. That is why the novel is so fragmented,"[79] the structure of the text is much more than an authentic recollection of the past. The free flow of the text and the vagueness of memory signal the artificiality of a linear life story and its teleological unfolding; however, a deliberate rationale guides its design.

The text is composed of fragmented sections of short chapters linking experiences, attitudes, and memories. The sequences of memories, along with letters, political manifestos, quotations from novels and gardening books, all organized non-chronologically, create different perspectives but remain linked syntactically since the word that ends one chapter is the same word that starts the next chapter. Balaban called the novel an arabesque, a structure that preserves a central facet of the mother's roots in Egypt, whereas Nitza Keren suggested "quilt writing" as a way to describe the patchwork of interlocking materials. However, above all this is a portrait that demands a different approach, as shown through the only photo referred to in the text.

Photography plays a role in Matalon's novel. Her engagement with photography started with her first novel, *The One Facing Us*, where her dominant esthetic strategy was to refer to photos but to deliberately undermine their validity. The chapters begin with reproductions of pictures (or pictures that are only described), which launch the narrative. These pictures are fictional and they express the slippery dichotomy between facts and imagination. In fact, as noted by Omri Ben Yehuda, Matalon uses photography to instill doubt in regards to identification and to blur categories of identity.[80] In *Bliss*, she also describes Sara as being a photographer and her informal activity of taking photos of sleeping people, also with no reference to their identities.[81]

In *The Sound of our Steps*, only one photograph is described, but according to Nancy Berg the entire novel is in fact a portrait in which the artist generates a gaze from the outside and a dialogue with its observer/reader.[82] Whereas Oz's photo is a formal one in terms of its setting and also in its clarity as concrete evidence that appears in the text, Matalon writes about a picture of herself and her parents taken in Italy when she and her mother visited her father (23). The chapter "Piazza San Marco: First visit" (25) describes the photograph: "There were three of us in the photograph: him, the mother, and me at the age of a year and ten months" (25). The photo shows the relationship between the parents and the girl as a beloved infant (as opposed to many other incidents in the text).

> The photograph is split: three deep creases run down its right side, passing through Maurice, the square, the group of pigeons on the right. It looks as if it has been glued together, or as if it has been fished out of something, rescued despite itself, as if it has become fiction or was always fiction. A fictitious photograph. She says: "It was when I took you to Italy, for him to see you when you were about two years old." It never happened. (26-7).

Matalon goes back and forth from photo to text. The photo is only described in the text so the reader cannot see it or be sure it exists. In an interview with Dalia Ben-Ari, Matalon showed this specific picture and stated that "this is the only family photo in which I have a mother and a father together, and the photo seems delusional and fictitious to me, on the borderline between 'was' and 'wasn't' Figure 2."[83]

In the novel, the photo becomes a literary figure preserving the tension between its existence and its fictitious quality. It also correlates with other figures and portraits,

Figure 2. Ronit Matalon with her mother, Emma, and her father, Felix. Courtesy of the Matalon family.

such as Monet's picture that is hanging on the walls of the shack.[84] The constant reexamination of the photo portraying a normative family underscores how unrepresentative and fantastic this event was since its intimate and optimistic content refutes the "the history of the *familia* and her place in it tiptoed around holes, pits of heavy, ambivalent silence: the eyes troubles were there in the silence, the partial blindness, the flaws"(12).

These two family photographs can serve as a metonym for the nature of Oz's and Matalon's autobiographical writings. They reveal an instant of joy and a wish for normativity, but they clash with the misery of the families. Neither of them articulates the specific Israeli space, and thus negates the ideological demand for national rooting. They both reveal that facts, photos, and documents cannot tell the whole story and that grasping the autobiographical narrative is a constant dialectical movement between pedagogical narrative and the performativity of the intimate and the personal, between a photo and what is hiding behind it.

However, the Oz family photo, which is real and evidence, enables him, for the first time, to remove his cover story and reveal his childhood and his uprooted parents. This diasporic picture, with its typical setting, represents a historical moment, makes the tragedy vivid, and corresponds to the lives of many readers who can identify with his story. Thus it brings together the authoritative voice (Oz the persona who shows his childhood photo) and an emotional and empathetic reaction.

Matalon's photo tells a different story. It does not exist in the text, and thus cannot immediately draw the attention or elicit the emotions of the reader. Its validity is undermined all the time since, above all, it does not represent any historical moment. This photo expresses a much more modest position of the author/narrator that counters and subverts any authoritative voice: when times and places, memory, and speculations, truth and fiction are merged, and the hierarchies are broken, the suffering is real but empathy is always evasive. This creates a feeling of unease and demonstrates the power of "empathetic unsettlement" in any collective narrative or ideology.

A Tale of Love and Darkness and *The Sound of Our Steps* are clearly two monuments of contemporary Israeli literature. They both relate to the trauma of immigration and cast doubt on Israeli meta-narratives by revealing the tension between the personal and the national and between formal autobiographical writing and the narration of fragmented memory and recollection. Their mutual focus on the relationship between mother and child and their representation of home, garden, and the question of the land reveal the disparity between them. Oz's combination of an authoritative voice, the acknowledgment that it is Oz, the ultimate sabra and the renowned author who reveals his secret, and the poetics of empathy that conveyed this strong feeling, gave him the power to openly discuss and criticize the cost of Zionism. Matalon, on the other hand, adopted poetics that rupture emotional identification and create "empathic unsettlement," as a means to subvert the national endeavor. With her unauthoritative voice that undermines its own realization, her story shows that it is possible to tell an Israeli story with no harmony or happy end.

Notes

1. Gilmore, *Autobiographics*, 11.
2. Hess, *Self as Nation*, 5.
3. Ibid., 2.
4. Lejeune, "The Autobiographical Pact," 5.
5. See: Gilmore, *The Limit of Autobiography*, 2; and Miller, "Representing others."
6. Smith and Watson, "Introduction," 20.
7. Olney, *Metaphors of Self*, 38; and *Memory and Narrative*.
8. Kaplan, "Amos Oz's A Tale of Love and Darkness," 122.
9. See for instance: Ashkenazi, "Ha-hakhi yafa," 170.
10. Ibid., 11.
11. Gili Izikovitz, "Ha'im janer ha-auto-fiction hoo be-sakh ha-kol sifrut shel narkisistim [Is the Auto-fiction Genre Merely the Literature of Narcissists?]," *Haaretz*, February 1, 2019. https://www.haaretz.co.il/gallery/literature/.premium-MAGAZINE-1.6803878#hero__bottom. Accessed November 8, 2020.
12. Hess, *Self as Nation*, 2.
13. Ben-Dov, *Haim ktuvim*, 15.
14. Oz, *Sippur*, 36 (in Hebrew). see also Ben-Dov, *Haim ktuvim*, 14–15; and Hess, *Self as Nation*, 9.
15. See: Schwartz, *Pulhan ha-sofer ve-dat ha-medina*, 30.
16. Ari Shavit, "Ha-yehudi ha-sored – re'ayon im Amos Oz [The Surviving Jew – Interview with Amos Oz]," *Haaretz*, March 1, 2002. http://www.haaretz.co.il/misc/1.775818. Accessed November 13, 2020.
17. Elkad-Lehman, "Ha-bait hu ha-makom"; Balaban, *Teysha imahot ve-ima*, 82–99; Keren, "Hed psi'otenu."
18. Matalon, *Kro u'khtov*, 13–4.
19. Matalon, *The Sound of Our Steps*, 133. All quotations from the novel are from the translation by Dalya Bilu, and are marked by page numbers only.
20. Although the father in the novel has many traits in common with the author's biological father, his name in the story is Maurice, not Felix. The real name of Matalon's mother is Emma, but she is called Lucette or Levana in the novel (11). The girl is described throughout the novel in the third person, although it is clear that the character is identified with the narrator. Her name is not identical to the author's name either.
21. Dinah Assouline Stillman, "The Sounds of Memory in Writing: A Conversation with Ronit Matalon," World Literature Today, May 2015, https://www.worldliteraturetoday.org/2015/may/sounds-memory-writing-conversation-ronit-matalon-dinah-assouline-stillman. Accessed November 8, 2020.
22. Matalon, *Ad argi'ah*, 156.
23. Tsal, "haster astir panay," 73. Tsal sees this novel as the "third try to tell the story of the family."
24. Smith and Watson. "Introduction," 27. See also: Huddart, *Postcolonial Theory and Autobiography*.
25. Spivak, "Can the Subaltern Speak?" and Spivak, "Three Women's Texts."
26. Matalon, *Kro u-khtov*, 45–6.
27. See for example: Anderson, *Imagined Communities*.
28. Bhabha, "DissemiNation," 299.
29. On the dialectic between the narrative of *aliyah* and the narrative of *immigration* and their manifestations in Hebrew literature, see Mendelson-Maoz, "Amos Oz," 70–76.
30. See also Porat, "Hayah be-yerushalayim pahad," 143–154.
31. Feige, "Introduction: Rethinking Israel Memory and Identity," vi.
32. Schwartz, *Pulhan ha-sofer ve-dat ha-medina*, 151.
33. Zerubavel, "The 'Mythological Sabra,'"18.

34. All quotations from the novel are from the translation by Nicholas de Lange, and marked by page numbers only.
35. Hall, "Cultural Identity and Diaspora," 394.
36. Shapira, "Ha-sippur ha-tziyoni," 164.
37. Jaffee, "The Victim Community."
38. Schwartz, *Pulhan ha-sofer ve-dat ha-medina*, 145.
39. Schwartz, "Sus troyani," 90–91.
40. Matalon, *Kro u-khtov*, 48.
41. Mendelson-Maoz, *Multiculturalism in Israel*, 120–122.
42. Deborah Starr discusses the role of this novel in Matalon's writing. See: Starr, "Kriah, ktiva, ve-hizakhrut."
43. See for example the grotesque descriptions by Dan Benaya-Seri in which the characters' sexuality changes and bodily organs become autonomous, as well as detailed physical descriptions of characters who fail to comply with the Sabra bodily ideal which enable literature to deviate from the ideological concept of the Zionist body.
44. Caruth, *Unclaimed Experience*, 8.
45. The literature on empathy is intensive. See Coplan and Goldie, *Empathy – Philosophical and Psychological Perspectives*; Hoffman's *Empathy and Moral Development*. For more on empathy in literature, see Keen, *Empathy and the Novel*.
46. On the criticism of empathy see Amiel Hauser's and Mendelson Maoz' reading of Levinas in "Against Empathy" and Mendelson-Maoz on the risk of imperialism, in "The Fallacy of Analogy."
47. LaCapra, *Writing History, Writing Trauma*, 78.
48. LaCapra argues that the film *Schindler's List* works in this direction.
49. Ibid., 41.
50. Ibid., 78.
51. Hochberg, *In Spite of Partition*, 63.
52. Bachelard, *The Poetics of Space*, 4–6.
53. Gurevitz and Aran, "Al ha-makom," 11.
54. See: Robinson, "Exiled in the Homeland," 66.
55. Almog, *The Sabra*, 164–171.
56. Gluzman, *ha-guf ha-tziony*.
57. Schwartz, *ha-yadata et ha-arets*, 13.
58. Ibid., 32.
59. Ibid., 448.
60. Milner, "Sippur mishpahti," 74.
61. See also: Ben-Dov, "Ne'ilah she-hi be'ila," 117–129.
62. Gertz, "ha-nofim shelo," 216.
63. Yosef, *The Politics of Loss*, 143.
64. See: Mendelson-Maoz, "The Fallacy of Analogy."
65. Alon and Markovich, "Yalda shehora," 10–12.
66. Shimoni, *Al saf ha-geula*, 256.
67. Tsal, "He is missing," 310.
68. This strategy also appears in the last line of her novel *Sara Sara* (Bliss): "They've murdered your Rabin," which does not give the reader any relief from the political context. Matalon, *Sara Sara*, 262.
69. Koopman, *Reading the Suffering of Others*, 237.
70. Ibid., 240.
71. Miller, "I Killed My Grandmother," 323.
72. Shaked, "Matzeva le-avot ve-siman le-banim," 17.
73. Laor, "Be-mehozot ha-zikaron," 39–40.
74. Avirama Golan considers the success of this novel to be a literary trick in which those at the margins are set within the consensus as a device for the return of the Zionist narrative. Golan's claim that "the power of *Love and Darkness* resides in the use it

makes of the legitimacy conferred by the multicultural concept to the marginal narrative simply in order to strengthen the central (or previously central) narrative" and presents the idea that by transforming the trauma of immigration from a private event into a collective trauma, he creates a counterfeit homogeneous text. See: Avirama Golan, "Ha'im ha-sippur shelo hu ha-sippur shelanu? [Is his story our story?]," *Haaretz sfarim*, August 31, 2005. https://www.haaretz.co.il/literature/1.1040323. Accessed November 8, 2020.

75. Matalon, *Kero u-khetov*, 47.
76. On Matalon, bell hooks and the black female autobiography, see Galon and Mendelson Maoz, "An Autobiography of Her Own."
77. hooks, "Taking Back," 6, 9.
78. Smith and Watson, "Introduction"; and Galon and Mendelson Maoz, "An Autobiography of Her Own."
79. Assouline Stillman, "The Sounds of Memory."
80. Ben Yehuda, "Le-lo panim," 86.
81. See note above 64.
82. Berg, "Mabat sheni."
83. Dalia Ben-Ari, "Tmunot me-ha-haim: Re'ayon im Ronit Matalon [Pictures from life: An Interview with Ronit Matatlon]," *La-isha*, 2008. Re-published in "Ha-biographia ha-metzulemet shel Ronit Matalon" [The Pictured Biography of Ronit Matalon], *La-isha*, December 12, 2017. https://xnet.ynet.co.il/articles/0,7340,L-5063182,00.html. Accessed November 6, 2020.
84. Berg, "Mabat sheni," 134.

Acknowledgments

The author would like to thank the anonymous reviewers for their helpful comments.

Disclosure statement

No potential conflict of interest was reported by the author(s).

Bibliography

Almog, O. *The Sabra: The Creation of the New Jew*. University of California Press: Berkeley, 2000.
Alon, K., and D. Markovich. "Yalda shehora, pere atzil ve-avaryan tza'atzua: ha-giborim ha-hadashim shel ha-safrut ha-Ivrit. [A Black Girl, a Noble Savage, and a Petty Criminal: Hebrew Literature's New Protagonists]." *Ha-kivun mizrah* 8 (2004): 10–12.
Anderson, B. *Imagined Communities: Reflections on the Origin and Spread of Nationalism*. Rev ed. London: Verso, 1991.

Appelfeld, A. *Sipur ha'im*. [The Story of a Life]. Jerusalem: Keter, 1999.

Ashkenazi, Y. "Ha-hakhi yafa: ha-behira ha-estetit shel kol tze'adenu ke-bituy la-mifgash she-bein ma'arekhet ha-sifrut be-Israel shel shnat 2018 le-nekudat ha-mabat shel ha-mehaberet [The "Prettiest Girl" – The Aesthetic Choice of The Sound of Our Steps as an Expression of the Encounter between Israel's Literary Establishment in 2008, and the Author's Perspective]." *Mikan* 18 (2018): 155–194.

Bachelard, G. *The Poetics of Space*. Translated by Maria Jolas. Boston: Beacon Press, 1964.

Balaban, A. *Teysha imahot ve-ima*. [Nine Mothers and a Mother]. Tel-Aviv: Ha-Kibbutz Ha-Meuhad, 2010.

Barthes, R. "The Death of the Author." In *Image Music Text*, edited and translated by Stephen Heath, 142–148. London: Fontana Press, 1977.

Be'er Haim. *Havalim* [The Pure Element of Time]. Tel-Aviv: Am Oved, 1988.

Ben Yehuda, O. "Le-lo panim: al ha-anonimiyut ba-roman ze im ha-panim eleynu [Faceless: On Anonymity in The One Facing Us]." *Mikan* 18 (2018): 76–88.

Ben-Dov, N. "Ne'ilah she-hi be'ila - al he'adrut, al eros ve-al teshuka be-yetzirotav shel Amos Oz [On absence, Eros and Lust in Amos Oz's work]." *Israel* 7 (2005): 117–129.

Ben-Dov, N. *Haim ktuvim: al autobiographyot sifrutiot Israeliot*. [Written Lives: On Israeli Literary Autobiographies]. Jerusalem: Schocken, 2011.

Berg, N. "Mabat sheni: iyun mehudash ba-dyokan [A Second Look: Re-visioning The Portrait]." *Mikan* 18 (2018): 126–140.

Bhabha, H. "DissemiNation: Time, Narrative, and the Margins of the Modern Nation." In *Nation and Narration*, edited by H. K. Bhabha, 291–322. New York and London: Routledge, 1990.

Caruth, C. *Unclaimed Experience: Trauma, Narrative and History*. Baltimore: Johns Hopkins University Press, 1996.

Castel Bloom, O. *Ha-roman ha-mitzri* [The Egyptian]. Bnei-Brak: Ha-Kibbutz Ha-Meuhad, 2015.

Cixous, H. "The Laugh of the Medusa." *Signs* 1, no. 4 (Summer, 1976): 875–893.

Coplan, A., and P. Goldie, eds. *Empathy—Philosophical and Psychological Perspectives*. Oxford: Oxford University Press, 2011.

de Man, P. *Allegories of Reading*. New Haven: Yale University Press, 1979.

Elkad-Lehman, I. "Ha-bait hu ha-makom she-mimenu mathilim: le-sugiyat ha-(auto)biographia be-ktivata shel Ronit Matalon [Home is Where it all Begins: Ronit Matalon's (Auto) Biographical Writing]." *Iyunim ba-safa u-ba-hevra* 2, no. 2 (2009): 23–99.

Feige, M. "Introduction: Rethinking Israel Memory and Identity." *Israel Studies* 7, no. 2 (2002): V–XIV.

Foucault, M. *The Order of Things*. London: Tavistock Publication, 1970.

Frade-Galon, T., and A. M. Maoz. "An Autobiography of Her Own—Matalon's the Sound of Our Steps." *The Comparatist* 43 (2019): 228–251.

Frankel, A. *Yalda* [Girl]. Tel-Aviv: Mapa, 2004.

Gertz, N. "Ha-nofim shelo ve-ha-nofim sheli." *Israel* 7, no. 2 (2005): 211–217. His landscapes and My Landscapes.

Gilmore, L. *Autobiographics: A Feminist Theory of Women's Self-representation*. Ithaca and London: Cornell University Press, 1994.

Gilmore, L. *The Limit of Autobiography - Trauma and Testimony*. Cornell University Press: Ithaca and London, 2001.

Gluzman, M. *Ha-guf ha-tziony: Leumiut, migdar u-miniut ba-sifrut ha-ivrit ha-hadasha* [The Zionist Body: Nationalism, Gender and Sexuality in Modern Hebrew Literature]. Tel-Aviv: Ha-Kibbutz Ha-Meuhad, 2007.

Gurevitz, Z. *Al ha-makom* [On place]. Ra'anana: Am Oved, 2007.

Gurevitz, Z., and G. Aran. "Al ha-makom [On place]." *Alpayim* 4 (1993): 9–44.

Hall, S. "Cultural Identity and Diaspora." In *Colonial Discourse and Post-Colonial Theory*, edited by P. Williams and L. Chrisman, 392–404. Hertfordshire: Harvester Wheatsheaf, 1994.

Hall, S. "Ethnicity: Identity and Difference." In *Becoming National*, edited by G. Eley and R. Grigor, 339–48. Oxford: Oxford University Press, 1996.

Hess, T. S. "A Mediterranean Mayflower? Introducing Ronit Matalon." *Prooftexts* 30, no. 3 (2010): 293–302.

Hess, T. S. *Self as Nation – Contemporary Hebrew Autobiography*. Waltham: Brandeis University Press, 2016.

Hochberg, G. Z. *In Spite of Partition: Jews, Arabs, and the Limits of Separatist Imagination*. Princeton: Princeton University Press, 2008.

Hoffman, M. L. *Empathy and Moral Development: Implications for Caring and Justice*. Cambridge: Cambridge University Press, 2001.

hooks, bell. *Talking Back: Thinking Feminist, Thinking Black*. Routledge: New York and Oxford, 2015.

Huddart, D. *Postcolonial Theory and Autobiography*. London and New York: Routledge, 2008.

Irigaray, L. *This Sex Which is Not One*. Translated by Catherine Porter with Carolyn Burke. New York: Cornell University Press, 1977.

Jaffee, M. "The Victim Community in Myth and History: Holocaust Ritual, the Question of Palestine and the Rhetoric of Christian Witness." *Journal of Ecumenical Studies* 28 (1991): 223–238.

Kaniuk, Y. *Tashah [1948]*. Tel-Aviv: Yediot Sfarim, 2010.

Kaplan, E. "Amos Oz's A Tale of Love and Darkness and the Sabra Myth." *Jewish Social Studies* 14, no. 1 (2007): 119–143.

Karen, G. *Place and Ideology in Contemporary Hebrew Literature*. Syracuse: Syracuse University Press, 2011.

Keen, S. *Empathy and the Novel*. Oxford: Oxford University Press, 2007.

Keren, N. "Hed psioteynu be-ginat ha-em ha-gdola [Our Steps Echo in the Garden of the Great Mother]." *Moznaim* 83, no. 1 (2009): 24–26.

Keren, N. *Ka-yeri'a be-yad ha-rokemet: nashim kotvot ve-ha-text* [Like Fabric in the Hand of the Embroideress: Women Writers and the Text]. Ramat Gan: Bar-Ilan University Press, 2010.

Koopman, E. "Reading the Suffering of Others—The Ethical Possibilities of 'Empathic Unsettlement." *Journal of Literary Theory* 4 (2010): 235–252.

Kristeva, J. *Desire in Language: A Semiotic Approach to Literature and Art*. Translated by L.S. Roudiez. New York: Columbia University Press, 1980.

LaCapra, D. *Writing History, Writing Trauma*. Baltimore: Johns Hopkins University Press, 2001.

Laor, D. "Be-mehozot ha-zikaron: biografiyah, idiologiyah ve-sippur be-ktivato shel Amos Oz [In the lands of memory: biography, ideology and story in the writing of Amos Oz]." *Israel* 7 (2005): 25–38.

Lejeune, P. "The Autobiographical Pact." In *On Autobiography*, edited by P. J. Eakin, 3–30. Minneapolis: University of Minnesota Press, 1989.

Levy, L. *Poetic Trespass: Writing between Hebrew and Arabic in Israel/Palestine*. Princeton: Princeton University Press, 2014.

Matalon, R. *Kero u-khetov* [Read and Write]. Tel Aviv: Ha-Kibbutz Ha-Meuhad, 2001.

Matalon, R. *Bliss [Sarah, Sarah]*. Translated by Jessica Cohen. New York: Metropolitan Books, 2003.

Matalon, R. *The Sound of Our Steps [Kol tze' adenu]*. Translated by Dalya Bilu. New York: Metropolitan Books, 2015.

Matalon, R. *Ad Argiah*. [Literary Essays]. Ramat-Gan: Afik, 2018.

Mendelson-Maoz, A. "Amos Oz's 'A Tale of Love and Darkness' in a Framework of Immigration Narratives in Modern Hebrew Literature." *Journal of Modern Jewish Studies* 9, no. 1 (March, 2010): 71–87.

Mendelson-Maoz, A. "ha-bait ha-na'ul shel Amos Kenan ve-Amoz Oz [Identities in transition in Israeli Culture, a book in Honor of Prof. Nurit Gertz]." In *Zehuyot be-hithavut ba-tarbut ha-Yisraelit: sefer ha-yovel li-khvod Nurit Gertz* [The Locked House of Amos Kenan and Amos Oz], edited by S. Meiri, Y. Munk, and A. Mendelson-Maoz, 482–496. Ra'anana: The Open University Press, 2013.

Mendelson-Maoz, A. *Multiculturalism in Israel – Literary Perspectives*. West Lafayette, Indiana: Perdue University Press, 2014.

Mendelson-Maoz, A. "The Fallacy of Analogy and the Risk of Moral Imperialism: Israeli Literature and the Palestinian Other." *Humanities* 8, no. 3 (2019): 1–18.

Miller,, K. N. "Representing Others: Gender and the Subjects of Autobiography." *Differences: A Journal of Feminist Cultural Studies* 6, no. 1 (1994): 1–27.

Miller, K. N. "I Killed My Grandmother: Mary Antin, Amoz Oz, and the Autobiography of a Name." *Biography* 30, no. 3 (2007): 319–341.

Milner, I. "Sippur mishpahti: Mitos ha-mishpaha be-sippur al ahavah ve-hoshekh u-ve-yitzirato ha-mukdemet shel Amos Oz [A Family Story: The Myth of the Family in A Tale of Love and Darkness and in Amos Oz's Early Work]." *Israel* 7 (2005): 73–105.

Netiva, B.-Y. *Bein ha-sfirot: Roman al hathalat ha-milhama 1948.* [Between Calendars]. Yerushalem: Keter, 1981.

Netiva, B.-Y. *Bein ha-sfirot: roman al hathalat ha-milhama 1948.* [Through the Binding Ropes]. Yerushalem: Domino, 1985.

Netiva, B.-Y. *Kshe'prtsa ha-medina.* [when the State of Israel Broke Out]. Yerushalem: Keter, 1991.

Olney, J. *Metaphors of Self: The Meaning of Autobiography.* Princeton: Princeton University Press, 1972.

Olney, J. *Memory and Narrative: The Weave of Life-Writing.* Chicago and London: University of Chicago Press, 1998.

Oz, A. *A Tale of Love and Darkness [Sippur al ahavah ve-hoshekh].* Translated by Nicholas De Lange. London: Vintage Books, 2005.

Porat, D. "Hayah bi-Yerushalayim pahad: sho'ah ve-antishemiyut be-sifro shel Amos Oz sippur al ahavah ve-hoshekh [There was Fear in Jerusalem: Holocaust and Antisemitism in Amos Oz's A Tale of Love and Darkness]." *Israel* 7 (2005): 143–154.

Robinson,, D. D. "Exiled in the Homeland." *Shofar – an Interdisciplinary Journal of Jewish Studies* 21, no. 2 (2003): 66–81.

Schwartz, Y. "Nikhnasta le-armon mekhushaf ve-shihrarta oto me-ha-kishuf: al sippur al ahava ve-hoshekh ke-sefer pulhan [You entered an Enchanted Place and Released it from the Spell: A Tale of Love and Darkness as a Cult Novel]." *Israel* 7 (2005): 173–210.

Schwartz, Y. *Ma she-ro'im mikan: sugiyot ba-historyographia shel ha-sifrut ha-ivrit.* [What We See from Here: Issues in the Historiography of Hebrew Literature]. Tel Aviv: Dvir Publishing House, 2005.

Schwartz, Y. *Ha-yadata et ha-arets sham ha-limon pore'ah? handasat ha-Adam u-mahshevet ha-merhav ba-sifrut ha-ivrit ha-hadasha* [Did You Know the Land where the Lemon Tree Blooms? Human and Spatial Engineering in Modern Hebrew Literature]. Tel Aviv: Dvir Publishing House, 2007.

Schwartz, Y. *Pulhan ha-sofer ve-dat ha-medina* [The Cult of the Author and the State Religion]. Or Yehuda: Dvir, 2011.

Schwartz, Y. "Sus troyani: ha-knisa ha-metuhkhemet shel Ronit Matalon le-lev ha-stzena shel ha-sifrut ha-Yisraelit [Trojan Horse: Ronit Matalon's Subtle Entry into the Heart of the Israeli Literary Scene]." *Mikan* 18 (2018): 89–103.

Shaked, G. "Matzeva le-avot ve-siman la-banim: ha-otobiyografiya shel Oz al reka otobiografiyot shel Guri, Kaniuk ve-Appelfeld [A Tombstone for Fathers and a Sign for the Sons: Oz's Autobiography in the Context of Guri's, Kaniuk's and Appelfeld's Autobiographies]." *Israel* 7 (2005): 1–24.

Shapira, A. "Ha-sippur ha-tzioni shel Amos Oz [Amos Oz's Zionist narrative]." *Israel* 7 (2005): 163–171.

Shimoni, B. *Al saf ha-geula: sipur ha-ma'abara: Dor rishon ve-sheni* [On the Verge of Redemption: The Story of the Ma'abara: The First and Second Generation]. Be'er-Sheva: Heksherim – Kinneret Zmora Bitan, 2008.

Smith, S., and J. Watson. "Introduction: Situating Subjectivity in Women's Autobiographical Practices." In *Women, Autobiography, Theory: A Reader*, edited by S. Smith and J. Watson, 3–52. Madison: University of Wisconsin Press, 1998.

Soker-Schwager, H. "Hasvaa shkufa—taktikot shel mered aher—al 'Kakha ani medaberet im ha-ruah' me'et Sami Berdugo [Transparent Camouflage—Tactics of a Different Rebellion: Sami Berdugo's 'And Say to the Wind']." *Mehkarey Yerushalaim ba-safrut ha-ivrit* 22 (2008): 153–175.

Spivak, G. C. "Can the Subaltern Speak?" In *Marxism and the Interpretation of Culture*, edited by N. Cary and L. Grossberg, 271–313. London: Macmillan, 1988.

Spivak, G. C. "Three Women's Texts and Circumfession." In *Postcolonialism and Autobiography*, edited by A. Hotnung and E. Ruhe, 7–22. Amsterdam: Rodopi, 1998.

Starr, D. "Kriah, ktiva ve-hizakhrut: Ronit Matalon ve-sifrut ha-zikron ha-mitzrit [Reading, Writing, and Remembrance: Ronit Matalon and the Jewish-Egyptian Memorial Literature]." *Mikan* 18 (2018): 141–154.

Tammy, A. H., and A. M. Maoz. "Against Empathy: Levinas and Ethical Criticism in the 21st Century." *Journal of Literary Theory* 8 (2014): 199–218.

Tsal, N. "Haster astir panai: hitmodedota shel Ronit Matalon im ha-steriotip ha-mizrahi [I Will Hide My Face: Ronit Matalon's Encounter with the Mizrahi Stereotype]." *Mikan* 18 (2018): 54–75.

Tsalka, D. *Sefer ha-alef bet [Alphabet Book]*. Tel Aviv: Hargol, 2003.

Yosef, R. *The Politics of Loss and Trauma in Contemporary Israeli Cinema*. New York: Routledge, 2011.

Zerubavel, Y. "The 'Mythologial Sabra' and Jewish Past: Trauma, Memory, and Contested Identity." *Israel Studies* 7, no. 2 (2002): 115–144.

Amos Oz: The lighthouse

Yigal Schwartz

ABSTRACT

Yigal Schwartz, Amos Oz's long-time editor and a prominent Oz scholar, reflects on the author's impact on Israel culture.

The moment I learned of Amos Oz's death, the first thought that came to my mind – and, I am certain, to the minds of other Israelis as well – was that this event marks an end of an era. Apparently, this is what comes to mind instinctively when a great artist and a distinguished human being passes away. Amos Oz was an exceptional author and an outstanding man. And yet, as a matter of fact, the period in which he was considered undisputedly to be one of the heroes of Israeli culture has ended long before his death. Oz knew this. With his sharp senses and extraordinary ability to transform feelings and insights into creative works, he was the first to document carefully the erosion processes and the collapse of this era in real-time. In the 1980s, or more precisely from 1982 to 1991, he wrote a series of requiems for his world and his bygone era. It was there that he foresaw, as he had already done in the story "The Way of the Wind," which was included in *Where the Jackals Howl* (1965), what would be the alternate routes leading to other people, who would be the heroes of the next period. I remember this decade, and especially the second half of it, exceptionally well because I had the privilege of being Oz's editor at the Keter publishing house at the time. The first of these requiems was *A Perfect Peace* (1982).[1] It was followed by Oz's attempt to prevent the demise and ultimate collapse of Israel's old elite in the form of the travelogue, *In the Land of Israel* (1983),[2] in which Oz attempted to open doors and windows to the winds of time and to recalibrate his own navigational instruments. Next, he wrote a series of three funeral books. The first, with its postmortem title *Black Box* (1987), is a sensational epistolary novel in the style of Pierre Choderlos de Laclos's *Dangerous Liaisons*.[3] In it, Oz describes a total war – over territory, over a woman, and over a legacy – between the arrogant and depressive Dr. Alexander A. Gideon, who wanders between universities in the United States and England, a representative of the white aristocracy whose legitimacy has expired, and Michael (Michel-Henri) Sommo, a Mizrachi, religious, pious man, who is, in essence, a representative of the rising class. The second requiem in the series was *To*

Know a Woman (1989).[4] The novel's protagonist, Yoel Raviv, an Israeli Security Services retiree, serves as a monument to a rich and fascinating bygone era, who spends his time renovating his home and maintaining contact with a few kindred souls. Fima (Efraim Nisan), the protagonist of *The Third Condition (Fima)* (1991),[5] the third requiem in the series, is a wonderful Jewish-Israeli version of Ivan Alexandrovich Goncharov's character Oblomov.[6] Both Fima and Oblomov are aristocrats who have lost their spiritual assets and spend their days in useless wandering and pondering. The character of Fima, for whom I have a great fondness (he is somewhat reminiscent of the late Prof. Menachem Brinker,[7] who was one of Oz's close friends), anticipates the captivating figure of the detached "eternal student" Shmuel Ash in the novel *Judas* (2014).[8]

The fifteen years between the early 1980s and the mid-1990s were problematic years in Oz's career in Israel. They came after fifteen exceptionally productive years during which Oz took the Israeli literary scene by storm and later (especially after *My Michael* was translated into English) became one of the most popular and well-known voices in world literature. During those years, the first of his career, from the appearance of *Where the Jackals Howl* to the publication of *A Perfect Peace*, Oz enjoyed almost unlimited literary and public recognition. The only exception, perhaps, was of some grating voices of members of the kibbutz community, who were not particularly enamored of their images as they were reflected in Oz's kibbutz stories.

In *Where the Jackals Howl* (1965),[9] which was published when he was only 26 years old, Oz already managed to draw a depth map of the fault line of Israeli culture, which threatens its existence more than anything. This fault line is the enormous tension between two vectors of desire, represented by the two largest political camps in Israel. Most of the Israeli public perceives Oz as a typical representative of the Left. This is true, but only on a superficial, political level. As an artistic personality, throughout his life, and especially during his first creative period, Oz was torn between two incompatible desires: first was the vision and Zionist Revisionist romantic imagery that he imbibed from his parents and his great uncle Joseph Klausner[10] at his home in Jerusalem, from which he ran away for his entire life following his mother's suicide, and the second was the moderate socialist-Zionist vision, which he adopted at Kibbutz Hulda, where he went to live at the age of fifteen. Oz was ambivalent about the authors of the literary generation that preceded him – the Palmach Generation – mainly S. Yizhar and Moshe Shamir, the latter of which was, from the beginning of his career (when he was still closely associated with the Ha-Shomer Ha-Tzair movement), a completely devoted Revisionist Zionist. In complete contrast to the claims of major Israeli literary critics, especially Gershon Shaked and Gabriel Moked, Oz never rebelled against the "generation of his fathers," who were, in fact, his "elder brothers." On the contrary, he admired S. Yizhar, who encouraged him in letters but also did not spare the rod in dealing with him, and he greatly appreciated Moshe Shamir. He also saw them mainly as the standard-bearers of the national literature who paved the way for him. He studied them, reread them, was in conversation with them in his stories, and took from them, together with A. B. Yehoshua, the torch of national literature, which had drawn from the "native" culture of the Land of Israel.

In the stories in the collection *Where the Jackals Howl*, Oz created the Israeli chronotope,[11] depicting a small tribe that perceives itself as an island of culture in an animal-like, barbaric world, surrounding itself with fences, to protect them from the area beyond which is teeming with hostile creatures, jackals, and murderous Arabs. It pretends to be closed and withdrawn from everything that is beyond the fences. But in fact, "the stalker? is in the room" (and the paradigmatic story in this context is, of course, "Nomad and Viper"). The protagonists' heart goes out to what is beyond the fence, and because it is a taboo, and a voluntary taboo at that, the soul rebels. The body crosses the fences and meets the "others" in situations in which fantasy takes control of reality. The forbidden contact, which remains unrealized, is perceived as rape, and in its wake, an "act of reprisal"[12] takes place.

Amos Oz's projection of the depth map of the Israeli fault line, which he refined in his first novel, *Elsewhere, Perhaps* (1966),[13] has not received the attention it deserves. It reached the peak of its complexity and precision in *My Michael* (1968),[14] one of the great novels of the twentieth century. The publication of *My Michael* was a formative event in the collective literary imagination of readers of Hebrew literature, first and foremost because in it Oz (who was then only 28) gave us Hannah Gonen, a larger-than-life woman, a real blue-and-white femme fatale, the Jewish sister of Anna Karenina,[15] Hedda Gabler,[16] Madame Bovary,[17] and Effi Briest.[18] But unlike these characters, and Tzeruya Shalev has noted her uniqueness in this regard,[19] she needs no one, neither husband nor child, with the exception of the Arab twins about whom she fantasizes and literary protagonists from other worlds (for example, Michael Strogoff[20]). She is a woman who despises the ordinary and has a passionate affair with death and its representatives beyond the fence. Hannah also captivated readers due to the fantastic combination of her character and that of Jerusalem, where she lives. Oz drew Jerusalem in the image of Hannah and vice versa. Jerusalem in *My Michael* is a remote, gray place on the fringe of the Middle East, but beneath its surface, the "Jerusalem syndrome" is erupting once again with great bursts of dreams and messianic, apocalyptic spirits. *My Michael* is an amazing map that predicts the forces and drives that eventually gave birth to the 1967 Six-Day War and the components of the moral epidemic that spread after it – the arrogance and visions of imperial grandeur, the blurring of physical and emotional boundaries, the fanaticism, the messianism, the terrible violence.

The third most prominent period in Amos Oz's literary career began with his novel *The Same Sea* (1999)[21] and ended, according to him, with his book of conversations *What's In An Apple?*.[22] Oz loved *The Same Sea* very much, and for a good reason. In this innovative novel, he made a courageous move of rejuvenating this writing career, which he had done years before, in other ways, in his marvelous novella *The Hill of Evil Counsel* (1976) and later in his young adult novel *Soumchi* (1978). He entered his warehouse of images, gleaned from it various materials, and created from them mighty and imaginative syntactic and rhythmic chains. It is possible to say, with caution, that he allowed himself, after many years, to approach the materials of his life and the mementos that were gathered in that warehouse of images in his childhood. After years of wandering in the desert, *The Same Sea* allowed Oz to get back on track. In my opinion, without *The Same Sea*, he would not have written *A Tale of Love and Darkness* (2002),[23] which is one of his finest works and indeed one of the greatest works of Hebrew literature in particular and modern Western literature in general.

In *A Tale of Love and Darkness*, Oz allowed himself for the first time to write an imaginary autobiography. After writing dozens of books in which he made every effort to avoid touching the fire, the shame, the anxieties, and also the brightness of the epiphanic moments he experienced in childhood, in writing this book he has opened to us, as much as he opened to himself, a window to his primal growth chamber. Here, too, he touched the fire with the gloves of reason (he was a man who had lived all his life as someone who had been burned by fire). But these were remarkably thin gloves that made it possible to feel Oz more powerfully than in any of his previous books. It is no wonder that the book was so successful in Israel and abroad (to Oz's great surprise, by the way), since it gave us, its readers, what we need most and receive only in genuinely great works – the deepened, tangible, rich, almost eternal feeling of time as we experienced it only in childhood.

And now is the moment, it seems, to say something almost personal. In the minds of many, Amos Oz seemed to be an arrogant man. Maybe because of his "unbearable" eloquence, maybe due to his decisive tone, maybe because he was handsome, and indeed for many other reasons that belong to the socio-pathology of Israeli culture (an issue to which I devoted an entire book[24]). I want to testify, as someone who knew him for thirty years, during which I had quite a few opportunities to look at him closely, that the term "arrogant" does not in any way relate to the man I knew. I would not address this point if it was not of real importance in understanding his entire oeuvre. Oz, as he said in one of the first interviews with him, was a man who was wounded on the most intimate level. He was in contact with thousands of people, many of whom were showered by him with affection and kindness. There are few people as generous as he was. But certainly, at least according to my sense of the issue, intimate contact with people was not easy for him. It was difficult for him to let go of the glorious towers of defense he had erected in his youth in order to protect himself, in order to survive. Sometimes he seemed to me like a medieval knight who had to manage in our fast-paced world in a heavy suit of armor. And at times I imagined him as the figure of the poet in the brilliant poem "The Albatross" by Baudelaire: The poet resembles "the prince of the clouds/Who is friendly to the tempest and laughs at the bowman;/Banished to ground in the midst of hootings,/His wings, those of a giant, hinder him from walking."[25]

In any event, the playground that Oz created for himself in *The Same Sea* and later also in the hauntingly beautiful fable *Suddenly in the Depth of the Forest* (2005)[26] heralded the sense of liberation that was later realized in a tremendous explosion of creativity in *A Tale of Love and Darkness*. The same sense of freedom was realized in another way in his gentle return to his early stories: *Judas*, which returned in a well-meaning way to the extremist, murderous Christian narrative of *Unto Death* (1971),[27] through the inter-mediate station of *The Third Condition*, to stories from kibbutz life in *Scenes from Village Life* (2002)[28] and *Between Friends* (2012),[29] which return in a calm version, albeit one charged with new anger, to the same spaces which Oz occupied when he began his remarkable writing career, with the collection *Where the Jackals Howl* and the novel *Elsewhere, Perhaps*.

Then came the cursed disease. I remember my conversation with him a year or slightly more before he died. He told me he would not write another novel. A short story, perhaps. I was dumbstruck. I did not know what to say. And he added, as he had told me many times before, and certainly not only me: "Write, write! Friends want to hear your voice."

Amos Oz was a lighthouse that helped many people to navigate through the darkness – family, marital, social, and political darkness. He always remained in the same place. One knew he was there, that he would not move. One knew that he would not turn off the light. And like the spectator in Hans Blumenberg's *Shipwreck with Spectator*,[30] he remained standing on the beach with a divided heart. The magical storm, the capsized ship, and the drowning people attracted him; but as one forced by a demon, and with him, it was the "demon" of the wisdom and vision that had been fighting all sorts of demons all his life. He remained in position and continued to illuminate. He did this, as he testified, twice, once at the beginning of his career in *Under this Blazing Light* (1979)[31] and once at the end of his career, in an exciting interview with Shira Hadad in *What's In An Apple?*: like a blind man who knows how to guide people through the darkness, in a landscape which is intimately familiar to him, and therefore does not prevent him from making his way through.

Translated by Dr. Hannah Komy

Notes

1. Original Hebrew title: *Menuhah nekhonah* (literally: "a proper rest," an expression that appears at the opening of the liturgical prayer "El malei rachamim" ["To the Merciful One"] usually recited at the graveside during the burial service for the soul of a person who has died. Translated into English as *A Perfect Peace*.
2. Original Hebrew title: *Poh ve-sham be-Erets-Yisra'el bi-setav 1982* (literally: "here and there in the land of Israel in the autumn of 1982"). The book records various encounters Oz had during that year with various segments of Israeli society, including members of an ultra-Orthodox community, settlers, Palestinians, and more. Though the interviews Oz conduct were first published in the weekly *Davar ha-shavua* between November 1982 and January 1983, Oz did not consider the book to be merely a journalist or documentary piece but a hybrid fusing together journalistic and literary elements. Translated into English as *In the Land of Israel*.
3. Original Hebrew title: *Kufsah shehorah*. Translated into English as *Black Box*. *Les Liaisons dangereuses*, de Laclos's sensationalist novel, was first published in 1782, and tells the story of a rivalry between to French aristocrats who used seduction to control and exploit other.
4. Original Hebrew title: *La-da'at ishah*. Translated into English as *To Know a Woman*.
5. Original Hebrew title: *ha-Matsav ha-shelishi* (literally: The third condition). Translated into English as *Fima*.
6. An 1859 Russian novel whose main protagonist, the lazy and dreamy aristocratic Ilya Ilyich Oblomov, is often read as the literary incarnation of the superfluous man, a symbol of the old order in 19th-century Russian literature.
7. Menachem Brinker (1935–2016) was a professor of literature and philosophy at the Hebrew University. He was one of the founders of the Peace Now movement, served as literary editor at Keter Publishing, and as the inagural Henry Crown professor of Hebrew Studies at the University of Chicago. Notoriously prolific and interdisciplinary thinker, Brinker's works deal with philosophy, esthetics and the theory of literature and interpretation, Hebrew and general literature, modern Jewish thought, literary criticism and journalism.
8. Original Hebrew title: *ha-bsora al-pi Yehuda* (literally: The Gospel According to Judah). Translated into English as *Judas*.
9. Translated into English as *Where the Jackals Howl and Other Stories*.
10. Joseph G. Klausner (1874–1958): a Jewish historian and professor of Hebrew Literature at Hebrew University, and chief redactor of the Encyclopedia Hebraica. Klausner was the uncle of Dr. Yehuda Arieh Klausner (1910–1970), Amos Oz's father.
11. A term used by the Russian literary theorist Mikhail Bakhtin to refer to the configurations of time and space invoked by a given narrative.
12. In the present context, the term "act of reprisal" echoes the name used in Israel in the 1950s and 1960s to describe the IDF's raids and various deterrence operations, which were carried

out in response to terrorist acts against Israeli residents or military provocations carried out by the armies of the countries bordering Israel.

13. Original Hebrew title: *Makkom Aher* (literally: a different place). Translated into English: Oz as *Elsewhere, Perhaps.*
14. Translated into English as *My Michael.*
15. The protagonist of Leo Tolstoy's 1878 novel.
16. The protagonist of Henrik Ibsen's 1891 play.
17. The protagonist of Gustave Flaubert's 1856 novel.
18. The protagonist of Theodor Fontane's 1895 novel.
19. Shalev, "Aharit davar," 293–300.
20. The protagonist of Jules Verne's 1876 novel.
21. Original Hebrew title: *Oto ha-yam.* Translated into English *The Same Sea.*
22. Oz and Hadad, *Mi-mah `asui ha-tapuah?*
23. Original Hebrew title: *Sipur al ahava ve-hoshekh.* Translated into English as *A Tale of Love and Darkness.*
24. Schwartz, *Ha-ashkenazim.*
25. Baudelaire, Charles. "The Albatross." Translated by Eli Siegel. In Eli Siegel, *Hail, American Development.* New York: Definition Press, 1968, 78. The French poet Charles Baudelaire (1821–1867) included the poem "L'albatros" in the second edition (1861) of *Les Fleurs du mal* (The flowers of evil), famously comparing the large seabird to the poet. In the French original: *"Le poète est semblable au prince des nuées/Qui hante la tempête et se rit de l'archer;/ Exilé sur le sol, au milieu des huées,/Ses ailes de géant l'empêchent de marcher."*
26. Original Hebrew title: *Pitom be-omek ha-yaar.* Translated into English as *Suddenly in the Depths of the Forest.*
27. Original Hebrew title: *Ad mavet.* Translated into English as *Unto Death: Two Novellas: Crusade and Late Love.*
28. Original Hebrew title: *Tmunot mi-hayei ha-kfar.* Translated into English as Oz, Amos. *Scenes from Village Life.*
29. Original Hebrew title: *Ben haverim.* Translated into English as *Between Friends.*
30. Blumenberg, *Shipwreck with Spectator.*
31. Original Hebrew title: *Be-or ha-tekhelet ha-azah.* Translated into English as *Under This Blazing Light: Essays.*

Disclosure statement

No potential conflict of interest was reported by the author(s).

Bibliography

Blumenberg, H. *Shipwreck with Spectator: Paradigm of a Metaphor for Existence.* Translated by Steven Rendall. Cambridge, Mass: MIT Press, 1997.

Oz, A. *My Michael.* Translated by Nicholas De Lange. New York: Knopf, 1972.

Oz, A. *A Perfect Peace.* Translated by Hillel Halkin. San Diego: Harcourt Brace Jovanovich, 1985.

Oz, A. *Elsewhere, Perhaps.* Translated by Nicholas De Lange. San Diego: Harcourt Brace Jovanovich, 1985.

Oz, A. *Black Box.* Translated by Nicholas De Lange. London: Chatto & Windus, 1988.

Oz, A. *To Know a Woman.* Translated by Nicholas De Lange. San Diego: Harcourt, Brace, Jovanovich, 1991.

Oz, A. *In the Land of Israel.* Translated by Maurie Goldberg-Bartura. San Diego: Harcourt Brace Jovanovich, 1993.

Oz, A. *Fima.* Translated by Nicholas De Lange. New York: Harcourt, Brace, 1994.

Oz, A. *Under This Blazing Light: Essays.* Translated by Nicholas De Lange. Cambridge; New York, N.Y.: Press Syndicate of the University of Cambridge, 1995.

Oz, A. *The Same Sea.* Translated by Nicholas De Lange. New York: Harcourt, 2001.

Oz, A. *Suddenly in the Depths of the Forest.* Translated by Sondra Silverston. London: Chatto & Windus, 2010.

Oz, A. *Scenes from Village Life.* Translated by Nicholas De Lange. Boston: Houghton Mifflin Harcourt, 2011.

Oz, A. *Where the Jackals Howl and Other Stories.* Translated by Nicholas De Lange and Philip Simpson. Boston: Mariner Books, 2012.

Oz, A. *Between Friends.* Translated by Sondra Silverston. Boston: Houghton Mifflin Harcourt, 2013.

Oz, A. *A Tale of Love and Darkness.* Translated by Nicholas de Lange. Boston: Houghton Mifflin Harcourt, 2017.

Oz, A. *Judas.* Translated by Nicholas De Lange. London: Houghton Mifflin Harcourt, 2017.

Oz, A., and S. Hadad. *Mi-mah asui ha-tapuah?: Shesh sihot al ketivah ve-al ahavah, ʿal rigshe ashmah ve-taʿanugot aherim [What's in an Apple?: Six Conversations about Writing and about Love, about Guilt and Other Pleasures].* Ben Shemen: Keter, 2018.

Schwartz, Y. *Ha-ashkenazim: Ha-merkaz neged ha-mizrah* [The Ashkenazim: Center Vs. East]. Ramat Gan: Bar Ilan University Press, 2014.

Unto Death: Two Novellas: Crusade and Late Love. Translated by Nicholas De Lange. Boston: Houghton Mifflin Harcourt, 1971.

Love, compassion, and longing

Nurith Gertz

ABSTRACT

The year was 1973 when I read the story Late Love by Amos Oz, and underlined the following passage: [...] something must, absolutely must, reveal itself, a formula, a dazzling system, a purpose, surely it is inconceivable that you will go from birth to death without experiencing a single flash of illumination, without encountering a single ray of sharp light, without something happening, surely it is impossible that all your life you have been nothing more than a barren dream inside yourself, surely there is something, something must make itself known, there must be something. After reading these lines, I decided to write my MA thesis on Amos Oz. After Late Love, I went on to read My Michael and Where the Jackals Howl, as well as many of his articles and interviews he'd given. And only afterwards I was bold enough to write him, asking if we could meet. Quickly and succinctly, he replied: "What is there to discuss? You can find everything [you are looking for] in my books and essays." Still, just a few days later, we met at Café Peter for a lively conversation, which felt like a real dialogue. That conversation which was the basis for my book, What was Lost to Time: A Biography of a Friendship, is the essence of this article.

"I must admit, at first I was concerned because when we met, you spoke just the way you write in the book as if you were reciting a transcription, without the spontaneous beauty I expected from my hero. But I soon realized it was no recitation, not a trace of inauthenticity, but a considered choice by a man who believes in [the power of] language and in choosing his words with all his being. Your belief in words impelled you to choose them so judiciously - only words crafted by hard work, so your listeners feel what you wanted them to."

(Natalie Portman, 'Of Love and Light,' *Davar Rishon*, December 31, 2018).

"When I was four, I told him I was afraid of dying, and he said: "Don't worry, by the time you grow up, I'll create an invention that prevents people from dying." Some would say, probably correctly - I accept this criticism of my father with love - that a child who fears death shouldn't be told their father will come up with a death-beating invention. But that was so like my father, as if words alone could bring redemption, full recovery, or at least buy some time, just to keep at bay a child's anxiety about death, and also an adult's, and an old man's [...] to cradle them in a totally fabricated magic of future dreams."

(Fania Oz-Salzberger, Memorial Service, Tzavta Theater, December 31, 2018).

AMOS OZ'S TWO PENS

"[...] Zionism was founded on a messianic hope, but will only continue existing at the cost of abandoning the Messiah. Oz's message – not to renounce the dream yet not to abhor the reality which isn't a dream – is inherent in his Janus-faced suggestion at the end of In the Land of Israel: *"All those who secretly long for the charms of Paris and Vienna, for the Jewish shtetl, or heavenly Jerusalem: do not cut loose from those longings – for what are we without longings? - But let's remember that Ashdod is what there is." Dreams are infinite. Only a few mythic heroes in Oz's works merge with his flow. We, earthbound creatures, are left with a yearning."*

(Nitza Ben-Dov, "On the Endings of Amos Oz's Stories," *Ma'ariv* Literary Section, weekend edition, April 21, 1997, p. 48).

The year was 1973 when I read the story "Late Love"[1] by Amos Oz, and marked the following passage:

[...] something must, absolutely must reveal itself, a formula, a dazzling system, a purpose, surely it is inconceivable that you will go from birth to death without experiencing a single flash of illumination, without encountering a single ray of sharp light, without something happening, surely it is impossible that all your life you have been nothing more than a barren dream inside yourself, surely there is something, something must make itself known, there must be something.

After reading these lines, I decided to write my MA thesis on Amos Oz. After "Late Love," I went on to read *My Michael*[2] and *Where the Jackals Howl*,[3] as well as many of his articles and interviews with him. And only then I dared writing to him, asking if we could meet. Quickly and succinctly, he replied: "What is there to discuss? You can find everything [you are looking for] in my books and essays."

Still, just a few days later, we met at Café Peter[4] for a lively conversation, which felt like a real dialogue. But it wasn't. Because Oz was using his talent – which I later recognized very well – for letting his interlocutors believe that what they were saying is precisely that which should have been said. After all, he would already phrase it in almost the same terms. Yet his own words were different, carefully crafted and designed. He would employ structuring sentences like "the writer has a map in his heart of paths leading to the murkiest regions," and "I know the devils' dark fire, I've seen it close-up." A different language, hovering a few centimeters above mundane language.

We spoke extensively about his works, particularly *My Michael* and "Late Love." I was a student in the Department of Literature at Tel Aviv University. There I'd become confident that I knew what the author and his protagonists meant to say, better than the author; my role was to reveal this to him and his readership. Actually, I knew what they wanted, not because I had learned about unreliable narrators and how to interpret them; it was because they wanted exactly what I did – to reach that land where, according to that Zionist song written in 1922, "all our dreams will come true."[5] They called it, variously, "the Russian steppes," "eternal silent spaces," "heavenly Jerusalem." For me, at that time, that promised land was the kibbutz.

Or, more precisely, it was what I had heard about the kibbutz – a just, egalitarian society, "from each according to his ability, to each according to his needs" – I'd been seeking things that the protagonists of *My Michael* and "Late Love" had already sought elsewhere, in places populated only by imagination and longing. If what we both were seeking was not here at all, in the actual kibbutz, in the Israeli state, in making the desert bloom, surely it was worthy pursuing it there, in those silent spaces, in a heavenly

Jerusalem. To fail to find something, one can look for it everywhere, even if it's not there. That was what I liked in the imaginary journeys taken by Oz's protagonists in "Late Love" and *My Michael.*

The heavens are, indeed, silent, and God resides only in the hearts of those who seek but fail to find him.[6] Amos Oz had read Pascal[7] as I had, but his protagonists were forced to speak; they imagine and insist on hearing. And in the background, the author tries to find "the hearing with which we hear the voices, and the one with which we hear the silence."[8]

That is what I tried to tell him, in a slightly more scholarly manner. Yet I stammered and abandoned the idea. Later, sitting with my typewriter, in that pre-computer era, after erasing quite a lot (with Tipp-Ex[9]), I attempted to phrase my thoughts in complete sentences, without stammering: You might say that I did not inhabit the empty world that lies under Pascal's eternal silence of infinite spaces, but the empty world of Hannah in *My Michael* and Shraga's in "Late Love." Like them, I too could talk of past harmony and long for it, although it was getting hard to recall, and, in any case, the road leading there was blocked. In Amos Oz's books, that distance could only be traversed with wild hallucinations, violent frenzy, and yet, reading his stories, I could envisage that path.

It was well-phrased, and it seemed right to transfer to the books everything I once thought might still be fulfilled in reality. That's why I sat with Oz that morning in Café Peter. I was hoping to understand what captivated the crowds who attended his lectures, read his works, and hung on his words. I had the same feeling during our conversation, just like when reading his stories, that there is a harmonious world out there, somewhere; a world which he knew because he had been there and could provide an account of it. I debated saying: "Amos, but you're lying. That's a false promise; you don't have the key to that other world, just beautiful words. What kind of promise is that?" But I didn't. I also thought about his fictional characters: how they engage with that world only by the violence, devastation, and destruction that they bring on themselves and others. So, I questioned him about it: "I understand the need to be part of something greater, to flow, to never remain static; to reach people who are burning, to merge with them. But why through violence? Such savage impulses? Why must it be so destructive?"

Oz replied: "Because that is an innate aspect of human nature." And I wanted to say (but did not): "What kind of answer is that?". To come up with a better answer, I wrote about violence in Oz's writing in my MA thesis. I argued that the protagonists in Oz's novels achieve their dreams through war, murder, and violence because they live in a society that fulfills its dreams through wars. But they do not dream their dreams in the right place and send them elsewhere, not to an earthly destination, but far away in the distant skies.

I didn't come up with that answer in our conversation because we only spoke generally about the connection of dreams to war. It was late September 1973, and the Yom Kippur War lay two weeks ahead. Amos would be called up and sent to the Golan Heights, and the question "why such violence, why such savagery?" would grow less relevant.

Not long ago, when he was already tired and ill, we discussed several things, and I returned to that question. Now his answer was very different: "There was tremendous rage within me at that time, during those years. But it left me completely, nothing remains."

We returned to the same theme in other talks, some of which were recorded, assuming they might eventually appear in book form. Here is a fragment from one such conversation:

- NG: You always gave the sense that there's something so complete, and you're showing it exists because you write about it so powerfully, and even if you say it's non-existent, we will still believe it is.

- AO: Yes.

- NG: When Hannah speaks of the infinite spaces, and Shraga of distant galaxies, and Guillaume of Touron about heavenly Jerusalem, I can envisage them, even though they are nonexistent, marked by a minus sign as you like to say, but a minus is not a negation. It does not mean they do not exist.

- AO: Yes. I am now far from those books and stories; I haven't read them in years.

- NG: But you are not far from yourself. What I mean is, you would tell people: "There is a Jerusalem, it is somewhere, a heavenly Jerusalem." Your books created the sense it existed somewhere, that you could describe it to us.

- AO: True. I scattered many promises, but at tough times I think they were perhaps the false promises of someone whistling to himself because he is walking in the dark. Others take his whistling seriously, thinking, "great, maybe there's something in the darkness. If a person whistles, he's probably doing it for a reason; he must see something."

Now, years after that conversation at Café Peter, after *A Tale of Love and Darkness*[10] and so many other discussions and books, I know he did not promise us, his readers, that there is a place where nothing ever cracks and breaks. He promised it to himself. We just listened and observed.

Because now, when I am less curious about the link between the dreams of his characters and the society's dreams that resulted in war, I'm trying to understand how those dreams are associated with his journeys toward his mother, who committed suicide when Oz was twelve and a half.

A Tale of Love and Darkness ends with an account of the last day in the life of Amos Oz's mother. At first, Oz described her walking through the streets of Tel Aviv. A monologue follows, perhaps by the adult narrator, or perhaps the child who was there:

If I had been there with her in that room overlooking the back yard in Haya and Tsvi's flat at that moment [...], I would have certainly tried my hardest to explain to her why she mustn't. And if I did not succeed, I would have done everything possible to stir her compassion, to make her take pity on her only child. I would have cried, and I would have pleaded without any shame, and I would have hugged her knees, I might have even pretended to faint, or I might have hit and scratched myself till the blood flowed as I had seen her do in moments of despair. Or I would have attacked her as a murderer. I would have smashed a vase over her head without hesitation. Or hit her with the iron that stood on a shelf in the corner of the room. Or taken advantage of her weakness to lie on top of her and tie her hands behind her back, and taken away all those pills and tablets and sachets and solutions and potions and syrups of hers and destroyed the lot of them. But I was not allowed to be there. I was not even allowed to go to her funeral.[11]

That place where Amos Oz was not allowed to go was, in fact, the place he had been going to continuously, ever since he was twelve, and his protagonists accompany him: Guillaume of Touron (*Unto Death*) leading his crusade to the Holy Land to share in its redemption and bring it tranquility; Shraga ("Late Love") who tries to reach the "vast ... empty gray steppes," rebuild a heavenly Jerusalem of sorts, where he can know "Peace ..., perfect, final peace. And maybe even love;" Hannah (*My Michael*) setting out for the expanses where everything is flowing and living; Fima (*Fima*), and the mother in *The Hill of Evil Counsel*. They all go there to help him to shake her, throw out her pills, hit her to stop her from swallowing them, to amend the verdict. And, I, the reader, follow in their footsteps, stringing along as they move toward the calamity, and still further back, beyond death; to when his mother was still "white and elongated, as if moonstruck," going back with him, so she could hug him again and say "Of all my children, you're the one I love best. Can you tell me once and for all what it is about you that makes me love you the most?" Going back, to hear her again, her tale of a village emptied of its inhabitants, or a tale of an old man, Alleluyev, who lived together with three blacksmiths, beyond the mountains in the Land of Enularia.[12]

But the way back is obstructed by her suicide, impassable. These characters, together with Amos who created them, arrive at the locked gate, convinced that a herald of good news awaits them there, sure that behind it someone calls to them.' They persevere nonetheless. Reaching that complete place, unreachable but by stories, words and plots, is the fuel of the books in which they live. If such a place had never existed, and if it hadn't been blocked by the disaster, perhaps all that was written would never have been written.

Still, in Amos Oz's early books, his protagonists could pass barriers by killing or by being killed, by destroying or abusing. An alternative way is revealed only in his last works. Not a path leading to the catastrophe – the mother's suicide – but rather a path leading back to the sick mother and the attempts to understand her and, ultimately, to forgive her. For this reason, the journey back upon which he takes the protagonists of his last books wasn't an expedition intended to reach his mother, but paths toward comprehension and pardon: to sit next to her in front of that window, where she sat motionless for days on end. To see what she must have seen. To remember her memories, to dream her dreams. And to weep together with her over everything that was destroyed in her life.

Following their author, Oz's later novels' protagonists no longer seek remote galaxies nor the heavenly city they had previously dreamed about. They no longer need to slay others in order to get there. Instead, they seek out their fellow men, and they reach each other through compassion and forgiveness. That decision – to forgive and to understand – is what I find in the final chapter of *A Tale of Love and Darkness* as well, in the depiction of the last walk his mother took through the streets of Tel Aviv shortly before she died.

Every few years, each year anew, I read this description together with my students to teach them about point of view. How can we sense exactly what the protagonist feels, enter his head, look at what he's looking at, see what he's seeing? This is how the lesson unfolds, more or less: First, we read the entire passage, and then read it once again – but this time halting after each sentence: "My mother left her sister's flat in 175 Ben Yehuda Street at eight or eight thirty. She may have crossed Ben Yehuda Street and turned left, or northwards, towards Nordau Boulevard." At this point, the narrator still does not know what happened during that walk, where his mother was going and why; he only assumes, though he already knows what she would see: "My mother saw the rows of plastered buildings that already, three or four years after they were erected, showed signs of dilapidation: peeling paint, crumbling plaster turning green with mildew, iron railing rusting in the salt sea air [...]." As he continues, he can already recognize what is inside her and he explains it without relying on the metaphorical setting: "My mother was very tired that morning, and her head must have been heavy from lack of sleep [...] so that she would walk slowly like a sleep-walker." He hesitates for a moment, steps back, unsure: "She may have left Ben Yehuda Street before she reached Nordau Boulevard and turned right into Belvedere Alley, which despite its name had no view [...]" and immediately knows that "now she was really lost, she hadn't got the faintest idea how to get back to her sister's and why she had to get back, and she did not know why she had come out [...]". He knows yet doesn't know; he is outside her but also within her mind.[13]

Word by word, line by line, I show the students how Amos Oz merges with his mother and becomes part of her while still remaining the little boy she will leave forever in a few hours. I show how the author splits into three different people: Amos Oz the child, Amos Oz the adult, and the mother of them both. In this way, I tell them he manages to entirely merge two people into one, something that years ago, Hannah had tried to achieve through fantasized wild and violent orgies.

The ability to see, to accept, and to forgive that Amos Oz revealed in *A Tale of Love and Darkness* is also present in his other works from that period. The protagonists of those works no longer seek metaphysical unity with the world and humanity and do not seek another form of redemption either. They settle for less – understanding and forgiveness. *Between Friends*,[14] for example, returns to the former kibbutz, seeking remnants of the old socialist dreams of social redemption and creating a new message thereby. A humble message that does not pertain to offer a light unto the Gentiles, and certainly not unto the people of Israel. Nor does it aspire to unite people under one banner, whether religious, ethnic, or national; it does not presume to effect change nor to uncover heavenly Jerusalem. Instead, it seeks mutual compassion, concern, and responsibility between a few people. In the same place where old hopes have faded, in landscapes of the past, this book searches for small promises – human connections, nothing more.

We spoke a lot about this:

- AO: What happens there is a kind of miracle. I call it a minor miracle.

- NG: Why a miracle?

- AO: Why do I call it a miracle? Because it almost contradicts human nature, the connection between people, for me it's a miracle. It happens, I know it does, it happens. It happens [...] to people, but it is a miracle.

- NG: Isn't that too little for you?

- AO: I'm not sure it's too little for me, not nowadays. Once, it wouldn't have been enough, but not now.

- NG: Really?

- AO: Yes, now it's all I need.

192 AMOS OZ'S TWO PENS

- NG: And at night too, when you dream?

- AO: I don't need more. Compassion, softness, attentiveness, an occasional signal of solidarity. What more does a person need?

- NG: Sometimes just a bit more.

- AO: Yes, I don't deny it. What I'm saying is that a possibility takes shape, a gleam of light in the darkness. It isn't enough. I would gladly bring redemption to the world, so everyone is happy, and that's it – no one ever suffers again, or is lonely, feels abandoned or hurt, that we might all live contentedly, but I can't do that, Nurith. And I never believed in such a sweet redemption, never, not really.

- NG: But if you didn't, why was it still there, in your protagonists' dreams?

- AO: Because who in the world doesn't dream of redemption?

- NG: That isn't an answer.

This last conversation took place after his disease was first diagnosed, when it was still clear that treatment would help, that he would enter remission and continue seeking an answer in the years ahead, not settling for this humblest of messages. As he had searched before, he would continue seeking something to replace it. But he was not granted those years, and that is what we are left with – love and compassion. And it is also what he left behind for me, personally, together with longing and memories. Our friendship, which began 45 years ago in Café Peter, has ended.

Notes

1. One of the two novellas included in Oz's fourth book, '*Ad Mavet* (Editor's note).
2. Oz, Amos. *My Michael.*
3. Oz, Amos. *Where the Jackals Howl, and Other Stories.* This was Oz's first story collection, originally published in 1965.
4. A coffee house in the German Colony in Jerusalem, named after its owner, a Hungarian Jew, and renowned for its fine pastries and coffee and its Austro-Hungarian atmosphere. A favorite meeting place for Jerusalemite Bohemia and academics at the time. (Editor's notes)
5. A reference to the Zionist song "*Po be-eretz hemdat avot*" ("Here in the Land of Ancestral Yearning") written by the songwriter and teacher Yisrael Dushman (1884–1947) and the composer Hanina Karchevsky (1877–1925). A Hebrew adaptation of the Yiddish "Exile Hymn" (*golos marsh*), the song was written following the request from Haim Bograshov, the principal of the Hebrew Gymnasium in Herzliya at the time, to create a Hebrew hymn that would be sang by students during in trips and outdoor activities. Oz paraphrases the famous opening verse of the song: "Here in the land of ancestral yearnings/All hopes will be fulfilled." The oft-quoted phrase made its way to the title of one of Oz's collection of political essays, *Kol ha-tikvot* (Editor's note).
6. Gertz references here Oz's literary essays on S. Y. Agnon, *The Silence of Heaven* (Editor's note).
7. Blaise Pascal (1623–1662): French mathematician, physicist, and philosopher, known for his posthumous book, the *Pensées de M. Pascal sur la religion et sur quelques autres sujets* (1670), a collection of fragments that were planned as his defense of Christianity. Warning against the tyranny of reason, Pascal feared that it would rob from religion all that is mysterious or supernatural.
8. Oz, *Where the Jackals Howl*, 214.

9. A brand name for a white liquid used for painting over mistakes in a piece of writing.
10. Oz's memoir, *A Tale of Love and Darkness*.
11. Oz, *A Tale of Love and Darkness*, 532.
12. Reference to the tales Oz's mother used to tell him, as reported in *A Tale of Love and Darkness* (Editor's note).
13. Oz, *A Tale of Love and Darkness*, 530.
14. Oz's last collection of short stories, set in a kibbutz of the late 1950s, the time and place where his writing began:*Between Friends*.

Disclosure statement

No potential conflict of interest was reported by the author(s).

Bibliography

Oz, Amos. *'Ad Mavet* [Unto Death]. Jerusalem: Hakibutz Ha-artzi Ha-Shomer Ha-Tzair, 1971.

Oz, Amos. *A Tale of Love and Darkness* [Sipur al ahava ve-hosheh]. Translated by N. R. M. De Lange. London: Chatto & Windus, 2004.

Oz, Amos. *Between Friends* [Bein haverim]. Translated by Sondra Silverston. Boston: Houghton Mifflin Harcourt, 2013.

Oz, Amos. *Kol ha-tikvot: Mahshavot al zehut Yisraelit* [All Our Hopes: Reflections on the Israeli Condition]. Jerusalem: Keter, 1998.

Oz, Amos. *My Michael* [Michael sheli]. Translated by N. R. M. (Nicholas Robert Michael) De Lange. New York: Knopf, 1972.

Amos Oz. *The Same Sea* [Oto ha-yam]. Translated by N. R. M. De Lange. New York: Harcourt, 2001.

Oz, Amos. *The Silence of Heaven: Agnon's Fear of God*. Translated by Barbara Harshav. Princeton, NJ: Princeton University Press, 2000.

Oz, Amos. *Where the Jackals Howl, and Other Stories* [Be-artzot ha-tan]. Translated by N. R. M. De Lange and Philip Simpson. Boston: Mariner Books, 2012.

Afterword
Reading Amos Oz Today
Lilah Nethanel

Understanding is an intimate mode of attachment literature can offer us. It is a generous offer. It is a vital human possibility of contact between two: writer and reader. Strangers, but familiar. Distant, they do recognize each other even from afar.

For about five decades, from the 1970s until his death in 2018, Amos Oz had readers-addressees, a readership that found a language of understanding in his literary work. With these readers – new Israeli Jews, immigrants and natives alike – it was possible to correspond in the animistic language of cypress, wind, and the approaching evening, where "The soft gray light embraces the treetops with great tenderness".[1] One might invoke, for instance, Hannah Gonen's dream language, in *My Michael*: "They have been sent to wake me. Someone imagines I am asleep."[2] With this readership, it was possible to transport the inanimate into imagined motion, to yoke together one thing with something radically other, like the bells: "From the east, the bells rang out continuously, high bells and deep bells, Russian bells, Anglican bells, Greek bells, Abyssinian, Latin, Armenian bells as if a plague or a fire were devastating the city. But all the bells were doing was to call the darkness dark."[3]

More than anything, though, it seems to me, one could turn to these readers in the language of fear, and even spark it. Lust for it, even. To compel fear, as though it was something essential without which there was no language, not here in any case, in Israeli-Hebrew, and not now. The first lesson in Oz's fictional world – a world whose texture begins to emerge in the stories collected in *Where the Jackals Howl* and evolves until the final novel, *Judas* – is that without fear there is no knowledge. Neither of humans nor of animals. Neither of places nor of memory. Nothing.

> In the distance were more and more strange mountains and strange villages stretching to the end of the world, minarets of mosques, Shu'afat, Nabi Samwil, the outskirts of Ramallah, the wail of the muezzin borne on the wing in the evening twilight, dark women, deadly sly, guttural youth. And a slight hint of brooding evil: distant, infinitely patient, forever observing you unobserved.[4]

The imaginary space in which the stories in *Where the Jackals Howl* occur is cracked. Along one path you can walk, and then there is another, hidden one, along which no one goes: "The inner circle, the circle of lights, keeps guard over our houses and over us, against the accumulated menace outside. But it is an ineffective wall, it cannot keep out the smells of the foe and his voices."[5] This is why around Oz's world, a fence is always being erected: "Searchlights are mounted on wooden posts set out at regular intervals along the perimeter fence."[6] Beyond the fence, there is the wasteland,[7] or the eastern mountain range, "bare and rocky".[8] For Oz, the fence is not a boundary. It is neither identical to the political fence dividing the land nor to Israel's sovereign border, but mainly signals an always looming possibility of transgression. This is the nature of the fantasy about the Bedouin nomads invading the kibbutz's fields in the story "Nomad and Viper" and of the hallucination in the story "Where the Jackals Howl", a hallucination which carries the desire for desertification, the erasure of even the merest sign of settlement:

> In a flash the throngs of tiny people appear in the gullies. Like little black ants they swarm and trickle from their hiding places in the crevices of the mountain, sweeping down like a cataract. Hordes of thin dark people streaming down the slopes, rolling like an avalanche of stone and plunging in a headlong torrent to the levels of the plain. Here they split into a thousand columns, racing westward in furious spate. Now they are so close that their shapes can be seen: a dark, disgusting, emaciated mass, crawling with lice and fleas, stinking. Hunger and hatred distort their faces. Their eyes blaze with madness. In full flood they swoop upon the fertile valleys, racing over the ruins of deserted villages without a moment's check. In their rush toward the sea they drag with them all that lies in their path, uprooting posts, ravaging fields, mowing downs fences, trampling the gardens and stripping the orchards, pillaging home-steads, crawling through huts and stables, clambering over walls like demented apes, onwards, westward, to the sands of the sea.[9]

"Where the jackals howl" designates another space which would seem to stretch beyond Israel's sovereign borders. In actual fact rather than defining the limits of sovereignty, it stakes out the most intimate elements of its identity. This is a political symbolism that renders a specific, though never explicit, truth regarding the Zionist left's doctrine of separation: the fence assembles itself around the breach which it already includes. It is built to be ravaged. Not there to draw a line, it comes to pave a way for the refugees who will uproot it returning to their land, for nomads who will breach it on their way to the Jewish settlement, a passage to wind and dreams. Oz's early political symbolism situates the separation fence in the domain of language. It represents the vanishing point of violence – the threatened collapse of the possibility of language. In Oz, the image, the allusion, and the symbol all threaten to squash the possibility of rational, historical, contextual mediation in the voracious void of the animal's shriek, of ill intentions, profanity, and desire:

> And suddenly you too are surrounded, besieged, paralyzed with fear. You see their eyes ablaze with primeval hatred, mouths hanging open, teeth yellow and rotten, curved daggers gleaming in their hands. They curse you in clipped tones, voices choking with rage or with dark desire.[10]

What in Oz's early writings sounds like the disintegration of rational language, returns as the language of political debate in his late books. His final novel, *Judas*, is a novel of ideas, in which the jackals' howl has turned into a nocturnal conversation in the Jerusalem apartment of Gershom Wald, bereaved father and aging political ideologue, who is waiting for his death:

> What shall we do if the Arabs send an army of a half a million? Or a million? Or two million? Nasser is equipping himself right now with huge quantities of the best Soviet armaments and

is talking openly about a second round of war. And what are we doing? We are drunk of victory. Drunk on our power. Drunk on biblical clichés."

"And what does your Honor suggest?" Wald asked, "That we turn the other cheek?"[11]

The novel *A Tale of Love and Darkness*, the centre piece of Oz's late oeuvre, in many ways marks his turn from the symbolic foreboding of the howling jackals, to the exchange of ideas required by political justification. It also brings together his literary writing and the essayistic writing in which he engaged throughout his writing life, starting with his collection of essays *Under This Blazing Light*, until the final three essays that make up *How to Cure a Fanatic*. *A Tale of Love and Darkness* reflects the effort to reconcile the symbolic language of darkness by matching it with a "tale" which includes justification, in the language of love perhaps.

Thus for instance the image of the fence being built around the vegetable patch in the yard of the Jerusalem childhood home of the boy Amos Klausner is a late adaptation of the fence in the same garden, in the early story "The Hill of Evil Counsel". But while the garden in that latter story was "a lonely island of clear, sober sanity in the midst of a savage, rugged wasteland, of winding valleys, of desert winds,"[12] in *A Tale of Love and Darkness*, Oz, refraining from evoking this wildness, the rugged land, and the winds, writes: "from here to there was inside, in fact our vegetable garden, and everything beyond was outside, in other words the rest of the world".[13]

From the symbolic realism of his early writing through to the representations of ideas in his late output, Oz is an eloquent spokesperson for Israeli secular metaphysics: All that exists prevails against the possibility of destruction. The lanterns on the settlement's fence "strive to light up the fields and the valleys that stretch away to the foothills of the mountains."[14] The walls of the houses face whoever, outside, comes knocking at the door: "Sharp waves of chill autumn air clung to the outer walls of the houses, seeking entry."[15] "The rain beat furiously against the darkened windows, as if it was demanding that we listen with rapt attention to some urgent message it had to deliver."[16] And from above the night bears down: "Damp and close and hot the night fell on the kibbutz, tangled in the dust-laden cypresses, oppressed the lawns and ornamental shrubs."[17] The name Oz – Hebrew for strength – which Amos Klausner adopted in adulthood, indeed, comes as a stand against a painful heritage. It is a heritage of fear – fear of strangers, fear of the dead, and fear of the living. The Israeli language of understanding, which Oz commanded so masterfully, is the language of fear.

I am not writing this from an antiseptic, remote perspective. My reading is involved, in the sense that reading finds signs of life in literature. And in the sense that, at times, reading takes us to a place we already knew before. I remember my childhood in Israel of the 1980s. Oz's early books – *Where the Jackals Howl, Elsewhere Perhaps, My Michael, The Hill of Evil Counsel* – written in the first decades of statehood, were still recognizable and familiar even then, about 20 years after they were written. What I remember more than anything is not fear itself, as such, but the routines of that fear. The ritual of locking up the home towards the night, exactly the way Oz writes it: "Seal the lattice, close the window, keep the light on."[18] Evening brought the childish fear that held the adults in its grip. A hidden struggle about fear was being fought between them: the older and the younger adults – between the generation of the parents born in the 1950s and that of their parents, born in the 1920s and 1930s. Sometimes it was about ostensibly dismissing the fear, with casual contempt, derision – for instance: "What's the worry. There're people whose job it is". Often, the ridicule developed into fickle arrogance of the following type: "You have to talk to them in the only language they know," or – succinctly: "Brute force – that's all." Such things could be heard in nearly every home, whenever there was a family get together or friends came around. The same expression later appeared as the election slogan of one of the new political parties that emerged in Israel of the 1990s.

Sometimes though it was the opposite. Then the struggle was about whipping up worries, with phrases like "We have nowhere else to go", or "God knows what will be the end. Not 20 years from now. Tomorrow, or even in just another hour, what will be?" I remember my grandfather, thin and tall on the threshold of his house in the village, an early trembling shadow of night in the entrance hall, and instead of saying goodbye, he tells my father, always in the plural: "Take care on the road." A heart-harrowing expression of strange love. And he lingered in the open door. Watching us drive into the distance, and maybe, always this maybe, feeling wordlessly pained and enraged, maybe we would not be back. Neither to our home nor to his.

Home was a lock. Home was defense against outside. I remember the hush that fell when the radio played the newsflash jingle. Always, the children were told to be quiet (5 p.m., 7 p.m.). At 8 p.m., the main news of the day came on. It happened that the dial had to be turned to maneuver between Arab stations which broke out in foreign voices between Radio Two and the IDF Channel. As if those voices had no words, just a jarring, or as Oz writes: "a slight hint of brooding evil". It had to be silenced, quickly. There was, at home, a special deafness, terrible and very wonderful in its kind, it was intimate and protective, a deafness that was a vigorous refusal to hear what went on outside, beyond the Hebrew speaking news flash, beyond the Israeli gaze, and beyond sovereignty. A refusal to listen to this country, speak its language and for me turned Israeli-Hebrew into the language of refusal of the place.

And so it came to pass that the first words in Arabic I heard were *alte sachen*. A kind of local Palestinian Yiddish idiolect, these words were broadcast through a megaphone attached to an old Volkswagen van that was trailing through the new housing projects of Netanya-South and Gdud Haivri street, Avihayil's main road. The van came around every week, driving up from one of the nearby towns, Taybeh or Kalansuah, paying cash for old furniture, rugs, exactly what I don't know. It was a crackling jingle, over and over again, in a melodious guttural accent, like an Arab-Israeli afternoon prayer: "*Alte sachen* everything bought *alte sachen*". In the summer months, sometimes, this van, a bleached blue or green, would carry watermelons. The driver, accompanied by two or three boys, would stop on the corner to sell watermelons, whole or halves, which they would tap with flat, grooved hands. And the big knife, I remember, held in strange hands. Once I ate a sliver right off the blade, my fingers touching, it tasted sweet.

Because this wasn't just simple fear. It was a mixed fear, very dense, coming with a kind of aggression too. Fear that holds a desperate need for mercy as well as hate and contempt, and it also carries a plea for life alongside harsh repression and domination. Oz's Jerusalem night, with its eastern wall of Israeli sovereignty – the lands of the Judean desert, the West Bank, the wastelands of occupation and refugeehood – also touched on the secular sands of Israel's coastal strip. With their square apartments, verandas walled in to add extra room, the children of the 1970s and 1980s, second or third generation in Israel, their schooldays and tattered textbooks passed from one student to the next, and public TV from 4 p.m. till 6 or 7 p.m. in the evening, Saturday walks to the beach, green grapes in a basket and a towel. All of this on the sundrenched flatlands, the facades of new building projects and white shutters already cracked and turned yellow, and the buildings' pillars firm in the sand, and the orchards bordering the village, dusty for the best part of the year, erect on thin, white-chalked stems. There too the same deep valleys lay exposed, the same howl at night:

> At night the valleys all around were alive with sounds. The wildness of the rocks and mountains reached out to touch the house. Jackals howled nearby, and the blood froze at the thought of them padding softly, tensely, among the saplings, up to the shuttered windows, perhaps even onto the veranda. A single Mandatory streetlamp, encased in small, square panes and topped with a green dome, cast a solitary light on the unpaved road. The fingers of the fig tree at the bottom of the garden were empty. There was nobody outside the dark. The square-paned lamp cast its light in vain. All the residents were in the habit of shutting themselves up in their houses as soon as the darkness fell.[19]

Literature's language of understanding is a gift of grace. Meaning, recollection, recognition – these things are what a perceptive writer with a knowing heart may offer readers. Still, the precious asset of Oz's oeuvre notwithstanding, certain doubts arise, some dogged questions. A wish, ostensibly impossible, because it is hard to ask for something we don't know. And yet perhaps one should insist. To ask, over and beyond what Oz's literature actually is, what, and perhaps mainly, it isn't. What it never was and might perhaps have been in different circumstances, different times. What it did not hold out, and what, just maybe, it should have held out. I want to ask, very much in my own name, what I miss in this literature. And a harder question still: May I venture to express a wish for a different Israeli literature? And anyway, can one ask a literature for what it does not have?

I ask these questions here because what is absent in the literature Oz wrote is growing ever more apparent. It can no longer be sidestepped. It can no longer be refused, delayed, and we can no longer look away. Misunderstanding is right at the gate and knocking. Like a person, say, my grandfather or anybody else like him, still there, at the door, worrying, all these years, and waiting. And who cannot be made to wait any longer. It has to be decided. Whether to open or to close. To break through or to lock. Because what Oz's literature did not offer, and perhaps was unable to offer, was an imagined picture of blending and plurality. A blending and plurality that is the dream of some, but the nightmare of many. Oz's *is not* a regional literature, *it isn't* a bilingual literature, *it isn't* Arab-Jewish literature, and *it isn't* Hebrew-Palestinian literature. That would be against the very axioms of Oz's literary world: like a flowing fence, like soft rocks, like arid rain.

Oz's writing is in the language of separation. It is the foundation of what may very well be read as the central, major scene of his work. What I have in mind is chapter 44 in *A Tale of Love and Darkness*, in which Oz describes the night of 29 November 1947, when the UN General Assembly voted to end the British Mandate in Palestine, and decided on the establishment of two separate, independent states: one Jewish and one Arab. This is the moment of the political inception of bi-national separation. The residents of Jerusalem's Kerem Avraham neighborhood, Amos Klausner's boyhood scene, are outside that night, listening to the radio broadcast of the UN vote, witnessing its outcome:

(…) and after a couple more seconds of shock and disbelief, of lips parted as though in thirst and eyes wide open, our faraway street on the edge of Kerem Avraham in northern Jerusalem also roared all at once in a first terrifying shout and tore through the darkness and the buildings and trees, piercing itself, not a shout of joy, nothing like the shouts spectators in sports grounds or excited rioting crowds, perhaps more like a scream of horror and bewilderment, a cataclysmic shout, a shout that could shift rocks, that could freeze your blood, as though all the dead who had ever died here and all those still to die had received a brief window to shout, and the next moment the scream of horror was replaced by roars of joy and a medley of hoarse cries and "The Jewish People Lives".[20]

There's truth in fiction. It holds historic truth, the truth of the moment, as well as other truths. For instance, that when the wind rattles the doors of the houses, someone eventually will open. When the bells ring out on behalf of the night, the night will eventually end. When rain pelts against the window and, with fear in its heart, demands to be heard, somebody surely will listen. After all, even when speaking the language of understanding, even when it discloses what's familiar and nearby, literature is always written in very close proximity to absolute strangeness, very near incomprehension. The question is when incomprehension is beyond tolerable, when it is rejected by writers and readers alike, and when, on the contrary, the other's incomprehensible language, the story of what appears unreasonable and impossible, grow imperative.

There are historical conditions, it appears, pressures exerted by one reality or another, that require us to replace the language of understanding by a language that exceeds our understanding. To read not in order to get to know or to identify, but to head out beyond, to what cannot be here and yet will exactly have to.

The UN vote episode in *A Tale of Love and Darkness* concludes with a long parenthesis. This parenthesis serves as a kind of appendix, a prosthesis to the description of the Klausner family standing among the crowd in Kerem Avraham that night. The father, Amos the boy, and the mother, who "was also trying to share with him and me in our shout and with the whole street the whole neighborhood the whole city and the whole country my sad mother was trying to participate this time"[21] At this point, in the original Hebrew, Oz starts a parenthesis in which he accommodates the residents of Jerusalem's Arab neighborhoods. They too are listening for the results of the vote:

No, definitely not the whole city but only the Jewish areas, because Sheikh Jarrah, Katamon, Bakaa and Talbieh must have heard us that night wrapped in a silence that might have resembled the terrified silence that lay upon the Jewish neighborhoods before the result of the vote was announced. In the Silwanis' house in Sheikh Jarrah and in Aisha's home in Talbieh and the home of the man in the clothes shops, the beloved man Gepetto with the bags under his compassionate eyes, there were no celebrations tonight. They must have heard the sounds of rejoicing from the Jewish streets, they must have stood at their windows to watch the few joyful fireworks that injured the sky, pursing their lips in silence. Even the parrots were silent. And the fountain in the pool in the garden. Even though neither Katamon, Talbieh not Bakaa knew or could know yet that in another five months they would fall empty, intact, into the hands of the Jews and that new people would come and live in those vaulted houses of pink stone and those villas with their many cornices and arches".[22]

The same Jews into whose hands those Arab owned houses fell are still waiting for disaster to strike, same as in the past, they lock all entrances, defend and expel, protect homes and demolish. Oz's parenthesis, that conclude the UN vote for bi-national separation of the land – this parenthesis in which other people stand with their different hopes and different fears – constitutes a literary boundary which has yet to be crossed. Perhaps Oz's work, especially this parenthesis, missing from the English translation, stakes out a path for those who are still to enter the pages of Israeli literature, enter the stories that compose its fiction. Others, already, in the future to come – Jews-Arabs-Palestinians-Israelis – are waiting on the other side. I cannot recognize them from here. I need a good fiction, wise and perceptive, to make them out. Without fiction I cannot approach them. Reality is such a small crack to look through, and much will not be captured from it. That is why I need literature to see what is not quite yet, those who are not yet politically feasible, in terms of identity, or culturally, even though they do have a face and come with a name, in fiction. That is why somewhere out there, I am sure, a different Israeli literature is beginning to be written and will surely come. Because "it is the way of the wind to come and to go"[23], writes Oz," and to come again"[24] (p. 61).

Notes

1 Amos Oz, *Where the Jackals Howl*, trans. Nicolas de Lange and Philip Simpson, (Boston and New York: Mariner books, 2012), p. 7.
2 Amos Oz, *My Michael*, trans. Nicholas de Lange in collaboration with the author, (London: Vintage, 1988), p. 89.
3 Amos Oz, *The Hill of Evil Counsel*, trans. Nicholas de Lange in collaboration with the author, (New-York and London: A Helen and Kurt Wolff Book, 1978), p. 6.
4 Oz, *The Hill*, p. 18.
5 Oz, *Where the Jackals*, p. 9.
6 Ibid, p. 7.
7 Oz, *The Hill*, p. 18.
8 Amos Oz, *Elsewhere, Perhaps*, trans. Nicholas de Lange in collaboration with the author, (New York: Penguin Books, 1979), p. 11.
9 Oz, *Where the Jackals*, p. 16.
10 Ibid., p. 16–17.
11 Amos Oz, *Judas*, trans. by Nicholas de Lange, (Boston and New York: Mariner Books, 2016), p. 104.
12 Oz, *The Hill*, p. 14.
13 *A Tale of Love and Darkness*, p. 227.
14 Oz, *Where the Jackals*, p. 7.
15 Ibid., p. 18.
16 Oz, *My Michael*, p. 4.
17 Oz, *Where the Jackals*, p. 26.
18 Ibid., p. 77.
19 Oz, *The Hill*, p. 29.
20 Amos Oz, *A Tale of Love and Darkness*, trans. Nicholas de Lange, (London: Vintage, 2017), p. 343.

21 Ibid., p.343.
22 Ibid., p. 343–344 .
23 Ibid, P. 61
24 Ibid, Ibid.

Acknowledgments

I would like to express my gratitude to the early readers of this work for their attentive reading and friendship: Arie Dubnov, Michal Ben-Naftali and Ilai Rowner. I would also like to thank Mirjam Meerschwam Hadar for remarkably translating my thoughts and words into English.

Index

Page numbers followed with "n" refer to endnotes

ahuslim 27–8
Alboim-Dror, Rachel 108
aliyah (immigration to Israel) 10, 156–7
Alon, Ktzia 165
Alterman, Nathan 142
Alter, Robert 73, 75, 86
American Jews 77–8, 87
Americanness 44
Amir, Aharon 109
"Amos Oz 1939–2018: The President of the White
    Tribe has Died" (Ziffer) 27
Amotz, Dalia 37
Anderson, Perry 3
Anderson, Sherwood 44–7; American
    grotesque 52–60; short stories: related-tale
    format 49–52, 62; small town of 47–51, 57,
    58, 61, 62
Appelfeld, Aharon 86
Arabs 28, 118; Jews and 105, 164–5;
    Palestinian 35
Arafat, Yasser 101–2
Aran, Giddeon 162
Asali, Ziad 98
Asch, Shmuel 147, 180
Ashkenazi 29, 34, 37
Ashkenazim 15, 29, 35
Asscher, Omri 13
autobiographical pact 5, 153
autobiography 153–4
Avidan, David 16, 17
Avneri, Uri 109

Bachelard, Gaston 162
Badiou, Alain 39
Baker, A. T. 75
Balaban, Abraham 7, 169
Barnett, Michael 77
Baron, Salo 31
"Baruch of Magenza" (Tchernichovsky) 100
Baruch, Y. L. 100
Bayley, John 76
Be'er, Haim 108
"Before his time" (Oz) 79

Begin, Menachem 30, 31, 33, 34, 107
Bellow, Saul 86
Ben-Amotz, Dan 31–2
Ben-Gurion, David 8–10, 31, 54, 96;
    messianism 107–8
Benvenisti, Miron 97
Berdichevsky, Micha Yosef 97, 107, 109, 110
Bergman, Samuel Hugo 109
Berg, Nancy 170
Bernhard (Hoffmann) 136, 138–41, 146
Between Friends (Oz) 7, 51, 59–61, 123, 127–30,
    182, 191
Bhabha, Homi 157
Black Box (Oz) 15–17, 37–8, 179
Bnei Akiva 108
"Book of Josef, The" (Hoffmann) 141
"Book of the Grotesque (Anderson), The"
    52–7, 59, 60
Brenner, Yosef Haim 63n16, 84, 110
Broyard, Anatole 79
Buber, Martin 31

Camus, Albert 3, 96, 98
canaanism 108–10
Canaanite messianism 108–10
Caruth, Cathy 161
Christ of Fish, The (Hoffmann) 136, 138–42, 144
Coetzee, J.M. 167
colonialism 98
Crowley, John W. 47, 49
crusaders 98–103
"Crusaders" (Shalev) 101

Dayan, Moshe 12, 83
Dear Zealots (Oz) 104–5, 111n38
de Lange, Nicholas 4, 73–6, 83, 85, 142
Derrida, Jacques 119–20
Dickstein, Morris 75
Dumas, Alexandre 160
Dunne, Robert 53, 57

Edwards, Thomas 75
elgnena 166

INDEX

Eliav, Lova 105
Eliot, T. S. 11
Elsewhere, Perhaps (Oz) 10, 75, 85, 125–6, 181, 182, 196
empathic unsettlement 161, 167, 171
empathy 161
English translations 74, 83–5

Facing the Forests (Yehoshua) 99
family photographs of Oz and Matalon 167–71
Faulkner, William 47, 62
Feige, Michael 157
Fima (Oz) 7
First Man, The (Camus) 96
first-person plural narration 124–30
first-person singular narration 118, 124, 126, 127
Flusser, David 104
Franco, Rachel 54

Gan, Alon 12, 18
Gertz, Nurith 12, 30, 32, 135, 147, 164
Gilmore, Leigh 153
Golan, Avirama 117, 118
Gold, Nili 136
Gordis, Daniel 31, 32
Gordon, A. D. 54
Greenberg, Uri Zvi 109
Gretz, Nurith 6
grotesque 52–62
Grumberg, Karen 7, 117, 165
Gurevitz, David 137
Gurevitz, Zeli 162
Gush Emunim 13, 105, 107–9
Guwein, Daniel 36

Ha-Am, Ahad 109, 110
Halevi, Yehuda 162
Halkin, Hillel 85–6
Hassan, Ihab 136
Havel, Václav 2
Hebrew Labor 35
Herzl, Theodor 156
Hess, Tamar S. 153
Hill of Evil Counsel, The (Oz) 28, 75–7, 181, 190, 196
Hirschfeld, Ariel 16
Hirsch, Herbert 142
Hoffmann, Yoel 135, 147; critique of Zionist culture 141; postmodernism and Oz, Amos 136–46
Holtzman, Avner 137
"Horns of Hattin, The" (Ravikovitch) 100–1
Horwitz, Talia 137
Howe, Irving 57, 78
How to Cure a Fanatic (Oz) 105

identity politics, Oz, Amos 27–39
Imagining the Kibbutz (Omer-Sherman) 51
immigration 156–62
indeterminacy 136
Ingram, Forrest 49

In the Land of Israel (Oz) 13, 15, 28, 33, 36–7, 83, 97, 179
Israeli-Palestinian conflict 13, 14, 80, 83, 85, 165
Israelism 108

Jesus 103–4
Jewish history 31–3
Jews 99, 104, 106; and Arabs 105, 164–5
Jews and Words (Oz) 106
Judaism 104, 108, 109
Judas (Oz) 18–19, 103, 182, 194, 195
Judeophobia 14

Kaplan, Eran 3, 116–17, 154
Karamazov, Ivan 32
Kartun-Blum, Ruth 137
Kayser, Wolfgang 53
Kennedy, J. Gerald 50, 52, 56
Keren, Nitza 169
Khirbet Khizeh (Yizhar) 83
kibbutz 7–9, 12–13, 50–1
"Kibbutz at the Present Time, The" (Oz) 61
kibbutz movement 12
Kimchi, Rami 37
Kimmerling, Baruch 3, 27–8
Klausner, Joseph 6, 103–5, 110, 158, 180
Kleinberg, Aviad 18
Kook, Rabbi Abraham Hacohen 110; disciples of 106, 107
Kotker, Norman 75
Kurzweil, Baruch 11, 108–9

Labor Zionism 6, 8, 29, 33, 36, 45, 58
LaCapra, Dominick 161
La dame aux Camélias (Dumas) 160
land 164–5
Laor, Dan 30, 33, 168
Laor, Yitzhak 3, 38, 123
"Late Love" (Oz) 187, 188
Lauck, Jon K. 48
Lawrence, Ben 129
Lebensraum 12
Lefevere, André 71–2
Lehmann-Haupt, Christopher 125–6
Lejeune, Philippe 5, 153–4
Likud 28–30, 33, 34
Lindsay, Clarence 44, 47, 49–50, 52
linguistic Judaism 110
literary norms 140, 142, 143, 145, 146
Locke, Richard 75
Lundén, Rolf 49
lyrical fluidity 118, 122, 123, 129
lyrical I 119–20
lyrical suspense 121

Maalouf, Amin 98
Mann, Susan 49
Markovich, Dalya 165
Matalon, Ronit 17, 155–6, 165, 169; empathic unsettlement 161, 167, 171; family

photographs 170–1; garden 166; home 165–6; immigration156, 159–62; land 166; motherhood 160–2; shack 165; *see also* Oz, Amos
"Meaning of Homeland, The" (Oz) 84
Mediterranean 96–8
Mediterranean Cruise 97
Mediterranean humanism 96
Mediterraneanism 16
Mendelson-Maoz, Adia 17
Messiah 103–4, 106–7
"Messiah's Mule, The" 107
Messianic Idea in Israel, The (Klausner) 104
messianism 103–8; of Gush Emunim 13, 107–8
Mickiewicz, Adam 104
Miller, Laura 124
Miller, Nancy 167
Milner, Iris 163
Mintz, Alan 75
Miron, Dan 37, 39
Mitelpunkt, Shaul 78
Mizrahim 15, 27, 29, 34, 35, 38, 167
Moked, Gabriel 180
Myers, David 30
My Michael (Oz) 10, 11, 13, 72–5, 80, 181, 187, 188, 194, 196

Nagel, James 49
Nazarene, The (Asch) 147
Ne'eman, Yael 125
Neo-Revisionism 30, 31
Nesbit, Tara Shea 124–5
Netanyahu, Benjamin 18, 30–2, 39
Netanyahu, Benzion 30–1
New Heart, New Spirit (Eliav) 105
New York Times 75, 76
"Nomads and Vipers" (Oz) 11, 126–8, 195
Novak, William 75

Ohana, David 14
Omer-Sherman, Ranen 51, 116
One Facing Us, The (Matalon) 170
Oppenheimer, Yochai 160
Oz, Amos: anti-Israelism 81; Ben-Amotz, Dan and 31–2; Camus, Albert and 96, 98; and canaanism 108–10; childhood home 163; commentary on Israeli policy 82; critics on 74–6; and crusaders 98–103; early publication and reception history 72–4; essays for translation 82–7; family photographs 167–9, 171; first-person plural narration 124–30; *galut/golah* 84, 85; garden 163–4; genesis of 45–7; grotesque 53–6, 61; identity politics 27–39; immigration 157–9, 161; Israeli policies, critic of 13; Jews and the Arabs 164–5; as kibbutz 7–8; land and 164–5; life story 5–6; lyrical fluidity 118, 122, 123, 129; Mediterranean and 16, 96–8; meetings with Ben-Gurion 8–10; and

messianism 103–8; motherhood 157–9, 161; mother's suicide 6, 54, 143, 157, 158, 180, 189, 190; photo of 167; political commentary 72, 77, 84, 87; as political spokesman 76–8; political writings 13–14; postmodernism and Hoffmann, Yoel 136–46; probe into Israeli psyche 74–6; protagonists of 187–91; realism 143, 144, 146, 147; related-tale format 50–1; self-representation in the American press 81–2; short stories: related-tale format 50–2; smallness as strategy 43–5; translation of Oz's memoir 22n54; works in North American universities 79–81; Zionism 7, 14, 29–33, 45, 110, 180

Pacht, Michelle 50
Palestinian Arabs 35
Palestinian Versailles 15
Panther in the Basement (Oz) 19
Peleg, Ilan 30–2
Peres, Shimon 34
Perfect Peace, A (Oz) 7, 85, 179, 180
photographs (family) of Oz and Matalon 167–71
phylactery Judaism 109
political zealotry 105, 111n38
postmodernism: defined 136; Hoffmann, Yoel and Oz, Amos 136–46
Promethean 108
Publishers Weekly 75

Rabbi Jesus 103–4
Ratosh, Yonatan 108, 109
Ravikovitch, Dahlia 99–102
religious zealotry 104; neo-messianism of 107
Remnick, David 78
Revisionist Zionism 30
"Revolt from the Village", The (Van Doren) 47–8, 50
Rhyming Life and Death (Oz) 146
Richardson, Brian 124
Rosenblum, Doron 33
Rotbard, Sharon 97
Roth, Philip 86
Rubinstein, Amnon 76

Sabra 3, 28, 160, 162, 168, 169, 171
Said, Edward W. 15
Saladin 101–2
Same Sea, The (Oz) 16, 98, 119–24, 129–30, 134, 135, 137–43, 145–8, 181, 182; lyrical I 119–20; orgy 122; polyphony of prose 120–2
Scenes from Village Life (Oz) 51, 54–6, 59–61, 182
Schaham, Chaya 100, 137
Schevill, James 53, 57
Schmitt, Carl 107
Scholem, Gershom 107
Schwartz, Yigal 17, 135, 136, 157, 159, 162
secular Zionism 108, 109
Segev, Tom 18

Shaked, Gershon 32, 136, 180
Shalev, Yitzhak 101
"shaman of the tribe" 145–6; postmodernist and 136–45
Shamir, Moshe 180
Shamir, Yitzhak 17
Shapira, Anita 108, 117, 158
Shapira, Avraham 12
Shemtov, Vered K, 4
Shesher, Michael 34
Shimoni, Batya 165
Siah lohamim 12, 13, 17, 18
Slopes of Lebanon, The (Oz) 13, 83
social mobility 36
Soumchi (Oz) 181
Sound of Our Steps, The (Matalon) 17, 155, 159–61, 165, 166, 170, 171
Spivak, Gayatri Chakravorty 156
Stahl, Neta 17
Strachey, Lytton 19
Suddenly in the Depth of the Forest (Oz) 182

Tale of Love and Darkness, A (Oz) 5, 8, 16–17, 44–7, 86, 95, 103, 123, 130, 143, 146, 154–5, 157, 171, 181–2, 189–91, 196, 198, 199; "fluid I-Us" voice 115–19
Talmon, Jacob 105, 107
tchach'tchachim 34
Tchernichovsky, Saul 6, 100
Third Condition, The (Oz) 180, 182
To Know a Woman (Oz) 7, 180
Trevitte, Chad 54, 57
Tsa'irim 109
Tsal, Na'ama 156, 165

Under This Blazing Light (*Be-or ha-tkhelet ha-aza* (*Be-or ha-tkhelet ha-aza* Oz) 13, 30, 83–5, 183, 196
Unto Death (Oz) 32, 99, 102, 103, 182

Van Doren, Carl 47–8, 64n22
Vendler, Lawrence 119–22
Venuti, Lawrence 71
Viadomsky, Pan 147
Victorianism 19

Waxman, Anat 144
"Way of the Wind" (Oz) 79
Weiss, Hillel 14
What's In An Apple? (Oz) 181
Where the Jackals Howl (Oz) 10, 44, 51, 53, 55, 59, 61, 147, 179, 180, 187, 182, 194–6
Winesburg, Ohio (Anderson) 44, 46–52, 54, 57–9, 61

Yehoshua, A. B. 2, 11, 17, 62, 82, 86, 99, 102, 109, 137, 180
Yehuda, Omri Ben 170
Yeshurun, Helit 103
Yingling, T. 58
Yizhar, S. 11, 17, 109, 180
Yosef, Raz 165

Zach, Nathan 140
zealotry 105, 111n38
Ziffer, Benny 27–9, 33, 35, 39
Zionism 11, 14, 15, 29–33, 75, 78, 80, 81, 83, 87, 98, 102–9, 117, 156, 187; *see also* messianism
Zionist-Crusaders analogy 98, 99, 102, 103
Zionist Left 78, 79

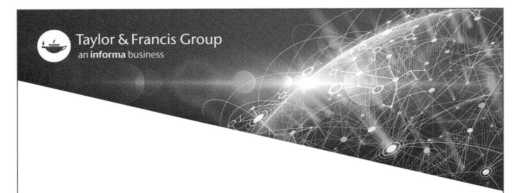

Taylor & Francis eBooks

www.taylorfrancis.com

A single destination for eBooks from Taylor & Francis with increased functionality and an improved user experience to meet the needs of our customers.

90,000+ eBooks of award-winning academic content in Humanities, Social Science, Science, Technology, Engineering, and Medical written by a global network of editors and authors.

TAYLOR & FRANCIS EBOOKS OFFERS:

- A streamlined experience for our library customers
- A single point of discovery for all of our eBook content
- Improved search and discovery of content at both book and chapter level

REQUEST A FREE TRIAL
support@taylorfrancis.com